Interpreting Judaism in a Postmodern Age

New Perspectives on Jewish Studies

A Series of the Philip and Muriel Berman Center for Jewish Studies
Lehigh University, Bethlehem, Pennsylvania

General Editor: Laurence J. Silberstein

Interpreting Judaism in a Postmodern Age
Edited by Steven Kepnes

*The Other in Jewish Thought and History: Constructions of Jewish
Culture and Identity*
Edited by Laurence J. Silberstein and Robert L. Cohn

*Jewish Fundamentalism in Comparative Perspective: Religion,
Ideology, and the Crisis of Modernity*
Edited by Laurence J. Silberstein

New Perspectives on Israeli History: The Early Years of the State
Edited by Laurence J. Silberstein

Interpreting Judaism in a Postmodern Age

Edited by
Steven Kepnes

NEW YORK UNIVERSITY PRESS
New York & London

Library of Congress Cataloging-in-Publication Data
Interpreting Judaism in a postmodern age / edited by Steven Kepnes.
    p.   cm. -- (New perspectives on Jewish studies)
    Includes bibliographical references and index.
    ISBN 0-8147-4674-8 (cloth : alk. paper). -- ISBN 0-8147-4675-6
(pbk. : alk. paper)
    1. Judaism--20th century. 2. Postmodernism--Religious aspects-
-Judaism. 3. Hermeneutics--Religious aspects--Judaism. 4. Judaism-
-Sacred books--Hermeneutics. I. Kepnes, Steven, 1952-   .
II. Series.
BM565.I58 1996
296'.09'045--dc20   95-22103
                        CIP

New York University Press books are printed on acid-free paper,
and their binding materials are chosen for strength and durability.

To my sisters, Jennine and Susan, and to the memory of my mother, Janet Kepnes "zl"

Contents

Kabbalah

Liturgy

Pedagogy

Hebrew Literature

Jewish Thought

Holocaust

Zionism

Feminism

Foreword

The essays in this volume address issues and problems that stand at the center of current academic debate. Specifically, each chapter undertakes to relate contemporary theories of interpretation to the study of Jewish culture and history. After outlining his or her theoretical orientation, each author seeks to demonstrate the value of that theoretical orientation by applying it to a specific set of texts. These essays thus show how a diverse group of contemporary Jewish studies scholars utilize new theoretical perspectives in their work.

By inviting this group of imaginative scholars to both reflect on and apply their theoretical frameworks to different areas of Jewish culture and history, the editor, Steven Kepnes, has rendered a significant contribution to the field of Jewish studies. This volume provides provocative examples of the ways in which a group of imaginative scholars in the field of Jewish studies utilize contemporary theories of interpretation. Thus, these articles may be seen as expanding the parameters of the prevailing academic discourse in the field of Jewish studies.

This is the first volume in the series New Perspectives on Jewish Studies not based on a major Berman Center conference. However, several of the essays were discussed at three seminars on postmodernism, cultural studies, and Judaism sponsored by the Center. Also, many of the problems and issues addressed here have already been raised in previous series volumes. Thus, this volume complements earlier ones, particularly the most recent, *The Other in Jewish Thought and History,* and carries forward conversations that have taken place at the Center since 1992.

LAURENCE J. SILBERSTEIN

Acknowledgments

This volume initially grew out of presentations and discussions held at the Association for Jewish Studies and at the spring seminars on postmodernism at the Philip and Muriel Berman Center for Jewish Studies at Lehigh University. The conceptualization of the collection was further shaped through conversations with Peter Ochs and the discussants of the Postmodern Jewish Philosophy E-Mail Network (POMO@JTSA.EDU). I want to thank all the contributors to this volume, whose oral and written remarks taught me an immense amount about contemporary theory and Jewish studies.

Special thanks go to Laurence Silberstein, editor of the Berman Center's New Perspectives on Jewish Studies series, for his encouragement, advice, and suggestions; to Shirley Ratushny and the staff of the Berman Center for their painstaking manuscript preparation; and to Philip and Muriel Berman for their continuing support of the work of the Berman Center. I also wish to thank Colgate University for contributing to the early editing that was carried out by Nicole Grant and to the preparation of the index. Finally, I wish to express my gratitude to the Hebrew University of Jerusalem and the Shalom Hartman Institute of Jerusalem for providing me with a sabbatical home during the final editing of the volume.

The Berman Center and I wish to acknowledge the following publications and publishers: *Prooftexts* for permission to reprint Edward Greenstein's article, "Deconstruction and Biblical Narrative" (January 1989); the University of Chicago Press for permission to reprint Susan Handelman's article, "The Torah of Criticism and the Criticism of Torah," which appeared in the *Journal of Religion*, vol. 74, no. 3 (July 1994); and Paulist Press for permission to print an adaptation of chapter 1 of *The Return to Scripture in Judaism and Christianity*, edited by Peter Ochs, © 1993 by Peter Ochs.

Introduction

Postmodern Interpretations of Judaism: Deconstructive and Constructive Approaches

Steven Kepnes

One of the most radical statements of postmodern Jewish interpretation in this collection is found in the opening lines of the essay by
Elliot Wolfson. Here the words of the decidedly premodern Hasidic
master, R. Zadoq ha-Kohen, when recontextualized through postmodern theories of interpretation, strike an eerie resonance. "Thus
I have received that the world in its entirety is a book that God,
blessed be He, made, and the Torah is the commentary that He
composed on that book." Here we see the written word, whose
primacy to language was asserted by Derrida, pushed to become the
basis of a cosmology. And here we see the notion of commentary or
interpretation, one of the key terms of poststructural criticism,
elevated to the status of holy scripture.

In this volume the reader will find many more "eerie resonances"
between postmodern theories of interpretation and culture and
Jewish texts. The essays collected display the fruits of the application of an array of postmodern hermeneutical[1] approaches to the
study of Judaism. By the term "postmodern" I mean to designate a
number of philosophical, social, and cultural transformations that
have come together in the contemporary period and that include a
movement away from the modern ideal of a universal rational
culture and toward a multicultural reality that celebrates the value
of the local and particular and attempts a new openness to premodern forms and motifs.[2]

Postmodern hermeneutical approaches were produced in the
wake of the failure of modern Enlightenment attempts to create

1

positivistic, "objective" methods that could determine univocal meanings of sacred and literary texts. These hermeneutical approaches were developed in an open spirit that has not only seen a whittling away of barriers separating academic disciplines but has also witnessed the creative possibilities of scholarship that emerge when long-held distinctions between the sacred and profane, philosophy and literature, text and interpretation, high and low culture, and politics and aesthetics are put aside.

Postmodernity is a transitional period. Coming after modernity without distinctly having emerged from modernity's political, social, and intellectual institutions, postmodernity is a period of creative conflict where the voices of the "other" and the different that were rendered silent or "minor" by modern culture are being heard in all their particularity and uniqueness. It is also a time of deep uncertainty and insecurity where the rational structures of modernity that were to replace the institutions and intellectual traditions of premodernity are being called into question and giving way to a simultaneous rebirth of antimodern fundamentalism along with a culture of continuing skepticism and nihilistic doubt. In this period the hermeneut attempts to be open to the pluralism of voices in a text while not being drowned out by all the noise or rendered silent or incoherent by the swirl of ever-available new theories and methodologies.

The postmodern Jewish hermeneut finds herself with texts, problems, traditions that are both unique to her and shared in the wider world. True to their position in Western culture as both inside and outside, a part of, yet set apart, the Jews have texts, like the biblical texts, that are both shared with non-Jews and that have a unique position in Jewish cultures. Jews have their own metaphysical views of their texts and thousand-year-long traditions of interpretation that supply them with both a sense of lineage, pride, and resources in approaching contemporary hermeneutical discussions and a series of entrenched prejudices, distortions, and morally suspect images of "others" like women and non-Jews that are difficult to dislodge.

Postmodern Jewish hermeneutics does not have a long history in Judaism. Although we can point to Buber and Rosenzweig as predecessors (Silberstein 1989; Kepnes 1992; Gibbs 1992), the tools of postmodern hermeneutics were not fully available when these figures did their most creative work. Emmanuel Levinas is, perhaps, the best representative of postmodern Jewish philosophy, and there is also Edmond Jabès.[3] But if we look outside of Jewish philosophy to Jewish studies in general, we see that the ruling methodological paradigm for the study of Judaism, since its nineteenth-century beginnings in *Wissenschaft des Judentums*, has been historical criticism. Cataloging and dating Jewish literatures and determining their meaning by philological analyses and establishing historical context have occupied and continue to occupy a great deal of the energies of scholars and thinkers in Jewish studies. However, not only has the claim to "objectivity" of historical criticism been radically challenged by contemporary historiography, but Gadamerian hermeneutics (Gadamer 1982) as well as literary theory has shown that historical criticism is radically deficient in helping us to understand and perform the crucial interpretive task of making texts of the past speak to the contemporary situation. In addition, narratology and semiotics have shown that explaining the way texts "mean" requires much more sophisticated linguistic analyses than history and philology can provide. This does not necessarily mean that historical critical methods have to be cast aside, for as Paul Ricoeur (1976) has argued and the most recent work in the "new historicism" shows (see Boyarin in this volume), historical methodologies can be used in tandem with a variety of literary perspectives (cf. Kepnes 1992, chap. 3). But the hegemony of the historical paradigm certainly has been broken.

Feeling constrained by the limitations of historical criticism and becoming aware of the sophistication and power of contemporary theoretical paradigms for the understanding of textually based traditions, an increasing number of those who work in Jewish studies have begun to utilize interpretive approaches grounded in neo-phenomenological hermeneutics, semiotics, discourse theory, and deconstruction. Given that exegesis has always been of paramount importance to Judaism, the turn to interpretive approaches is particularly apt for Jewish scholarship. Scholars are finding fascinating points of contact between contemporary hermeneutical theories and older Jewish methods of interpretation. Scholars of Judaism are beginning to explore these points of contact in a large variety of texts and schools of interpretation from the biblical and rabbinic to the mystical and philosophical.[4]

Although I used the word "paradigm" in describing the older Jewish scholarship, I would not say that the work represented in this volume represents a "paradigm shift" in the Kuhnian sense of a movement to a shared new model with commonly accepted methodological and evaluative criteria.   In a context where a central leitmotif is *différance*, it would be somewhat contradictory to assert and celebrate the emergence of new dogma and doctrine to replace the old. Rather, what we see in the essays collected here are "family resemblances" and "electives affinities." We see shared problematics and questions. We see recurring themes such as the importance of language and discourse in the construction of Jewish cultures. We see a movement away from fixed foundations and essentialized notions such as the "Jewish soul," "Jewish civilization," "Jewish values," and "Jewish traits." These essays also reflect an increased appreciation for the constitutive role of ritual and liturgy, of education and pedagogy, of text and interpretation, in short, of social and collective factors in Jewish cultures.

If modern historical methodology is cast in a new light in the emerging postmodern Jewish scholarship, so too is the determinative role of modern historical events in Jewish self-consciousness. Jews living in and through the conditions created by postmodernity are beginning to find that the great transformative events of the modern period—Emancipation, Holocaust, and the establishment of the State of Israel—no longer have the same power to generate ideologies that determine their existence. Thus part of the Jewish postmodern condition means to live in a world that is postassimilatory, post-Zionist, and post-Holocaust. Where much of modern Jewish scholarship on the events of modernity argued about the meaning and lessons of modern Jewish history, postmodern Jewish scholarship sees historical events as far too complex and opaque to reveal clear and univocal meanings and has given up on figuring out the lessons Jews are to take from each historical event. Scholars are turning their attention instead to analyzing the ideological uses and abuses of Jewish history and to showing the ways in which Jewish historiography functions to exclude some groups of Jews and non-Jews and include others.

Postmodern scholars of Jewish history are turning their attention to problematizing the neat metanarratives of the Jewish past so that different versions of Jewish history can emerge and different constituencies of Jews and non-Jews can have a voice in the present. This scholarship can be seen as a metadiscourse that attempts deconstructive and reparative analyses of Jewish historiography to the end of greater inclusiveness of those who were hitherto seen as "other."

In this volume the essays of both Daniel Boyarin and Hannan Hever illustrate the historiographical approach I have just outlined. Boyarin seeks to uncover forces in Talmudic cultures that opposed the dominant androcentrism. Boyarin uses evidence of the power and creativity of some women in the Talmud to "deconstruct" the monolithic image of them as powerless. By carving out a place for women in Talmudic cultures in the past, Boyarin aims to secure a place for women in the Judaism of the present. In Hever's essay the reader will find a deconstruction of modern scholarship on early-twentieth-century Hebrew literature that reveals the political motivations behind the construction of the canon of modern Hebrew literature. This deconstruction opens to a reparative analysis that illuminates the creative work of Galician Hebrew authors who have been marginalized by mainstream Hebrew literary history.

Differences

Lest I obscure some very real differences in the writings I have collected under the rubric of postmodern Jewish hermeneutics, let me begin to make some distinctions. Most generally the essays in this collection can be grouped around two different poles, each of which finds its roots in different hermeneutical traditions of Western intellectual life. These traditions can be described as "deconstructive hermeneutics" with Nietzsche, Marx, and Freud as modern progenitors and Derrida and Foucault as their postmodern successors, and "constructive hermeneutics" with Schleiermacher, Dilthey, and Heidegger[5] as modern progenitors and Gadamer and Ricoeur as postmodern successors.[6] The former type of hermeneutic attempts to uncover the conditions and processes that lie behind the ostensive meanings of human cultural expressions and the latter seeks to disclose new possibilities of meaning within the fabric of cultural products themselves.[7] Thus where a Freudian interpretation would find the conflicts of desire behind a symbol and a Marxian interpretation would find class conflict, a Gadamerian interpretation would recommend a playful engagement with the symbol that multiplies its explicit meanings. In my book, *The Text as Thou* (1992), I have used Martin Buber's categories and described the deconstructive approach as the "hermeneutics of I-It" and the constructive approach as the "hermeneutics of I-Thou."

In practice, the work of no hermeneut represents a pure type, and one can therefore find in every act of interpretation a mixture of deconstructive hermeneutics with constructive hermeneutics (cf. Kepnes 1986). Nonetheless, the reader will certainly sense that each essay collected here can be placed closer to one hermeneutical pole or the other. And the reader will also find that the essays associated with each different pole display their hermeneutical prejudices not only in content, theme, and argument but also in elements of rhetorical presentation and style.

The distance between the two hermeneutical approaches was emphasized by Wilhelm Dilthey, who distinguished between the *Naturwissenschaften* (the Natural Sciences), and the *Geisteswissenschaften* (the Human Sciences) and their corresponding approaches of *erklären* (explanation) and *verstehen* (understanding) (1959, xv–xix; 1958, 79–88). Dilthey saw the natural sciences and the human sciences and each of their respective methods of explanation and understanding as ontologically different. Each form of academic discourse proposes not only different ways of studying the world but also different forms of living or being-in-the-world. Although I will argue shortly that postmodern epistemology allows us to bridge the ontological gap that Dilthey established, we can still recognize differences in tone, style, and goals in the different hermeneutical approaches. Thus, in this volume, the tone of the essays by Silberstein and Ophir, which could be classified as examples of deconstructive hermeneutics, is decidedly different from the tone and rhetoric one finds in the essays by Wolfson and Handelman, which represent examples of constructive hermeneutics. In the former essays the authors maintain a distance from their materials and attempt to employ the neutral tone and rhetoric of social science to deconstruct, expose, and problematize the ideologies behind Zionist texts and discourse. In the latter essays the authors take an apologetic stance toward certain traditional Jewish texts. They offer readings that augment and enlarge the horizon of meanings in their texts and attempt to introduce them as constructive contributors to debates in contemporary academic discourse.

As to Dilthey's suggestion that the different hermeneutical approaches can be correlated with different forms of life, one could, if one investigated, find differences in political activity and in Jewish ritual and religious practice among the representatives of the different hermeneutical approaches. Thomas Docherty (1993, 5–26) suggests that deconstructive hermeneutics follows a trajectory from

Nietzsche, Marx, and Freud through the Frankfurt School of critical theory to poststructuralism and then to radical political praxis. Although not all of the authors in this volume who employ deconstructive hermeneutics follow Docherty's trajectory exactly, many are affiliated with movements for social change in Israel and America. On the other hand there is an attraction for those who are attempting to restore meaning and rehabilitate the imaginary world of Jewish texts to a renewed commitment to Jewish religious practice. Coming after the unfulfilled redemptive and utopian promises of modern ideologies, coming after the frustrations with democratic capitalism and socialism, and after the frustrations with correlative Jewish utopian movements of Reform Judaism and Zionism, many postmodern Jews have followed Franz Rosenzweig in his revalorization of ritual practice and sought contact with the transcendent in Judaism through liturgy and sacred texts.

Where modern Judaism tended to focus on the Hebrew Bible as the text that validated the connection of the Jews to the land, to a place in history, and also to a universal messianic vision for all of humankind, much of postmodern constructive Jewish hermeneutics has turned to rabbinic texts. For these are decidedly nonuniversalistic texts. They are the particularistic and idiosyncratic texts that formed the basis of the cultures of the Jews of the Diaspora. These rabbinic texts validate what Jacob Neusner once called the nonmessianic time "between time and eternity." The texts replace Temple and Priest with the Yeshiva and Rabbi and thus allow for Jewish life lived outside of the land of Israel.

Although some have labeled postmodern constructive hermeneutics a form of political "neo-conservatism," the designation has extremely limited applicability in the Jewish case. Rather, Jews who use this hermeneutic approach are often responding to the radical sense of insecurity and homelessness initiated in the modern break with tradition and brought to further extremes in the postmodern questioning and deconstruction of the rational structures that were to replace tradition. For some, the hermeneutics of retrieval of Jewish texts involves the retrieval of the model of the Yeshiva, traditional Jewish study house, as a Jewish "home" in an inhospitable environment. The environment is inhospitable not, essentially, because of anti-Semitism but because this environment is incapable of providing Jews with a sense of a genuine supportive community that could supply what Buber called "interhuman" connectedness and enriching interpersonal relationships. The model of the Yeshiva is the model of a moral world built in and through the language games of the Jewish texts. The postmodern "retrieved" Yeshiva is not the closed in and ghettoized Yeshiva of old but a Yeshiva modified by critique to include both men and women and to welcome visits by non-Jews. It is a Yeshiva not only open to internal critique but capable of mounting sustained ethical critique of the injustices in the larger Jewish and non-Jewish worlds outside of it.[8]

At this point, when we speak of the efficacy and necessity of critique, it is obvious that postmodern constructive hermeneutics, in order to function in accordance with its ethical aims, must incorporate critical deconstructive hermeneutics within it. And indeed that is what one finds in most postmodern Jewish constructive hermeneutics.[9] And, likewise, in the work of postmodern deconstructive hermeneuts, one never sees suspicion and deconstruction without an attempt to open a clearing for a new and different interpretation, another human voice, a productive ethical critique, or even the passing by of the back of the God, who cannot be seen or heard.[10]

So despite differences in styles of interpretation and forms of life, postmodern Jewish hermeneuts of all kinds come together to argue and converse in public and private conferences and in written and electronic correspondence. And although one could suggest that this is merely a function of the limited number of Jewish scholars who employ postmodern hermeneutical approaches in their work, I believe there is a substantive reason for the dialogues and therefore have sought to bring together essays by authors representing the different postmodern hermeneutical poles.

Postmodern Epistemology, Postmodern Hermeneutics

The substantive basis for dialogue between the two hermeneutical poles is to be found in the movement from modern to postmodern epistemology.[11] The specifically postmodern step involves a movement beyond the ontological gap established in the modern world between science and humanities and between "objective" and "subjective" forms of knowing. From the dawn of the modern age in seventeenth-century science through Enlightenment philosophy to the nineteenth-century social science, the dream of modernity has been to use technical and calculating reason to subsume all reality under objective universal laws and thereby achieve increasing domination and control of the natural and human worlds (Toulmin 1990; Brockelman 1992). As Richard Rorty suggests, modernity erected "physical sciences as the paradigm of knowledge" (1979, 322), and all other forms of knowing either had to ape this paradigm or appear as secondary, ancillary, subjective, and therefore inferior.

With all modern "interpreters," be they Marx or Freud, Schleiermacher or Dilthey, there is an attempt to arrive at objectivity in interpretation. Freud saw himself as discovering psychological laws and Marx believed he had discerned sociological and historical laws under which human behavior could be subsumed. These laws allowed Freud to reduce the meaning of all texts to the conflicts of desire, and Marx, to the conflicts of class and dialectical materialism. Schleiermacher and especially Dilthey believed that the "empathic method" could yield interpretations of human expressions that were of a different cultural order than science but that retained scientific validity and objectivity.

The postmodern hermeneutical revolution came with the realization that the person who initiates and plans the scientific or humanistic research can never be sealed off from the research; her prejudices, preferences, and choices will always have effects on the outcomes. Because it is impossible to neutralize the researcher's subjective involvement in the research, the dream of scientific objectivity will forever remain a dream. The move to hermeneutics began with the original insight of historicism—that personal, social, and cultural factors condition all forms of knowledge. But the specific positive postmodern hermeneutical turn came with the recognition that not only could these conditioning factors not be eradicated or "bracketed out" but that this task was counterproductive for scholarship. The postmodern hermeneut argues that the conditioning factors of person, time, place, and history do not limit the acquisition of knowledge but, quite the contrary, they supply the epistemological tools and traditions that make knowing possible. Postmodern hermeneutics suggests that scholarly arguments within and without the academic disciplines should not be viewed as arguments to establish the one objective "truth." Instead, each discipline represents a tradition or community of inquiry that proposes interpretations of texts, behaviors, data. Academic debates then are best seen as "conflicts of interpretation" rather than attempts to establish objectively verifiable truths. "Truth" is a function of agreement in a community of inquiry about the most adequate interpretation of a text or data rather than something that objectively inheres in the data or text itself (Bernstein 1983; Tracy 1987).

Through the hermeneutic turn, Marxist and Freudian sciences become "perspectives" that supply interpretations of human cultural products that can be viewed as different from, yet alongside of, perspectives supplied by Dilthey or Heidegger or an array of literary forms. From a postmodern point of view the social-scientific and literary forms of analysis are not separated by a large ontological gap; they are, instead, seen as different forms of discourse, different language games, that follow different rules of interpretation.

What is interesting, however, is that although the academic spokespersons for the different language games of the sciences and humanities struggle to keep their distinctiveness by upholding their rules of discourse and purifying their technical jargon, the language that they use to communicate both in their writings and in conversations with colleagues is one of the common natural languages of humanity: English, French, German, Hebrew. Thus, there is a constant admixture of languages and a constant process of translating from technical to common vocabulary, and we see this especially in teaching and in the practical and applied art of interpreting texts and data and conversing about these interpretations. So as postmodern scholarship appreciates the distinctions and differences that separate language games establish, it simultaneously recognizes a rich interpenetration of discursive practices, especially at the crucial point of lived conversation.

This rich linguistic mixing and hybridization of language has been pointed to by a number of poststructuralist critics who have sensitized us to the ways in which literary tropes appear in philosophical and scientific discourse (de Man 1979; White 1978; Gerhart and Russell 1984) and, vice versa, to the ways in which scientific rhetoric appears in literature. The multiple ways in which language games interpenetrate one another were especially appreciated by the Russian literary critic Mikhail Bakhtin, who coined the phrase "heteroglossia" (1981, 262–63) to refer to linguistic admixtures. We may say that the linguistic fact of heteroglossia and the underlying human proficiency in languages—the ability to master a multiplicity of languages—provide reason to hope that humans can both appreciate differences and at the same time perform basic acts of translation that allow them to speak to one another across their differences.[12]

The collective impact of these postmodern insights into interpenetration of discourses has led to the erosion of barriers separating the social sciences and humanities. This has not only increased interdisciplinary work but has led to a sense that the strict divisions into academic disciplines are antiquated if not unnecessary. Postmodern scholars see that it is highly artificial to divide the world up as the academic disciplines do and attempt to study human texts and behaviors in isolation. Postmodern scholarship uses a variety of interpretive approaches to study not literature, not society, not economy, not religion in isolation, but something that includes within it literature, society, economy, religion, but can be limited to none of these. This larger "something" some postmoderns have called "culture," and the analysis of it has been dubbed "cultural studies." Cultural studies have sensitized us to the ways in which common themes, meanings, motivations for behavior run through the multiple institutions and expressions of human cultures and are articulated in hegemonic "metanarratives" that define what is in and outside, like and different, good and bad in a culture. What could be called Jewish cultural studies in this volume, such as the essays of Boyarin, Ophir, Hever, Silberstein, and Levitt, analyze metanarratives and hegemonic discourses in Jewish cultures and attempt to open up these cultures to that which hitherto was seen as outside, "other," bad.

The structure of this volume follows a rough chronology from the biblical to the contemporary period. All authors were asked to include a methodological discussion in which they outline and distinguish the characteristics of the theoretical model they are using. Authors were also asked to illustrate the applicability of a particular postmodern approach to Jewish studies by performing an act of interpretation on specific Jewish texts. Therefore, in each essay the reader will find a different presentation of the recent theoretical movement in academic scholarship and its implications for Jewish studies. I have tried, in this introduction, to present my own reading of the massive changes that are occurring in the world and in scholarship, but the authors collected here certainly do not all agree with my interpretation and categorization. Therefore, I encourage readers to look to the methodological discussions in each of the essays to receive additional and highly perceptive analyses of both overarching contemporary developments and particular definitions of terms such as "postmodern," "deconstruction," "new historicism," "semiotics," "discourse," "tradition," "culture," and "postcritical."

Although most of the approaches used were developed outside of Jewish studies, I have attempted to include essays by scholars who work primarily in Jewish studies. This was done to distinguish this collection from others such as that of Hartman and Budick (1986) and also to encourage more postmodern hermeneutical scholarship within the field of Jewish studies by displaying the creative possibilities of this type of work.

The scholars in this collection utilize a wide range of postmodern approaches. One will find a Derridean analysis in the essay by Edward Greenstein, a Gadamerian analysis in the essay by Martin Jaffee, a Deleuze and Guattarian analysis in the essay by Hannan Hever, a semiotic analysis in the essay by Peter Ochs, a new historicist analysis in the essay by Daniel Boyarin, and an analysis employing feminist theory in the essay by Laura Levitt. These approaches represent a diverse group of theories that often clash with one another and are hard to organize and categorize. I have used the terms "deconstructive hermeneutics" and "constructive hermeneutics," provisionally and heuristically, to provide a structure to my collection.

At the risk of insulting creative scholars who by definition hate to be defined, I will provide a rough categorization. The essays of Greenstein, Boyarin, Ophir, Hever, Wyschogrod, Silberstein, and Levitt mainly utilize deconstructive hermeneutics, and the essays of Ochs, Jaffee, Wolfson, Handelman, and Greenberg mainly utilize constructive hermeneutics. As I mentioned before, the practical act of interpretation displays a mixture of hermeneutical modalities. Indeed, even in the work of the master deconstructor, Jacques Derrida, one could deconstruct his deconstruction to reveal constructive moments. The semantic richness of every word we use defeats any attempt to limit either the language of a text or the language of interpretation to univocal expression. Certainly many of the essays presented here show a mixture of hermeneutical moments. For example, Edward Greenstein shows how deconstruction can be used to multiply creative and constructive possibilities in the interpretation of the Bible, and Edith Wyschogrod shows how the philosophy of negation in poststructuralism leads to a retrieval of the Hasidic tale as a form of religious discourse uniquely appropriate for giving expression to the absent God of Auschwitz. On the other hand, representatives of constructive hermeneutics like Elliot Wolfson and

Yudit Greenberg use notions of writing, textuality, interpretation, and temporality in the works of Derrida and Levinas to illuminate the hermeneutics of the Gaon of Vilna and Franz Rosenzweig, respectively.

By including essays from different hermeneutical poles in the same volume, I hope not only to display the wide spectrum of scholarship opened up by postmodern Jewish hermeneutics but also to underscore the ways in which the varied interpreters and their interpretive approaches can work together.

NOTES

1. I realize that for some the word "hermeneutics" is too tied to the Dilthey-Heidegger-Gadamer pole of interpretation and to phenomenological philosophy (see Greenstein in this volume) that they feel preceded the move to poststructuralism, postfoundationalism, and postmodernism. Yet I use the word "hermeneutics" in the neutral sense of "theories of interpretation" to refer to a large variety of schools of interpretation that includes deconstruction, semiotics, new historicism, and "new" phenomenological approaches (cf. Madison 1988). Furthermore, I identify neo-phenomenological figures like Gadamer and Ricoeur (and one could include Bakhtin here) as postmodern rather than as predecessors to postmodern hermeneutics. I do this, in part, because they share the postfoundational epistemology of the postmoderns. In addition, they contribute to the articulation of a constructive hermeneutics of culture that represents a corrective response to the absence in postmodernity of images of hope, trust, and community (cf. Bauman 1992; Giddens 1990).

2. The literature on the notion of the "postmodern" is extensive and growing. The semantic field of the term is large and ranges from certain aesthetic and epistemological premises, to a social and cultural "condition," to a temporal period. The term received its first systematic definition through the related notion of "postmodernism" in art and architecture (Howe 1959; Fiedler 1965; Jencks 1977; cf. Calinescu 1987; Hassan 1987). It took on its now classic philosophical formulation in Lyotard's *The Postmodern Condition* [1979] and is currently commanding increasing attention of sociologists and social theorists. These writers have expanded the notion beyond art and philosophy and articulated the presence of the postmodern condition in social, economic, cultural, religious, and psychological spheres. Social critics look to postindustrialization and late-capitalism, post-Marxism and postcolonialism, postsecularism and the renewal of religion, and the ubiquitous presence of computer resources of information as signals of the emer-

gence of a new temporal period or era that they label "postmodernity" (Jameson 1984; Bauman 1992).

Among the most succinct sociological commentators is Barry Smart, who favors a cautious notion of postmodernity "as a contemporary social, cultural, and political condition . . . as a form of life, a form of reflection upon and response to the accumulating signs of the limits and limitations of modernity" in its ability to produce intellectual certainty and existential security (Smart 1993, 12). This conception does not present postmodernity as an epoch that is clearly distinct from modernity but presents postmodernity in relation to modernity "as a condition necessarily articulated with modernity" (12).

As to the temporal origins of postmodernity, Arnold Toynbee (1939), who first used the term "postmodern," placed the beginnings of the era before the end of the nineteenth century. Others have located the beginnings after the First World War or in the aftermath of the Second World War and the Holocaust (Greenberg 1977; Bauman 1989), and Marxist critics often place the beginning of the period at the end of the 1960s and the end of hopes for socialist revolutions in Europe. But if the origins of postmodernity are to be found in the beginning and middle of the twentieth century, most people associate the term with the impact of French poststructuralism in the 1970s and 1980s. The term seems to grow in popular use as we move toward the twenty-first century.

3. See Jacques Derrida's essays on Emmanuel Levinas (1964b) and Edmond Jabès (1964a) (for both in English, see Derrida 1978). For postmodern studies of Levinas, see Gibbs 1992 and Handelman 1991. For the relevance of Jabès to the study of Jewish texts and kabbalah in particular, see Wolfson in this volume. For a persuasive argument that Max Kadushin deserves to be seen as an American Jewish pragmatist predecessor to postmodern Jewish thinking, see Ochs 1990. Ochs argues, throughout much of his recent work, that postmodern Jewish thinking is better served by American pragmatism than continental phenomenology because the former is better suited to help philosophy get beyond the dichotomous options—subject/object, tradition/modernity, science/religion—offered by modern philosophy.

4. For overviews of recent postmodern Jewish scholarship, see Silberstein 1993 and Ochs 1993a and 1993b. For current and future monographs, see other volumes in the series in which this volume appears, New Perspectives on Jewish Studies, edited by Laurence J. Silberstein and published by New York University Press; and Daniel Boyarin and Chanah Kronfeld's University of California Press series, Contraversions. For articles focusing on Israel, see the journal *Theory and Criticism* (Hebrew) edited by Adi Ophir and published by the Van Leer Institute of Jerusalem. For current dialogue, see Peters Ochs and David

Seidenberg's Postmodern Jewish Philosophy E-Mail Network at POMO@JTSA.EDU.

5. Although I have placed Heidegger on the side of constructive hermeneutics, a number of postmodern hermeneuts have used Heidegger's critique of Western metaphysics as a basis for a deconstructive hermeneutics. John Caputo (1987) puts Heidegger together with Derrida to produce what he calls "radical hermeneutics."

6. My categorization is loosely based upon Paul Ricoeur's distinction between the "hermeneutics of suspicion" and the "hermeneutics of retrieval" (1970). However, where Ricoeur tries to provide an overarching framework to relate the two traditions and form a comprehensive hermeneutic system, I have resisted such a totalizing move in order to preserve the separateness of the different hermeneutical strategies. In my book *The Text as Thou* (1992), I use Buber's dialogic thought to thematize a version of the constructive hermeneutics of retrieval that I called "dialogic hermeneutics" and that includes such figures as Gadamer, Ricoeur, Jürgen Habermas, Mikhail Bakhtin, Wayne Booth, and David Tracy. Peter Ochs labels this type of hermeneutic when applied to Jewish and Christian scriptures "postcritical interpretation" (see Ochs in this volume). For a scale of hermeneutical approaches with more gradations, see Shaun Gallagher (1992, chap. 1), who divides the figures whom I mention in my deconstructive hermeneutics and constructive hermeneutics into four groups: conservative, moderate, critical, and radical.

7. For a good introduction to and collection of articles showing the relations and differences between what I call deconstructive hermeneutics and constructive hermeneutics, see Silverman and Idhe 1985.

8. Real-life examples of such Yeshivot are few, but there is at least one, the Hartman Institute in Jerusalem.

9. For a more elaborate explication of this type of hermeneutical approach, see my *The Text as Thou* (1992, chap. 4).

10. The issue of theology is a divisive one for deconstructive hermeneutics, and we can see this in this volume in the different positions taken by Ophir and Wyschogrod. Ophir argues that postmodern critique has rendered God language nonsensical: "Whereas modernists who have killed God sought to replace Him, postmodernists look calmly at the corpse and care little about what is done with it . . . [and] His representation in human language" (186). Wyschogrod, on the other hand, suggests that postmodern critique clears the way for a negative articulation of God, an articulation which, with the Jewish mystics, gives utterance to God as "abyss or non-ground." For another deconstructive postmodern theology, see Taylor 1990, cf. Altizer et al. 1982. For a constructive postmodern Jewish theology, see Borowitz 1991 and Ochs 1993b.

11. Zygmunt Bauman (1987) argues that postmodern epistemology neces-

sarily requires a movement to hermeneutical modes of knowing and requires social and cultural elites to move from "legislative" to "interpretive" approaches in addressing issues of social policy.

12. This assumption, the assumption that human understanding of difference is possible, has been articulated most strongly by representatives of constructive hermeneutics. It has been elevated to something of a principle of faith by theological representatives of this school who argue that the principle should hold even when differentials in power relations and histories of oppression make it extremely difficult for conversations to occur between victims and their oppressors (Buber 1974; Tracy 1987). If we do not want to take the principle as far as the theologians do, we can simply say that it points to some kind of common humanity on the basis of which all human conversation is possible.

REFERENCES

Altizer, Thomas J. J., Max A. Myers, Carl A. Raschke, Robert P. Scharlemann, Mark C. Taylor, and Charles E. Winquist. *Deconstruction and Theology*. New York: Crossroad, 1982.

Bakhtin, Mikhail. *The Dialogic Imagination*. Ed. M. Holquist. Trans. C. Emerson and M. Holquist. Austin: University of Texas Press, 1981.

Bauman, Zygmunt. *Legislators and Interpreters*. Ithaca, N.Y.: Cornell University Press, 1987.

———. *Modernity and the Holocaust*. Oxford: Polity, 1989.

———. *Intimations of Postmodernity*. London: Routledge, 1992.

Bernstein, Richard. *Beyond Objectivism and Relativism: Science, Hermeneutics, and Praxis*. Philadelphia: University of Pennsylvania Press, 1983.

Borowitz, Eugene. *Renewing the Covenant: A Theology for the Postmodern Jew*. Philadelphia: Jewish Publication Society, 1991.

Brockelman, Paul. *The Inside Story: A Narrative Approach to Religious Understanding and Truth*. Albany: State University of New York Press, 1992.

Buber, Martin. "Genuine Dialogue and the Possibilities of Peace." In *Pointing the Way* [1953], ed. and trans. M. Friedman. New York: Schocken, 1974.

Calinescu, Matei. *Five Faces of Modernity: Modernism, Avant-garde, Decadence, Kitsch, Postmodernism*. Durham, N.C.: Duke University Press, 1987.

Caputo, John. *Radical Hermeneutics: Repetition, Deconstruction, and the Hermeneutic Project*. Bloomington: Indiana University Press, 1987.

de Man, Paul. *Allegories of Reading*. New Haven: Yale University Press, 1979.

Derrida, Jacques. "Edmond Jabès et la question du livre." *Critique* 201 (January 1964a).

———. "Violence et métaphysique: Essai sur la pensée d'Emmanuel Levinas." *Revue de métaphysique et de morale* 3, 4 (1964b).

———. *Writing and Difference*. Trans. Alan Bass. Chicago: University of Chicago Press, 1978.

Dilthey, Wilhelm. *Der Aufbau der geschichtlichen Welt in den Geisteswissenschaften*. Ed. B. Groethuysen. Vol. 7 of *Gesammelte Schriften*. Stuttgart: Teubner, 1958.

———. *Einleitung in die Geisteswissenschaften*. Ed. B. Groethuysen. Vol. 1 of *Gesammelte Schriften*. Stuttgart: Teubner, 1959.

Docherty, Thomas. "Postmodernism: An Introduction." In *Postmodernism: A Reader*, ed. Thomas Docherty. New York: Columbia University Press, 1993.

Gadamer, Hans-Georg. *Truth and Method*. New York: Crossroads, 1982.

Fiedler, Leslie. "The New Mutants." *Partisan Review* 32, 4 (Fall 1965).

Gallagher, Shaun. *Hermeneutics and Education*. Albany: State University of New York Press, 1992.

Gerhart, Mary, and Allan Russell. *Metaphoric Process: The Creation of Scientific and Religious Understanding*. Fort Worth: Texas Christian University Press, 1984.

Gibbs, Robert. *Correlations in Rosenzweig and Levinas*. Princeton, N.J.: Princeton University Press, 1992.

Giddens, Anthony. *The Consequences of Modernity*. Stanford, Calif.: Stanford University Press, 1990.

Greenberg, Irving. "Cloud of Smoke, Pillar of Fire: Judaism, Christianity, and Modernity after the Holocaust." In *Auschwitz: Beginning of a New Era?* ed. E. Fleischner. New York: KTAV, 1977.

Handelman, Susan. *Fragments of Redemption: Jewish Thought and Literary Theory in Benjamin, Scholem, and Levinas*. Bloomington: Indiana University Press, 1991.

Hartman, Geoffry, and Sanford Budick, eds. *Midrash and Literature*. New Haven: Yale University Press, 1986.

Hassan, Ihab. *The Postmodern Turn*. Columbus: Ohio State University Press, 1987.

Howe, Irving. "Mass Society and Postmodern Fiction." *Partisan Review* 26, 3 (Summer 1959): 420–36

Jameson, Fredric. "Postmodernism or the Cultural Logic of Late Capitalism." *New Left Review* 146 (1984).

Jencks, Charles. *The Language of Post-Modern Architecture*. London: Academy Editions, 1977.

18   *Steven Kepnes*

Kepnes, Steven. "Bridging the Gap between Understanding and Explanation Approaches to the Study of Religion." *Journal for the Scientific Study of Religion* 25, 4 (December 1986): 504–13.
———. *The Text as Thou: Martin Buber's Dialogical Hermeneutics and Narrative Theology.* Bloomington: Indiana University Press, 1992.
Lyotard, Jean-François. *The Post-Modern Condition* [1979]. Minneapolis: University of Minnesota Press, 1984.
Madison, G. B. *The Hermeneutics of Postmodernity.* Bloomington: Indiana University Press, 1988.
Ochs, Peter. *Understanding the Rabbinic Mind: Essays on the Hermeneutic of Max Kadushin.* Atlanta: Scholars Press, 1990.
———. "Borowitz and the Postmodern Renewal of Theology." *Cross Currents* 43, 2 (Summer 1993a): 164–84.
———. *The Return to Scripture in Judaism and Christianity.* New York: Paulist Press, 1993b.
Ricoeur, Paul. *Freud and Philosophy.* New Haven: Yale University Press, 1970.
———. *Interpretation Theory.* Fort Worth: Texas Christian University Press, 1976.
Rorty, Richard. *Philosophy and the Mirror of Nature.* Princeton, N.J.: Princeton University Press, 1979.
Smart, Barry. *Postmodernity.* London: Routledge, 1993.
Silberstein, Laurence J. *Martin Buber's Social and Religious Thought.* New York: New York University Press, 1989.
———. "Reading/Writing Judaism: Literary Theory and Modern Jewish Studies." *Religious Studies Review* 19, 1 (1993).
Silverman, Hugh, and Don Idhe. *Hermeneutics and Deconstruction.* New York: State University of New York Press, 1985.
Taylor, Mark. *Tears.* Albany: State University of New York Press, 1990.
Toulmin, Stephen. *Cosmopolis: The Hidden Agenda of Modernity.* New York: Free Press, 1990.
Toynbee, Arnold. *A Study of History.* Vol. 5. Oxford: Oxford University Press, 1939.
Tracy, David. *Plurality and Ambiguity: Hermeneutics, Hope, Religion.* San Francisco: Harper and Row, 1987.
White, Hayden. *The Tropics of Discourse.* Baltimore: Johns Hopkins University Press, 1978.

Bible and Midrash

Chapter 1

Deconstruction and Biblical Narrative

Edward L. Greenstein

[D]econstruction is nothing if not a way of reading.[1]

Derrida is clearly out to do more than develop new techniques of reading.[2]

[T]he implications of deconstruction for the study of literature are far from clear.[3]

As one of the most radical and difficult expressions of postpositivist thinking, deconstruction has unsurprisingly provoked both enthusiasm and dread. The *Literary Guide to the Bible* specifically excludes the bugaboo deconstruction, along with Marxism and feminism, as an unsympathetic approach to reading biblical literature (Alter and Kermode 1987, 5–6). The editors of the *Guide*, Robert Alter and Frank Kermode, maintain quite correctly that deconstruction does not share the New Critical and structuralist view of the literary text as a contained and unified system of codes (cf. 5).[4] Jacques Derrida, who first developed deconstruction, clearly aimed "to unlock and break out of what have been seen as the constricting forms and patterning of structuralism" (Brooks 1981, xvii). Deconstruction contends not only that the present center does not hold; it holds that no center can hold (see Derrida 1972). Although Alter and Kermode claim to allow for an eclectic pluralism in their *Guide* (1987, 6), this openness must draw the line at a criticism such as deconstruction in which a text is shown to be "necessarily divided against itself" (Alter and Kermode 1987, 6).

The unity of the literary, or any artistic, work has been adopted by Alter and Kermode as the common, unifying presupposition of all the authors in their *Guide*. The assumption of the Bible's unity in ancient times, by classical midrash, for example, reflects a belief in the unity of God and the revealed character of the sacred text. The assumption of the Bible's literary unity by contemporary critics stems from a Western notion of the integrity of the human personality. Freudian psychoanalysis, however, as Geoffrey Hartman has noted, "has intensified our suspicions concerning the unity of art by suggesting that the unity of the person is at best synthetic or adaptive and more likely to be multiple and self-divisive" (Hartman 1982, 185–86).[5] If so, one might consider the possibility that texts, like those of us who read them, can be "divided against themselves," and one might entertain a criticism such as deconstruction that would by not presuming unity reveal internal division and instability within texts.

Little has been published as yet[6] on the applications of deconstruction to the Hebrew Bible, and I have seen virtually no purely deconstructive readings of it.[7] An issue of *Semeia* devoted to Derrida talked about rather than did deconstruction (Detweiler 1982). There is, however, rapidly growing interest and decided influence in certain quarters.[8] Biblicists will quite naturally hesitate to work deconstructively, partly (*pace* Alter and Kermode) because that would demand a suspension of conventional beliefs and partly, perhaps, too, because reading deconstruction is a demanding enterprise. In any event, one cannot assess the potential benefits of deconstruction without understanding it and seeing how it might be applied, and so I have endeavored to explain something of the background and philosophy of deconstruction as the context for my own reading of certain biblical texts, in particular the narrative of the deaths of Aaron's sons Nadav and Avihu. While I shall be indicating below those aspects of deconstruction that clearly militate against the Bible's own professed positions, I shall also suggest the values or uses of deconstruction for reading biblical narrative. These values or uses may be not only hermeneutical but theological as well.

Before proceeding, there is one more preliminary matter I should like to address. As a mode of discourse, deconstruction has strong implications for the way we write. Nietzsche developed an aphoristic, fragmented style as a reflex of his understanding that we cannot attain completeness and true coherence in knowing (cf., e.g., Kaufmann 1961, 14–15). To write continuous, straightforward prose would be to deny or suppress the kaleidoscopic character of our knowledge. The critical discourse to which we are accustomed is composed in a narrative form that by its nature presupposes completeness—a beginning, a middle, and an end (cf. McGann 1985). Derrida seeks to decenter and liberate from (always superimposed) structure, on the one hand, and to underscore the dynamic play within language, on the other, by expressing himself in unconventional form and rhetoric (cf., e.g., Hartman 1981 and Culler 1982, 134–56). A new way of thinking prompts a new way of writing. Though hardly going all the way, I have attempted to incorporate certain aspects of this quite earnest and provocative mode of discourse into the present essay. The style is not intended to distract but to call attention to the question of how we make meaning and how all discourse is in a real sense a composite—what Derrida terms a "bricolation"—and an echo of prior discourse.

Another deconstructive rhetorical tradition, if one calls it that, is that one reads texts such that they are not merely the object of a concern with language but are themselves *about* a concern with language in the most basic sense.[9] While this convention manifests the fundamental Derridean idea that it is we who inscribe what we read with sense, it is a strategy that has independent merit for returning us always to text. Derrida has cogently broken down the boundaries between theoretical, philosophical discourse and literature (cf., e.g., Norris 1987), so that it will make sense for us to track the philosophical development of Derrida's critical process through a reading of—in this case—biblical texts.

We begin with difference. In the beginning was difference, according to what we read in Genesis (cf. Kendrick 1986, 25). God began creation by speaking the word "light," *'or*, before it referred to anything. In the theory of Saussure, the starting point for all modern linguistic investigation, the sign comprises two concurrent, indivisible, yet distinguishable elements—the concept, the "signified"; and the "sound-image" that represents it in speech, "the signifier" (de Saussure 1966, esp. 65 ff.). "The bond between the signifier and the signified is arbitrary" (67, 113), by which Saussure means conventional (cf. 68). A language is a system of signs. Meaning is determined by speakers observing the relations among signs. Signs are distinguished from one another by their differences. Words, as signifiers, have no intrinsic relation to the concepts they signify. They are the product of relations with no positive value: "In language there are only differences *without positive terms*" (de Saussure 1966, 120); "Their most precise characteristic is in being what the others are not" (117); "Proof of this is that the value of a term may be modified without either its meaning or its sound being affected, solely because a neighboring term has been modified" (120). Once values have been assigned to signifiers by linking them with signifieds, the resultant sign does carry a positive value (120). In Gen. 1:3 the word *'or* does not yet signify a signified, is not yet a signifier (cf. Greenstein 1983, 26). It differs from the word the narrator uses to denominate the preexisting darkness, *hoshekh* (v. 2), but the narrator is telling in retrospect. There was no differentiation yet, no definition. Differentiation (of signifieds) comes only after "there was light"—*vayhi 'or* (v. 3). Light is defined only by its contrast with darkness: "He divided, God did, between the light and between the darkness" (v. 4).[10] It is this division, this difference, between light and dark, that creates them (cf. Westermann 1984, 87). Had there been light to begin with and had God created darkness, in this respect it would have made no difference, as it would have produced difference. One without the other could not be said to exist in any intelligible way. Their meaning, and in fact all meaning, is relative—the product of difference.

The word for light, *'or*, however, preexisted both the darkness and the light as it differs from the only word that precedes it—*yehi*, "Let there be . . ." (v. 3). In the narrated time of the Genesis 1 narrative the words *yehi* and *'or* anticipate becoming and light, respectively. The signifiers do not represent the signifieds, they precede them. They are meaningful only by virtue of their difference from each other and from all other possible words. They seem to exist as words that stand for something, as verbal signifiers. But signifiers cannot be signifiers unless they signify some signified. In the presence of signifiers without signifieds, we hear the sound of one hand clapping.

There is a further paradox in the word we now know as the verbal form *yehi*, "Let there be!" As we read on, we contrast it with the verbal form *vayhi*, "there was." The two forms differ in tense (future/past) or aspect (incompleted action/completed action). (Grammarians are divided.)[11] Either way, the word *yehi*, were it already to signify anything, would precede any difference in time. Time could be indicated only after the contrast of signifiers *yehi/vayhi* came into be(com)ing. This is further problematic, for the concept of time itself is only introduced after light begins to alternate with darkness (cf. Westermann 1984, 112). It is their difference that creates time: "He divided, God did, between the light and between the darkness. He called, God did, the light 'day,' and the darkness he called 'night'" (vv. 4–5). We anticipate the creation of time by projecting our already-formed concept of time onto the text (more on which below).

By the time God named day and night, they had already become, like the animals the first man *(ha'adam)* will name in the Garden of Eden (Gen. 2:19–20). Day and night as signifieds might seem to precede the words "day" and "night" as signifiers. But that is not so. Day and night are not the same as light and darkness. More precisely, "day" and "light," on the one hand, and "night" and "darkness," on the other, are not variable signifiers of the same signified. "Day" denotes all the light between two periods of darkness, and "night" denotes all the darkness between two periods of light (cf. Cassuto 1961, 29). Each term entails a presence following an absence, or an absence following a presence; each involves time. As I have said, it is the sense of difference between periods of light and dark that creates the contrast day/night, and with it the concept of time. In the realm of the signifier, tense precedes time. In Genesis, signifiers play by themselves before they are attached to signifieds.

In Saussure's system signifier and signified are paired within the sign, yet distinct. Derrida will find this distinction to be "problematical at its root" because "every signified is also in the position of a signifier" (Derrida 1981, 20; cf. Derrida 1974, 7). In order to appreciate the dynamic nature of signification, consider the Tower of Babel story. "It was, all the land was one language and one speech" (Gen. 11:1).[12] That language was "the holy tongue" (so Rashi ad loc.), Hebrew, the language God reportedly spoke in creating the world. Because it was God's language, it was not conventional; the bond between signifiers and signifieds was not arbitrary but authoritatively determined. At first, linguistic harmony obscured an underlying cultural differentiation. The narrator notes that the easterners—the builders of Babel—and the Hebrews, despite the unity of their language, had different building systems: "For them [i.e., the easterners] bricks were as stone, and bitumen was for them as mortar" (v. 3). The function of the building blocks was served by culturally differentiated materials. The easterners used man-made bricks, the Hebrews would have used

God-made stone. Westermann, in line with many other critics, calls this comment in verse 3 "an explanatory note," "a parenthesis," implying its secondary interpolation into the text (Westermann 1984, 546). The deconstructor seeks to read in these margins; it is no less text than the rest. Indeed, the allegedly parenthetic aside may serve as the key to the entire story.

According to Benno Jacob, "one speech" *(devarim 'ahadim)* in contrast to "one language" *(safa 'ehat)* refers to syntax (connected discourse) and vocabulary, respectively (Jacob 1934, 297, following S. D. Luzzatto's commentary [1871] 1965). If so (and even if not), because the narrative foregrounds wordplay and language (cf. Fokkelman 1975, 11–45), one can draw an analogy between the building of the city and tower and the linguistic practice of the builders. Syntax binds words as mortar/bitumen binds stones/bricks. The building can be read as an allegory of language. The builders operated under certain false ideas about language and signification. First, they thought that different signifiers could represent the same signified. The phonological difference between *hemar*, "bitumen,"[13] and *homer*, "clay," i.e., "mortar," on the one hand, and between *levena*, "brick," and *le'aven*, "(for) stone," on the other hand (cf. Jacob 1934, 298; Leibowitz 1969, 75; and Fokkelman 1975, 27), seemed so slight that it would make no difference. Small phonological distinctions can make all the difference in the wor(l)d, however. A greater error was that they thought they could, like the God of Genesis, establish unique and permanent unities between a signifier and a signified. They sought to make for themselves "a name" (v. 4)—a permanent and irreplaceable signifier of themselves, or rather of extensions of themselves, the tower, and city. As Derrida observes, these builders are the sons of Shem, "Name" (Derrida 1985, 100ff.). Bearing the name of Name, these mortals would "impos[e] their tongue on the entire universe on the basis of this sublime edification" (101). The name, they believed, would forever signify themselves as signified. The story, in which YHWH shattered their linguistic cohesion and renamed their city, proves otherwise.

To explain a third, more profound error, we return to our reading of the narrative. So long as the builders of the tower and city bind the same signifiers to the same signifieds, they proceed smoothly. But God endeavors to undo their plan by collapsing their foundation—the fact that they employ a single language (see v. 6), a consistent set of signs. "Come, let us go down that we may confuse their language there, so that one man cannot understand his neighbor's language" (v. 7). Rashi (ad loc.) insightfully suggests how the confusion occurred: "This one would ask for a brick, and the other would bring him mortar." The words in the two languages were homophonous! The same signifier would signify one signified to one person and a different signified to another. It is the reverse of the error we noted above. The inevitable frustration and anger that would ensue would lead to a lot of head-bashing (so Rashi).

Perhaps Rashi was particularly sensitive to the capacity of the same "sound-image" to represent different "concepts" in different languages because he perceived that even within the same language a signifier can have more than one signified. The bond between signifier and signified may be unstable. Meaning flickers. Rashi understood (albeit differently from Saussure) that meaning is derived from the contrasts among signs. Gen. 11:1 reads that all the land was one language *(safa 'ehat)* and one speech *(devarim 'ahadim)*. As "speech" contrasts with "language," they must, Rashi felt, differ in sense. In extraordinary fashion, even for him, Rashi proffers no fewer than four meanings for "one speech." First, their speech was one—they plotted in unison against the prerogatives of God. "One" refers to the subject of the discourse. Second, they spoke One-talk—talk directed against God, the One in the world. Third, "one" *('ahadim)* by its phonetic similarity to "sharp" *(haddim)* evokes another sense. The builders spoke *sharply:* they calculated that the sky would imminently fall and attempted to avert the disaster by propping it up. In this construal of meaning "one" modifies "speech" in a quasi-adverbial manner. To get this sense, Rashi must read the signifier *'ahadim* not as the direct signifier of a signified but—and this is quite typical of midrash (cf., e.g., Heinemann 1970, 96 ff.; Rojtman 1986)—as the signifier of a signified that itself becomes the signifier of another signified. It sets off a (limited) chain of signification.

We find an analogous trigger of signification in the name that YHWH gives to the newly built city, *bavel,* "Babylon."[14] The name serves first to denominate the city: it signifies a concrete signified. God, however, charges it with a second signification. The name *bavel* must signify another signified, the verbal stem *b-l-l,* which in turn signifies the signified concept, "confusion"—". . . he called its name Babylon *(bavel),* for there he confused *(balal),* YHWH did, the language of all the land" (v. 9).

According to Rashi's fourth comment on the locution "one speech," the phrase need not be interpreted in immediate relation to what follows—building the city and tower. Rashi, at verse 9, summing up, at a remove from the narrative's beginning, "forgets" his earlier proximate readings of "one speech" and interprets it as the harmonious state in which the builders lived before embarking on their (self-)project(ion). Rashi's repeated substitutions of signifieds for the same signifier, along with his awareness of how signifieds can themselves become signifiers, exemplifies the dynamic play of signification.

In a close critical reading of Saussure, Derrida demonstrates that not only does Saussure fail to allow for this dynamic play, his semiology is fraught with questionable assumptions of Western metaphysics (Derrida 1974, 27–73). By distinguishing signifier and signified within the sign, he "leaves open the possibility of thinking a *concept signified in and of itself*, a concept simply present for thought, independent of a relationship to language, that is of a relationship to a system of signifiers" (Derrida 1981, 19). In order to expose those faulty assumptions, Derrida locates contradictions, inconsistencies, and incoherencies in Saussure's writing and explains how such a difficulty *(aporia)*[15] must inevitably follow. The analytical method, or, more precisely, the critical mode of discourse that Derrida develops, is deconstruction—taking apart the unacknowledged presuppositions of a text by identifying how, on their account, the text deconstructs itself.[16] Derrida both illustrates deconstruction's mode of operation and propounds its core ideas in his reading of the founder of phenomenology, Husserl (Derrida 1973b, 1–104). "It is perhaps the essay which I like most," Derrida has said (1981, 4). One can see why: it says what it does, and it does what it says. In establishing the rationale for deconstruction it is always already (as Derrida likes to say) deconstructive.

Husserl took up the project of Descartes, to establish that which we can know for certain and proceed to explain how we know what we know (Husserl [1913] 1962, esp. 97 ff.). By bracketing out all phenomena that depend on some prior concept or mediating sense, Husserl sought, on the one hand, to expose our assumptions and beliefs and, on the other, to identify what we perceive immediately, purely, without the interference of something we already know or feel. The only thing, in the end, that we can posit absolutely, Husserl thought, is the "I," the Ego—pure self-consciousness (11 and passim). All else can be shown to be a construct of some sort, the product of ideas, not unmediated perception. We apprehend not by direct perception but by directing our consciousness and objectifying our ideas. Through a Cartesian method of radical skepticism, Husserl attempted to create the science of science itself, "the one science that criticizes itself at the same time" (165–66).

Derrida would seem to be engaged in a similar project. His target, however, is not merely epistemology but the most pervasive assumptions of metaphysics, those which even Husserl uncritically accepted. Derrida's distinctive (though not unique) mode of operation is not to attack one position by posing against it a superior one. Accordingly, Derrida, though heavily indebted to Nietzsche (cf., e.g., Spivak 1974, xxi–xxxviii; Norris 1982, 56–89), does not demolish Husserl's notion that self-consciousness is immediately perceptible by referring to Nietzsche's teaching that self is it-self an ideational construct, a "synthetic concept" (Nietzsche 1968, 216; cf. 1986b, 198–203). We begin with difference. Nor will Derrida undermine Husserl's theory of signs by adducing Saussure. Rather, Derrida works within Husserl's text to puncture and deflate it from the inside out. He deconstructs Husserl.

Husserl had not recognized the mediating role of language in affecting consciousness.[17] Derrida challenges this denial. Without even defining "sign," Husserl distinguished between signs that "indicate" directly and signs that "express" as a result of will and consciousness. Derrida shows that even Husserl's "expressive" signs involve subjective associations, reflections, re-presentations to one's consciousness, intention. Husserl's distinction between two types of sign implicitly manifests the body/soul dichotomy of ancient Greek and subsequent Western philosophy. Meaning presupposes the *presence* of will or intention to the self. It is impossible, as Husserl asserted, to separate reality from representation in language. Language already represents. Husserl wanted to remove the sign from immediate self-consciousness in order to save the metaphysical idea that something is always *present* to us. But even the sole survivor of Husserl's most extreme bracketing, the "I," already implies an opposition between the "I" who lives and is and the "I" who will be dead and is not.

Derrida proceeds to show how retention as a mode of perception that is continuous with the now involves time. Time, by definition, is relational, more extensive than an ever-present instantaneous moment. Derrida has caught Husserl in a serious inconsistency. Moreover, the very concept of the present implies the non-present. Meaning (like being in the Creation narrative) is always already the product of difference. When Adam and Eve chose to disobey God and eat from the Tree of Knowing, they applied a sense of discrimination that was not to be theirs until they had already eaten from the Tree (cf. Luzzatto [1871] 1965 on Gen. 3:24).

Expression, Husserl maintained, must be immediately present. Derrida has delineated two ways in which it is not. Now Derrida attacks the same central point in Husserl's phenomenology from a different angle. Expression must be conveyed by a medium that is purely unworldly, unobjectified. That medium is the voice. The voice precedes consciousness, or, contends Derrida, is consciousness (cf. Derrida 1981, 22). Auto-affection, "the exercise of the voice," conditions self-presence; in consequence, "no pure transcendental reduction [bracketing of all intermediation] is possible" (Derrida 1973b, 82). In other words, a priori one cannot bracket out all effects of consciousness because pure self-consciousness itself is conditioned. Signification is conditioned by difference, or rather *différance*, a hybrid term incorporating both spatial difference and temporal deferral. Time itself is the product of metaphor: it does not literally "move." Accordingly, "the living present . . . is always already a trace" (Derrida 1973b, 85). One can be aware only of what has been. The very sense of time cannot occur to us until time has past. Tense, as in Genesis 1, precedes time.

If signification involves *différance*, a subject cannot perceive in Husserl's unmediated sense. Metaphysics is grounded in a belief in some absolute presence. With the insight that presence is never fully there and is realized in traces—indications of absence—metaphysics, Derrida avers, has come to an end.[18] The presence of the signified to the signifier, of even the sign itself, is a fundamental notion in Saussurean theory that is supplanted, or plowed under, by Derrida (Derrida 1973a). Signs do not indicate presence; they "represent the presence in its absence; they take the place of the present . . . the movement of signs defers the moment of encountering the thing itself" (1973a, 138).

With this Derrida lays the groundwork for his second, more devastating critique of Saussure. Saussurean semiology posits speech as the primary model of language.[19] This conforms to the metaphysics undone by Derrida in which voice manifests presence and writing "obscures" and "disguise[s]" that presence (de Saussure 1966, 30). Through a deconstruction of many Western philosophers, Derrida exposes the *aporia* in their arguments precisely at those points where speech is privileged over writing. In fact, Derrida argues, if the sign represents but the traces of presence, of absence, then a better model of consciousness than speech is writing (see Derrida 1974). Semiology, the science of signs patterned on spoken language, is replaced by "grammatology," the science of writing. In writing we understand the trace of presence that is absent; writing, therefore, serves as the better model of experience. Experience, then, is textuality, a tissue of traces (cf. Atkins 1983, 23).

Meaning is not present in writing—*écriture*, anglicized as ecriture (Hartman 1981, 8)—but emerges from the play of *différance* —anglicized as differance with an "a" (Derrida 1973a, 129 ff.)— among the traces of presence. "Like differance, the trace is never presented as such. In presenting itself it becomes effaced; in being sounded it dies away" (154). "Play is the disruption of presence. The presence of an element is always a signifying and substitutive reference inscribed in a system of differences and the movement of a chain" (1978, 292). The text, the tissue of traces, does not embody or convey meaning. It is the scene of activity in which the reader inscribes meaning. Meaning, then, is unstable, it shimmers, like the self-effacing traces that are the scene of sense:[20] "The unconscious text is already a weave of pure traces, differences in which meaning and force are united—a text nowhere present, consisting of archives which are *always already* transcriptions" (211). Clearly Derrida is describing a totally different way for understanding experience. Deconstruction is a different way of thinking. Derrida suggests in his deconstruction of Freud that the mind is it-self already structured from made meaning. Reading a text is writing a text, inscribing it with the meaning that we find in it.[21] Recall God's creation of light in Genesis 1. Texts, written texts, are made of texts already made (a fact I have been highlighting in the composition of the present essay). All language echoes other language (cf. Hartman 1981).

The implications for reading biblical narrative can reach as far as one will let them.[22] But before entering into that barely charted territory, it will be worthwhile to note that while language for Derrida is written—ecriture—it is not literal.[23] Language is always other than what it says, always already figured. Consider the number of obvious metaphorical usages in the first sentence of this paragraph: "implications" (do I not draw them out?), "can" (what "can" an implication by itself do?), "reach" (with what arms?), "let them" (see how the implications have been personified). Think of my repeated usage of "on the one hand . . . on the other hand . . . ." To what extent is our habit of contrasting two elements in an opposition conditioned by our two-handedness? The root of language, of assertion, of "truth" itself is metaphor.[24] Conviction follows from the tentatively apt analogy, as Nietzsche, in an oft-cited passage, proclaims:

> What, then, is truth? A mobile army of metaphors, metonyms, and anthropomorphisms—in short, a sum of human relations, which have been enhanced, transposed, and embellished poetically and rhetorically, and which after long use seem firm, canonical, and obligatory to a people: truths are illusions about which one has forgotten that this is what they are; metaphors which are worn out and without sensuous power; coins which have lost their pictures and now matter only as metal, no longer as coins. (1986a, 219)

One of deconstruction's projects is to lay bare the figurative, nonliteral, false—or perhaps rather, untrue—within commonly accepted language.

In order to accomplish this task the deconstructor must, ironically, use language, perhaps the very terms that one is deconstructing. To catch the thief one must use the thief herself. Deconstruction, like Husserl's phenomenology, must subject itself to deconstruction. In order to use language differing from itself in sense, free from the meanings by which it has been inscribed, Derrida adopted from Heidegger the practice of writing "under erasure" (cf. Spivak 1974, xiv–xviii). To indicate, for example, that when we speak of textuality as traces that ~~are~~ no longer, we can write the word "are"—representing an elusive, always deferred presence—under erasure since we confine ourselves by our linguistic habits to speak of that which ~~is~~, when, in theory and in fact, it ~~is~~ not. There ~~is~~ no present.

The technique, or style, of writing under erasure could be useful in making ourselves aware of the metaphors and theology by which we live in reading biblical narrative. I might read Gen. 1:3–4, then, as follows:

> ~~He said~~, God did, "~~Let~~ there ~~be~~ light!" and there ~~was~~ light.
> ~~He saw~~, God did, the light, that it ~~was~~ good.

Most premodern readers would not read any of this passage under erasure. What we might read as the anthropomorphism and personification of God they would interpret literally. But a committed deconstructor could not rest contented with the above reading. Another important term to place under erasure would be "God."

Deconstruction, as modeled by Derrida, seeks, as we have seen, to pull out the bottom from under all metaphysics. Husserl had already felt compelled to bracket out a transcendent God as a "highly mediated" construct of consciousness (Husserl [1913] 1962, 157–58). In Derrida's view Western thought has posited God in order to prevent the chain of signification from extending endlessly into oblivion (cf., e.g., Derrida 1978, 280). By setting up God, as Genesis does, as the author(ity) behind language, signifiers will always reach an ultimate signified. God has been the "transcendental signified" in which meaning has inhered, the one assurance of presence behind the phenomenological curtain of absence. The transcendental signified is inconsistent with Derrida's theory of signification: "I define writing as the impossibility of a chain arresting itself on a signified that would not relaunch the signified, in that the signified is already in the position of the signifying substitution" (Derrida 1981, 82; cf. Derrida 1974, 7). The builders of Babel, in attempting to produce a permanent signification, were doomed to failure. So, for Derrida, is the God idea.

God is one of those concepts the West has cherished in order to hold the center, impose structure and finitude, a sense of order and arrangement—the sense we get in any conventional reading of Genesis. When, in the history of Western metaphysics, physical realities evolved into language and "everything became discourse," "it was necessary to begin thinking that there was no center, . . . that it was not a fixed locus but a function, a sort of nonlocus in which an infinite number of sign-substitutions came into play" (Derrida 1978, 279–80). Deconstruction would subvert any presumption of a center, implying a given structure; it would deny any guarantor of such structure, such as God, or any foundation of absolute knowledge, such as the mind of God. There can, then, be no unity of text, as Alter and Kermode would have it.[25] For theology, "deconstruction . . . is in the final analysis *the death of God put into writing*" (Raschke 1982, 3).

"Deconstruction," Derrida insists, "is not *neutral*. It *intervenes*" (1981, 93). To deconstruct the Bible would reduce it to the same nothingness to which other texts have been deconstructed. One would be left in the end with a Nietzschean vision of the void. Derrida's clearing the ground, Hartman has suggested, might allow for some other, nonmetaphysical building in its stead (1981, 28–29).[26]

Deconstruction might pave the way for types of constructive theology—confecting models of God—in place of the descriptive theologies
that have typified Western religions (cf. Winquist 1982, esp. 50,
citing the work of Gordon Kaufman). On the other hand, the
explicit antitheology of Derridean thought might find constructive
systems to be as antithetical as YHWH found the Tower of Babel.
It had to be smashed. Perhaps for this reason, Miscall, who had
applied certain deconstructive techniques in his reading of biblical
narratives (1983),[27] felt compelled to demur in his subsequent
work: "This is not a deconstructive reading, since I see no need to
deconstruct the Bible in the same sense that de Man or Derrida feels
the need to deconstruct the texts he reads" (1986, xxiv). Deconstruction takes apart the system it reads. It would be ironic indeed to
read the Bible according to an approach so out of sympathy with the
Bible's own outlook (cf. Polzin 1980).

One might nevertheless find good reasons to perform deconstructive operations on the Bible. It is the deconstructor's tack, as
we have seen in Derrida's reading of Husserl, to dismantle the text
from within. One could say that in so doing one is fulfilling the
destiny of the text itself. Husserl presented his phenomenological
criticism "as [if] it were the secret longing of the whole philosophy of
modern times" ([1913] 1962, 166). It is basic to Derrida's position
that the texts he reads are self-deconstructing. Derrida, the reader,
teases out their implications. Now what if one were to view the
Bible as a model of deconstruction? One could then perform deconstruction in response to the Bible's inherent tendency. Herbert
Schneidau has characterized the Hebrew Bible as a text that
continually subjects its own values to criticism in a sort of proto-
deconstructive fashion (Schneidau 1975; cf. 1982). With respect to
God, the Bible does not present the deity systematically, and rarely
through description. YHWH becomes known through his acts, by
later retrospective interpretation, through displacement (cf. Atkins
1983, 43). One might challenge Schneidau on his admittedly
Lutheran emphasis on prophecy at the expense of law, or on his
relativistic readings of self-proclaimed absolute texts. There is,
however, something of the subversive, or at least the restive, within
the complex arrangement of materials in so textured a text as the
Torah, and we shall reconsider this matter below.

One could further argue for the consonance of the Bible with the
deconstructive program by pointing to the indivisibility of signifier
and signified that is reflected in the fact that Hebrew *davar* means

"word" and "act" and "thing" (cf., e.g., Handelman 1982, esp. 3–4, 31–33). Derrida himself has connected his views on the primacy of writing and the dynamic nature of signification within the Hebraic tradition (cf. Atkins 1983, 45–47). Yet, one can hardly overlook the central importance of God's presence in biblical narrative, literalized (or literally) in the aura, the *kavod*, that so often was made manifest before the eyes of the Israelites (e.g., Exod. 40:34–38; Lev. 9:23). The Torah's reiteration that YHWH "walks" among the people (cf., e.g., Exod. 33:16; Deut. 23:15), even if interpreted metaphorically, gives a strong impression of presence. Israel's worship of YHWH was predicated on its witness of the divine presence in their present, albeit often a recollected present. The point can be underscored by noting the verbal resemblance between witness and worship in such a verse as Exod. 14:31: "It saw *[vayyar']*, Israel did, the hand, the great one, that he had done, YHWH had, against Egypt; they feared *[vayyir'u]*, the people did, YHWH." Deconstruction must blow away the cloud of God's presence that hovers over virtually all biblical narrative.

One might do better to exploit deconstruction as a means of liberating ourselves from what Harold Bloom has termed "facticity" —"the state of being a fact, as an inescapable and unalterable fact" (Bloom 1984, 1). By exposing the root ideas supporting biblical narrative, we become aware of the extent to which we are entangled in them ourselves. Our critical reading of the Bible, or of any other text, is liable to be compromised by our unconscious acceptance of the views of which we are supposed to be critical (cf. Polzin 1980). Like the fruit of the Tree of Knowing, deconstruction may open our eyes to facts so commonplace we had not noticed them before. We might, like the couple in Eden, blush at our nakedness. Certain recent feminist criticism of the Bible, for example, has had this effect (cf., e.g., Bal 1987; Fuchs 1985a, b; Fuchs 1987). Similarly, we have assumed more than we are apt to realize of traditional perspectives on the biblical text. The mode of deconstruction, by its denial of given centers and structures, favors the roads not taken, the margins, even the unthinkable, or more precisely, the unthought. To get a better look, it likes to invert.

Bloom, for example, escapes the powerful facticity of conventional readings of the Garden story by reading it Gnostically: the Serpent is not Satan but hero (Bloom 1984). This is not how the story has been generally read. J has been read straight, not ironically. But if meaning is indeed inscribed within the traces, the product of presuppositions that are always already in the reader's mind, then an ironist will find an ironist in J just as a traditionalist will find a traditionalist. Consider again the Tower of Babel text. When YHWH marks the builders' initial progress, he says: "Now they will not be blocked from all that they had schemed to do" (Gen. 11:6b). YHWH sounds worried. Rashi, our proto-deconstructor, subverts this sense. A pious traditionalist, Rashi does not allow a God who could feel alarm at the idea that the builders might succeed. Accordingly, Rashi inscribes the text with the interrogative and reads it as a question: "Shall they not be blocked from all that they had schemed to do?" The alternatives of meaning are always already with the reader. Center and margin, top and bottom, all depend on perspective. An ironist will find an ironist, and a religious reader will find God in the Torah. The Derridean incisor, to cut at all, must cut both ways.

I hope to show that by implementing strategies of deconstruction as hermeneutical tools one can both pry open and plumb more deeply into biblical narrative. One can perhaps even enhance the presence of God, at least by virtue of having inscribed it. Rather than venture to summarize here the reading strategies that one might adopt from deconstruction (see, e.g., Spivak 1974, esp. lxxiv–lxxvii; Culler 1982, esp. 180 ff.; Atkins 1983). I apply various of those strategies to a reading of a brief, opaque narrative—the story of how Aaron's eldest sons, Nadav and Avihu, died. I choose this passage for a number of reasons, not least of them the fact that the text has been read (inscribed) by many readers, over many centuries, in numerous ways. All along we shall be asking whether the text deconstructs itself. We shall find it a model of undecidability. Here is my rendering of the passage (Lev. 10:1–5; verse numbers are in square brackets):

> They took, sons of Aaron, Nadav and Avihu, did, each man his tray; they put in them fire; they placed on it incense; they brought near before YHWH fire, strange (fire), that he did not command them. [2] It came out, fire did, from before YHWH;[28] it consumed them; they died before YHWH. [3] He spoke, Moses did, to Aaron: "It is that which he spoke, YHWH did, saying, 'Among my near-ones I shall be hallowed, and before all the people I shall be honored.'" He was still, Aaron was. [4] He called, Moses did, to Mishael and to Elzaphan, sons of Uzziel, uncle of Aaron, and he said to them: "Draw near, carry your brothers away from before the holy-place to outside of the camp." [5] They drew near, and they carried them in

their tunics to outside of the camp, according to that which he spoke, Moses did.

The text is rife with ambiguities. The most obvious of them result from undefined pronominal antecedents. Who, in verse 1, is the subject of "*he* did not command"?[29] To what does "that which" in verse 3 refer? In whose tunics did Mishael and Elzaphan remove the detritus of their hapless cousins (v. 5)? Each of these ambiguities has been exploited by exegetes as a clue to solving one of the several mysteries of this episode—the story of what looks to most readers like a punishment in search of a crime (cf., e.g., Rashi ad loc.; Leibowitz 1980, 66; Kirschner 1983, 380). Some assume that it was YHWH who "did not command" Nadav and Avihu to bring the fire (e.g., Wenham 1979, 155). Others assume it was Moses, in which case Nadav and Avihu were usurping prerogatives of Moses' authority (e.g., R. Eliezer, cited in Rashi ad loc.; cf. Shinan 1978/-1979, 205). As for "it is that which" in verse 3, most commentators, like Aaron, are silent, stymied perhaps. Ehrlich foregrounds the issue: "It *[hu']* cannot refer to what YHWH had said because YHWH had never said any such thing. It must refer, rather, not to what precedes but to what follows" (Ehrlich 1899, 221). By incinerating Aaron's sons YHWH has quite flamboyantly made a point: "Among my near-ones I shall be hallowed." "Near-ones" here, Ehrlich contends, means Aaron alone. (One should not be thrown off the track by the plural suffix on "near-ones.") We shall discuss the ambiguity of "near-ones" below; for now we turn to the third ambiguous reference in this passage, "their tunics" (v. 5).

"Their" could, of course, refer to Mishael and Elzaphan. That would be too simple, it would seem, for virtually all commentators—or they have been so caught up in the facticity of prior readings that they have not even seen this possibility. Assuming the pronoun refers to Nadav and Avihu, the puzzle is more intriguing. How could they have been borne out in their own clothes after they had been consumed by fire? (cf., e.g., Noth 1965, 85–86). The midrash *Mekhilta demillu'im* explains how the priests' bodies were all that was burned: the fire entered their nostrils and consumed them from the inside out, stopping at their garments (cf. Goldberg 1981, 117). Philo is more "rational" but presupposes more background: Nadav and Avihu stripped naked before making their offering—naturally, their clothes were untouched by the fire (cf. Kirschner 1983, 388–89).

None of these ambiguities can be resolved, except by controlling their references, incorporating them into a specific (pseudo-)comprehensive interpretation of the story—shaving the pieces until they fit into the puzzle one has imagined. Deconstruction holds that ambiguity is not an occasional property of literature, selectively enriching the sense of the text. Ambiguity is characteristic of language itself, the dynamic play in the scene of reading (cf. Eagleton 1983, 146). While other critical approaches attempt to solve the puzzle, deconstruction denies the objectivity of order and "renounce[s] the ambition to master or demystify its subject (text, psyche) by technocratic, predictive, or authoritarian formulas" (Hartman 1980, 41). Meaning is always indeterminate.

Most readers, in their efforts to circumscribe sense, enlist a particular hermeneutic to decide the interpretation. Most are transfixed by the fire: there was something foul about the fire (cf., e.g., Noth 1965, 84–85; Laughlin 1976, esp. 561). Haran (1978, 232), for example, elaborates the view of R. Abraham Ibn Ezra (12th c.):

> Nadab and Abihu intended to make an offering of incense in their censers (Lev. 10:1–3). They were punished because they offered it to Yahweh in "strange fire," that is, fire other than that which was kept burning on the altar for the daily sacrifice. Nadab and Abihu *apparently* [emphasis added] took their fire from somewhere outside the altar-area and placed it in their censers, as it is stated: "each took his censer and put fire in it."

It should be remarked at the outset that the certainty of this exegesis is belied by the exegete's evocation of doubt when he honestly introduces the word "apparently." We are being cautioned: assumptions are being made. The prooftext cited is certainly no proof—it says nothing about the source of the fire. Indeed, a persistent problem with this reading is the fact that the "fire" is presented first as mere, unqualified "fire." It is modified as "strange" (more on which below) only *after* it had been offered with incense before YHWH (cf. Noordtzij 1982, 108).

We may then raise other possibilities of meaning. Perhaps there was something wrong with the priests bringing incense (cf. Ehrlich 1899, 221). Compare Noordtzij: "*Apparently* [emphasis added] they intended to offer daily incense that only the high priest was authorized to do" (1982, 108). The tell-tale "apparently" admits to a high degree of doubt, leaving room for the contrary claim: "Along with

Aaron and their brothers, Eleazar and Ithamar, [Nadab and Abihu] had just been ordained as priests. It *may be assumed* [emphasis added], therefore, that they had the right to offer incense" (Wenham 1979, 154). The need to "assume" bespeaks the undecidability of the sense. Perhaps, as Wenham suggests, the fire was made "strange" because YHWH (or Moses) had not commanded it (1979, 155; cf. Leibowitz 1980, 67–68; Friedman 1987, 205). Though possible, this reading can be challenged. The phrase "that he did not command them" can be understood as a description of the "strange fire" after the fact rather than as an explanation of its cause. The nature of the fire, in other words, conditioned its being not-commanded.

Perhaps, alternatively, Nadav and Avihu were in fact unauthorized to offer incense (contra Laughlin 1976, 559–60; Wenham 1979, 154). In support of this interpretation Gradwohl adduces Lev. 16:12, which prescribes that the high priest remove fire from the altar and bring incense into the holy of holies (1963, 290). One cannot, however, deduce from this prescription a proscription of incense offerings by other priests.

On the other hand, the term for "strange," *zar*, may serve as a clue. Milgrom has made a respectable philological case that *zar* refers to unauthorized cultic personnel (1970, 5 ff.). The verb "to draw near," *qarev*, denotes encroachment of the sacred precincts. In our passage, however, the verb "to draw near" is not predicated of Nadav and Avihu. They brought the fire near (*hiqriv*), and it is not at all clear that *zar* has the same force when said of objects such as "fire" as it has of personnel (cf. Kirschner 1983, 381 n. 28). Moreover, when Moses orders Mishael and Elzaphan to "draw near" (*qarev*), and they do so (vv. 4–5), it is hardly a matter of encroachment. There is a play in our text of only five verses among the *hiqriv* of Nadav and Avihu's offering, the *qarev* of Mishael and Elzaphan's response, and the enigmatic statement of YHWH: "Among my near-ones [*qerovay*] I shall be hallowed" (v. 3). Does this imply that Nadav and Avihu were not YHWH's "near-ones" (emphasis on "near ones")? Or does this mean to condemn what Nadav and Avihu, as priests who should have known better, did as a desecration of YHWH's cult (emphasis on "I shall be hallowed")? The succeeding phrase, "before all the people I shall be honored," is prone to the same alternatives in emphasis. Assuming that Nadav and Avihu acted in view of the assembled Israelites (end of chap. 9), one could read it: *"Before all the people"* is the place to honor me. Or one could read: "Before all the people" *you had better show me honor!* This clause seems less critical than the preceding one, but it cannot be used to decide the meaning of the preceding. Back to square one.

Shinan wants to settle the issue simply, using two strategies (1978/1979, 201). One capitalizes on the parallelism of "fire" and "fire": since the supposed punishment is divine fire, the sin, too, must have related to the fire (cf. Laughlin 1976). One can go further and note that the phrase describing the incineration of Nadav and Avihu—"It came out, fire did, from before YHWH; it consumed them" (Lev. 10:2)—echoes the description of the divine ignition of the altar immediately above (9:24). The notion of measure-for-measure retribution is well known in the Bible (cf. Marcus 1986). It is, however, neither universal nor predictive. The man gathering wood on the Sabbath was, after all, stoned to death (Num. 15:32–36). He was neither burned nor impaled. Moreover, as we have seen above, "fire"/"fire" is not the only motivic-linguistic parallelism in our passage. One could argue, along similar lines, that YHWH's declaration, "Among my near-ones I shall be hallowed," points the accusing finger at Nadav and Avihu as the culprits, not at the fire that they brought. Again, we recall that the fire only explicitly became "strange" after it had been "brought near" by the young priests.

The second of Shinan's strategies is to interpret Scripture by Scripture. He cites three other passages in the Torah in which the death of Nadav and Avihu is mentioned: Lev. 16:1, Num. 3:4, and Num. 26:61. In his text Shinan states that the expression "strange fire" repeats three times (1978/1979, 201). But in a footnote (n. 17) and through independent checking, one finds that not every passage refers to the "strange fire." It is telling that in order to proffer any interpretation, one must select and suppress textual data, forcing the square peg into the round hole. The Torah resists such over-simplification. As Gradwohl observes, even within the so-called priestly material of the Torah, the death of Nadav and Avihu is differently motivated (1963, 289). Num. 3:4 and 26:61 both describe the deaths "when they brought near fire, strange (fire), before YHWH." Lev. 16:1, however, reads differently: "When they drew near before YHWH, and they died." Here, the deaths seem attributed to the priests' encroachment of the sacred precincts.[30] Such an interpretation is consistent with the following verse, which warns Aaron against entering the inner sanctum "at any time." Had Lev. 16:1 conformed to the other passages, one might submit to the uniform interpretation that would result (though it would still be no less an interpretation). The verse, however, impedes any attempt at harmonization.

The ancient Aramaic targum, Onkelos, seeks harmony. In consequence, it does violence to our text. It renders Lev. 16:1 *beqaro-vehon 'eshata nukhreta*—"when they brought near fire, strange (fire)." Other ancient versions similarly succumb to the Hellenistic penchant for order (cf. Gradwohl 1963, 289–90). The integrity of the Hebrew source in its diversity stands intact against the efforts of interpreters, ancient and modern, to domesticate it. It is as stubborn as Job in the face of his friends' contentions. In the end God supported Job. Interpretation runs into difficulty—Derrida's *aporia*—at precisely those points at which it seeks to impose order.

The Torah's three references to the story of Nadav and Avihu in Lev. 10:1–5 present two alternative readings of the passage.[31] Each, we have seen, is problematic. The Torah would seem to exemplify the play of reading that deconstruction assumes for any text by inscribing the passage one way—placing the onus on the fire (Num. 3:4 and 26:61); and by inscribing it another way—placing the onus on the personnel (Lev. 16:1–2). It would seem to self-deconstruct.

Our reading is hardly exhausted. We had been assuming that the sense of the passage could be located within verses 1–5 of Leviticus 10. Frames, however, are artificial, superimposed at will.[32] Let us expand the frame and look at the succeeding text. Rashi cites another classical midrash, this in the name of R. Yishmael (cf. Shinan 1978/1979, 208). Most readers view the death of Nadav and Avihu as an effect and look for a cause. The midrash sees the death scene as a cause and looks for an effect. The effect holds the key to the cause. In Lev. 10:8–9 YHWH commands the priests to beware entering the sacred precincts drunk with wine or beer—"so that you do not die" *(velo' tamutu)*. If this be the effect, Nadav and Avihu died because they approached YHWH in an intoxicated state.[33] The impulse to interpret, to subordinate the text, and not simply to inhabit it, leads some to read words into the text (see Shinan 1978/1979).

Others read more in words. Philo spins a reading out of the protagonists' names. The names are not incidental but crucial to his sense of the text. Like a deconstructor who "castles" the center and the margin, exposing the merely relative position of each, Philo reads the plot in the names. Nadav, from the verbal stem *n-d-b*, "to donate," denotes the one who serves God willingly, without compulsion. Avihu, "My Father is He [i.e., God]" (or "Yah is my Father"), represents pious submission to the sovereignty of God (cf. Kirschner 1983, esp. 386). The young priests, in a fit of ecstasy, purposely transgress the danger limit of the divine presence so that they would be immolated and translated into immortality, like Enoch and Elijah. A text as mystifying as ours prompts far-reaching exercises to make it intelligible. One grasps for clues.

Another midrash returns us to Num. 3:4. Immediately after relating the deaths of Nadav and Avihu, in the context of the Aaronide genealogy, the text adds "and sons, they were not theirs"—that is, Nadav and Avihu had fathered no sons (cf. Shinan 1978/1979, 209). Could this seeming disregard for the divine commandment to procreate (cf. Gen. 1:22, 9:1) and continue the priestly line have motivated their deaths? Did they, like Esau, belittle their hereditary vocation? Could the genealogical note in Numbers 3 hold the key to the mystery in Leviticus 10? The midrash has made the connection. How long will it remain inscribed?

It is ironic that within the Bible's narrative patterns or typologies Nadav and Avihu never had a chance to survive. It is well known that in the Bible's global scheme firstborn sons must yield to their juniors (cf., e.g., Goldin 1977).[34] In accordance with this pattern, Aaron's eldest sons must be eliminated to allow Eleazar and Ithamar, the next youngest pair, to receive the mantle of priestly leadership (cf. Licht 1985, 33–34; Damrosch 1987, 278). Note the sequence of events related in 1 Chron. 24:1–2:

> . . . sons of Aaron: Nadav and Avihu, Eleazar and Ithamar. They died, Nadav and Avihu did, before their father, and sons, they were not theirs. (So) they served-as-priests, Eleazar and Ithamar did.

One could say that the fact of Eleazar and Ithamar's succession conditioned both the sonlessness (it would not have mattered had they had daughters) and the death of Nadav and Avihu—the extinction of their line.

If, indeed, the young priests had to die, the search for a reason for their deaths within the local narrative may be misguided from the start. To put it differently, the narrative may not motivate their deaths at all; there may be no reason to look for. The search for a reason reflects a drive for order within the interpreter (*pace*

Nietzsche). The presupposition that there is a reason not only motivates the search (the reader already "knows" that some explanation lurks within the text); it necessarily posits, or superimposes, the structure of sin and punishment on the story. The doctrine of retribution is found widely in the Torah (cf., e.g., Fokkelman 1975, 32–39). But one cannot know but only assume that that doctrine is assumed by every Torah text.[35] Its presence is a sign of its facticity, the product of a tradition of reading. One service of deconstruction, as noted, is its capacity to break facticity. If, for argument's sake, the narrative of Nadav and Avihu meant to challenge or subvert the absolute rationality of the Torah, the scrutability of divine retribution, we could never find such a meaning were we to posit the pervasiveness of the sin-and-punishment pattern. Perhaps in the way that metaphysicians were never aware that they presupposed presence because they had been indoctrinated with the idea itself, readers will not be able even to consider the possible irrationality or disorderliness of the Nadav and Avihu narrative if they first assume orderliness.

A story in which incinerated bodies are transported on intact garments gives pause/cause to suspend our presumption of reason and order. A scene of reading/writing in which the modifier "strange" stubbornly clings to the second, not the first, mention of the "fire" foregrounds its indeterminacy. The further we explore the possibilities of intelligibility, the denser we find the jungle. The quest for coherent sense has gone up in in-cense. Our search for the rational God of the cultic law has led us to ponder the imponderable *mysterium tremendum* of Otto (Otto 1957). Reading our story, Plaskow has written:

> The idea that divinity can be terrible and awesome, an unbreachable mystery and consuming fire, is far from modern notions which equate God's holiness with sanctity and moral purity or which find God's presence only in sustenance and care. Yet this terrifying aspect of God is found repeatedly in the *Tanakh*. (1986, 5)

Jewish tradition, as Plaskow, too, has noted, comments on the irrationality of the Nadav and Avihu episode by coupling it in the weekly Torah reading cycle with the *haftara*, relating the sorry story of Uzzah in 2 Sam. 6:1–8. In the course of David's bringing the Ark of YHWH to Jerusalem with his men, the wagon bearing the ark was about to topple. Trying to break the ark's fall, Uzzah touched it, provoking YHWH to "explode" *(parats)* against him.[36]   The intertextual connection of this tale to ours is more than thematic. The ark had just been removed from the house of Uzzah's father *Avinadav*, a name that is nothing but a reverse conflation of *Nadav* and *Avihu*.[37] The terrible destructive power that consumed Nadav and Avihu lurks within the story of Uzzah in a barely concealed permutation. Shades of Nadav and Avihu indeed!

The method, or mode, of deconstruction—of driving wedges into the spaces of the text and leaving them there—can be used as a means of remystifying the text, insisting on the unknown as we grope for the known. It is not that we can never produce a reading. We can never produce a certain, stable, or impregnable meaning. As Derrida says near the end of "Speech and Phenomena," "This does not mean that we know nothing but that we are beyond absolute knowledge" (1973b, 103). The beginning of wisdom is the ac-know-ledgment of our limitations in knowing. The God-belief, or ideal, entails our humanness; humanness implies human limitation. A way of thinking and doing such as deconstruction, which is dedicated to exposing the limits/borders of human understanding as a consequence of the instability of linguistic sense, can paradoxically facilitate a God-belief (though not the God of absolute order). If, as Ebner writes, the "foundation task" of religious education "is to foster awareness of Mystery" (1986, 484), deconstruction could be the prime hermeneutic of the unknown: it deepens our mystification as we read. It can inspire awe.

There has always been an intimate, perhaps necessary, correlation between the obscurity of texts and their sacredness. Sacred texts, the ones in which readers "find" God, can only function when their spaces are frequent and wide.

The heightening of the meaningfulness of a text as a whole is . . . often connected with a lowering of its meaningfulness at the level of ordinary linguistic communication. Hence, the typical process whereby incomprehensible texts become sacred: utterances that circulate in a given community but which are incomprehensible to it are given text significance. . . .[38] Inasmuch as a high degree of text meaning is perceived as a guarantee of truthfulness, and text meaning grows inasmuch as ordinary linguistic meaning is obscured, in many instances the tendency can be observed to make texts from which a high degree of truthfulness is expected incomprehensible for the addressee. In order to be taken as a text the message must be incomprehensible or barely comprehensible and must need further translation or interpretation.[39] (Lotman and Piatigorsky 1977/1978, 238)

In this regard the opaque story of Nadav and Avihu serves as a quintessential sacred tale, a text most obviously open to endless interpretation, as its numerous readings attest, or—to no interpretation. In its radical reduction of the text, deconstruction ironically reveals the sources of its sacredness.

The story of Nadav and Avihu, as narrative, intrudes into the exposition of cultic law that precedes and follows it. It may strike the reader as disrupting the text as violently as the flash of fire annihilated the young priests. As the narrative genre of the episode disturbs the legal landscape by its otherness, so does its representation of a possibly opaque and nonverbal—irrational—God upset the orderliness of the cultic system. Notwithstanding the cultic regulations, all of which posit that reward and punishment follow directly from obedience to or violation of divine prescriptions, God has not in fact explained everything. The system contains terrible dark secrets; YHWH may strike without warning. The system of the cult rationalizes, sets things in order. It reassures that there is a way to purify the polluted and expurgate sin; like the rainbow after the Flood it guarantees human life despite its imperfection. It entails, however, a theological danger: it renders God normative and predictable. It subordinates the deity to the system the deity is supposed to transcend.

"The value and force of a text may depend to a considerable extent on the way it deconstructs the philosophy that subtends it" (Culler 1982, 98). Lest God become altogether manipulable by the cult, the episode of Nadav and Avihu, I would suggest, subverts the orderly ritual's implication of orderliness by asserting YHWH's unpredictability and autonomy, YHWH's sheer transcendence. Consider Damrosch's more traditional perspective, first published in Alter and Kermode's *Literary Guide*: "Clearly the episode serves, in part, a monitory purpose, to warn against the invention of new practices or the importation of practices external to the cultic order" (Damrosch 1987, 267). This reading assumes the inviolability of order—even by God. YHWH's fire, in this view, restores order. But our deconstruction of the passage has made the search for a rational cause impossible in practice and possibly misguided in theory. In our reading, YHWH breaks up the orderliness to show he is above/beyond the cultic order. A God worthy of the name cannot be trammeled by rules any more than an infinite God can be contained by names, by language.

Wenham observes that the first verse of our passage, Lev. 10:1, employs the priestly vocabulary of the surrounding context: *laqah* ("to take"), *natan* ("to put"), *sim* ("to place"), *hiqriv* ("to bring near," i.e., to offer), *q-t-r* ("incense") (1979, 154). The words are at home in Leviticus; the story seems of a piece. By weaving the local vocabulary into a tale of the *mysterium tremendum*, the narrative of Nadav and Avihu can be understood to deconstruct the finely wrought cultic fabric. Order is subverted to expose disorder. The young priests are functioning as priests—the words seem right. It is not enough, however, to act the priest. The priest can only control what the priest does; he cannot control God. Behind the orderly veneer of priestly ritual, behind the *parokhet* that screens off YHWH's quasi-condensed presence from the human observer, is the unscrutable Other. YHWH can hardly be better comprehended than the motives of Nadav and Avihu and the question of whether they had done anything amiss.

As I have claimed in my deconstructive analysis, the very strangeness of the episode undercuts its susceptibility to rational explanation. There is no reason to assume that there is any reason for Nadav and Avihu to die, though, as we have seen, readers have cast about for reasons. One can always contrive some reason from fragments of text. But a deconstruction will both turn up other, ill-fitting fragments and show that the fragments themselves are plays of differance, no-longer-present constructions ready already for deconstruction.

NOTES

This essay originally appeared in *Prooftexts*, vol. 9, 1989. I presented versions of parts of this essay at the Columbia University Seminar for the Study of the Hebrew Bible (18 March 1987) and at a regional meeting of the American Academy of Religion (15 April 1988). I am grateful to the participants for their responses, and to the Abbell Research Fund of the Jewish Theological Seminary of America for stipends that supported this work. Professor Jacob Milgrom, Professor Baruch M. Bokser of blessed memory, and Joshua Levinson suggested helpful bibliographic references in the course of my research.

1. Atkins 1983, 3.

2. Eagleton 1983, 148.
3. Culler 1982, 180.
4. Alter and Kermode evince their kinship with structuralism when they write of literature as a "complex language" and define the role of "constructive" criticism as one that calls "attention to the operations of this language." "Its syntax, grammar, and vocabulary," they write, "involve a highly heterogeneous concord of codes, devices, and linguistic properties" (1987, 5). One is reminded here, for example, of the work of structuralist Roman Jakobson, such as Jakobson 1960, 1968, and 1980.
5. Cf. Freud 1965, 299: "But just as all neurotic symptoms, and, for that matter, dreams, are capable of being 'over-interpreted' and indeed need to be, if they are to be fully understood, so all genuinely creative writings are the product of more than a single motive and more than a single impulse in the poet's mind, and are open to more than a single interpretation." Cf. also Freud 1965, 182, 253, and passim.
6. Editor's note: This was written in 1988.
7. I refer to some of the pertinent literature, including Derrida's reading of the Tower of Babel story, below.
8. The Society of Biblical Literature's seminar on structuralism might be redubbed the "Post-Structuralism Seminar."
9. Notable examples are Jacques Lacan's reading of Edgar Allen Poe's "The Purloined Letter" in Lacan 1973, Derrida's reading of Lacan's reading of Poe in Derrida 1975, and Barbara Johnson's interpretation of Melville's *Billy Budd* in Johnson 1980.
10. I offer a brief word of explanation for the mode of translation I use. It is meant to highlight certain linguistic or rhetorical patterns in the Hebrew. Often certain Hebrew usages are more nuanced than any idiomatic English counterpart. For example, "between . . . and between" renders Hebrew *ben . . . uven*, which contrasts with *ben . . . leven*; the former indicates a parity relation while the latter places the inferior term after the preposition *l*. For more information, see Ehrlich 1899 ad Gen. 1:6; cf. vol. 3 [1901] ad 2 Chron. 14:10. For further discussion of my translation style and its indebtedness to Martin Buber and Franz Rosenzweig, see Greenstein 1983.
11. For a survey of the debate, see McFall 1982.
12. Cf. Skinner 1930, 225, who renders the difficult *devarim 'ahadim* as "a single set of vocables." More on this phrase below.
13. A number of commentators observe that Hebrew might otherwise have employed *kofer* to indicate "bitumen," as in Gen. 6:14 (cf., e.g., Driver 1904, 135; Westermann 1984, 534).
14. For a somewhat different treatment of the name, emphasizing the paradox of a proper name having a common noun's meaning, see Derrida 1985, 101–2.
15. Thanks to Professor Richard Corney for researching for me the background of this classical philosophical term, used by Plato, Aristotle, and

others, and now put to renewed use by Derrida. Diodorus speaks of "solving a difficulty by a difficulty," a notion, Corney observes, that might appeal to Derrida.

16. Helpful introductions to deconstruction are Atkins 1983, Culler 1982, Norris 1982, 1987, and Spivak 1974, ix–lxxxvii.

17. Cf. Husserl [1913] 1962, 123: "The spatial thing which we see is, despite all its transcendence, perceived, we are consciously aware of it as given in its *embodied form*. We are not given an image or a sign *in its place*" [emphasis in original].

18. Contrast Norris 1987, 53.

19. This fundamental belief was shared even by Nietzsche, who anticipated Saussure in saying, "Words are acoustical signs for concepts" (1968, 406).

20. Cf. Nietzsche 1986b, 213: "There are no facts, everything is in flux, incomprehensible, elusive."

21. Cf. Nietzsche 1986b, 204: "There are no 'facts-in-themselves,' for a sense must always be projected into them before there can be 'facts.'"

22. Some of the political implications are discussed in Jobling (1990).

23. This theme has been particularly treated by Paul de Man (1979), who made the deconstruction of figures the focus of his analysis.

24. For a discussion of this aspect of Derrida's writing, see Detweiler 1980.

25. Cf. Derrida 1981, 63–64; cf. Nietzsche 1986b, 202: "Man projects his drive to truth, his 'goal' in a certain sense, outside himself as a world that has being, as a metaphysical world, as a 'thing-in-itself,' as a world already in existence."

26. For a significant effort to develop a metatheological deconstructive discourse, see Taylor 1984. To convey an idea of what such a (heavily christological) discourse sounds like, I cite a brief passage from pages 106–7: "The death of the father opens the reign of the word that is embodied in scripture. Since this word enacts absolute passage, it is forever liminal and eternally playful. The play of the word is writing, and the drama of writing is word. In writing, fixed boundaries break down. Scripture, therefore, is always marginal. The/A word is nothing in itself; it is a play within a play."

27. For critical discussion of Miscall's use of "indeterminacy" here, see Lasine 1986, esp. 51–56.

28. The precise origin of the fire is debated. R. Samuel ben Meir (12th c.), comparing the ignition of the altar in Lev. 9:24 with that in 1 Kings 18:38, concluded that the fire came down from the sky, as in the latter verse. David Zvi Hoffmann, in his Leviticus commentary (1966, 203), cites the more widely held, as well as the classical rabbinic position, that the fire emerged from the holy of holies. The phrase *lifne YHWH*, "before YHWH," occurs several times in the preceding chapters of Leviticus as the site where offerings to YHWH were made (e.g., Lev. 8:26–28; 9:2, 4). In Lev. 9:5 the entire assembly (*kol ha'eda*) approaches

YHWH and stands *lifne YHWH*, awaiting the materialization of the divine aura *(kavod)* (v. 6). It would seem that the people are standing outside of and facing the tent of meeting, housing the holy of holies. This interpretation may be corroborated by 9:21. There Aaron displays animal parts that are offered *lifne YHWH*; then (v. 23) Moses and Aaron enter the tent of meeting. The locution *lifne YHWH* would seem to indicate a locus in front of and facing the divine abode. It is not, therefore, clear that the fire igniting the altar in 9:24 and consuming the young priests in 10:2 came from within the tent. It may have materialized outside the tent or, indeed, fallen from the sky.

29. Certain critics remove the phrase from the text altogether as a later scribal gloss (cf., e.g., Gradwohl 1963, 289 n. 5).
30. Recall Milgrom's treatment of the term *zar*.
31. Certain ancient (cf. Shinan 1978/1979; Kirschner 1983), medieval (e.g., Rashi, Abravanel), and modern (e.g., Gradwohl, Noth, Leibowitz) readers, too, propose alternative interpretations.
32. One midrash finds the cause of Nadav and Avihu's punishment, in the past, at the Sinai revelation (see Geller 1965). David Damrosch, in *The Narrative Covenant: Transformations of Genre in the Growth of Biblical Literature*, in an intricate and intriguing analysis, finds Aaron, not his sons, to be the focus of attention. Assuming the death of Nadav and Avihu is a punishment, Damrosch explains it as a displacement of the punishment that Aaron himself deserved for his role in making the golden calf (Damrosch 1987, 266 ff.). The fact that Nadav and Avihu revive in only slightly altered form, as the sons of King Jeroboam I, who himself made two golden calves, lends force to Damrosch's reading. See further below.
33. Rabbenu Asher (14th c.) elaborates that these prohibitions were transmitted to the priests prior to beginning their service. The fact that the Torah presents this law after the death of Nadav and Avihu has no chronological bearing. *'En muqdam ume'uhar battora*—the Torah does not adhere to a chronological sequence (quoted in Steinsaltz 1978, 36–37).
34. Goldin correctly notes that Aaron the high priest was not a younger brother but a firstborn (1977, 35). Aaron, however, in his own generation, is made subservient to his younger brother, Moses. Eleazar and Ithamar succeed to the position of their older brothers, Nadav and Avihu. The crucial relationship of older and younger is established *between brothers*. Consequently, it is of no consequence that Aaron's oldest surviving son, Eleazar, should serve as high priest under his unrelated contemporary, Joshua.
35. Wenham posits a normative situation: "The whole narrative from 8:1 has led us to expect God's ministers to obey the law promptly and exactly" (1979, 155). It is this expectation or presupposition that allows him to conclude that Aaron's two sons were killed for having brought

"something that had not been commanded." Similarly Leibowitz assumes that "normative religious discipline" precludes "religious ecstasy. . . . For this reason they were punished" (1980, 68).

36. Cf. the usage of *parats* to describe the destructive force of YHWH in Exod. 19:22.
37. This is not the place to discuss the further intertextual connection with the sons of Jeroboam I, Nadav and Aviyah, in 1 Kings 14, for which see Gradwohl 1963, 294–95, and Damrosch 1987, 268 ff.
38. This has been dramatized in Russell Hoban's 1980 novel *Riddley Walker* (Hoban) and in the "tell" sequence in the film "Mad Max III: Beyond Thunderdome."
39. Consider the assumptions of rabbinic midrash concerning the elliptical and allusive nature of Scripture; see now Rojtman 1986 and cf. Rawic̉o- wicz 1957. In comparing rabbinic midrash and deconstruction, as some—notably Handelman (1982)—do, one must be careful not to ᴘush the comparison too far. Hartman has succinctly encapsulated the two general problems with the equation: midrash posits an omnipresent, single, authoritative God; and it asserts the primacy of Scripture; see Hartman 1986, xi; cf., on the former point, Stern 1988, and, on the latter, Fisch 1986.

REFERENCES

Alter, Robert, and Frank Kermode. "General Introduction." In *The Literary Guide to the Bible*, ed. Robert Alter and Frank Kermode. Cambridge, Mass.: Belknap Press of Harvard University Press, 1987.

Atkins, G. Douglas. *Reading Deconstruction/Deconstructive Reading*. Lexington: University Press of Kentucky, 1983.

Bal, Mieke. *Lethal Love: Feminist Literary Readings of Biblical Love Stories*. Bloomington: Indiana University Press, 1987.

Bloom, Harold. "Criticism, Canon-Formation, and Prophecy: The Sorrows of Facticity." *Raritan* 3, 3 (1984): 1–20.

Brooks, Peter. "Introduction." In Tzvetan Todorov, *Introduction to Poetics*. Minneapolis: University of Minnesota Press, 1981.

Cassuto, Umberto. *Commentary on the Book of Genesis*. Vol. 1. Trans. I. Abrahams. Jerusalem: Magnes, 1961.

Culler, Jonathan. *On Deconstruction*. Ithaca, N.Y.: Cornell University Press, 1982.

Damrosch, David. *The Narrative Covenant: Transformations of Genre in the Growth of Biblical Literature*. San Francisco: Harper and Row, 1987.

de Man, Paul. *Allegories of Reading*. New Haven: Yale University Press, 1979.

Derrida, Jacques. "Structure, Sign, and Play in the Discourse of the Human Sciences." In *The Structuralist Controversy*, ed. Richard Macksey and Eugenio Donato. Baltimore: Johns Hopkins University Press, 1972.

————. "Difference." In *Speech and Phenomena and Other Essays on Husserl's Phenomenology*, trans. D. B. Allison. Evanston, Ill.: Northwestern University Press, 1973a.

————. "Speech and Phenomena: Introduction to the Problem of Signs in Husserl's Phenomenology." In *Speech and Phenomena and Other Essays on Husserl's Theory of Signs*, trans. D. B. Allison. Evanston, Ill.: Northwestern University Press, 1973b.

————. *Of Grammatology*. Trans. G. C. Spivak. Baltimore: Johns Hopkins University Press, 1974.

————. "The Purveyor of Truth." *Yale French Studies* 52 (1975): 31–113.

————. *Writing and Difference*. Trans. A. Bass. Chicago: University of Chicago Press, 1978.

————. *Positions*. Trans. A. Bass. Chicago: University of Chicago Press, 1981.

————. *The Ear of the Other*. Ed. Christie V. McDonald, trans. Peggy Kamuf. New York: Schocken, 1985.

de Saussure, Ferdinand. *Course in General Linguistics*. Ed. C. Bally and A. Sechehaye with A. Riedlinger, trans. W. Baskin. New York: McGraw-Hill, 1966.

Detweiler, Robert. "After the New Criticism: Contemporary Methods of Literary Criticism." In *Orientation by Disorientation: Studies in Literary Criticism and Biblical Literary Criticism*, ed. R. A. Spencer. Pittsburgh: Pickwick, 1980.

————, ed. *Derrida and Biblical Studies*. Semeia 23 (1982).

Driver, Samuel Rolles. *The Book of Genesis*. 2d ed. London: Methuen, 1904.

Eagleton, Terry. *Literary Theory: An Introduction*. Minneapolis: University of Minnesota Press, 1983.

Ebner, James H. "Talk about God." *Religious Education* 81, 3 (1986): 466–84.

Ehrlich, Arnold B. *Mikra Ki-Pheschuto*. Vol. 1. Berlin: Poppelauer, 1899.

Fisch, Harold. "Midrash and the Novel—An Afterword." In *Midrash and Literature*, ed. Geoffrey H. Hartman and Sanford Budick. New Haven: Yale University Press, 1986.

Fokkelman, Jan P. *Narrative Art in Genesis*. Assen: Van Gorcum, 1975.

Friedman, Richard Elliott. *Who Wrote the Bible?* New York: Summit, 1987.

Freud, Sigmund. *The Interpretation of Dreams*. Trans. J. Strachey. New York: Basic, 1965.

Fuchs, Esther. "The Literary Characterizations of Mothers and Sexual Politics in the Hebrew Bible." In *Feminist Perspectives on Biblical Scholarship*, ed. Adela Y. Collins. Chico, Calif.: Scholars Press, 1985a.

————. "Who Is Hiding the Truth? Deceptive Women and Biblical Androcentrism." In *Feminist Perspectives on Biblical Scholarship*, ed. Adela Y. Collins. Chico, Calif.: Scholars Press, 1985b.

————. "Structure and Patriarchal Functions in the Biblical Betrothal Type Scene." *Journal of Feminist Studies in Religion* 3 (1987): 7–13.

Geller, Stephen A.   "The Common and the Uncommon."   *Conservative Judaism* 19, 3 (1965): 57–62.

Goldberg, Abraham.   "Twice-Told Midrashim in *Mekhilta demillu'im*" (Hebrew).   *Sinai* 89 (1981): 115–18.

Goldin, Judah.   "The Youngest Son or Where Does Genesis 38 Belong?" *Journal of Biblical Literature* 96 (1977): 27–44.

Gradwohl, Roland.   "Das 'Fremde Feuer' von Nadab und Abihu."   *Zeitschrift für die alttestamentliche Wissenschaft* 75 (1963): 288–96.

Greenstein, Edward L.   "Theories of Modern Bible Translation."   *Prooftexts* 3 (1983): 9–39.

Handelman, Susan.   *The Slayers of Moses*.   Albany: State University of New York Press, 1982.

Haran, Menahem.   *Temples and Temple-Service in Ancient Israel*.   Oxford: Clarendon, 1978.

Hartman, Geoffrey H.   *Criticism in the Wilderness*.   New Haven: Yale University Press, 1980.

———. *Saving the Text*.   Baltimore: Johns Hopkins University Press, 1981.

———. "Jeremiah 20:7–12: A Literary Response."   In *The Biblical Mosaic*, ed. Robert Polzin and Eugene Rothman.   Philadelphia and Chico, Calif.: Scholars Press, 1982.

———. "Introduction."   In *Midrash and Literature*, ed. Geoffrey H. Hartman and Sanford Budick.   New Haven: Yale University Press, 1986.

Heinemann, Isaak.   *Darkhei ha'aggada* (The Ways of Midrash).   3d ed. Jerusalem: Magnes, 1970.

Hoban, Russell.   *Riddley Walker*.   New York: Summit, 1980.

Hoffmann, David Zvi.   *Sefer Vayikra'* (The Book of Leviticus).   Trans. Z. H. Shefer and A. Lieberman.   Jerusalem: Mossad Harav Kook, 1966.

Husserl, Edmund.   *Ideas: General Introduction to Pure Phenomenology*. Trans. W. R. B. Gibson.   New York: Macmillan, [1913] 1962.

Jacob, Benno.   *Das erste Buch der Tora: Genesis*.   Berlin: Schocken, 1934.

Jakobson, Roman.   "Linguistics and Poetics."   In *Style in Language*, ed. Thomas A. Sebeok.   Cambridge, Mass.: Harvard University Press, 1960.

———. "Poetry of Grammar and Grammar of Poetry."   *Lingua* 21 (1968): 597–609.

———. "A Postscript to the Discussion on Grammar of Poetry."   *Diacritics* 10, 1 (Spring 1980): 22–35.

Jobling, David.   "Writing the Wrongs in the World: The Deconstruction of the Biblical Text in the Context of Liberation Theologies."   *Semeia* 51 (1990): 81–118.

Johnson, Barbara.   *The Critical Difference*.   Baltimore: Johns Hopkins University Press, 1980.

Kaufmann, Walter.   *Critique of Religion and Philosophy*.   Garden City, N.Y.: Doubleday, Doran, 1961.

Kendrick, Walter.   "Confessions of a Deconstructor."   *Boston Review* 11, 3 (1986): 5–6, 25–26.

Kirschner, Robert. "The Rabbinic and the Philonic Exegesis of the Nadab and Abihu Incident." *Jewish Quarterly Review* 73 (1983): 375–93.

Lacan, Jacques. "Seminar on the Purloined Letter." *Yale French Studies* 48 (1973): 38–72.

Lasine, Stuart. "Indeterminacy and the Bible: A Review of Literary and Anthropological Theories and Their Applications to Biblical Texts." *Hebrew Studies* 27 (1986): 48–80.

Laughlin, John C. H. "The 'Strange Fire' of Nadab and Abihu." *Journal of Biblical Literature* 95 (1976): 559–65.

Leibowitz, Nehama. *Studies in Bereishit (Genesis)*. Trans. A. Newman. Jerusalem: World Zionist Organization, 1969.

———. *Studies in Vayikra (Leviticus)*. Trans. A. Newman. Jerusalem: World Zionist Organization, 1980.

Licht, Jacob. *A Commentary on the Book of Numbers 1–10* (Hebrew). Jerusalem: Magnes, 1985.

Lotman, Y. M., and A. M. Piatigorsky. "Text and Function." *New Literary History* 19 (1977/1978): 233–44.

Luzzatto, Samuel David. *Commentary on Humash*. Ed. P. Schlesinger. Tel Aviv: Dvir, [1871] 1965.

Marcus, David. "David the Deceiver and David the Dupe." *Prooftexts* 6 (1986): 163–71.

McFall, Leslie. *The Enigma of the Hebrew Verbal System*. Sheffield: Dove, 1982.

McGann, Jerome J. "Some Forms of Critical Discourse." *Critical Inquiry* 11 (1985): 399–417.

Milgrom, Jacob. *Studies in Levitical Terminology*. Vol. 1. Berkeley: University of California Press, 1970.

Miscall, Peter D. *The Workings of Old Testament Narrative*. Philadelphia and Chico, Calif.: Scholars Press, 1983.

———. *1 Samuel. A Literary Reading*. Bloomington: Indiana University Press, 1986.

Nietzsche, Friedrich. *The Basic Writings of Nietzsche*. Trans. and ed. Walter Kaufmann. New York: Modern Library, 1968.

———. "On Truth and Lie in an Extra-Moral Sense." In *Deconstruction in Context: Literature and Philosophy*, ed. Mark C. Taylor. Chicago: University of Chicago Press, 1986a.

———. "The Will to Power." In *Deconstruction in Context: Literature and Philosophy*, ed. Mark C. Taylor. Chicago: University of Chicago Press, 1986b.

Noordtzij, Arie. *Leviticus*. Trans. R. Togtman. Grand Rapids, Mich.: Zondervan, 1982.

Norris, Christopher. *Deconstruction: Theory and Practice*. London: Methuen, 1982.

———. *Derrida*. Cambridge, Mass.: Harvard University Press, 1987.

Noth, Martin. *Leviticus: A Commentary*. Trans. J. E. Anderson. London: Westminster, 1965.

54   *Edward L. Greenstein*

Otto, Rudolf. *The Idea of the Holy.* 2d ed. Trans. J. W. Harvey. London: Oxford University Press, 1957.

Plaskow, Judith. "Drawing the Awful Line between the Holy and the Profane." *Long Island Jewish World,* 4–10 April 1986.

Polzin, Robert M. "Literary and Historical Criticism of the Bible: A Crisis of Scholarship." In *Orientation by Disorientation: Studies in Literary Criticism and Biblical Literary Criticism,* ed. R. A. Spencer. Pittsburgh: Pickwick, 1980.

Raschke, Carl A. "The Deconstruction of God." In *Deconstruction and Theology,* ed. Thomas J. J. Altizer, Max A. Myers, Carl A. Raschke, Robert P. Scharlemann, Mark C. Taylor, and Charles E. Winquist. New York: Crossroad, 1982.

Rawidowicz, Simon. "On Interpretation." *Proceedings of the American Academy for Jewish Research* 26 (1957): 83–126.

Rojtman, Betty. *Feu noir sur feu blanc.* Lagrasse, France: Editions Verdiers, 1986.

Schneidau, Herbert N. *Sacred Discontent: The Bible and Western Tradition.* Baton Rouge: Louisiana State University Press, 1975.

———. "The Word against the Word: Derrida on Textuality." *Semeia* 23 (1982): 5–28.

Shinan, Avigdor. "The Sins of Nadab and Abihu in Rabbinic Literature" (Hebrew). *Tarbiz* 48 (1978/1979): 201–14.

Skinner, John. *Genesis: Critical Exegetical Commentary.* Edinburgh: T. and T. Clark, 1930.

Spivak, Gayatri C. "Translator's Preface." In Derrida's *Of Grammatology.* Baltimore: Johns Hopkins University Press, 1974.

Steinsaltz, Adin. *Perush hummiqra' besifrut hashe'elot uteshuvot* (Interpretation of Scripture in the Responsa Literature). Jerusalem: Keter, 1978.

Stern, David. "Midrash and Indeterminacy." *Critical Inquiry* 15 (1988): 132–61.

Taylor, Mark C. *Erring: A Postmodern A/theology.* Chicago: University of Chicago Press, 1984.

Wenham, Gordon J. *The Book of Leviticus.* Grand Rapids, Mich.: Eerdmans, 1979.

Westermann, Claus. *Genesis 1–11: A Commentary.* Trans. J. J. Scullion. Minneapolis: Augsburg Publishing House, 1984.

Winquist, Charles E. "Body, Text, and Imagination." In *Deconstruction and Theology,* ed. Thomas J. J. Altizer, Max A. Myers, Carl A. Raschke, Robert P. Scharlemann, Mark C. Taylor, and Charles E. Winquist. New York: Crossroad, 1982.

Chapter 2

Postcritical Scriptural Interpretation in Judaism

Peter Ochs

"Postcritical scriptural interpretation"[1] represents an emergent movement among Jewish and Christian text scholars and theologians to give rabbinic and ecclesial traditions of interpretation both the benefit of the doubt and the benefit of doubt: the former, by assuming that there are dimensions of scriptural meaning that are disclosed only by way of the hermeneutical practices of believing communities and traditions of Jews or Christians; the latter, by assuming, in the spirit of post-Spinozistic criticism, that these dimensions may be clarified through the disciplined practice of philological, historical, and textual/rhetorical criticism. Among Christian scholars, this tendency is displayed, for example, in what the late Hans Frei terms the attempt to recover Scripture's *sensus literalis* or in what George Lindbeck has called a "cultural-linguistic" approach to interpreting Church doctrine. Among Jewish scholars, the tendency is displayed, in its various forms, in Moshe Greenberg's "holistic" method of interpreting scriptural texts,[2] David Weiss Halivni's studies of the rabbinic principles of halakhic exegesis, Michael Fishbane's studies of "intra-biblical" exegesis, and also Steven Fraade's historico-literary approach to aggadic midrash. In this brief essay, I review the rules of specifically Jewish postcritical interpretation as they are displayed in works by the latter three scholars. I pick these three because, within the single context of rabbinic studies, they display three paradigmatic types of postcritical inquiry.

I first encountered the postcritical approach to interpretation in the rabbinic studies of Max Kadushin, z"l, then my teacher at the Jewish Theological Seminary. Through a series of five books, published between 1932 and 1969,[3] Kadushin sought to describe the complex conceptual structures of rabbinic Judaism. His method was to identify the collection of rabbinic exegetes as a community of interpreters whose work provided the context in which scriptural texts had meaning for the Jewish people. He argued that this meaning was embodied in the practice of rabbinic exegesis itself and that the rules which informed this practice represented the conceptual order of rabbinic Judaism. He devoted most of his work to examining these rules by examining the system of virtues, or what he called "value-concepts," that were displayed in rabbinic literature. Kadushin believed his work challenged those who assume that conceptual order is to be understood only on what he called a philosophical model. He argued that this assumption leads to one of two errors: either imposing an extraneous conceptual scheme on rabbinic Judaism, or else denying that rabbinic Judaism displays any conceptual order. Instead, he examined religions as indigenous systems of "value-concepts." The scholar's task, he said, is to observe how these concepts interrelate with one another and how they guide concrete behavior.

While I have since written several essays on Kadushin's method,[4] I did not realize that his approach underlay a movement in both Jewish and Christian theological hermeneutics until I sat in on a discussion of such matters among Greenberg, Fraade, Lindbeck, and Frei. After Greenberg's Bible seminar at Yale in 1987–88, these four gathered several times to discuss the meaning of "plain sense" exegesis. I recall that for Frei and Lindbeck "plain sense" reading respected the integrity of the words of a scriptural text in its intratextual context *and* displayed the performative force of that text as token of an authoritative community's code of religious behavior. On the other hand, Greenberg and Fraade tended to distinguish plain-sense and performative (or interpretive) readings, limiting the plain-sense or *peshat* to that aspect of the text that, in the integrity of its intratextual context, rendered all reference possible.[5] Nonetheless, impressed that all four shared in a broader consensus about how to discuss such matters, I set out to collect more examples of this consensus and to reduce the examples to their shared rules of inquiry. As reported in the collection *The Return to Scripture in Judaism and Christianity: Essays in Postcritical*

Scriptural Interpretation, I found that Kadushin's work displayed rules of inquiry that were comparable to those of the four discussants and of eight additional Jewish and Christian scholars. Borrowing a term from Lindbeck's book, *The Nature of Doctrine* (1984), I labeled the approach they all shared "postcritical" inquiry.

In his book, Lindbeck contrasts the "cultural-linguistic" approach of postcritical (or "postliberal") theology with precritical "propositionalist" and critical "experiential-expressivist" approaches. According to Lindbeck, the propositionalists are traditionalists who read Church doctrines as "truth claims about objective realities" and Scriptures as referential signs of those claims (Lindbeck 1984, 16). He says the experiential-expressivists are liberal scholars, for whom "doctrines [are] . . . nondiscursive symbols of inner feelings, attitudes or existential orientations" (16). They read Scriptures as nonreferential signs (for example, metaphors) that give expression to "common core experiences" that are available to all humans at all times (31). According to the "cultural-linguistic" alternative, "meaning is constituted by the uses of a specific language." Scriptures therefore display their meaning intratextually, that means within the context of Scripture as a system of symbols. These symbols are to be interpreted by the community for which they are meaningful as rules of conduct: first, the conduct of scriptural reading itself and, then, the everyday conduct that is enjoined by this reading.

In Lindbeck's terms, then, Kadushin was a postcritical scholar. The "propositionalists" against whom he argued were the philosophers who imposed extraneous conceptual schemes on the rabbinic texts, claiming that the texts referred ostensively to the objective meanings of Scripture. The "experiential-expressivists" were the philosophers (and irrationalists) who denied that rabbinic Judaism displayed any conceptual order; for them, the rabbinic texts expressed either the rabbis' subjective beliefs or else the root experiences that are common to all humanity. Against these two approaches, Kadushin offered his "cultural-linguistic" alternative: for the rabbis, Scripture was a system of symbols, or value-concepts, whose meanings were displayed, within the rabbinic community, in its everyday and its scholarly conduct. I believe Kadushin's approach reappears in a contemporary idiom in the recent rabbinic studies of Fraade, Halivni, and Fishbane.

Steven Fraade's Moderate Postcritical Interpretation

Fraade's recent book, *From Tradition to Commentary, Torah and Its Interpretation in the Midrash Sifre to Deuteronomy* (1991), displays the postcritical approach in what I will call its moderate form.[6] He presents his book explicitly as an alternative to two dialectically opposed tendencies in modern scholarship in rabbinics. He calls these "the hermeneuticist and historicist fallacies" (1993, 155). He argues that, on the one hand, by viewing "the historicity of commentary's *representations* apart from the hermeneutical grounding of its performance," historicists allow the text only to face "out upon history and society" (155). On the other hand, by "viewing the hermeneutics of commentary's *interpretations* apart from the sociohistorical grounding of its performance," hermeneuticists allow the text to "face in upon itself" (156). In Lindbeck's terms, historicists are modern propositionalists, for whom the meaning of rabbinic texts is to be found only in their objective reference; hermeneuticists are modern experiential-expressivists, for whom the meaning of rabbinic texts is to be found only in readers' subjective responses to them.

Fraade's response is that, however useful it may be "for the maintenance of our disciplinary boundaries" (156), the modern attempt to bifurcate these two tendencies distorts the meaning of rabbinic literature. His goal is to reintegrate the two tendencies by giving voice to a third mode of inquiry which, true to his approach, he identifies only by performing it. I have found the following characteristics of his performance to be most telling:

• Without disclaiming critical inquiry, he seeks to reclaim a dimension of textual meaning that is lost in the ancient texts themselves. His method is to find *within these texts* a mode of inquiry that, when reappropriated within the context of modern scholarship, would enable that scholarship to reclaim the dimension of textual meaning it had lost. His method is thus dialogic—in his terms—a "shuttling back and forth" between modern and ancient discourses in order to recover both the overlooked meaning of rabbinic literature *and* the appropriate method for disclosing it. He calls this the method of *commentary* and sets out both to *describe* rabbinic scriptural commentary *and* to *perform* his new variety of modern scholarly commentary.

• He notes that, like other commentaries, rabbinic commentaries "begin with an extended base-text, of which they designate successive subunits for exegetical attention, to each of which they attach a comment or chain of comments, which nevertheless remain distinct from the base-text, to which the commentary sooner or later returns . . . to take up the next selected subunit in sequence" (Fraade 1993, 143). Like other commentaries, rabbinic commentaries are therefore paradoxical, in that they derive their rhetorical framework from the sequence of subunits in their scriptural base-texts at the same time that they atomize and reorder those subunits for the sake of analysis (143).

• He sets out to engage the "rabbinic turn to commentary" in its aboriginal form, both by studying rabbinic commentaries in their textual entirety and integrity and by focusing on "one of our earliest compilations of rabbinic exegesis . . . against the backdrop of its only known antecedents as biblical commentary," the prophetic *pesharim* of the Dead Sea Scrolls and the allegorical commentaries of Philo (142).

• Through detailed studies of selected, individual texts, he isolates the major hermeneutical traits of these antecedents that are of relevance to a study of rabbinic commentary. As a type, the *pesharim* represent "deictic" commentary, which means they refer each phrase of their biblical base-texts to specific (in this case, allegorical) referents. As a type, Philo's allegories represent "dialogical" commentary, which allows the commentator to interact with the base-text by posing questions of it and proffering answers (145, 148).

• Examining the *Sifre* to Deuteronomy in its textual integrity, he notes how it integrates both deictic and dialogic forms of commentary, while emphasizing the latter. Consider, for example, *Sifre's* commentary on Deut. 32:7:

> Remember the days of old *(olam)*, consider the years *(shenot)* of each and every generation; ask your father and he will inform you, your elders and they will tell you. "Remembers the days of old": [God said to them:] Take heed of what I did to the earliest generations. . . . "Consider the years of each and every generation": You can find no generation without people like those of the generation of the flood. . . , but each and every individual is judged according to his deeds. "Ask you father and he will inform you": These are the prophets as it says, "When Elisha beheld it he cried out [to Elijah], 'Father, father'" (2 Kings 2:12). "Your elders and they will tell you": These are the elders, as it is said, "Gather for Me seventy men of the elders of Israel" (Num. 11:16).[7]

Fraade explains how the atomized element "father" is taken to refer deictically to "prophets" and "elder" to "elder" (1993, 157 ff.). *Sifre's* overall reading is dialogic, however. In this commentary, *Sifre* interprets the scriptural passage as referring to a biblical past, from earliest times to the present. In "another interpretation" brought after this one, *Sifre* interprets the passage as referring to the future, from the sufferings of the present ("whenever God brings sufferings to you") to the ultimate future ("'Consider the years of each and every generation': This is the generation of the Messiah.'")—a time when Israel will hear directly from her "father" (now referring to "the Holy One"). The only elements common to each interpretation are the "elders," referring each time only to "elders." Fraade interprets these "elders"—standing in between the prophets of the past and the God revealed in the distant future—to mean the rabbinic sages themselves: the "inspired class" that mediates between revelation and redemption. *Sifre's* commentary has thereby interacted dialogically with its base-text, eliciting from it a message about the role of the rabbinic sages in Israel's relation to God.

Here is a sampling of the other features of *Sifre's* commentary to which Fraade draws our attention:

· The commentary allows for multiple interpretation of the base-text, while still respecting the integrity of the text's plain sense. No matter how many interpretations it brings, it bases these on a reading of all the words of its Deuteronomic text in their intratextual setting.

· By bringing the base-text into dialogue with all of Scripture, the commentary provides a medium through which Scripture can refer to and interpret itself.

· The commentary presents itself as the product of collective and cumulative, rather than of merely individual, activities of interpretation.

· It effects a dialogical relationship between Scripture as a whole and the interpretive rabbinic community, through which textual meaning and communal practice are mutually transformative. Thus the words of Torah become the sages' words.[8] The goal of commentary is to stimulate continuous study and the continuously transformative activity that accompanies it. Fraade's comment about the "elder" as the rabbinic sage is a brief sampling of his analyses of ways in which the sages included themselves and their mode of inquiry into Scripture's subject matter.

• Fraade concludes that rabbinic commentary, so described, "requires that our own critical interpretation of its texts adopt two converging perspectives: that of their formation and that of their reception" (1993, 164). As literary historians, modern rabbinic scholars must examine how rabbinic redactors integrated various traditions into running commentaries. As hermeneuts, they must also receive and respond to the commentary as if they were its intended students, thereby achieving some understanding of its performative method and force. Fraade is proposing, in sum, "that the critical analysis of a rabbinic scriptural commentary take itself the form of commentary, one that in its own way is dialogical, alternating between the perspectives of the text's formation and reception, as between that of the ancient student of the text and the modern critic of it" (166).

• *The leading principles of his modern commentary thereby reappropriate the principles of rabbinic commentary:*
· to respect the integrity of rabbinic and prerabbinic base texts in their plain-sense;
· to bring these base-texts into dialogue with comparable texts, so that the modern commentary may serve as a medium for the ancient text's self-reference;
· to engage the modern reader in an activity of reinterpreting the base-texts as well as of reevaluating modern methods of interpretation;
· to contribute to the collective work of transforming modern rabbinic scholarship.

The Semiotics of Postcritical Inquiry

So far, I have offered a first-level analysis of some of the attributes of Fraade's method of inquiry. This is, in other words, a first-level analysis of Fraade's logic of inquiry. The next level is to describe these attributes more precisely through the use of the logical instrument of semiotics, a science developed by the philosopher Charles Peirce (d. 1914) for the logical study of sign systems. The purpose of all this precision is to provide simpler models of postcritical studies, which models may then be used to compare postcritical with other systems of interpretation and, for those interested, to provide standards against which to check the consistency and rigor of specific postcritical interpretations.[9] Philosophic theologians may want to apply the results of philosophic analysis to other uses, but that is another matter.

Charles Peirce's semiotics may be adapted to the study of postcritical inquiry in two ways: as an instrument for identifying the fundamental elements of Scripture as an interpretable text and as a model of the kind of reasoning that is displayed in postcritical interpretation in particular. I will begin with the latter, which is, strictly speaking, a model of the pragmatics, or performative pattern, of postcritical reasoning. According to Peirce's theory of pragmatism,[10] our everyday reasonings about the world and about what we are supposed to do in it are informed by deep-seated rules of knowledge that we do not ordinarily have reason to question. Instead, these rules set the largely unperceived context in terms of which we question and correct our understanding of particular facts and behavioral norms. At times, however, our incapacities to correct problems in everyday understanding stimulate a deeper-level questioning: what Peirce calls a "pragmatic" inquiry, designed to adjust our deep-seated rules of knowledge to changing conditions of life. Postcritical inquiry is a pragmatic inquiry of this kind, stimulated by the doubts certain text scholars have about the fundamental rules of scholarship they inherited from modern academia. More specifically, these are doubts about modern scholarship's capacity to sponsor pragmatic inquiry when it is called for and to recognize pragmatic inquiry when it is already in place. The postcritical claim is that modern scholarship tends to define rational inquiry on the model of everyday inquiry, as if reason operates only when a community's deep-seated rules of knowledge are in place and when the task of inquiry is strictly referential, that is, to identify facts and norms with respect to these rules. Modern scholarship therefore tends to reduce the pursuit of knowledge to the terms of a binary opposition between referential, rational inquiry (when the deep rules are in place) and nonreferential irrational inquiry (when they are not). In the case of scriptural studies, the effect is to assume either that scriptural texts are simply referential (in which case they display their meaning by pointing ostensively to certain facts or norms) or that they are nonreferential (in which case they are either silent or display their meaning only metaphorically). The postcritical complaint is that this binary opposition excludes the possibility that scriptural texts may have pragmatic reference, that is, that they may represent claims about the inadequacy of certain inherited rules of meaning and about ways of transforming those rules or adjusting them to new conditions of life. To the degree that they refer pragmatically, scriptural texts will not disclose their meanings to modern methods of study.

Semiotics functions, secondly, as an instrument for reclassifying the elements of scriptural texts as records of pragmatic inquiry. For Peirce, the fundamental unit of reference is the sign: a *signifier* that displays its *object* (reference or meaning) only with respect to a particular *interpretant* (context of meaning, interpretive mindset, or system of deep-seated rules). Among types of sign, an *index* (deictic sign) refers to its *object* by virtue of some direct force exerted by the object on the sign. In other words, an indexical sign is indifferent to its interpretant, the way modern scholars suppose a referential text simply refers to some facts independently of any particular context of reference. An *icon* (image) does not refer to its object ostensively; instead, it appears to its *interpretant* to share certain characters with its object. The icon therefore displays its meaning metaphorically, through similarity, the way modern scholars suppose a nonreferential text is either silent or fully subject to the interpreter's attributions. A *symbol,* finally, refers to its *object* by virtue of some implicit law that causes the symbol to be *interpreted* as referring to that object.[11] In other words, a symbol displays its meaning only to a particular interpretant, but it is not fully subject to the interpreter's attributions. Instead, a symbol *influences* the way its interpretant attributes meaning to it. The symbol therefore engages its interpretant in a dialogue, the product of that is *meaning.* As agent of a semiotic law, the symbol engages its interpreter in some tradition of meaning. Transferring agency to the interpreter, the symbol also grants the interpreter some freedom to transform the way in which that meaning will be retransmitted. *In this way, the symbol is the fundamental agent of pragmatic inquiry.* It is itself the interpretant of a community's deep-seated rules of knowledge (its semiotic law), of which it serves as an agent. At the same time, the freedom it grants its own interpreter serves as a sign (technically, an index) that these deep-seated rules are also subject to and, we presume, in need of change. The simultaneously conservative and reformatory activity of interpreting a symbol is what we call pragmatic inquiry. In the process of inquiry, the interpreter can use his or her freedom for nought—that is, without accepting the responsibility to hear the symbol's complaints, as it were, and to determine what changes need to be instituted in its semiotic law. Or the interpreter can use his or her freedom for the good of this law, inquiring after its needs for change.

For postcritical scholars, scriptural texts do not always function as genuine symbols and thus as signs of the need for pragmatic inquiry. When they do not—that is, when textual elements refer iconically or indexically—then modern scholarship offers useful instruments for scriptural study. To the degree that scriptural texts function as symbols, however, modern scholarship fails to serve as their agent. This is a serious failing, indeed, since it represents a failure to *hear* the text's call for help, as it were: a failure to make use of the freedom the text grants its interpreter to search after *(l'derosh)* those deep-seated problems of which it is a sign. Postcritical interpretation reforms the deep-seated rules of modern scholarship in order to render that scholarship useful as an agent of this kind of search.

In these terms, Fraade's inquiry illustrates the pragmatics and semiotics of postcritical interpretation. The pragmatics, or performative pattern, of his inquiry looks like this:

• His inquiry emerges, from within the setting of modern rabbinic scholarship, as a critique of the capacity of that scholarship to recognize pragmatic inquiry within the rabbinic corpus, that is, the rabbis' efforts to transform Scripture's semiotic laws in the process of transmitting them. Recognizing only ostensive reference or its absence, modern scholarship therefore tends to divide into two, contrary modes of inquiry: "historicists" misrepresent pragmatic inquiry in ways that overemphasize objective reference; "hermeneuticists" misrepresent pragmatic inquiry in ways that overemphasize subjective interpretation.

• To reform modern rabbinic scholarship, Fraade seeks to reclaim the rules of interpreting pragmatic inquiry from within the rabbinic literature itself. This move brings to mind the pragmatic philosophers' antifoundational claim that the rules of reasoning are to be found only within the conduct of particular forms of reasoning: there is no single, universal logic, in other words, but only various logoi indigenous to practices of reasoning (as operative logoi). At the same time, the pragmatists believe that there are generalizable methods of clarifying and evaluating such logoi (methods of rendering the indigenous logoi normative). Fraade labels the rabbis' indigenous pragmatic inquiry "commentary" and examines the earliest strata of rabbinic commentary for evidence of its operative logic. He takes pains to examine this logic within what he considers its indigenous setting: individual documents of rabbinic midrash, read in their textual entirety and integrity.

• He identifies the leading principles of rabbinic commentary and adopts them, as well, as norms for the reformulation of modern inquiry into the pragmatic inquiry he calls modern commentary. He calls the reformulation a "dialogue" between rabbinic and modern methods of inquiry. The product is what he calls a "literary-historical" approach to rabbinic scholarship, where literary-historical study is the modern scholarly instrument of a pragmatic inquiry.

Restated in the terms of semiotics, his logic of rabbinic commentary looks like this:

• Rabbinic commentary interprets Scripture both referentially ("deictically") and symbolically ("dialogically"). For symbolic, or pragmatic, commentary, the scriptural text is a genuine symbol that displays its reference with respect to a finite interpretant.

• The relation between Scripture, as symbol, and its rabbinic interpretant is dialogic. As the agent of a community's deep-seated rules of knowledge, Scripture engages the rabbinic interpreter in a tradition of meaning. Transferring agency to the interpreter, Scripture also grants some freedom to transform the way in which that meaning will be retransmitted. In the process, Scripture and its interpreter are mutually transformed. The product is a rabbinic commentary that serves as genuine symbol to its own interpretants, which serve as symbols to their interpretants, and so on. To capture the force of rabbinic commentary as symbol, the modern commentator engages it in a mutually transformative dialogue of a similar kind. Interpretation thus breeds interpretation, a phenomenon that is represented in the rabbis' norm of continuous study.

• The paradoxical character of commentary—both atomizing and respecting the integrity of its base-text—is an index of the conservative/reformatory character of pragmatic interpretation.

• Historicist scholars reduce the triadic character of scriptural semiosis to the two terms of text and reference; hermeneuticist scholars reduce it to the two terms of text and interpretant. Reformulating rather than abandoning these scholarly tendencies, Fraade transforms historicist reading into what he calls the study of "formation," or of the character of rabbinic commentary as symbol or agent of meaning. He transforms hermeneuticist reading into what he calls the study of "reception" or of the character of commentary as interpretant. These are the two scholarly instruments of his pragmatic inquiry.

Foundational and Radical Postcritical Interpretation: The Hermeneutics of David Weiss Halivni and Michael Fishbane

Postcritical interpretation assumes different forms in different contexts of interpretation. Because this interpretation is a form of pragmatic inquiry, these contexts are defined primarily by the forms of modern scholarship that the postcritical interpreter seeks to reform. The moderate form of Fraade's inquiry corresponds to his criticizing both historicist and hermeneuticist tendencies with generally equal force. In his recent book, *Peshat and Derash, Plain and Applied Meaning in Rabbinic Exegesis* (Halivni 1991), Halivni is responding primarily to the excessive subjectivity of contemporary legal interpretation; he therefore places particular emphasis on the foundational, or objectively referential aspect of his postcritical inquiry. On the other hand, in his recent book, *The Garments of Torah, Essays in Biblical Hermeneutics* (Fishbane 1989b), Fishbane responds primarily to the excessive objectivism in both traditional and modern text interpretation; he therefore places particular emphasis on the more radically interpretive aspect of his postcritical inquiry.

Read according to its own *peshat,* Halivni's *Peshat and Derash* offers a theological/hermeneutical recommendation about how observant rabbinical scholars may resolve conflicts they perceive between the *peshat,* or plain-sense, of the scriptural text and the *midrash halakhah,* or the scriptural readings the Talmudic rabbis have offered for the sake of making legal judgments. He offers a history-like account and justification of one Talmudic practice in particular: in cases where a conflict between *peshat* and *derash* would have consequences for legal decision making, the rabbis identify their *midrash halakhah* as the correct *peshat.* Two features of Halivni's account are most significant: his interpretations of the legal nullity of scriptural texts transmitted through the First Temple period and of Ezra's role in restoring the correct meanings of these texts and thereby initiating the rabbinic mode of corrective, midrashic exegesis.[12]

At the same time, as Halivni indicates in his Preface, the performative form of his book also delivers part of its message. Divided into separate scholarly and theological parts, "the structure of the book . . . mirrors its central theological proposition—that rabbinic exegesis and halakha (legal norms) are integrally, but not always inextricably, linked" (Halivni 1991, v). On the one hand, "the critical scholar . . . [has] an allegiance to the dictates of objective truth and accuracy—indeed, to *peshat*" (Halivni 1991, 92). Critical scholarship is historical "science," the work of the "intellect," guided by the standards of "logic" to observe "objective," "timeless" truth, "external reality" (92–99). On the other hand, Halivni's theological approach abandons "scholarly aloofness" and is charged with pragmatic, or what he calls "existential," concerns (viii–ix).

His theology is the "systematic mining of rabbinic theological sources," according to "two different methodologies." His first method is to draw "inferences" that relate these sources to issues of contemporary social and religious concern. One example is his reading of the Talmudic story of R. Eliezer and R. Joshua, in which the Heavenly voice sides with R. Eliezer, yet the law is nevertheless decided according to R. Joshua, who declares *lo bashamayim hi!*, that the Torah "is not in heaven!" (Halivni 1991, 91 and 107). Halivni cites the story as rabbinic evidence for his dichotomizing practical *halakhah* (represented in this case by the majority position) and intellectual study for its own sake (represented by the minority position, which may reflect the biblical *peshat*).

His second theological method is what he calls reasoning by analogy. This is to interrelate several rabbinic sources according to some freshly suggested paradigm and then to apply that paradigm, by analogy, to the solution of a contemporary problem. For example, interrelating the rabbis' history-like claims about errors in the transmission of the Torah and about Ezra's role in emending the Torah text, he reasons that Ezra restored the original *peshat* of the Torah. He then solves apparent contradictions between the *midrash halakhah* and the biblical *peshat* by supposing that, like Ezra, the rabbis' *midrash* has actually restored an original *peshat* that was errantly transmitted.

As a dialogue between these objective ("scholarly") and subjective ("theological") methods, Halivni's book as a whole represents a pragmatic inquiry: interpreting the rabbinic corpus (as symbol) as it bears on an issue of immediate pragmatic, or "existential" concern (its interpretant). This appears to be Halivni's concern to respond, on the one hand, to those in the Orthodox movement who criticize his antiauthoritarian Talmudic science and, on the other hand, to those in the Conservative movement who criticize his persistently Orthodox religious practice. In response, he suggests that all his critics share in the mistaken belief that science and practice share a common authority and that the results of each should therefore be harmonized. He believes that this leads contemporary Orthodox scholars to reduce their exegetical science to the changing standards of authority and convention that govern religious decision making *(halakhah)* and that it leads contemporary Conservative scholars to reduce their process of religious decision making to the objectifying standards of science that govern exegesis. As an alternative, he offers a historical-hermeneutical account and justification of the exegetical approach that is exemplified in the work of the medieval Bible commentator R. Samuel ben Meir (the Rashbam, c.1080– c.1174) (Halivni 1991, ix).

Halivni argues that, as text scholar, exemplifying "the highest genre of *Torah Lishmah*" (the study of Scripture for its own sake), the Rashbam searched for the *peshat,* even at the expense of his own legal readings (Halivni 1991, 103). As *posek,* or adjudicator ("one of the greatest *posekim* of his time"), he relinquished his fidelity to *peshat.* Responding to the needs of his community, he no longer, in Halivni's words, "had the luxury" of studying the text for its own sake (103).[13] By way of illustration, Halivni writes that, for the Rashbam,

> the Torah . . . was halakhically resonant and meaningful only through the prism of the Talmud. When read independently of its Rabbinic (halakhic) manual, it could be subjected to the scrutiny of *peshat.* His disposition toward *peshat* could reign supreme in his Torah commentary—leading him, for example, to interpret the traditional scriptural prooftext for tefillin ("a sign on your hand and a reminder on your forehead," Exod. 13:9) metaphorically, because halakha was not jeopardized in the process. By contrast . . , in a manifestly halakhic context, the explicit scriptural foundation of tefillin could not be denied. In Mishnah Sanhedrin 11:3, in the discussion of the deviant behavior of a "zaken mamreh" (rebellious elder), the scriptural basis of tefillin is presupposed, as the "zaken mamreh" is punishable only if he rebels against something that is not explicit in the Torah, such as the number of partitions in the tefillin, but not if he denies something that is explicit in the Torah, such as the existence of the precept itself ("if he says, 'There is no obligation wear phylacteries' so that he transgresses the words of the Law, he is not culpable . . . ."). In this setting, in which the Mishnah tacitly interprets the scriptural prooftext for tefillin literally and not metaphorically, the Rashbam must abide by the Rabbinic derash. . . . The Rashbam is not be accused here of exegetical inconsistency, or of a disloyalty to *peshat,* for he is simply

responding reasonably and judiciously to his exegetical setting. (Halivni manuscript, 168–73)

There is also a third dimension of Halivni's book: the critique of modernist reductionism implicit in his response to traditionalist reductionism. In this regard, Halivni's scholarly discussion of the evolution of rabbinic exegesis is most telling. Like Fraade, Halivni has sought to avoid the reductive tendencies of modern inquiry by reclaiming for a modern rabbinic commentary the indigenous rules of rabbinic exegesis. He has sought to examine these rules, however, as they are displayed not only in single documents, but also in what he considers the singular trajectory of rabbinic exegesis in its evolution from the Second Temple period to today. Reducing an extensive collection of rabbinic documents to their operative rules of interpretation, he has observed a tendency that links one to the other in historical sequence. He says this is a progressive tendency to respect the integrity of scriptural and rabbinic texts in their extended intratextual contexts *(peshat)* and the integrity of the halakhic process *(midrash halakhah)* in its time-bound, communal contexts.

Restated in terms of a postcritical semiotics, Halivni's thesis is that, in its evolutionary trajectory, rabbinic exegesis tends to draw a tripartite distinction among the *peshat* of the text (as *symbol*), time-bound interpretations of the text's references (as *meanings*), and the time-bound contexts of interpretation (as *interpretants*). Here, *peshat* (as "extended intratextual context") refers to the unburdened presentation of the symbol as locus of possible meaning. This means that referential, hermeneutical, and pragmatic studies of the *peshat* are true to the extent that they *do not fail to uncover* whatever possibilities of signification are displayed by the text in its intratextual contexts. They are false if they misrepresent those possibilities *or limit them* by attending preferentially to certain possibilities over others.[14] The plain-sense scholar *(pashtan)* displays the semantics of the text and identifies the range of meanings that might possibly attend such a text as interpreted with respect to the range of known interpretants. The interpreter *(darshan)* explores the possibilities of meaning that are available with respect to single interpretant.[15]

Halivni argues that "contemporary critics" misconstrue this evolutionary trajectory because they have evaluated it in terms of the modern standards of "original [authorial] intent" and of "literal sense" (Halivni 1991, 50). From this perspective, he says, these critics believe that rabbinic exegesis through the years has "zig-zagged" back and forth between concern for *peshat* and for *derash.* Thus,

> Talmudic interpretation of the Bible is generally considered by modern exegetes to be quite distinct from the peshat, out of tune with the 'natural' meaning of the biblical text it purports to explain. In contrast, medieval exegesis, especially that of Rashbam . . . and Ibn Ezra . . . is regarded as close to peshat (relatively speaking). . . . Postmedieval exegesis is again unacceptable, harking back to talmudic interpretation of the Bible. (1991, 49)

According to Halivni, however, authorial intent and literal sense are the preferred standards of only one, more recent phase in the evolution of rabbinic hermeneutics. To interpret earlier phases according to these standards is to remove them from their historical contexts and impose on them an alien intentionality. The result is to read into previous modes of exegesis a dichotomy between "natural" *peshat* and "artificial" *derash* that is not evident in those modes.[16] It is to be expected that the "theological" discourse in Halivni's book would itself present a dilemma for modern critics, who may prefer to classify it as explicitly "subjective" and thus something strictly other than his critical textual scholarship. Halivni's use of the terms "subjective" for his theology and "objective" for his critical work may lend apparent and unwitting support to this preference. Read, however, as a mode of postcritical inquiry, his theology puts critical scholarship to pragmatic use. His critical scholarship expands the range of possible readings available in the *peshat* of the *rabbinic* sources. His theology advances context-specific interpretations of selected elements of that expanded *peshat,* offered for the sake of resolving problems specific to his community/ies of interpretation.

In sum, uniting Halivni's explicit and implicit inquiries is a critique of interpretive tendencies either to overly harmonize *peshat* and *derash,* and thus, with traditionalists, to assimilate reference and interpretation, or to overly dichotomize the two, and thus, with the moderns, to ignore the relations between reference and interpretation. Each of these errors results from a failure to respect the integrity of the scriptural or rabbinic texts as genuine symbols. Halivni's alternative is to reclaim for modern rabbinic commentary the rabbinic tradition's progressive respect for the integrity of *peshat* as extensive intratextual context. Understood this way, the study of *peshat* does not compete with midrashic interpretation; instead, it prepares readers, in the integrity of their contexts of interpretation, to engage the text in the integrity of its context of symbolization.

Radical Postcritical Interpretation

In *The Garments of Torah*, Fishbane celebrates the maieutic voice of Scripture: the capacity of its mystery to challenge the limits of language, to deflate ontological pretensions, and to decenter out-moded traditions of reading. At the same time, he identifies the dialogic partner to whom this voice is addressed and for whom it would be redemptive. This is what he calls, after Martin Buber, the monologic modern self: left with nothing else than its autonomy, just as, in Roland Barthes' reading, the interpreter is left with nothing else than his or her "will-to-power" (Fishbane 1989b, 45). *Garments* records Fishbane's search for ways of renewing a modern culture that has lost its connection to sacrality, to community, and to the conditions of meaning that the biblical traditions once provided. He organizes the book into three parts, reflecting the "three typical moments whereby cultures renew themselves herme-neutically," as well as what I take to be the three elements of his own program for renewing the culture of scriptural reading. These elements are,

• first, to examine the range of exegetical possibilities inherent in the *peshat* of the scriptural text;

• second, to identify the forms of exegesis, in the Bible and in rabbinic literature, that emerged in response to epistemological dislocations in biblical and early rabbinic cultures;

• third, to identify the epistemological dislocations that stimu-late modern exegetical scholarship and, then, to reintroduce the forms of biblical and rabbinic exegesis which may respond to these dislocations.

Part I of *Garments* delivers the lesson of Fishbane's *Biblical Interpretation in Ancient Israel* (Fishbane 1989a and 1989b): that Scripture interprets itself and, thus, that scriptural revelation is a revealed activity of interpretation. The pragmatic force of this lesson is that Scripture is a living dialogue in which the modern reader has a part. This is what Halivni calls a "non-maximalist conception of revelation," and what a postcritical semiotician may term the genuinely symbolic character of Scripture which calls the reader to hear and respond to the complaints of which it is a sign. Fishbane interprets this pragmatic message through the language of the kabbalah:

> Rabbi Simeon said: If a man looks upon the Torah as merely a book presenting narratives and everyday matters, alas for him! . . . The Torah, in all of its worlds, holds supernal truths and sublime secrets . . . The tales related in the Torah are simply her outer garments, and woe to the man who regards that outer garb as the Torah itself, for such a man will be deprived of portion in the next world.[17]

The words of the Torah are garments; the inner message lies within. The question for Fishbane is how that message can be heard once again by the modern, solitary self for whom the words of Scripture have lost their sacrality.

Fishbane's response begins with his scholarly study of the genres of innerbiblical exegesis. These appear in his work to be signs of the Torah's inner life, sewn into the "garments" themselves. In the language of postcritical semiotics, these genres are tokens of the semiotic law according which the scriptural text, as symbol, displays its meaning to its various interpretants. To study them, in other words, is to study tokens of the divine semiosis. Fishbane catalogs the genres as "scribal," "legal," "aggadic," and "mantological"— exemplified in a plurality of specific exegetical strategies, or logia, of which there is no overarching logos. The lack of any single archetype means that the divine semiosis cannot be reduced ultimately to any language other than that of the biblical text as a whole, alive with all of its semiotic indeterminacies and, thus, with its drive to be actualized in as yet undisclosed ways. Kadushin described the rabbinic value-concepts in just this way, as having a "drive to concretization." He claimed the value-concepts named certain rules of knowledge-and-conduct, however, such as "lovingkindness" *(gemilut hasadim)*, "God's mercy" *(middat ha-rahamim)*, and "God's justice" *(middat ha-din)*. In Fishbane's work, the logia are strictly rules of exegetical conduct, such as scribal correction, "lemmatic legal exegesis" (legal interpretation bound to an authoritative legal text), analogical aggadic exegesis, and the recontextualization of historical narratives as oracular signs.

A logicist tendency in Fishbane's analysis of these rules is moderated by a series of disclaimers. The biblical text displays a plurality of interpretive logia, formed and ordered eclectically without any recommendation for reducing the plurality to a single set or, indeed, to some meta-logos. Some of the logia lend themselves to formalization, others only weakly so. The genres and subgenres are mixed, requiring "one to recognize that the human exegetical voice . . . is a subordinate voice" (Fishbane 1989a and 1989b, 272). In other words, the logia are themselves "soulful" garments of a divine logos whose presence cannot be reduced ultimately to any language other than that of the biblical text as a whole, alive with all of its semiotic indeterminacies and, thus, its drive to be actualized in as yet undisclosed ways. As a collection, the logia are signs of the dialogic character of a divine word that is revealed only in its relation to lives that are, in its own image, generative and interpretive.

Human suffering is the archetypical, but not the only, stimulus to interpretation. Other stimuli give rise to referential or iconic readings of the Bible, that is, efforts to identify precisely what the Bible means or how to live in its image. Only suffering gives rise to genuinely symbolic readings, by which I mean readings that engage the revealed word in a mutually transformative dialogue. Fishbane does not make such a claim explicitly, but I believe it is consistent with the analyses of chapter 2 of *Garments*, "Extra-Biblical Exegesis: The Sense of Not Reading in Rabbinic Midrash." Illustrating the force of biblical hermeneutics as it is taken up in early rabbinic exegesis, Fishbane identifies scribal corrections of the biblical text as occasions for the rabbis to playfully suspend the authority of the text as written and substitute for it some semantic marks of their own theology. By means of the formula, *al tikre . . . elah* ("do not read the text as . . . , but as . . . ."), the rabbis reveal hidden meanings beneath the garments of the text, thereby becoming "master of the text and its theology while simultaneously acknowledging the independent authority of the Scripture" (Fishbane 1989b, 27). Nevertheless, while independent of the Biblical mythoi, the "mythopoetic theology imbedded in rabbinic midrash" (23) bears an evident relation to its biblical antecedents. In this essay, Fishbane identifies two aspects of this embedded theology: "divine empowerment through ritual praxis and divine pathos in response to human suffering" (23).

To illustrate the rabbinic theology of divine empowerment, Fishbane notes how the homilist of the *Pesiqta de-Rav Kahana* rereads Job 17:9, "But the righteous one holds fast to his way, and the pure of hands will increase [his] strength *[yosiph ometz]*":

> God—who is both righteous and pure of action—gives strength *(koach)* to the righteous in order "that they may do His will." This construction concluded, the Joban passage is then further applied to both Moses and the righteous. On this last application, R. Azariah interprets the verse to mean: "Whenever the righteous do the will of the Holy One, Blessed be He, they increase strength *(mosiphin koach)* in the *dynamis*"—that is to say, they empower the divine principle of immanent power through their performance of the commandments. (Fishbane 1989b, 24)[18]

To illustrate the rabbinic theology of divine pathos, he notes how the homilist of *Exodus Rabbah* (XXX.24) rereads Isa. 56:1, "for My salvation is near to come *[ki qeroba yeshu'ati lavo]*":

> [The homilist] begins with a philologist's observation: "Scripture does not say '*your* salvation' (second person plural) but '*My* salvation.'" And he adds: "May His name be blessed! For were it not [so] written [in Scripture], one could not say it." . . . [the *derashah* continues] "If you [Israel] do not have merit, I shall perform [the salvation] for My *own* sake *(bishvili)*; for *kivyakhol* [as it were], as long as you are in trouble, I am with you, as it says [in Scripture]: "I am with him (Israel) in trouble" *('imo anokhi be-tzarah)* (Ps. 91:15). (Fishbane 1989b, 27–28)

If biblical exegesis is indeed a form of ritual praxis, then its appearance within the Bible itself would seem to illustrate, within the biblical context, the rabbinic concept of divine empowerment through biblical exegesis! If, furthermore, human suffering provides the occasion for biblical exegesis, then this exegesis may provide the occasion for divine pathos. I take this, in fact, to be the pragmatic message of parts 2 and 3 of Fishbane's book.

Part 2 displays Fishbane's conviction that crises and dislocations in Israel's hermeneutical life mark the occasions of symbolic, or dialogic, scriptural interpretation in traditional as well as modern practice.[19] These are occasions of when a community's rules of interpretation no longer apply—when, therefore, God's word has for the moment lost its referentiality and the loving God has become a hidden God. Paradoxically, by freeing the community to its solitary autonomy, God's absence stimulates it to fulfill its role as God's partner in dialogue. Searching *(l'derosh)* the scriptural sources for new conditions of interpretation, the human partner recovers the capacity to hear the scriptural word as God's call for help—help, that is, for the beloved sufferer.

Arguing that new midrashic systems insulate their disciples from immediate experience of their earthly conditions as well as from the dislocations they have previously suffered, Fishbane concludes that midrashic interpretation therefore represents only one moment in the dynamic process of scriptural reading and rereading. To describe this process, he reinterprets the medieval concept of a fourfold method of reading *(PaRDes)*. His notion of the first level of reading, *peshat*, corresponds to Halivni's: "The *Peshat* thus focuses on the givenness and autonomy of the text, on its independence from the words of interpretation" (Fishbane 1989b, 115). In the terms of a postcritical semiotic, this means that *peshat* displays the text as a semiotic field generative of all its possible meanings. Fishbane assigns to the second level of reading, *remez* ("suggestion"), "the determination of significance by means of factors independent of, and external to, the textual surface (the *Peshat)*" (116). In a postcritical semiotic, this represents the range of context-specific referents of which the text serves as indexical sign. The third level of reading, *derash* ("interpretation"), "includes the tropological and moral sphere of text interpretation." We might call this the range of interpretive practices by which the text delivers its meanings for a particular community of interpreters. The fourth level of reading, *sod* ("mystery"), refers to "the mystical sphere of text interpretation, . . . [its] eternal dimension," with respect to which all finite readings are transcended (120). For Fishbane, this dimension, epitomized in the kabbalah, frees midrashic systems of their "idolatrous" capacities. Within a postcritical semiotic, *sod* displays the text's capacity, from now into the future, to stimulate interpretation after interpretation toward some ideal limit which is the divine life itself, as imaged in interpretive practice. Fishbane's references to *sod* correspond in surprising ways to Halivni's references to *hashkafa,* or scientific speculation. For Halivni, *hashkafa* points beyond the context-specific subjectivity and vagueness of *derash* to the timeless, distinct truths of the text's ultimate referentiality. For Fishbane, *sod* points beyond the context-specific referentiality of *derash* to the timeless mysteries of the text's supralinguistic speech and, thus, relationality. References to *sod,* like those to *haskafa,* may or may not be consistent with a postcritical hermeneutic. They are other than postcritical if, in the name of mystery, they reify undisclosed ontological attributions or emotive responses. They remain within the orbit of postcritical readings if they refer indexically to the dyadic and thus silent relation that links hermeneutically dislocated readers to a God whose face is hidden by virtue of that dislocation.

In part 3 of *Garments,* Fishbane describes the hermeneutical dislocation of the modern reader, symbolized by the collapse of modern scholarship's dichotomous presuppositions—subjectivistic on the one side (in Fishbane's terms, "fideistic," or "personalistic") and objectivistic on the other ("philosophical," "objective," or "historical-philological"). Paradoxically, however, this dislocation both insulates modern readers from the sacrality of Scripture and offers them the occasion to rediscover the vitality of Scripture as a genuine symbol. In the approach of Buber and Rosenzweig, this is to rediscover Scripture as a *spoken* word: "Only responsiveness to the claims of the hour can open the heart of this monologic self and give him the one thing needful—speech" (Fishbane 1989b, 100). In Rosenzweig's terms, this is God's speech, which, addressing us by name, says "Love Me!" (Rosenzweig 1970, 98). For Fishbane, modernity is thus redeemed by its potential receptivity to God's love, as offered by the words of Scripture when they are read "from deep to deep," that is, from the depth of one's own suffering heart to the depth of Scripture's inner meaning.

In sum, Fishbane's and Halivni's theological hermeneutics display the following features of postcritical inquiry:

• Both are responding to their sense of the inadequacy of modern scholarly responses to crises in the social/religious communities they serve. For Fishbane, this crisis is the spiritual-epistemological malaise of the monologic self; for Halivni it is the inability of both Orthodox and Conservative movements to resolve apparent discontinuities between received traditions of legal interpretation and the claims of critical text scholarship.

• Both identify two features of this inadequacy. One feature is the incapacity of modern text scholarship to recognize the pragmatic dimension of the rabbinic and biblical sources: the fact that these sources may symbolize ways of repairing inherited rules of meaning that have lost their meaning or efficacy. The other feature is the tendency of modern scholars to reduce their interpretations of the source texts to the terms of unwarranted dichotomies: between "plain sense" and "use," between "objective fact" and "subjective interpretation," and so on.

• Both identify in these source texts prototypes for what are at once nondichotomous and pragmatic rules of interpretation and repair. And both describe these rules in ways they believe would contribute to repairing the social/religious crises that concern them.

AFTERWORD

If I may allow my own philosopher's voice to intrude, what moves me most about the postcritical scholars is the way they display the redemptive power of reason reengaged in the service of divine revelation. The failings of modern scholarship do not exhibit the failings of reason, but only the failings of the propositional or essentialist model of reason, along with its emotivist contraries. The propositional model separated reason from its hermeneutical task and introduced into medieval thinking—long before Descartes—the illusion of reason's autonomy, which is the autonomy of an indwelling logos. The model of postcritical inquiry redescribes reason as a relational, or dialogic, activity, assuming as many specific forms as there are contexts of suffering which call out for understanding—or which call out for divine love. Reason is the relationality of this love: touching us most intimately in the body of those deep-seated rules of knowledge which enable us, not to know the world—for such knowing is a transient, everyday activity—but to repair the errors that regularly arise in our everyday knowledge. As this form of relationality, reasoning is repairing—an activity without which we cannot live. The tragedy of modern scholarship is that it despairs of its capacity and responsibility to participate in the work of repair. For the postcritical scholars, this is the work of exegesis and interpretation, and they do not despair.

NOTES

1. Parts of this essay appear in expanded form in Ochs 1993. A briefer version also appears in Cohn-Sherbok 1992.
2. See, for example, Greenberg 1980, 143–63, and 1985, 49–67.
3. See Kadushin 1964 and 1972.

4. See, for example, Ochs 1990 and Marshall 1990.
5. At the same time, Greenberg (1980) offers a mediating alternative, in his method of reading the plain-sense as it would be received by what he calls an "ideal reader."
6. I will be quoting mostly from Fraade's synthesis of chapters 1 and 3 of his book that appeared as "The Turn to Commentary in Ancient Judaism: The Case of Sifre Deuteronomy" in Ochs 1993.
7. *Sifre Deuteronomy* §310, cited in Fraade 1991, 75–76 (Fraade translates from the MS Vatican) with commentary following, 76–79.
8. *Sifre* interprets "May my discourse come down as rain" (Deut. 32:2): "Just as rain falls on trees and infuses each type with its distinctive flavor. . . . so too words of Torah are all one, but they comprise *mikra* (Scripture) and *mishna* (oral teaching): *midrash* (exegesis), *halakhot* (laws), and *haggadot* (narratives)" (§306, cited in Fraade 1991, 96).
9. In another project, I am trying to show that intrabiblical and early rabbinic hermeneutics may serve, in fact, as the prototype of semiotics itself. For some preliminary suggestions, see Ochs 1992b. Jose Faur is engaged in a comparable project, although, in the Continental tradition of de Saussure, his semiotic draws a dyadic distinction between signifier and signified, in contrast with Peirce's triadic distinction among sign, meaning (reference), and interpretant (the context of meaning). For more information, see Faur 1986.
10. For his original statement of this theory, see Peirce [1877] 1934 and 1935, and [1905] 1934 and 1935.
11. These definitions of icon, index, and symbol are adapted from Peirce 1903, 247–49.
12. Halivni writes:

> According to our interpretation of the [concept of *chate'u yisrael*, or the legal nullity of the First Temple period], Ezra received an altered text of the Torah. At the same time he also possessed the knowledge and authority to indicate how the misleading *peshat* of certain passages should be corrected—although he lacked the authority actually to emend the faulty text in most cases. He initiated a process of textual rehabilitation, partly by providing a system of marking certain words of the Torah as spurious, and, more comprehensively, by disseminating an oral tradition of restorative exposition, or *midrash*. We are thus left with a scriptural text whose *peshat* is not always authoritative or decisive, but whose tradition of midrashic interpretation *is*. . . . Our *halakha* is codified according to rabbinic *derash* because *derash*, and not *peshat*, always conforms to the dictates of Sinaitic revelation. (1993, 112–13)

13. Halivni notes that the Rashbam "could afford to adhere strictly to peshat even when it ran counter to practical halakha because," in these cases, he tended to ground his halakhic expositions on some redundancy of word or letter in the Scriptural text (Halivni 1991, 27). Separating

the realms of *peshat* and *derash* more radically, Halivni has no need to adopt this exegetical device.

One implication is that Halivni's work on the *peshat* of the Talmud might contribute to the process of halakhic decision making, but not directly. Its contribution would come, if at all, only in the way its readings might in the long run filter into reformulations of centuries of accumulated patterns of legal argumentation. Halivni reminds us repeatedly that law is not guided by the text alone, but also by precedent and by the time-bound contingencies of social life. God, he says, has withdrawn from direct participation in the legal process; the eternal is the immediate subject matter only of intellectual speculation *(haskafa)*, not of *halakhah.*

14. This does not imply that the possibilities are endless, since an accurate intratextual reading would warrant discounting most possibilities.

15. Halivni may also attribute to the speculative scholar the capacity to display the ideal meaning of a text with respect to an ideal ("eternal") interpretant. If so, his approach in this regard either reflects a medieval-modern concern to privilege one context of meaning as transcendent or supracontextual, or a postcritical scholar's context-specific effort to offset subjectivist tendencies.

16. The most striking illustration of the force of Halivni's critique is his study of *pilpul* ("farfetched casuistic deductions") in halakhic scholarship of the sixteenth century and after (1991, 42–44). He notes that, when *peshat* is identified with natural sense, the pilpulists appear to deviate most problematically from rabbinic Judaism's progressive concern to protect the integrity of the *peshat.* *Pilpul* appears to ignore the text's literal reference. When *peshat* is identified, however, with extended intratextual context, the pilpulists appear to exemplify this concern! They fully respect the contextual integrity of their base-texts as stimuli for additional deductions.

17. *Zohar*, vol. III, 152. Translation from *Zohar, The Book of Splendor: Basic Readings from the Kabbalah*, Scholem 1963, 121f. Cited in Fishbane 1989b, 34.

18. Fishbane cites *Pesiqta de-Rav Kahana*, vol. II, Mandelbaum, 379–81.

19. Fishbane examines the "axial ruptures in cultural system" that stimulated ancient Israel's two major hermeneutical innovations. The first was Israel's primary break with the mythic cosmology of the ancient Near East: inserting its conception of the transcendent, supernatural God into the immanental cosmologies of its contemporaries. For Fishbane, this crisis of separation corresponded to the emergence of Torah as an autonomous source of meaning and law. The second was Israel's secondary movement "from a culture based on direct divine revelations to one based on their study and reinterpretation." Beginning in the time of Ezra, this shift corresponded to the emergence of

hermeneutics as Israel's prototypical mode of religious discourse (1989b, 64–65).

REFERENCES

Cohn-Sherbok, Dan, ed. *Torah and Revelation.* Lewiston/Queenston/Lampeter: Edwin Mellen, 1992.

Faur, Jose. *Golden Doves with Silver Dots.* Bloomington: Indiana University Press, 1986.

Fishbane, Michael. *Biblical Interpretation in Ancient Israel.* Oxford: Oxford University Press, [1985] 1989a.

———. *The Garments of Torah, Essays in Biblical Hermeneutics.* Bloomington: Indiana University Press, 1989b.

Fraade, Steven. *From Tradition to Commentary, Torah and Its Interpretation in the Midrash Sifre to Deuteronomy.* Albany: State University of New York Press, 1991.

———. "The Turn to Commentary in Ancient Judaism: The Case of Sifre Deuteronomy." In *The Return to Scripture in Judaism and Christianity: Essays in Postcritical Scriptural Interpretation,* ed. Peter Ochs. Mahwah: Paulist Press, 1993.

Greenberg, Moshe. "The Vision of Jerusalem in Ezekiel 8–11: A Holistic Interpretation." In *The Divine Helmsman: Studies Presented to L. H. Silberman,* ed. J. L. Crenshaw and S. Sandmel. New York: KTAV, 1980.

———. "How Is the Torah to be Interpreted in Our Time?" (Hebrew). In *Hesegulah vHakoach,* 49–67. Haifa: Sifrit Poalim, Hakibutz Hameuchad, 1985.

Halivni, David Weiss. *Peshat and Derash, Plain and Applied Meaning in Rabbinic Exegesis.* New York and Oxford: Oxford University Press, 1991.

———. "Plain Sense and Applied Meaning in Rabbinic Exegesis." In *The Return to Scripture in Judaism and Christianity: Essays in Postcritical Scriptural Interpretation,* ed. Peter Ochs. Mahwah: Paulist Press, 1993.

———. "The Impact of Halakha on Peshat." Appendix 4 to *Peshat and Derash.* Prepublication manuscript.

Kadushin, Max. *Worship and Ethics.* Evanston: Northwestern University Press, 1964.

———. *The Rabbinic Mind.* New York: Bloch Publishers, 1972.

Lindbeck, George. *The Nature of Doctrine, Religion, and Theology in a Postliberal Age.* Philadelphia: Westminster, 1984.

Marshall, Bruce, ed. "A Rabbinic Pragmatism." In *Theology and Dialogue.* Notre Dame: University of Notre Dame Press, 1990.

Ochs, Peter. "Max Kadushin as Rabbinic Pragmatist." In *Understanding the Rabbinic Mind: Essays on the Hermeneutic of Max Kadushin*, ed. Peter Ochs. Atlanta: Scholars Press for South Florida Studies in the History of Judaism, 1990.

———. "Postcritical Scriptural Interpretation in Judaism." In *Torah and Revelation*, ed. Dan Cohn-Sherbok. Lewiston/Queenston/Lampeter: Edwin Mellen, 1992a.

———. "Theosemiotics and Pragmatism." *Journal of Religion* 72, 1 (January 1992b): 59–81.

———. "Introduction." In *The Return to Scripture in Judaism and Christianity: Essays in Postcritical Scriptural Interpretation*, ed. Peter Ochs. Mahwah: Paulist Press, 1993.

Peirce, Charles. *Charles Peirce: Collected Works*. Vol 2. Ed. Charles Hartshorne and Paul Weiss. Cambridge, Mass.: Harvard University Press, 1903.

———. "The Fixation of Belief." *Popular Science Monthly* 12 (1877): 1–15.

———. "The Fixation of Belief" [1877]. In *Charles Peirce: Collected Papers*. Vol. 5, 358–87. Ed. Charles Hartshorne and Paul Weiss. Cambridge, Mass.: Harvard University Press, 1934 and 1935.

———. "What Pragmatism Is." *The Monist* 15 (1905): 161–81.

———. "What Pragmatism Is" [1905]. In *Charles Peirce: Collected Papers*. Vol. 5, 411–37. Ed. Charles Hartshorne and Paul Weiss. Cambridge, Mass.: Harvard University Press, 1934 and 1935.

Rosenzweig, Franz. *The Star of Redemption*. Trans. William Hallo. New York: Holt, Rinehart and Winston, 1970.

Scholem, Gershom, ed. *Zohar, The Book of Splendor: Basic Readings from the Kabbalah*. New York: Schocken, 1963.

Talmud and Halakhah

Chapter 3

Halakhah as Primordial Tradition: A Gadamerian Dialogue with Early Rabbinic Memory and Jurisprudence

Martin S. Jaffee

I. Gadamerian Tradition and Rabbinic Halakhah

The hermeneutical thought of Hans-Georg Gadamer has had a broad impact upon North American humanistic scholarship since the first English translation of *Wahrheit und Methode* (1960) in 1975.[1] His account of the crucial nineteenth- and twentieth-century reorientation of interpretation theory—from methods of recovering the original meaning of texts (e.g., Schleiermacher) to a universal theory of historical being (e.g., Heidegger)—has been influential in opening many fields of American humanistic learning to a series of fresh interpretive discourses which move well beyond Gadamer's own philosophical and historical perspective.

The academic study of the history of the Jews and Judaism is not one of these fields. For example, in my own areas of interest— the history of rabbinic Judaism in antiquity and the appropriation of rabbinic thought for contemporary theological construction— Gadamer's thought remains essentially untapped.[2] My purpose in what follows is to show what might be gained by paying attention to him. The present essay, therefore, attempts to interpret an important theme of early rabbinic literature—the primordiality of *halakhah* as part of oral Torah—from a standpoint opened up by Gadamer's hermeneutical work. I will try to show that a Gadamerian perspective can be of value not only for the historical interpretation of early rabbinic Judaism, but also for shaping theologically motivated engagements with the rabbinic corpus. Here I will focus on one issue in particular, the relationship between the truth of rabbinic historical memory and the appropriation of the halakhic praxis developed in early rabbinic sources.

An important strand of Gadamer's hermeneutical theory addresses the problem of how received tradition relates to the interpretation of texts. I believe that Gadamer's philosophical formulation of the problem of tradition and textual understanding, and his recognition of its application to the interpretation of historical being itself, enables fresh approaches to rabbinic formulations of the relation of halakhic norms to revelation. As a case in point, I shall focus in what follows upon early rabbinic texts which construe *halakhah* as a particular modality of tradition.

By the sixth century C.E., rabbinic reflection on scriptural and extrascriptural law had reached a high degree of literary formalization and ideological self-consciousness, an object of sustained jurisprudential and historical reflection.[3] In jurisprudence, *halakhah* was recognized as a distinctive sphere of learning overagainst others (e.g., *aggadah*) and defined in relation to other sources of legal norms (e.g., *mitzvot*, "biblical commandments"; *torah*, "Scripture"). At the same time, *halakhah* was endowed with a historical dimension, one bearing great theological weight. Its origins were located in an orally preserved Torah revealed at Sinai, and its development was seen as proceeding under the guidance of sages whose development of halakhic principles and practice were governed by their reception and preservation of the original teachings of Moses.[4]

In both its jurisprudential and historical/theological contexts, then, *halakhah* had come, within the classical rabbinic corpus, to signify a body of tradition constituting the normative interpretive application of the Torah to the ongoing life of Israel. This is in fact what originally aroused my interest in Gadamer. Tradition, in the special sense he assigns to it (and to which we shall turn momentarily), is for Gadamer a fundamental element in the constitution of our capacity to understand not only texts, but our own selves as we come to know them in the matrix of history. What I attempt to do below is to review early rabbinic discussions of *halakhah* that recognize its character as tradition so as to better grasp the hermeneutical foundations of rabbinic thought itself. I shall try to show that Gadamer's insights into tradition as a hermeneutical phenomenon help us to see rather familiar rabbinic discussions of *halakhah* anew. We observe, as it were, rabbinic tradition thinking about itself and coming to create itself as an object of reflection and a mode of historical being.

In the spirit of Gadamer's model of hermeneutical inquiry, my reflections upon *halakhah* in early rabbinic literary culture try to recover a way of thinking received from the past and to re-present it in such a way that its claim to represent the truth about things is given a full hearing. In the first instance, then, I attempt to trace the ways in which *halakhah*, as a technical term, appropriates to itself a variety of related but distinguishable nuances as it passes through successive generations of the scribal culture responsible for the compilation of rabbinic literary sources.

I claim in this part of the exercise that Gadamer's theoretical perspective enables us to see in this complex of meanings more than the inevitable "evolution" of a term in a variety of novel applications. Rather, the shifting significations of *halakhah* testify to successive reconstructions of the conception of tradition itself as rabbinic authorities pass on a corpus of texts and an estimation of their meaning. In these reconstructions both jurisprudential concerns— for the rationalization of received legal knowledge—and historiographical concerns—for locating that knowledge within a comprehensive conception of the past—play important roles. My concern here is to suggest ways in which jurisprudence and historical memory function hermeneutically to inform the sages' interpretation of their increasingly complex inheritance of legal knowledge.

This inquiry into the rabbinic construction of *halakhah* as a form of tradition is mounted in service of a broader concern, the outlines of which are suggested in the concluding portion of the essay. There I ask what consequence a Gadamerian appreciation of rabbinic *halakhah* as tradition might have for those who would weave classic halakhic texts into the texture of contemporary Judaic religious commitment. It seems clear to me that anyone who regards the rabbinic halakhic literature as a possible source of Jewish nourishment must confront the problem of the historical claim which has grounded the authority of halakhic norms—that *halakhah*, with the Torah as a whole, comes from Sinai. The conclusion of this essay, therefore, attempts to speak of *halakhah* as primordial tradition— oral Torah—without falling into the sophisticated historicist strategy of relativizing it as "myth" (what was once believed but which can no longer be trusted as truth) or the naive historicist strategy of concretizing it as "historical fact" (what once happened exactly as a venerable text describes it). I ask, then, how a Gadamerian reading of the hermeneutical dimension of early halakhic tradition might contribute to a retrieval of that tradition as a discourse with a serious claim on contemporary Jews.

II. Tradition and Historically Effected Consciousness

This discussion cannot proceed further without a more formal presentation of Gadamer's perspective on the hermeneutics of textual understanding and its relation to historical truth. Central to his notion of textual understanding are two interrelated concepts. The first is "tradition," understood most basically as a more or less formal body of assumptions and perspectives within which the meaning of a text is transmitted and configured as it passes through successive communities of readers. The second is "historically effected consciousness," the awareness that one's own understanding of a text is achieved not *despite* one's historical situatedness at a particular moment in the transmission of tradition, but precisely *in and through* it. Both conceptions are crucial to Gadamer's general critique of the failure of the hermeneutical theorists of the nineteenth century in particular to account for the role of the historical interpreter in the creation of textual meaning as well as conceptions of the past.

As I understand Gadamer, tradition is a kind of fusion of three analytically distinct phenomena: the text transmitted, the process of transmitting it to new audiences, and the interpretation that begins to accompany the text as it passes through its varied audiences. Some estimate of the meaning of a transmitted text, by virtue of its having generated an interpretive discourse among earlier readers/hearers, is transmitted to its new audience prior to their personal engagement with it. The complex of text and interpretation, mediated together into the present and presented to the audience as the accepted meaning of the text, is tradition.

On this construction of matters, tradition is the very foundation of textual meaning. It enables understanding insofar as it supplies the complement of assumptions concerning the text that constitute a culturally informed reader's first orientation to its meaning. These assumptions, which Gadamer terms the reader's "prejudices" or prejudgments, are not, contrary to the methodological caveats of historicism, barriers to interpretation. Rather, insofar as without them the text is silent, they constitute the very ground of interpretive possibility. "They are," as Gadamer points out in one of his essays, "simply conditions whereby we experience something—whereby what we encounter says something to us" (1976, 9). But here, of course, one must ask what prevents prejudice borne by tradition from reproducing itself in the text and substituting its own meaning for that of the text?

In Gadamer's view tradition is ultimately incapable of totally substituting itself for the meaning of the text. The reason is that prejudices ground our interest in those elements of the text that fail to confirm them. In the essay just quoted, he asks, "is not our readiness to hear the new also necessarily determined by the old that has already taken possession of us?" (1976, 9). There will, it appears, always be for Gadamer some gap between transmitted expectations and what a given reader may discover. Indeed, the paradigmatic form of textual understanding, and the transformative moment in the ongoing life of tradition, occurs precisely when a reader's prejudices about a text's meaning are disappointed in the act of reading. The gap between what tradition postulates as the text's meaning and what the reader finds present in the text generates the reader's own efforts to restore coherence between her own reading of the text and what she has understood as the tradition.

Interpretation, therefore, is in Gadamer's terms an "infinite process. Not only are fresh sources of error constantly excluded, so that all kinds of things are filtered out that obscure the true meaning; but new sources of understanding are continually emerging that reveal unsuspected elements of meaning" (Gadamer 1989, 298). The interpretive construction of a text's meaning achieved at one moment in the unfolding of tradition becomes immediately a point of alienation, which, even as it brings the reader into the circle of a text's meaning, enables the reader to stake out an independent perspective on the text overagainst tradition. If temporal distance from the text contributes to the failure of understanding that makes tradition necessary and interpretation possible, this very same distance constitutes the productive power of hermeneutical understanding as it attempts "to distinguish the true prejudices, by which we *understand*, from the *false* ones, by which we *misunderstand*" (298–99; original italics). Thus, precisely as the work of tradition seeks to displace the text with a global account of its meaning, tradition creates the foundation for its own inadequacy to continue to comprehend the text in its entirety; it creates the possibility of new readings that, if successful, will enter into tradition as the ongoing meaning of the text.

Hermeneutics in the Gadamerian formulation, therefore, is devoted to the twin task of constructing the meaning of a text in the present overagainst received tradition even as it discloses the power of tradition to bring the text to productive interpretation in the present and for the future. Hermeneutical thinking, that is to say, must become historical in a way unanticipated by the romantic conviction that to think historically is to rethink another's thoughts rather than one's own. "Real historical thinking," says Gadamer, "must take account of its own historicity. Only then will it cease to chase the phantom of a historical object that is the object of progressive research, and learn to view the object as the counterpart of itself and hence understand both" (1989, 299).

This historical thinking, which takes account of its own historicity, is what Gadamer means by the term "historically effected consciousness." Most simply, it is the recognition that one's own interpretive activity is grounded in one's historical relationship to tradition and, as a matter of necessity, is in turn enabled and hindered by that relation. Thus one never moves *beyond* tradition to the "original" meaning of a text, but only *within* tradition toward a dialogical discourse about the text's meaning, a dialogue within which tradition itself alternates as interpreter of the text and text-to-be-interpreted. It is this very dialogue which opens the results of interpretation to the future, enabling fresh meaning to enter the tradition that preserves the text.

A crucial consequence of Gadamer's estimation of tradition in the process of understanding is that there is no Archimedean point beyond historically mediated tradition from which a scientific historical interpreter may survey the "original" meaning of a literary work, whether such originality is construed as the intended meaning of the author or the understanding of the work's first audience. The reason is that the very meaning located in the past by historical reconstruction is always also a meaning achieved and construed in a concrete present on the basis of a historically mediated tradition, that is, that of scientific historiography. Historical understanding is, therefore—precisely to the degree that it is governed by methodological models inherited in academic tradition—always, by definition, contemporary understanding, a mediation between past and present achieved here and now. It is never the past itself for itself, but always a composition of the historical imagination in conversation with historiographical tradition. A historian's conversation, there-fore, is not with the "author" of a text. Rather, as historical readers we hear the collective voices of earlier and contemporary reader-interpreters whose contributions have helped to define our orienta-tion for the present reading. The meaning of a text, therefore, is not separable from the history of its interpretation, for it is only by a reader whose understanding has been shaped by some sort of historically effective tradition that the text can be understood at all.

Gadamer's stance on textual meaning is intimately bound up with another crucial issue: the question of truth and the historian's relationship to it. If the historian has no epistemologically reliable methods for recovering the true (i.e., original) meaning of a text as it emerged into the light of history, must methodological discipline be left behind in order to recover the truth of a text? If so, by what hermeneutical mysteries is truth grasped? As we shall see, Gada-mer is not thoroughly clear on these questions. There is, however, a good deal of warrant for arguing that Gadamer sees historical method and the hermeneutical appropriation of a text's truth as complementary.

To be sure, there are passages in Gadamer that seem to suggest that the use of historical methods in the reconstruction of a text's original meaning often includes within itself a fundamental negation of the possibility that the original meaning of the text can also remain true for the interpreter (e.g., 1989, 304). On such a view, it is important for the critic of the text to know what it "once" meant, apart from what has been laid upon it over time, so that one can understand the text as a product of its own period, of a conscious-ness or worldview distinct from one's own.

Under such circumstances, Gadamer argues, interpretation is, more properly, an exercise in cross-examination, a forensic disquali-fication of the text's truth rather than a sharing in the possibility of its truth. To the degree that such interrogation is made the goal of historical interpretation, Gadamer regards it as hermeneutically incomplete:

> [S]imply establishing facts, elicited from possible prejudiced witnesses, does not make the historian. What makes the historian is understanding the significance of what he finds. Thus the testimony of history is like that given before a court. . . . In both cases testimony aids in establishing the facts. But the facts are not the real objects of inquiry; they are simply material for the real

tasks of the judge and of the historian—that is, respectively, to reach a just decision and to establish the historical significance of an event within the totality of his historical self-consciousness. (Gadamer 1989, 338)

The truth of a text, therefore, if it is genuinely understood at all, can be apprehended only after it has returned from the historian's cross-examination and been invited to engage us as a discursive equal. Only at this point is the text enabled to challenge the interpreter's own standpoint and assert its own truth overagainst that of the historian.

This should not be misunderstood, as some of Gadamer's critics have, as an expression of uncritical submissiveness to authoritative textual utterance (e.g., Habermas 1988, 168–70; cf. Hoy 1988, 319–29). Nor is it an absolute rejection of the value of philological, sociological, or other historical methods of textual analysis. His understanding of the mutual dependence of method and understanding, I think, can be summarized in a brief sentence from his essay, "The Universality of the Hermeneutical Problem" (Gadamer 1976, 6), written in 1966, a few years after the original German edition of *Wahrheit und Methode*:

No one disputes the fact that controlling the prejudices of our own present to such an extent that we do not misunderstand the witnesses of the past is a valid aim, but obviously such control does not completely fulfill the task of understanding the past and its transmissions.

Gadamer's point is that the moment at which method has concluded its task, which, as he puts it in *Truth and Method*, is to highlight "the experience of a tension between the text and the present" (1989, 306), the true work of interpretation begins. That task is, first of all, "to project a historical horizon that is different from the present" so that "historical consciousness is aware of its own otherness and hence foregrounds the horizon of the past from its own" (306).

The purpose of creating a horizon of the past is, from Gadamer's point of view, to be able to fully reclaim that past while retaining critical consciousness of one's own role in producing it. Such a creation is "only something superimposed upon continuing tradition, and hence it immediately recombines with what it has foregrounded itself from in order to become one with itself again in the unity of the historical horizon that it thus acquires" (306). The methodologically constructed meaning of the text is always under reconstruction as that meaning becomes, in its own right, part of historiographical tradition. As such, its power to shape the meaning of texts is overcome as the refinement of method requires the revisioning of textual meaning.

This observation has important implications for Gadamer's evaluation of the competing claims, say, of historiography and theology regarding the meaning of a biblical text. The past meaning of a text disclosed by historical reconstruction has no ultimate epistemological privilege over the meaning that is mediated to the present through the tradition that transmits the text as Scripture. The reason is that the theological tradition is indeed willing to pay greater attention to the fundamental claim of the text to speak the truth. "To interpret the law's will or the promises of God is clearly not a form of domination [as in historical method] but of service" (311). Each tradition, to be sure, constructs a statement of the meaning of the text which holds true within the type of discourse that itself constitutes the sole meaningful framework within which one may address questions to the text in the first place. For this reason a theological statement of scriptural meaning is indeed incomplete if it ignores methodologically constructed meaning. But at the same time, methodologically constructed meaning silences the living address of the scriptural text unless, in attending to what the text itself requires of readers, theological interpretation draws the text into conversation with the present.

Gadamer, then, explicitly links the distancing strategies of historical reconstruction and the appropriative moment of theological reading into a single hermeneutical process by which reconstructive thought is enabled to serve the possibility of the text's theological application in the present. The implications of this reading of Gadamer for research in rabbinic Judaism are important. The conception of tradition as a hermeneutical organ helps us to see that the study of rabbinic hermeneutics includes far more than an account of the explicit interpretive methods employed in rabbinic texts for the discussion of Scripture, the Mishnah, or other early literary sources. Rabbinic exegetical *middot*, codified or implicit, are only the superficial (because consciously formulated or deployed) phenomena behind which lie the broader hermeneutical processes that mediate the culture represented in literary sources.

Furthermore, insofar as the critical establishment of a past historical horizon is a fundamental, if preliminary, step in Gadamer's theory of historical understanding, hermeneutical inquiry in the Gadamerian mode is eminently open to synthesizing results achieved through the methodological paths of philology and the other textual- and historical-critical disciplines. All of these research domains must be exploited in order to gain the fullest appreciation of the various interpretive fields within which specific rabbinic views of the past are constructed and amplified. Gadamer's understanding of tradition as the ongoing construction of past meaning in the present helps us to see that the rabbinic past, known primarily insofar as it is transmitted by rabbinic literature, is indeed a kind of historical memory the truth of which remains to be grasped, both in terms of its reality as a past historical horizon as well as a continued claim to truth. Hermeneutical research has as its goal to identify and elucidate this dialogue of present and past within the memory of rabbinic tradition, even as it tries to reflect upon ways in which the memory's meaning can be uttered with contemporary lips. In what follows, we make a beginning by attempting to grasp how tradition itself becomes an object of jurisprudential and historical thought in early rabbinic literature.

III. Halakhah as an Object of Rabbinic Thought

A. The Construction of Halakhah as Tradition

We are now in a position to focus on the real concern of this study, the way in which a Gadamerian orientation to the historical study of texts can guide our own reflections upon *halakhah* as a legal and historical phenomenon within rabbinic culture. First, by way of establishing methodologically the historical horizon in terms of which *halakhah* must first be grasped, a word or two about the social, semantic, and literary range of the term *halakhah* itself.

In the surviving Hebrew literature of postbiblical Jewish antiquity, the noun, *halakhah*, used as a technical term equivalent to "law," appears only in rabbinic literature.[5] Thus, while other nonrabbinic Jews must certainly have acknowledged some customary law as distinctive to their group, and while rabbinic law clearly draws on nonrabbinic Jewish custom, *halakhah* remains distinctive to the circle of rabbis and their disciples. In its most common applications, the term suggests origins in jurisprudential reflection upon the sources of legal authority in a society governed in principle by the disciplined interpretive application of scriptural law. *Halakhah* derives its basic meaning in relation to a complementary term derived from the scriptural legal lexicon, *mitzvah* (commandment). The pair together identify and distinguish two sorts of authoritative legal norms: those stemming from scriptural commandments, *mitzvot*, and those stemming from the instructions of sages, *halakhot*.

The distinction between Scripture *(hatorah*[6] or *miqra')*, the primal revelation of divine will, and the rabbinic teachings within which that will is embodied, is in jurisprudential theory an absolute one, although the two sorts of norms are often found in interactive connection where specific problems of law are concerned. Thus, in a well-known passage, the Mishnah claims: "The *halakhot* of the Sabbath, pilgrimage offerings and sacrilege are like mountains hung by a hair, with little Scripture *(miqra')* and many *halakhot*" (Hagigah 1:8: cf. T Hagigah 1:9; T Eruvin 3:23–24). The point is that certain areas of law in which biblical legislation is sparse may be supplemented by ample rabbinic prescriptions. It is assumed that such prescriptions, in the absence of scriptural legislation, are to be regarded as normative application of scriptural commandments. In this sense (and in tune with its etymological connection to the root *h-l-k*), *halakhah* may best be rendered as "procedure," a rabbinically ordained directive for carrying out scriptural covenant norms.

This jurisprudential sense of *halakhah* is quite common throughout the Mishnah and later sources. But there is a second sense of *halakhah* that is of particular interest to our present study. This second sense becomes noticeable in texts that supply *halakhah* with an institutional history as a distinctive body of knowledge under sages' unique province, they alone determining its character by majority vote in their own legislative bodies (e.g., M Eduyyot 1:5; M Shabbat 1:4). Any specific sage, furthermore, is assumed to represent, in his own person, the deposit of halakhic learning as it has been transmitted to him by his teacher. *Halakhah* is the product of the sages' own judicial activity, nurtured in their own institutions and mediated within their own framework of master-disciple instruction. Thus, as in M. Oholot 16:1, one sage can criticize the accuracy with which another has reported a prescription received from the past: "Said R. Tarfon: May I bury my children if this isn't a corrupt *halakhah*! For the one who heard it misheard it." Similarly, an opinion reported correctly by a sage is to be followed, insofar as he speaks "in accordance with the *halakhah*" (M Peah 4:1–2), the authoritative complex of norms received from the past.

In such usage the jurisprudential sense of "procedure" is retained, but recedes in salience. The focus now is not on how the halakhic dictum, as a legal genre, relates to other generic norms, such as the commandments of Scripture. Prominent now is the matter of the halakhic utterance itself and its relation to the sage, the one who transmits accurately knowledge that he has received from a reliable source. This shift from concern to place *halakhah* in a system of textual authority (in relation to Scripture) to a concern for its origins in social authority is important. It signals the awareness of *halakhah* as a cultural possession of an order slightly more nuanced than "law" need imply; it has begun to be conceived as well as "tradition" per se, something received from the past which must be passed to the future by means of authoritative transmitters. It is as "tradition" of this basic sort that *halakhah* becomes an object of reflection in both jurisprudential and historiographic settings as the mishnaic corpus is received, reflected upon and amplified in its course of transmission through rabbinic scribal culture.

Of most importance for our present discussion are the ways we can trace, in the early postmishnaic literature, a progressive elaboration and enrichment of the mishnaic image of *halakhah*. The Mishnah's sense of *halakhah* as tradition quickly gathers around itself a range of semantic nuances that can be discerned particularly in the ways successor texts to the Mishnah restate and reformulate mishnaic materials regarding *halakhah*. We shall see that the later literature discloses the emergence of a tradition, in the Gadamerian sense, that has reached and begun to transmit a certain consensus about the nature of *halakhah*. This consensus discloses itself in ways in which later rabbinic texts subtly reformulate materials received from the Mishnah itself.

Two striking examples of this appear in the following contrasts between a mishnaic report of a particular judicial process and its rendering in the Tosefta. Neither mishnaic passage makes reference to the term *halakhah*, and both have little interest in the Mishnah's overall conception of *halakhah* as the representation of tradition per se. The toseftan renditions, however, differ from the mishnaic reports in ways which might often be dismissed in textual scholarship as variant versions of an underlying, no longer extant statement or utterance. I would suggest that, with Gadamerian sensitivities to the way in which textual meaning is constructed by passage through tradition, we might rather interpret what is before us as ways in which mishnaic tradition, coming to fresh expression in the later Tosefta, has already synthesized and extended senses of *halakhah* inherited from the mishnaic corpus itself. The toseftan usage of *halakhah*, then, represents a fresh investment of meaning in the term, even while the sources of that meaning can clearly be traced back to the Mishnah.

The first case concerns the process by which questions of normative law during the Second Temple period were brought to progressively higher courts for resolution until, ultimately, they came before the High Court in the Gazit Chamber on the Temple Mount. The Mishnah, at Sanhedrin 11:2, points out that, if a lower court had heard no tradition on a particular matter taught by a given sage, that sage and his challengers "come to the High Court in the Gazit Chamber, since from there does Torah go forth to all Israel."

The Mishnah's reference to "Torah" in this context requires comment, because it does not signify the revealed Torah of Moses alone. Rather, it must be rendered as "teachings of the sages regarding the enactment of the Torah." This usage is not uncommon in the Mishnah and its fundamental sense as primordial tradition is made clear by the context of its usage in the very first paragraph of Mishnah Avot, "Moses received Torah from Sinai." The Sage's teaching is Torah because it has its origins with Moses.

In this light, the expanded description of the Court's procedure, as found in T Sanhedrin 7:1, is of great interest:

> If they [the judges] had heard [a tradition], they would inform them [the petitioners]; but if not, they would place it up for a vote. If those declaring "unclean" were in the majority, [the matter was decided as] unclean; if those declaring "clean" were in the majority, [the matter was decided as] clean. From there did *halakhah* become widespread in Israel.

From our perspective, the crucial difference between the mishnaic and toseftan versions is that the judges' teaching is reached by means of a vote, and that the result is designated not Torah but *halakhah*. Is this revision of the mishnaic scenario and displacement of one technical term for tradition by another simply evidence of a dual transmission of some bit of historical memory which is no longer before us in its pristine form? I think not, because of the nature of the differences.

The toseftan text reveals two important assumptions on the part of its tradent, assumptions which differ dramatically from those of the mishnaic text. The first is that since *halakhah*, not Torah, is known to the Mishnah to emerge from a vote (e.g., M. Eduyyot 1:5. Shabbat 1:4), *halakhah* is the most appropriate designation of the decision reached by the Court in the present case as well. Thus, a mishnaic notion of halakhic origins by judicial vote is now woven by the toseftan passage into M Sanhedrin, which prefers Torah, ancient tradition, to *halakhah* as a designation of the judicial ruling. Second, the toseftan displacement of Torah by *halakhah* allows the latter to participate in Torah's semantic value as uniquely authoritative teaching tinged by the charisma of revelation itself. If *halakhah* can stand in the place of Torah, even though it is reached by human adjudication, it is seen to share in the primordial character which the term Torah will bear in any Judaic setting.

In sum, M Sanhedrin 11:2 is understood and reformulated by the toseftan tradent in light of the Mishnah's own amply attested conception of *halakhah* as tradition. At the same time, the Mishnah's notion of Torah is redefined as *halakhah* by virtue of the Tosefta's displacement of the former with the latter. The toseftan revision of the mishnaic scenario, therefore, testifies already to the development, grounded in the mishnaic text, of an interpretive tradition that had already reached some tacit judgments about the meanings and nuances that could be applied to technical terms such as Torah and *halakhah*. The terms are borrowing values from each other and becoming, to a degree, interchangeable. This interchangeability, however, seems to move in one direction—toward the preference for *halakhah* as a comprehensive term for tradition as a primordial inheritance.

We may turn now to a second toseftan signpost in the early development of *halakhah* as a reference to tradition. Mishnah Parah 7:6 records a ruling concerning the extent to which a particular act performed in the course of a purification ritual might impair the rite's effectiveness. The ruling is glossed as follows:

> This [issue] went *(halakh)* to [the Patriarchal Court at] Yavneh on three successive festivals [for adjudication]. And on the third festival they declared the act suitable as a temporary measure.

Note the Tosefta's amplification (T Parah 7:4):[7]

> In regard to this *halakhah* did the residents of Asya go up to
> Yavneh on three successive festivals. And on the third festival, etc.

To regard the Tosefta's version of the Mishnah as simply an alternate or variant transmission of some "source" underlying both the Mishnah and the Tosefta is to miss the hermeneutically important element of this transmission. The assonance of *halakh* (went) and *halakhah* (procedure) proves irresistible to the literary traditionist, who filters the Mishnah's perfect verb through the many other mishnaic instances in which items of legal interest are identified as *halakhah*. Since what "went up to Yavneh" is a question of ritual law, it must also have been "a *halakhah*"; those who "went up to Yavneh" are the villagers of Asya who bring the halakhic question with them. Thus the toseftan traditionist brings a mishnaic text more fully into conversation with conceptions of halakhic tradition mediated in the first instance by the Mishnah itself and transmitted within the interpretive milieu, the Gadamerian intercourse of text and interpretive discourse, that underlies the toseftan reformulation of the Mishnah.

These examples, I hope, suggest the way in which the term *halakhah* is enriched within the hermeneutical processes of rabbinic textual transmission itself. As an object of thought, *halakhah* is reconstructed in constant dialogue with the texts received from the past, texts which now serve as the basis of historical memory and the foundation for new hermeneutical constructions of the past as it ought to have been. The figure of *halakhah* as tradition is even read back into texts in which it had not originally appeared.

B. Halakhah, Divrei Soferim, and Scripture

The foregoing cases are relatively simple examples of how apparent variants of a single transmission of information can disclose the interpretive milieu within which a text's information is transmitted. In what follows, I would like to explore another aspect of this process a bit further in an area of signal importance for the ultimate transformation of *halakhah* into what rabbinic Judaism has come to call "oral Torah." We turn our attention to the way in which *halakhah*, established in the Mishnah as a model of tradition, finds its place in relation to yet another source of legal knowledge, identified in the Mishnah as the "words of the scribes" *(divrei soferim).*[8] Like *halakhah* itself, *divrei soferim* have more than a single value in early rabbinic jurisprudential and historical reflection. Shifts in the term's signification, which correlate with its applications in jurisprudential and historiographic contexts, will prove instructive in our present discussion.

The distinction between *halakhah* and *divrei soferim* as sources of authoritative tradition is drawn most clearly by reference to a third source of authority, Scripture *(hatorah)* itself. This is clear on the basis of the one place in the Mishnah in which scribal opinion is explicitly juxtaposed with *halakhah*. At issue in M Orlah 3:9 is the extent to which the consumption of produce grown outside the Land of Israel is subject to certain restrictions which, according to Scripture, must be applied to all native Israelite crops:

> I. The consumption of new produce [i.e., tree-fruit in its first year of bearing] is forbidden anywhere [in the Land and in the Exile] on the basis of the Torah (Lev. 24:13).
> II. But the prohibition against consuming tree-fruit [grown in the Exile] prior to its fourth year of bearing is *halakhah*.
> III. And the prohibition against sowing a field [in the Exile] with seed of diverse kinds is based upon *divrei soferim*.

The Mishnah's interest in distinguishing the sources of the various prohibitions is jurisprudential: on what authority do the several legal statements rest? The appeals to halakhic authority (II) and scribal teaching (III), however, assume that we know the legal force of the distinction between *halakhah* and "the words of the scribes."[9] But the Mishnah itself provides no explicit explanation. Both clearly constitute sources of legal guidance. Are the sources, however, distinct in origin, but equal in authority? Or is there a distinction to be made in their respective authority as well?

We may frame an answer to this question by pointing out, first of all, that there is an important difference in the way *halakhah* and *divrei soferim* are assumed in the Mishnah to correlate with scriptural commandments. As I have argued elsewhere (Jaffee 1992), the Mishnah understands halakhic dicta to constitute a source of legal material not merely supplementary to Scripture, but genuinely definitive of its application. As "tradition," halakhic norms govern the embodiment of the scriptural code.

Therefore, as in the following example from M Yevamot 8:3, disputes about the application and extension of scriptural command- ments are resolved not by appeal to logical exegesis of Scripture, but rather by appeal to authoritative received tradition. In a dispute regarding the naturalization of Egyptians and Edomites into the Israelite community, R. Shimon argues that, while the males must wait three generations, as required by Deut. 23:8–9, the females may be naturalized immediately. His view is itself based upon the Mishnah's own exemption of females from Deut. 23:4's stricture against Ammonites and Moabites in general. When R. Shimon explains that his own view merely constitutes a logical extension of what the anonymous mishnaic dictum already holds, an instructive interchange follows:

> [Sages] replied: If this is *halakhah* we will accept it. But if this is
> [a conclusion reached through] argument, it can be overruled.
> He replied: Not all! I report *halakhah*!

It is assumed here that the extensions of scriptural law offered by the sages stand not on their own individual authority as reasoners, but upon their ability to summon *halakhah*, received legal tradition, in their support. Nobody challenges Shimon to demonstrate a scriptural basis for his opinion. Indeed, he is explicitly told that unless he can link his view to an halakhic report, all arguments based upon exegetical deduction from scriptural facts are subject to dismissal (cf. M Nazir 7:4). The assumption is that one can dispute a halakhic report only on the basis of some other halakhic report. Naturally, this is precisely what Shimon claims to have at hand. As in our earlier example from M Hagigah 1:8, *halakhah* is conceived as a framework for the application of scriptural laws, a framework that is itself independent of the explicit content of Scripture, even though its authority is in part drawn from connection to it.[10]

Keeping in mind the dominance of halakhic principles over the scriptural word in the actual construction of covenantal law, we may profitably compare the Mishnah's jurisprudential conception of the "words of the scribes" as an authoritative source of knowledge. In the handful of such reports preserved in the mishnah,[11] *divrei soferim* appear, like halakhic dicta, to constitute legal views supple- mentary to those of Scripture. In nearly all mishnaic contexts, however, it is quite clear, as Sanders has recently reminded us (1990, 115–17), that *divrei soferim* that have passed into the legal corpus are treated as less authoritative than strictures believed to be located explicitly in scriptural revelation.[12] Thus, for example, in the potentially catastrophic realm of cultic contamination, items explicitly declared unclean by the Torah are treated as capable of greater continued virulence than those declared unclean on the strength of scribal teaching (M Parah 11:4–5; cf. M Tohorot 4:7, 4:11). The point is that, while *divrei soferim* are deemed to constitute a legal source, their force as law is always subordinate to Scripture and ancillary to it. While *divrei soferim* may clarify the meaning of Scripture, they can never displace its primacy. *Halakhah*, to the contrary, constitutes Scripture's contemporary and legitimate embodiment as living law. The Mishnah never says, and cannot be imagined to say, that where Scripture and *halakhah* come into conflict, Scripture takes precedence. But this is precisely what is possible with regard to scribal teaching.

From the Mishnah's nascent jurisprudential perspective, then, *halakhah* is primarily conceived as the embodiment of Scripture's imperatives in the life patterns of the community of Israel. Scribal teaching, while having to do with matters of scriptural law, is represented primarily as learned or scholastic formulas supplying information essentially supplementary to Scripture. Not only are *halakhah* and *divrei soferim* distinct; more importantly, it is the former, not the latter, which constitutes Scripture's hermeneutical extension into living authoritative forms. The covenantal law of Scripture, in other words, is embodied in and through *halakhah*; scribal teaching lives only as a source of knowledge that may or may not find itself incorporated in the embodied covenant of *halakhah*.

C. Halakhah, Divrei Soferim, and the Emergence of Primordial Tradition

The Mishnah's perspective on the relationship between *halakhah* and scribal learning suggests that, for the Mishnah at least, there is a distinction not only between these two forms of tradition, but between its bearers as well. *Halakhah* is the tradition of the sages themselves, the recent masters whose disciples transmit their teachings in the very text of the Mishnah. *Divrei soferim*, to the contrary, stem from a group—the "scribes"—who are more ancient than the sages, yet, in some unarticulated sense, are connected to them.[13] Put in another way, *halakhah* has the value of tradition established in the recent past and present, while *divrei soferim* represents a deposit of learning stemming from a group of greater antiquity than the sages. It is the sages who selectively determine the degree to which such ancient learning enters into the more recent living halakhic forms.

The nature of the connection between the sages and the scribes, and the relationship between the types of knowledge transmitted within each group, remains relatively unexplored in the Mishnah. In the postmishnaic literature, however, jurisprudential reflection is supplemented with a historical perspective on the relations of scribes to sages. Specifically, the gulf in time and authority between the two seems to narrow. The groups are gradually assimilated to each other in status and function; halakhic contributions appropriate to the sages are attributed increasingly to the scribes, just as ancient scribal learning is assimilated into more recent formulations of sages' tradition.

The Talmuds offer rich evidence of this process. In PT Sheqalim 48c, for example, Ezra, the Bible's prototypical scribe, is reported as having "counted the words of the Torah as well as the words of the sages," both Scripture and the traditions of the sages coming under his scribal competence. Similarly, in an explicit ascription to scribes of the traditions of the sages, BT Sanhedrin 106b (parallel, Hagigah 15b) announces that the scribes would pore over the sages' traditions of halakhic argumentation in addition to deriving "three hundred *halakhot*" concerning a legal conundrum presented in the Mishnah's laws of uncleanness. What is important here is that people specifically portrayed as scribes *(soferim)*, rather than sages *(hakhamim)* produce not *divrei soferim*, but halakhic rulings themselves on a par with those of the sages.[14]

The hermeneutical activity which underlies and supports this new construction of the distant past is evident in the way in which material known in earlier texts as scribal contributions is assimilated, in later texts, to *halakhah*. I present as an example the remarkable variations by which rabbinic literature from the Mishnah through the Babylonian Talmud transmits a brief periscope that affirms that Abraham, despite having lived prior to the sinaitic revelation, practiced the divine commandments in their entirety. As we move through the various versions of the text, we will be able to track as well the way in which developing concepts of *halakhah* as tradition structure the reception of earlier texts and replicate themselves in the production of new texts, texts that gradually link *halakhah* and *divrei soferim* into an indistinguishable unity of primordial sinaitic tradition.

The basic conviction of Abraham's loyalty to the sinaitic covenant enters rabbinic literature in the Mishnah, where it appears in M Qiddushin 4:14 as a brief midrash-like inference drawn from Gen. 26:5. After commenting on this passage, we will attempt to track its resonances in the body of traditions preserved in the Tosefta, the tannaitic midrashim, and the Talmuds.

The Mishnah states:

> We find that Father Abraham observed the Torah *(hatorah)* in its entirety before it was given, as it is said: "Since Abraham obeyed my voice, and kept my observances, commandments, statutes and my teachings *(torotai)*." (Gen. 26:5)

Abraham's obedience to the Torah prior to its revelation, asserted in the introduction to the paragraph, is implied by the scriptural text itself, which lists a series of virtual synonyms for divine law as testimony to Abraham's obedience to God. The Mishnah, therefore, offers little beyond a restatement of the scriptural claim. At best it highlights for a rabbinic audience the centrality of Abraham as a model of obedience—in all, hardly an original or controversial thought in ancient Judaism.

Later appropriations of this reading of Gen. 26:5, however, take their points of departure from a detail of the verse which seems to hold little interest for the framer of the mishnaic passage. This is the appearance of the word *torah* in its plural form, "my teachings" *(torotai)*. Consider, for example, the versions of the two main toseftan manuscripts, shown in bold below, which spell out the implications of Scripture's use of the plural form of *torah*.

> And the Omnipresent blessed him [Abraham] in his old age more than in his youth. And why so? For he enacted the Torah even before it came, as it is said: "Since Abraham obeyed my voice . . . and my teachings." "My *torah*" is not stated; rather, "my *torot*." **This teaches that the principles of the Torah and all its specifications *(diqduqeiha)* were revealed to him [so that he could observe them].** (T Qiddushin 5:21, MS Vienna)[15]

> And the Omnipresent blessed him [etc.] . . . "My *torah*" is not stated; rather, "my *torot*." **This teaches that the words of the**

> **Torah** *(divrei torah)* **and the words of the scribes** *(divrei soferim)* **were revealed to him**. (T Qiddushin 5:21, MS Erfurt)[16]

The Tosefta, representing a rather common pattern of postmishnaic exegetical thought,[17] draws attention to the implications of the plural form of *torah* and tries to supply the form with fresh content drawn from beyond the range of explicit scriptural law.

Of genuine interest, however, is the distinction between Vienna and Erfurt in the kind of extrascriptural content each imports into the biblical text. Here we have yet another example of how what a text-critic might view as a variant appears, from a hermeneutical perspective, to constitute an example of a tradition's construction of its own circle of meaning. For Vienna, Abraham receives as revelation all knowledge available to anyone possessing the present text of Torah, that is, its principal topics as well as the details of their enactment. It is not clear where, of course, these details are to be found. The Erfurt text, however, supplies the answer: the dual reference of Scripture implies Abraham's reception of two corpora of revealed knowledge, the text of the sinaitic Torah and the body of scribal teaching in which the "specifications" of the text's application are to be found.

The Erfurt version of the Tosefta, sharpening the implication of Vienna, reveals a tendency toward the homogenization of all genres of rabbinic teaching into revelation which, as I have suggested elsewhere (Jaffee 1992), begins to dominate discussion of halakhic tradition as a whole in all texts reaching redaction from the late third century and onward. A striking passage of Sifra is only the most commonly cited example of this tendency:

> "On Mt. Sinai, by the hand of Moses" (Lev. 26:46)—this teaches that the Torah was given with all its procedures *(hilkhoteiha*; viz., "its *halakhot"),* specifications *(diqduqeiha)* and interpretations through Moses on Sinai.

Here, as is clear, the revelation at Sinai ranges well beyond what can be found in the scroll of the Torah: in addition to a body of exegesis it includes the entire body of knowledge contributed by sages *(halakhot)* and scribes *(diqduqim).*

At this point, scribal knowledge and halakhic norms appear to be following the same path toward assimilation to the concept of revelation. An important marker on this path appears in the

Palestinian Talmud, where a dictum ascribed to the third-century sage, R. Yohanan, whose name is frequently associated with the nascent doctrine of Oral and Written Torah,[18] holds that in certain specific instances, *"divrei soferim* over-rule the words of the Torah" (PT Maaser Sheni 53c). R. Yohanan's view, echoing other claims that *halakhah* can supersede words of the Torah (Mekhilta D'Rabbi Ishmael Mishpatim 2, PT Qiddushin 59d, BT Sotah 16a), indicates the degree to which scribal knowledge has begun to occupy a jurisprudential role reserved in the Mishnah and other early texts for *halakhah* alone. Like mishnaic notions of *halakhah* (e.g., M Yevamot 8:3, cited above), R. Yohanan's *"divrei soferim* are related to words of the Torah and are as beloved as words of the Torah" (PT Berakhot 3b; cf. Sanhedrin 30a, Avodah Zarah 41c). They are capable of being definitive statements of practice overagainst the textual record of the Torah itself.

The move toward a complete assimilation of scribal knowledge to the full embodiment of covenantal norms implied in the term *halakhah* comes to closure in an important passage of the Babylonian Talmud, Yoma 28b, which resumes and applies the toseftan traditions cited above from T Qiddushin.[19]

> Said Rav, and some say, Rav Ashi: [Before Sinai] Father Abraham fulfilled even the requirement to place a dish of food in a courtyard to create a shared Sabbath domain *('eruv). As it is said: "my teachings." All the same are the words of the Torah and the words of the scribes.*

Here the words of Torah, revelation, are regarded as sharing an authority equal to that of scribal tradition—they are "all the same," part of a single divine teaching stemming from Sinai. The knowledge of the scribes, that is, has become like the halakhic reports of the sages, part of a single line of tradition linking the present to the primordial past that began with the revelation of the Torah.[20] They are aspects of the same body of law, a single, primordial tradition.[21]

D. Summary

Perhaps now we can summarize the ground we have covered. Appearing in the Mishnah as a source of law complementary to *halakhah*, "words of the scribes" become assimilated to halakhic tradition in both a jurisprudential and historical sense, as scribal teaching becomes historically reconceived as the equivalent of the *halakhah* embodied in the decisions and teachings of rabbinic sages of the third and fourth centuries. The concept of *halakhah*, preserved in the Mishnah as a source of tradition quite unrelated to *divrei soferim*, comes during the course of rabbinic usage to assimilate the latter to itself. As I have argued, this reconceptualization testifies to a hermeneutical development immanent in the process of early rabbinic tradition, as sages reflect upon, apply, and recast their own deposit of legal, jurisprudential, and historical texts.

IV. Halakhic Primordiality and the Question of Truth

Our attempt to employ a disciplined methodological program to sketch the historical horizon of early rabbinic texts regarding *halakhah* is completed. Is it possible now to move beyond methodological constraints to engage these texts hermeneutically as formulations of the truth? If so, what sort of truth might lie in the particular rabbinic claim that *halakhah* is received in Israel as primordial tradition, "from Moses at Sinai"?

The question is crucial, for halakhic dicta are sources of living law in Judaism only to the degree that the historical memory that makes them worth preserving is compelling in its claim to truth. As Robert Cover points out with great eloquence, law and historical memory, nomos and narrative, interpenetrate at every moment:

> [A legal tradition] includes not only a corpus juris, but also a language and a mythos—narratives in which the corpus juris is located by those whose wills act upon it. These myths establish the paradigms for behavior. They build relations between the normative and the material universe, . . . [they] establish a repertoire of moves—a lexicon of normative action—that may be combined into meaningful patterns culled from the meaningful patterns of the past. (Cover 1983, 9)

Cover joins the issue in a pointed way. If *nomos* (in our context, *halakhah*) requires mythic narrative in order to live as law, then the death of the myth is the death of the law. A *halakhah* without a ground in historical memory has no more compelling a claim to the religious attention of Jews than the Code of Hammurabi.

By uncovering the interdependence of *nomos* and myth in the hermeneutical life of law, however, Cover prevents its deployment in the hermeneutical appropriation of the truth of rabbinic memory. Cover can help us understand, as methodological outsiders to the hermeneutical community of *halakhah*, why *halakhah* is accompanied by judgments of its primordiality. But he cannot provide, for those standing within that hermeneutical community, guidance in appropriating the truth of halakhic primordiality.

To represent the sinaitic origins of *halakhah* as "mythic" and to decode the myth in terms of its function in the economy of rabbinic imagination in late antiquity is precisely the victory of method over understanding against which Gadamer's work is directed. Confined by method solely to the horizon of the past, the narratives of halakhic primordiality are safely trapped there, fixed in an ancient frame of mind which can now be diagnosed but neither lived in nor engaged as one's equal, let alone one's teacher. Within the historicist frame of reference, then, the primordiality of *halakhah*, taken as "myth," is irrelevant to the historical truth, while taken as a claim to historical truth it is simply false.

There are important implications here for the academic study of rabbinic Judaism and its relation to a truly hermeneutical theory of halakhic praxis within Judaism itself. To the degree that historical scholarship on rabbinic tradition in universities and rabbinical seminaries remains committed to historicist assumptions and methods, its impact upon the hermeneutical life of non-Orthodox forms of Judaism will remain (as it has for most of the past two centuries) either negligible or subject to vulgarization. On the one hand, the most rigorous historicist constructions of the meaning of rabbinic texts will have little application to contemporary Judaic discourse, because such analyses will show how firmly the texts are anchored in the particularities of their own time and place. On the other hand, the results of historicist research, passing as they normally do from technical publications into the presses of the various ideological movements of Judaism, will be selectively and unselfconsciously mined by ideological entrepreneurs so as to project onto the past any version that suits a given contemporary agenda. What begins in serious historical curiosity becomes fodder for the construction of histories which serve only the perpetuation of institutional ideologies.

Within Orthodox forms of Judaism, the scenario differs, but hardly to the benefit of historicist models of research. To a certain degree, historicism and modernist Orthodoxy could be excellent partners where philological or sociological reconstruction of the language and circumstances of the rabbinic *nomos* is concerned. To reconstruct an authentic text, to delimit what a given halakhic dictum could have meant in its setting, and to disclose its interpretive history in the life of the later halakhic commentaries and codes could be of great value in providing added information by which contemporary halakhic decisions could be reached.

But, as in the field of biblical criticism, historicist inquiry into rabbinics ultimately touches questions of the historical truth of the sacred text's narrative, its "myth." It is at this point that historicist research into the rabbinic literature ceases to be of interest to modernist Orthodoxy, for it continues to cling to a naive historicism which holds that what the sacred text reports indeed occurred in precisely that way. *Halakhah* must ultimately come from Sinai, just as the sages claim. But a critically reconstructed truth of the *nomos* shorn of an equally critical reconstruction of the truth of its accompanying narrative is, ultimately, a hermeneutical failure. Its failure to construct a single ethic of interpretation for all aspects of the text denies it an integrated standpoint or coherent horizon from which to begin the work of fresh understanding.

If this admittedly broad analyses is at all convincing, it would seem that there can be only one legitimately hermeneutical relationship to the corpus of rabbinic law, that which emerges in various forms from the circles of ideologically antimodernist halakhic traditionalism. Here the contradiction of modernist Orthodoxy— commitment to historical reconstruction of the *nomos* without a historical analysis of the narrative—does not exist. The reason is simple: the category of "myth" in relation to halakhic tradition could never occur, and the methodological constraints of historical method in establishing meaning are irrelevant. To the contrary, from the antimodernist perspective, no gulf exists at all between the texts of the past and the diverse hermeneutical horizons that bear them into the present. When the question of historical truth is raised, therefore, one is confident that this might be grasped immediately through the words of the text, mediated by the sacred tradition printed in smaller script on the margins of the page, as if no interpretive moment intervened between the historical object and its representation in tradition.

Is the destiny of academic research into rabbinic Judaism, then, to be either misinterpreted and selectively mined within the modernist branches of Judaism, or entirely ignored within the antimodernist branches? Does the dichotomy between "myth" and "real history" serve as the stumbling block that will, for one or another reason, consign academic historiography to Judaic irrelevance and Judaic religion to historical naivete? As we brush hard against the apparently firm dichotomy of myth and history, the importance of Gadamer's hermeneutic approach to the truth of the past may now be fully appreciated.

In my view, the question of historically effected consciousness is the kernel of a Gadamerian critique of antimodernist Orthodoxy. If Gadamer holds that the ultimate task of hermeneutics is to submit to the truth of the text and engage it in dialogue, what quarrel would he have with the hermeneutics of such Orthodoxy? It would seem that precisely this is its strength. The answer is rather simple: never having passed through the solvent of historicism, an antimodernist hermeneutics cannot pass to full hermeneutical self-consciousness. It cannot achieve full awareness of its own role in the creation of tradition and the mediation of textual meaning, for it has never come to recognize the embeddedness of all texts in a matrix of concrete historical causes and effects that fully shape how they are understood.

The antimodernist hermeneutical posture, therefore, is unavailable for anyone who has tasted the eye-opening fruit of historicism and fully digested it, for once consumed, that fruit alters any hermeneutical system which has absorbed it. Insofar as nearly all forms of contemporary Jewish thought have fully digested historicism, accordingly, Judaic religious discourse can only move beyond historicism. It must attempt to bring its effects to full self-consciousness in all our interpretive engagements with the texts of Jewish tradition.

This point brings us, at last, to our constructive proposal regarding the retrieval of the truth of rabbinic discourse concerning *halakhah* in particular. The historical horizon we have constructed through method in the first part of this essay yields a picture of rabbinic tradition constructing, through its own processes of textual mediation and revision, a progressively richer conception of *halakhah* as tradition. *Halakhah* begins its life as a set of legal dicta, the sole possession of a learned class of sages. Yet within a few centuries it comes to represent the entire corpus of nonscriptural legal learning received by the great heroes of the Israelite past, from Moses through the scribes and on to the sages. Once, that is, the nomos of rabbinic Judaism comes into clear jurisprudential consciousness, it is immediately drawn into a narrative web, a system of historical memory, which obsessively extends the origins of the nomos indefinitely into the past.

There are some useful truths to be entertained here. One, as Cover suggests, is a truth about law: it requires a historical dimension before it can be a living force in a culture. The second, I think, is a truth about early rabbinic Judaism: as soon as it realizes the gap between its own operative legal system and that of Scripture, it must begin to close that gap through the construction of a historiography which links *halakhah* to Sinai. The question, however, is: Is that all the truth there is? How do we represent within the conventions of our own discourse the truth of what is said in rabbinic texts about the primordiality of *halakhah*? How do we move from truths *about* law or rabbinic Judaism to the truth *of* the discourse of rabbinic texts themselves?

We begin to do so, I believe, as soon as we recall the structure of our own hermeneutical consciousness as Gadamer has helped us to discern it. We recognize an important correspondence between the structure of historical understanding and the historical unfolding of *halakhah* as tradition that mediates between Sinai and the present. The assimilation of *halakhah* to primordial tradition in rabbinic historiography restates, in narrative, the hermeneutical assertion that there is no textual meaning without the intervention of an interpretive tradition between text and reader. The hermeneutical situation, in which textual understanding is at all moments bound up with the authoritative voice transmitted from the past, is not only illustrated in the historical development of rabbinic ideas of *halakhah*; it finds there an echo and confirmation.

In other words, halakhic primordiality is the narrative formulation, within the conventions of rabbinic historiography, of the Gadamerian postulate that all understanding is necessarily grounded in what is received from the past. For Gadamer, the authority of the past has the quality of primordiality, even if critical historiography can reconstruct a point before which tradition did not exist. What matters in hermeneutical understanding is that a tradition, whatever its origins, now confronts one as inescapable—thus, primordial—in the moment of one's work of understanding. Understanding is unthinkable without it.

So, too, as we have seen in our study of the foregrounding of *halakhah* as primordial tradition, the halakhic norm as legal directive proves ultimately unthinkable within rabbinic jurisprudence without a simultaneous perception of its rootedness in the past, a rootedness which alone constitutes the possibility and the necessity of its application to the present. The truth to the claim of halakhic primordiality lies in the constructive element of historical memory that, as always, is an interpretive synthesis of tradition from the past brought into concrete expression in terms of some present concern for meaning.

The proposition that halakhic tradition stems from Sinai is and must forever be in error *if it is judged as a claim critically to represent a vanished past*. But to judge it as such is to mistake the authentic sphere within which its claim rings with irrefutable truth. That sphere lies in the realm of halakhic praxis, where the primordiality of *halakhah* constitutes the distinctively rabbinic formulation of the hermeneutical situation in which all application of past meaning in the present takes place. This is the claim to truth to which those on the near side of the historicist moment must attend.

NOTES

1. The second German edition of 1965 was the basis of the first English translation (Gadamer 1975). All citations in the present essay are from the second revised edition (Gadamer 1989), based on the fifth German edition. This is not the place for an extended rehearsal of the English-language discussion of Gadamer's work. Excellent analyses of Gadamer, with ample reference to secondary discussions, may be consulted in Warnke 1987 and Weinsheimer 1985.

2. The one possible exception is recent literary and hermeneutical studies of rabbinic midrash. Paul Ricoeur and, more recently, Jacques Derrida are probably the most frequently acknowledged inspirations for scholars working on the hermeneutical dimension of midrashic literature. Ricoeur in particular has been an important mediator of Gadamer's thought to English readers. See, for example, Ricoeur 1973 and the essays collected in Ricoeur 1981. Explicit reference to Gadamer in studies of midrashic literature may be found in Handelman 1982, 21–25; Fraade 1991, 183–84, 187, 190; Bruns 1990, 189–213, and 1991, 1–21. In all, one must say that Gadamer's direct impact on the study of midrashic hermeneutics remains minor.

3. The principal works stemming from this period are the Mishnah (ca.

200 C.E., hereafter cited as M), the Tosefta (ca. 250–200, hereafter T), the various exegetical compilations attributed to teachers of the mishnaic era (ca. 300–400), the Palestinian Talmud (ca. 375, hereafter PT), and the Babylonian Talmud (ca. 525, hereafter BT).

4. The work of Jacob Neusner has been most important in tracing the stages in the development of the notion of Oral Torah through the classical rabbinic corpus. See, for example, Neusner 1985, 26, 53, 61, 74, 105, 110, 114, 144. Recent discussions of the dating of the notion of Oral Torah within rabbinic circles may be consulted in Schaefer 1978, 153–97, and Kraemer 1989, 175–90.

5. For a rough chronology of the literature, see n. 3. The most comprehensive discussion of the semantic range of *halakhah* in rabbinic sources is that of Bacher 1965, I:42–43, II:53–56. See also the etymological discussion in Lieberman 1950, 83, and Urbach 1986, 2–3.

   Unless renewed publication of the Qumran literature yields some surprises, *halakhah* in its rabbinic sense makes no appearance within the scrolls. In my view, scattered references to *dorshei halaqot* ("interpreters of smooth things": cf. Isa. 30:10 and CD [Damascus Covenant] 1:18, 1QH [Thanksgiving Scroll] 2:15, 32; 4Q169 [Nahum Commentary] 2:7) are not convincingly explained as punning or dismissive allusions to pharisaic *halakhot* and so cannot attest to the existence of the term in its jurisprudential sense. For a recent discussion of the meaning of *halaqot* in the scrolls, see Bronsnik 1991, 653–57. Furthermore, while the verbal noun, *halakhah*, in the sense of "going," is known in these texts (e.g., 1QS [Manual of Discipline] 1:25, 3:9), it is not a technical, jurisprudential term. Thus, while it might share a common semantic field with the rabbinic usage, it is an error to suppose, as have some (e.g., Rabin 1957, 106), that a common tradition of usage links covenanters and sages.

6. *Hatorah* (the Torah) and *torah* (Torah) are not equivalent. The former refers to Scripture per se, while the latter signifies rabbinic instruction in law and ethics. This distinction is crucial, and its implications will be developed below.

7. Compare T Hullin 3:10 and T Miqvaot 4:6, both of which record that a particular *halakhah* regarding ritual cleanness was brought to Yavneh by the residents of Asya (Etzion-Gever, known in Eusebius as Aisia: see Alon 1975, 145). In neither case is the toseftan formulation generated by the presence of the verb *halakh* in the Mishnah, although T Hullin does make reference to the corresponding mishnaic ruling at M Hullin 3:2. It appears, then, that the toseftan transformation of M Parah is the point of origin for the development within the Tosefta of a stereotypical description of the process of bringing halakhic questions.

8. Most studies of *divrei soferim* done by professional historians collapse the question of their jurisprudential function into that of the historical role of the scribes in the society of Second Temple Palestine. The one

important exception, the article *"divrei soferim"* in the *Entsiklopedyah Talmudit* (Berlin and Zevin 1947, 7:91–106), is very useful jurisprudentially, but is written without sensitivity to historical method. For useful surveys of current opinion on the scribes as a class and the nature of their contribution to ancient Jewish learning, see Schuerer 1979, 322–25, and Bar-Ilan 1988, 21–37.

9.   PT Orlah 63b and BT Qiddushin 38b–39a record a dispute over this issue between the third-century Amoraim, Samuel and R. Yohanan. The former holds that *halakhah* in this context simply refers to local custom *(hilkhot hamedinah;* cf. M Baba Metziah 7:8), while the latter maintains that the reference is to Mosaic *halakhah* received at Sinai. Neither party expresses an opinion on the import of *divrei soferim,* yet the ensuing analysis in Qiddushin 39a (bottom) makes it clear that, for the editors of this discussion at least, the "scribes" are merely sages who enacted an edict against diverse kinds in the Diaspora *(bahus la'ares nami gazru beho rabbanan).* As I hope my own discussion makes clear, this editorial understanding must be seen as reflecting already the process by which various sources of tradition have come to be homogenized into a monolithic *halakhah* stemming from the distant past, yet incorporating within it mechanisms of innovation reserved for the sages. Compare on this point Urbach 1986, 102.

10.   The point is reflected in Mekhilta d'Rabbi Ishmael, Nezikin 2, a midrashic compilation most probably dated to the third to fifth centuries: "The Torah says . . . , but the *halakhah* says . . ." Reformulated within the Talmuds, and ascribed to R. Ishmael, the material becomes one of the classic understatements of rabbinic jurisprudence: "In three cases does the *halakhah* overturn Scripture" (PT Quiddushin 59d, BT Sotah 16a).

11.   See Kasovsky 1957, 3:1287.

12.   The one exception, upon examination, turns out to be no exception at all. M Sanhedrin 11:3 states: "The words of the scribes bear greater sanction than the words of the Torah." In the context of the passage, the point is merely that, as far as the teaching of the law is concerned, misrepresentation of scribal teaching is more serious than a misrepresentation of scriptural law, for scriptural law is publicly known while scribal teaching remains the professional, therefore private, possession of the scribes. It is in this light that I interpret the other early passage, this from T Taaniyot 2:6/T Yevamot 2:4, which holds that scribal teachings should be more strictly enforced than scriptural rules. The reason is that they are less well known and bear lesser intrinsic authority.

13.   Cases in which sages are represented as referring to their contemporaries as "scribes" are very rare, occurring once in the Mishnah (Kelim 13:7=Tebul Yom 4:6) and occasionally in the later compilations (e.g., Sifre Numbers Naso, 8). In such instances the activities of the

sage/scribes is assumed to be creative of tradition, in line with the general estimate of halakhic tradition in these sources as innovative. In PT Erubin 25c and BT Sanhedrin 113a, this view of halakhic innovation among the sages/scribes is projected back into the Second Temple period, with scribes "innovating the *halakhah*." I read such comments as part of the larger tendency to assimilate scribal activity to those appropriate to sages. For works dealing with the social/historical context of the scribes, see works mentioned in n. 8.

14. See, for example, R. Aqiva's report (T Sanhedrin 11:5) of R. Eliezer's power to derive three hundred halakhic norms from study of the scriptural text. The Talmuds' reports about scribes are obviously modeled upon this earlier toseftan report of the prolific halakhic creativity of the early mishnaic sages. Thus behavior once ascribed solely to sages is, in the Talmuds, the province of scribes as well. See also n. 21.

15. I cite the text of Lieberman 1967, 299.

16. I cite the text of Zuckermandel 1970, 344.

17. See, e.g., Sifra Behuqotai to Lev. 26:46, and Jaffee 1985, 391–92.

18. See the discussion in Kraemer 1989, 186–89.

19. I cite the manuscript versions discussed in a brief but illuminating article by M. Gruber (1990, 225–28). Gruber points out that the version of the text found in printed editions since the sixteenth century that mentions Oral Torah explicitly is actually a medieval revision grounded in Rashi's commentary on Gen. 26:5.

20. Compare the approbation of R. Yohanan b. Zakkai's learning, which also links *halakhah* and scribal learning into a continuum of tradition: "They said of Rabban Yohanan b. Zakkai that he did not neglect Scripture, oral recitation, legal dialectic, *halakhot* and *aggadot*, the specifications *(diqduqei)* of the Torah or the specifications *(diqduqei)* of the scribes" (BT Sukkah 28a).

21. In this connection, Yoma's reference to the creation of a Sabbath-domain *('eruv)* as one of Abraham's practices is particularly instructive. Elsewhere, the Babylonian Talmud (Eruvin 21b/Shabbat 14b) regards the laws of the Sabbath-domain as a legislative act, a *taqqanah*, introduced into halakhic tradition by King Solomon. The assumption is that, like other biblical heroes such as Moses (PT Megillah 74c, 75a; BT Berakhot 48b; and Bava Qamma 82a), Joshua (BT Eruvin 17a), and Ezra (PT Megillah 75a, BT Megillah 31b, and Bava Qamma 82a), Solomon inherits and contributes to a legislative tradition that has its origins with Moses and that reaches its current fullness under the authority of the sages. It appears, then, that as the qualitative distinction between scribal and halakhic tradition closes, so too is obscured the perception of scribes and sages as distinct institutional embodiments of separate sources of tradition. In the jurisprudential and historiographic imagination of the Babylonian Talmud, then, *divrei*

soferim have become identified with the corpus of halakhic legislation, the *taqqanot*, reserved in the earlier literature as the distinct prerogative of the sage. See also n. 14.

REFERENCES

Alon, Gedalyahu. *History of the Jews in the Land of Israel in the Period of the Mishnah and Talmud* (Hebrew). Vol 1. Tel Aviv: HaKibbutz HaMeuhad, 1975.

Bacher, Wilhelm. *Die exegetische Terminologie der juedischen Traditionsliteratur.* Vol 2. Reprint, Hildesheim: Georg Olms, 1965.

Bar-Ilan, Meir. "Scribes and Books in the Late Second Commonwealth and Rabbinic Period." In *Mikra: Text Translation, Reading, and Interpretation of the Hebrew Bible in Ancient Judaism and Early Christianity*, ed. Martin Jan Mulder. Assen/Maastricht and Philadelphia: Van Gorcum and Fortress, 1988.

Berlin, Meir, and Shelomoh Yosef Zevin. *Entsiklopedyah Talmudit.* Vol. 7, s.v., *"divrei soferim."* Jerusalem: Mossad Ha-Rav Kuk, 1947, 91–106.

Bronsnik, Nahum M. "On the Meaning of the Epithet *Dorshei Halaqot"* (Hebrew). *Tarbiz* 60 (1991): 653–57.

Bruns, Gerald L. "The Hermeneutics of Midrash." In *The Book and the Text: The Bible and Literary Theory*, ed. Regina Schwartz. Cambridge, Mass.: Basil Blackwell, 1990.

———. "What Is Tradition?" *New Literary History* 22 (1991): 1–21.

Cover, Robert M. "The Supreme Court 1982 Term—Foreword: *Nomos* and Narrative." *Harvard Law Review* 97 (1983): 4–68.

Fraade, Steven A. *From Tradition to Commentary: Torah and Its Interpretation in the Midrash Sifre to Deuteronomy.* Albany: SUNY Press, 1991.

Gadamer, Hans-Georg. *Wahrheit und Methode.* Tübingen: J. C. B. Mohr (Paul Siebeck), 1960.

———. *Truth and Method.* Ed. G. Barden and J. Cumming. London: Sheed and Ward, 1975.

———. *Philosophical Hermeneutics.* Trans. and ed. David E. Linge. Berkeley: University of California Press, 1976.

———. *Truth and Method.* Trans. and rev. J. Weinsheimer and D. G. Marshall. New York: Crossroad, 1989.

Gruber, Mayer. "Rashi's Torah Commentary as a Source of Corruption in Talmudic *Aggadah"* (Hebrew). *Sinai* 106 (1990): 225–28.

Habermas, Jürgen. *On the Logic of the Social Sciences.* Trans. S. W. Nicholsen and J. A. Stark. Cambridge, Mass.: MIT Press, 1988.

Handelman, Susan A. *The Slayers of Moses: The Emergence of Rabbinic Interpretation in Modern Literary Theory.* Albany: SUNY Press, 1982.

Hoy, David Couzens. "Interpreting the Law: Hermeneutical and Poststructuralist Perspectives." In *Interpreting the Law and Literature: A Hermeneutical Reader*, ed. Sanford Levinson and Steven Mailloux. Evanston, Ill.: Northwestern University Press, 1988.

Jaffee, Martin S. "*Halakhah* in Early Rabbinic Judaism: Innovation beyond Exegesis, Tradition before Oral Torah." In *Innovation in Religious Tradition: Essays in the Interpretation of Religious Change*, ed. Michael A. Williams, Collet Cox, and Martin S. Jaffee. Berlin: Mouton de Gruyter, 1992.

———. "Oral Torah in Theory and Practice: Aspects of Mishnah-Exegesis in the Palestinian Talmud." *Religion* 15 (1985): 387–410.

Kasovsky, Chaim. *Otzar Leshon HaMishnah*. Tel Aviv: Massada, 1957.

Kraemer, David. "On the Reliability of the Attributions in the Babylonian Talmud." *Hebrew Union College Annual* 60 (1989): 175–90.

Lieberman, Saul. *Hellenism in Jewish Palestine*. New York: Jewish Theological Seminary, 1950.

———. *The Tosefta: The Order of Nashim: Sotah, Gittin, Kiddushin*. New York: Jewish Theological Seminary, 1967.

Neusner, Jacob. *Torah: From Scroll to Symbol in Formative Judaism*. Philadelphia: Fortress, 1985.

Rabin, Chaim. *Qumran Studies*. Oxford: Clarendon, 1957.

Ricoeur, Paul. "Ethics and Culture: Habermas and Gadamerian Dialogue." *Philosophy Today* 17 (1973): 153–65.

———. *Hermeneutics and the Human Sciences*. Cambridge, U.K.: Cambridge University Press, and Paris: Editions de la Maison des Sciences de l'Homme, 1981.

Sanders, E. P. *Jewish Law from Jesus to the Mishnah: Five Studies*. London: SCM, and Philadelphia: Trinity International, 1990.

Schaefer, Peter. *Studien zur Geschichte und Theologie des rabbinischen Judentums*. Leiden: E. J. Brill, 1978.

Schuerer, Emil. *The History of the Jewish People in the Age of Jesus Christ*. Vol. 2. Rev. and ed. G. Vermes, F. Millar, and M. Black. Edinburgh: T. and T. Clark, 1979.

Urbach, Ephraim E. *The Halakhah: Its Origins and Development*. Trans. Raphael Posner. Tel Aviv: Massada, 1986.

Warnke, Georgia. *Gadamer: Hermeneutics, Tradition, and Reason*. Cambridge, U.K.: Polity, 1987.

Weinsheimer, Joel C. *Gadamer's Hermeneutics: A Reading of Truth and Method*. New Haven and London: Yale University Press, 1985.

Zuckermandel, Moses. *Tosephta, with "Supplement to the Tosephta."* New edition by Saul Lieberman. Jerusalem: Wahrmann, 1970.

Chapter 4

Rabbinic Resistance to Male Domination: A Case Study in Talmudic Cultural Poetics

Daniel Boyarin

Historicism as Resistance

> In short, genealogy as resistance involves using history to give voice
> to the marginal and submerged voices which lie "a little beneath
> history" the voices of the mad, the delinquent, the abnormal, the
> disempowered. It locates many discontinuous and regional strug-
> gles against power both in the past and present. These voices are
> the sources of resistance, the creative subjects of history. (Sawicki
> 1991, 28)

This essay seeks to answer two questions. The first is a theoretical,
historical, and textual question, and the second, a practical one. The
theoretical question is: Why does an ancient literature, in our case
the literature of rabbinic Judaism, preserve within its canonical
documents texts that stand in opposition to the dominant ideological
orientation of the culture? The practical question is: What good can
we do for a troubled world by studying ancient texts? I am going to
try to show that the answers to the two questions can be related to
each other. My immediate target in this essay is the marginalization of women in rabbinic Jewish culture.

I want to begin, however, by stating something of my personal/-
political commitments in this discourse, at least to the extent that I
am conscious of them. I desire to empower a change of gender relations within the communities of Jews who are dedicated to maintaining a powerful connection with the Talmudic tradition. This

statement, unpacked, demonstrates two motivations: a progressive feminist motivation and a conservative religious and cultural one. I wish to change the practice of Judaism out of a moral, political commitment, but I wish to change Judaism because of another urgency: the need to have a Judaism to hold on to and pass on. Jews (or others) who simply find the memory of Talmudic Judaism irrelevant will not respond to the political force of this inquiry except perhaps vicariously.

My assumption is that we cannot change the actual past. We can only change the present and the future; yet this involves changing our understanding of the past. Unless the past is experienced merely as a burden to be thrown off (which indeed it might be by many), then constructing a monolithically negative perception of the past and cultivating anger at it seem to be counterproductive and disempowering for change. Finding only misogyny in the past reproduces misogyny; finding only a lack of female power, autonomy, and creativity reifies female passivity and victimhood. In contrast to this, recovery of those forces in the past that opposed the dominant androcentrism can help put us on a trajectory of empowerment for transformation. Jana Sawicki has made a similar point in a different context, arguing that some feminist scholars portray the power of reproductive technologies over women's bodies as such that "our only options appear to be either total rejection of them or collaboration in our own domination" (Sawicki 1991, 14). Instead of this, Sawicki suggests a strategy of paying "constant attention to the ruptures, discontinuities and cracks in the systems of power," such that "multiple strategies for resisting their dangerous implications" can be developed without either collaborating in domination or total rejection. Since I do not wish to collaborate in domination and certainly not to reject Judaism, the latter type of research can be a powerfully redemptive tool. Precisely and paradoxically, where the culture did not work then, that is where we can make it work for us now. That is the strategy of the current project.

There are two lines of inquiry to be pursued. The first delves for evidence of women's power, autonomy, and creativity that the dominant discourse wishes to suppress but cannot entirely expunge. This line of research has been very fruitful for study of Ancient Greece, the biblical period, and the Hellenistic period.[1] The second line of inquiry, however, promises to be more fruitful for the Talmud, namely the search for male opposition, within the Talmud itself, however rudimentary, to the dominant, androcentric discourse.

In the rest of this essay, I propose to read two very familiar texts of very different origins and genres with this inquiry in mind. Before, however, pursuing this agenda, I wish to lay out something of the actual theoretical assumptions and methodology of my critical approach: cultural poetics.

Cultural Poetics and Talmudic Culture

The question of the relation of the literary text to the rest of culture has always been a live one in the modern interpretation of rabbinic texts. In traditional positivistic historiographical approaches to the study of rabbinic literature, the biographical narratives of the rabbis were considered to be legendary elaborations of "true" stories, that is, stories that contained a kernel of biographical-historical truth, which could be discovered by careful literary archaeology.[2] The biographical stories about the rabbis were treated as the "historical background" for the study of both their halakhic (ritual law) views and midrashic interpretations of the Bible. In my work, in direct contrast to that approach, these will be treated as the least transparent of texts, that is, precisely as fictions requiring foregrounding to explain them. Many critics have realized that these texts are essentially literary (that is, fictional) accounts about men and (occasionally) women who probably lived but functioned primarily as signifiers of values within the culture, as exempla (Frankel 1981). They have been analyzed, accordingly, with the methods of literary criticism, and particularly with varieties of formalist techniques of analysis.[3]

Once, however, we read the individual narratives as "fictions," it becomes increasingly difficult not only to imagine any "outside" to the text but even to connect the different moments of the Talmud itself one to another, that is, to read the biographical legends and the legal-ritual discourse together. Since we no longer imagine that the stories reflect the "real" events of "real" lives of the "authors" of the legal discourse, the latter seems to come from no one and nowhere.[4] Once the biographical narratives are bereft of referentiality, the legal texts have no authors and are disconnected from the stories.[5] However, the notion that rabbinic literature of any genre is autonomous (in the New Critical sense) seems counterintuitive in the extreme. If there was ever a literature whose very form declares its embeddedment in social practice and historical reality, it is these texts. How may we, then, historicize our readings of these stories, given the historical skepticism that I have outlined above? I propose that the older insight that there is connection between the genres of rabbinic textuality and between them and a society can be preserved when we understand literature as discourse, that is, discourse in the Foucauldian sense best defined by Hodge:

> When literature is seen as a contingent phenomenon produced in and by discourse, then a whole set of new objects and connections becomes immediately and directly available for study: social processes that flow through and irresistibly connect "literary" texts with many other kinds of texts, and social meanings that are produced in different ways from many social sites. This concept, following Foucault's influential usage, emphasizes literature as a process rather than simply a set of products; a process which is intrinsically social, connected at every point with mechanisms and institutions that mediate and control the flow of knowledge and power in a community. (Hodge 1990, viii)

This notion of literature as a process integrally connected with other social processes is a very powerful one for the study of Talmudic texts. It enables us to consider how the social meanings produced in the halakhic discussions and innovations that the documents preserve are reproduced in the stories (more properly literature) about the rabbis that the same documents tell. If we can no longer write biographies of rabbis that can then be used to explain (even partially) their halakhic interventions (as, for example, the classic biography of Rabbi Akiva by Louis Finkelstein [1964]), we can, it seems, use both halakhah and aggadah together to write the history of discursive processes and social sites, of communal mechanisms and institutions.

Having abandoned the notion that texts simply reflect the intentions of their authors or the extratextual reality of their referents, what alternative to a purely intratextual reading remains? The answer lies in an appropriate apprehension of the concept of intertextuality, and particularly the special form of intertextual reading pursued by a group of scholars called the "New Historicists."[6]

The research paradigm loosely known as the "New Historicism" is more a sensibility than a theory. Indeed, certain of its practitioners have defined themselves explicitly (if somewhat ironically) as being "against theory."[7] Nevertheless, I believe that we can discover one overriding principle that both constitutes the paradigm as a significant theoretical intervention and explains the convergence of sensibility between critics of otherwise very diverse interests and methods. This principle is rejection of the view that literature and art form an autonomous, timeless realm of transcendent value and significance and, concomitantly, the promulgation of the conviction that this view is itself the historical, ideological construction of a particular time and place in cultural history. Stated more positively, literature and art are one practice among many by which a culture organizes its production of meaning and values and structures itself. There follow from this hypothesis several postulates:

1. The study of a literary work cannot be pursued in isolation from other concurrent socio/cultural practices.
2. So-called "high" culture has no essential privilege over "popular" and "mass" culture. These very definitions are a cultural practice and an ideological intervention that must be examined.
3. Some kind of materialism must be assumed (not necessarily Marxian).
4. Much of the rigid barrier between the current humanities and social sciences must be dismantled.

These postulates require a radical restructuring of our understanding of critical practice and indeed of human culture altogether. Posing them as such and basing one's work upon them is an already transgressive practice vis-à-vis the ideology underlying the current division of scholarship into "humanities" and "social sciences."

Now, as a candidate for research in the narrower New Historicist mode, the Talmud provides little promise. For one thing, as already mentioned, we have almost no access to extraliterary written documents that could provide the raw material for the sort of thick description beloved of the Renaissance men and women of New Historicism.[8] The question is, then: How can we pursue a cultural poetics under such conditions, a new historicism whose typical rhetorical and epistemological moment is emblematized by that flash of the apparent real, the anecdote?[9] A founding assumption of that practice, rendered heavily problematic in theory, is nevertheless that the document, proclamation, deed, diary, private letter, provide access in some sense to a less processed, more transparent version of the discursive practices of the period and can thus serve as explanatory context for the "text."[10] However, when we study the Talmud, this illusion must be abandoned once and for all. All of the texts available are of the same epistemological status. They are all literature or all documents in precisely the same degree; indeed, they all occur within the same texts, between the same covers. There is literally (virtually) nothing outside of the text. However, under the rubric of cultural poetics, the problem disappears entirely. Since no assumption is made of an essential difference between literature and other texts or between textual and other practice, we read what we have as a textual practice, co-reading many different subtexts in search of access to the discourse of the society in which they were produced. We shall be engaged, then, in a kind of close-reading that aspires to be thick description at the same time.

Another important way in which cultural poetics can provide methods applicable specifically to Talmudic texts is the tools it furnishes for a unitary explanation of *halakhah* (religious law) and *aggadah* (narrative)—especially biographical legends about the rabbis—as participating in the same discursive formations. A word of explanation may help here. Where previous generations of researchers in Jewish history have seen the biographical legends as preserving a "kernel" of historical truth, which may be then used as explanatory "background" to explain legal opinions and innovations, and a later generation of scholars insisted on the "autonomy" of the aggadah qua literature (Frankel 1981), the method of cultural poetics recombines them, but in a new fashion. I assume that both the halakhah and the aggadah represent attempts to work out the same cultural, political, social, ideological, and religious problems. They are, therefore, connected but not in the way that the older historicism wished to connect them. We cannot read the aggadah as background for the halakhah. If anything, the opposite is the case: the halakhah can be read as background and explanation for the way that the rabbinic biographies are constructed. Not, I hasten to add, because the halakhah represents "reality" that the aggadah "reflects," but only because the halakhah is, almost by definition, ideologically more explicit. The assumption that I make is that the very assignment of a story or a halakhic view to a named rabbi, whether or not this assignment is "historically" true, is of semiotic significance and can be interpreted as part of the history of rabbinic discourse. This is not to contest the possibility that there is a kernel of "historical truth" in some, any, or even all of the stories, only to argue that this kernel is insignificant compared to the amount of history of discursive practice that can be written using these materials. Thus, for instance, in one of the examples below, I shall be studying, in detail, a romantic and clearly fictional story of the marriage of Rabbi Akiva. The story will be interpreted here as having very little to do with the life and times of Rabbi Akiva himself (Palestine, c. second century) and a great deal with Babylonian Jewish marriage and sexual practices in the fourth and fifth centuries. Nevertheless, the question of why the story is told about Rabbi Akiva is highly significant and interpreted here.[11]

We thus escape the stultifying paradigm of "rabbinic thought," as if rabbinic literature were a sort of philosophy manque and, instead, study culture as a set of complexly related practices both textual and embodied. We can see then that halakhic discussions and decisions as well as stories about the rabbis, and even the reading of the Bible, are all ways in which this culture expresses its concerns and unresolved tensions and attempts to work them out. We can accordingly learn quite a bit about the culture and its problems, and even about the differences between different branches of it, from studying these discursive practices together. In the rest of this chapter, I will summarize various analyses of narratives of tannaitic lives that I have carried out in detail in other venues, with a view to exemplifying more concretely and fully the theoretical points that I have been making here.[12] In particular, I am interested here in seeing how the methods of cultural poetics and the assumptions of a Foucauldian analysis of texts can help us to construct usable resources for a feminist transformation of rabbinic Judaism for our own time.

Rereading Beruria

The story of Beruria, the female Torah sage, has been interpreted many times; however, I think it has not yet been completely accounted for. Let me briefly recount the textual facts. In the Tosefta (third century, Palestine), we find two incidents reported in which a woman, once called Beruria and once the daughter of Rabbi Hananya ben Tradyon, states a halakhic opinion on a rather abstruse topic that is validated by an important tannaitic authority vis-à-vis a male who disagrees with her. Now the question is: Why does the Tosefta tell us these stories and report these halakhic decisions in the name of a woman? Just to point up the contrast, I will remark that the Mishnah reports the same points, without giving them a female genealogy. Recently Rachel Adler has attempted to answer this question in an article in *Tikkun* (1988, 28 ff.). In an insightful comparison of this narrative with halakhic texts that portray unrealistic situations as test cases for legal theory, Adler writes:

> What do these surrealistic situations represent if not a passionate attempt to capture some elusive truth by smashing context? Imagining Beruriah must be regarded as just such an effort a straining for a more encompassing context, an outrageous test case proposed as a challenge to all contextually reasonable assumptions: What if there were a woman who was just like us? (1988, 29)

Adler's interpretation is, then, that the stories of Beruria present a hypothetical, a "what if" scenario, which attempts to capture some truth that cannot otherwise be captured than by the construction of a legend. She never details, however, what that truth is. Indeed, by conflating the earliest tannaitic traditions of Beruria with later Babylonian and even medieval European ones, her only answer to this question can be: G-d forbid that there ever be a woman just like us. After all, in another kind of margin, Rashi's glosses to the Talmud (eleventh-century Europe), Beruria committed suicide in the end. Only catastrophe can result from a woman who does not know her place in the scheme of things. That is undoubtedly a fair representation of the ideology of women studying Torah as it developed in medieval and later Judaism. It is, moreover, a pretty fair account of the hegemonic practice of the Talmudic rabbis themselves. There are, after all, precious few accounts of women learned in the Torah, suggesting that, normatively, women were not encouraged and were probably prevented from studying Torah. They were, rather, confined to the reproductive and nurturing bodily sphere.

However, if we do not conflate the earliest texts with any later ones, then the question is sharpened. The earliest texts, the ones that I have just described, neither prescribe nor describe a horrible end for the woman learned in Torah. Not at all. There is not the slightest ambiguity about her status. She is approved of within the text, and that is all. It seems to me that the only way we can account for the presence in the Tosefta of these stories is by assuming that some man or men involved in the production of that text were uncomfortable with the exclusion of women from the study of Torah. Although, to be sure, he or they could not overturn society and culture and materially change the situation; what they could do was leave a record of their opposition, a record which constitutes a crack in the monolith of Talmudic androcentrism, a fissure into which we can creep. The later tradition in both the Talmuds and particularly in Rashi's story have made mighty efforts to replaster the crack, to foreclose once more the option it opened up, but a critical, historicized reading can uncover the plaster once more. In the next section I will take up a somewhat more complex example of this practice.

The Speaking of Female Desire

The second case with which I will deal has also to do with women and speaking, but in this case, not with the speaking of Torah but with the speaking of desire. Once more, the dominant ideological position within the Talmud is that women may not speak of their desire:

> Rav Avdimi said that Eve was cursed with ten curses, for it says, And to the woman He said: Greatly I will multiply [Gen. 3:16]: These are the two flows of blood, the blood of menstruation and the blood of virginity. your pain: this is the effort of rearing children. and your conception: this the effort of pregnancy. in pain shall you bear children: as it sounds. and to your man will be your desire: teaches that the wife desires her husband when he goes on a journey. and he will rule over you: that the woman bids [for sex] in her heart, while the man with his mouth. (Eruvin 100b)

To be sure, in contrast to certain Protestant interpretations, which held that the "curses of Eve" are normative and must be enhanced and enforced in human society, the rabbis understood them as natural descriptions of women's state and enforced their alleviation. So, in this case, the fact that a woman only asks for sex in her heart means that her husband must be particularly attentive to any signs or signals of her desire and respond. Nevertheless, this text, which became normative within rabbinic literature, reinforces gender asymmetry in such a way that the male is dominant and the female dominated with respect to the expression of desire. However, there is another tradition, as well: Rav Shmuel, the son of Nahmani, said in the name of Rabbi Yohanan:[13]

> Any man whose wife asks for sex will have children such as were unknown even in the generation of Moses, for in the generation of Moses it is written, Get yourself intelligent, wise and renowned men (Deuteronomy 1:14), and then it is written, And I took as the heads of the tribes renowned and intelligent men (Deuteronomy 1:16), but he could not find "wise men," but with regard to Leah it says, And Leah went out to him, and said 'You shall sleep with me tonight, for I have hired you' (Genesis 30:16) and it says, The children of Yissachar were acquainted with wisdom (I Chronicles 12:34). (Eruvin 100b)

Rav Shmuel's tradition praises the woman who requests sex openly in as vivid and strong terms as the rabbinic tradition knows by claiming that such a woman would have better children than even the children of that paragon generation, the generation of Moses. This principle is derived from a typically clever midrashic reading. Moses is sent by God to search for certain kinds of persons to be the tribal leaders, but when the results of that search are reported, one of the qualifications is absent. The midrash, with its usual literalness, assumes this to mean that he could not find people who had that quality: wisdom. On the other hand, the Bible tells us explicitly that Leah requested sex openly of Jacob, when she had paid her sister for the right to have him that night, and, with regard to her children, we are informed in another place in the Bible that they possessed exactly that characteristic found lacking in the generation of Moses. The inference is drawn that it was the open expression of their mother's desire to their father that produced that wisdom. Once again, the Talmud itself marginalizes this antithetical and oppositional position by harmonizing it with the repressive one. Rav Shmuel does not really mean that a woman may approach her husband sexually openly, but only that she may send him signals of her desire. The tradition of Shmuel represents a recognition that women and men are not as different from each other as the dominant tradition proposes, that Eve has not been accursed with silence. Here is another margin waiting for our redemption.

A closely related issue involves the practice of married men separating themselves sexually from their wives for the purpose of total devotion to the study of Torah, without reference to the wives' desires. This practice was heavily promoted, in particular, by the Babylonian Talmud. It will be seen that it is closely related to both of the previous issues of the subjectivity of women within the culture. The most famous example of such promotion is the story of Rabbi Akiva's marriage to Rachel, who voluntarily and cheerfully lived as a grass widow for twenty-four years, the best years of her life, so that her husband could fully devote himself to the study of Torah. It should be emphasized that this version of Rabbi Akiva's life-story is only told in the Babylonian Talmud, where we find also serious propaganda for just such a lifestyle, if in somewhat attenuated form. However, such a pattern, which runs roughshod over the notion that women have their own subjectivity and desires, even within the realm which is, at it were, assigned to them in this culture, namely the body, was clearly disturbing to other male rabbinic authorities of the time.

The opposition occurs, interestingly enough, within the very halakhic context in the Talmud that supports very extended absence from home on the part of scholarly husbands, and, moreover, it smuggles itself in as if it were support for the practice:

> [The students may go away from their homes for study of Torah without permission for thirty days . . .]; these are the words of Rabbi Eliezer: Rav Bruna said that Rav said: The halakha is in accordance with the view of Rabbi Eliezer. Rav Ada the son of Ahva said that Rav said: Those are [only] the words of Rabbi Eliezer, but the Sages hold that the students may go away for the study of Torah for two or three years without permission. Rava said that our Rabbis have relied upon Rav Ada the son of Ahva and indeed practice in accordance with his view.

We find here a relatively late Babylonian tradition, which, in contrast to all earlier authorities, reverses the ruling of Rabbi Eliezer that the married scholar may not absent himself for more than thirty days from his wife and permits absences of several years.[14]

The Babylonian Talmud's report of Rava's declaration that "our Rabbis have relied upon Rav Ada, the son of Ahva and indeed practice according to his view" constitutes evidence for a change in social practice that is associated by the tradition with Rava, that is, with the leading Babylonian rabbinic authority of the fourth century, although, to be sure, such attribution is not necessarily to be taken literally. It would seem, however, that the attempt to institute this change in marriage practice met with substantial opposition in spite of Rava's hegemonic prestige. The Talmudic text, at the same time that it is ostensibly recording the support for this innovation, reveals sharp dissension from it. These oppositional voices encoded within the text, I suggest, are intimations of the social conflict outside the text.

The Talmud proceeds to cite a story, which while overtly claiming to be a precedent for the practice of the "rabbis" who stay away from their wives for two or three years, is plausibly read as an index of ambivalence and opposition to this practice:

> Rava said that our Rabbis have relied upon Rav Ada the son of Ahva and indeed practice in accordance with his view. As in the case of Rav Rehume who was a disciple of Rava's in Mahoza. He would regularly visit his wife every year on the Eve of Yom Kippur. One day, his studies absorbed him. His wife was waiting for him, "Now he will come. Now he will come." He did not come. She became upset, and a tear fell from her eye. He was sitting on the roof. The roof collapsed under him and he died.

As I have said, on the overt level of the structure of the Talmud's argument, this text is cited as a support for Rava's contention that the rabbis depend legitimately on Rav Ada's tradition and practice accordingly. However, it does not take a very suspicious hermeneut to read it against the grain. The story, in fact, encodes a very sharp critique of the practice of married rabbis being away from home for extended periods. First of all, let us note that it is clear from this story that the rabbi did not study at any great distance from his home; for had he done so, one day of slightly extended study would not have made such a difference and prevented him from getting home for Yom Kippur. This consideration only enhances the irony that Yonah Frankel has pointed to in the phrase "would regularly visit his wife on the Eve of Yom Kippur" (Frankel 1981, 101). Further, the fact that he is portrayed as being so unmindful that he even forgets the one time of the year that he goes to visit his wife can only be read as an extremely critical and ironic representation of this rabbi's behavior.

The empathetic depiction of the eagerly waiting wife is calculated by the narrator to lead the reader/hearer of this story to a position of identification with her, a moral judgment that is confirmed on the explicit level when the rabbi is punished by death. To be sure, there is nothing in the overt narrative that condemns the practice of being away from home per se. The implication is that had he fulfilled, at least, his habit of visiting once a year, there would have been no stain on his behavior. Nevertheless, I would claim that the way that the entire story is presented provides rather a strong condemnation of the practice at the very same time that it is overtly supporting it.

Even sharper internal opposition to the practice is encoded in the following aggadic narrative:

> Rav Yosef the son of Rava was sent by his father to the House of Study to study with Rabbi Joseph. They set for him six years of study [i.e. he had been married and it was decided that he would be away from home for six years]. After three years, on the Eve of Yom Kippur, he said, "I will go and visit my wife." His father heard and went out to meet him with weapon. He said to him, "You remembered your whore?" And some say, he said, "You remembered your dove?"[15] They fought, and neither of them got to eat the final meal before the fast.

This shocking tale, with near-unique violence of language and more than a hint of violent behavior between a father and a son, testifies eloquently to the extent of the conflict that the Babylonian innovation associated with Rava's name aroused in his own community of Babylonia. Representing the strife as between Rava and his own son makes that conflict vividly real.

Further support for the claim of internal opposition to the practice of marital celibacy can be found in the tannaitic midrash on Miriam's complaint against her brother Moses (Numbers 12 and Sifre ad loc.). This narrative tells of a complaint that Miriam lodged with and against her brother Moses and the strong rebuke and punishment that she received from God for this insolent behavior. By diverting the interpretation of this complaint from one against the wife of Moses (as the biblical text seems to imply) to one on her behalf, the midrash produces strong opposition to celibate marriage.

The biblical story opens with the statement that Miriam and Aaron spoke against Moses regarding the Ethiopian woman (Tzipporah, according to the midrash)[16] he had married:

> And Miriam and Aaron spoke against Moses [Num. 12:1]: This teaches that both of them spoke against him but Miriam initiated it, for Miriam was not accustomed to speaking in the presence of Aaron, except for an immediate need.

The midrashic text is a response to an anomaly in the biblical text, namely that while the verb has two subjects, one male and one female, the verb-form is feminine singular.[17] The midrash interprets this to mean that it was on Miriam's initiative that the slander or complaint against Moses took place. The midrash continues to explicate the story:

> And Miriam and Aaron spoke with regard to the Ethiopian woman: And indeed, how did Miriam know that Moses had withdrawn from sexual intercourse?[18] She saw that Tzipporah no longer adorned herself with women's ornaments. She said to her, "What is the matter with you? Why do you not adorn yourself with women's ornaments?" She said, "Your brother does not care about the matter." And this is how Miriam knew. And she spoke to her brother [Aaron], and the two of them spoke against him.

Rabbi Nathan said Miriam was at the side of Tzipporah, at the time, when it says "And the youth ran . . . and said Eldad and Medad are prophesying in the camp" (Num. 11:28). When Tzipporah heard, she said, "Woe to the wives of these!"[19] And this is how Miriam knew. And she spoke to Aaron, and the two of them spoke against him.

In contrast to other early interpretative traditions that understand that Miriam and Aaron were complaining against the wife of Moses, the midrash understands it to be a complaint on her behalf. The midrashic rewriting of the story is, as is usually the case at least in these early midrashim, a response to a gap in the biblical text that demands interpretation. The story begins with Miriam complaining "with regard to the Ethiopian woman," but in the elaboration, the complaint of Miriam and Aaron is entirely different: "Did God only speak with Moses; He indeed spoke with us as well?" Rather than being a charge having to do with whom Moses had married, it seems to be a challenge to some power or privilege of his. Moreover, God's defense of Moses cum punishment of Miriam seemingly has nothing to do with his wife, being merely a statement of Moses' special holiness. There is accordingly an inner contradiction in the story: Was the complaint because Moses had married inappropriately or because Miriam was jealous of his status? The midrashic story fills this gap by connecting the two complaints as one; she complained on behalf of the wife, arguing that he had behaved toward her in a way that was arrogant and overbearing. Did she and her elder brother not share his status and yet they do not behave so toward their spouses? The midrash, moreover, knows precisely what the complaint of the wife was, and as plausible a resolution of the contradiction as this is, it is not straightforwardly accounted for as the "meaning" of the biblical text. As is typical for midrash, we seem to have a synergy of two factors in creating the interpretation; on the one hand, a genuine interpretative difficulty that is addressed by the interpretation, and, on the other hand, an ideological investment which is served by the interpretation.[20] Accordingly, the midrash doubly ventriloquizes the voice of the woman and her complaint, first because it is Miriam who is the initiator of the action and speaker here, and second, because the midrash reports, in her name, what she had heard from Tzipporah that had made her aware of the wife's distress.[21] The text communicates two forms of the woman's complaint against her husband. The first is more subtle in that only by indirection does it imply an indictment of Moses for not having intercourse with her, while in the second case, the grievance is sharp, direct, and clear. "Woe to the wives of these!" Woe to the wife of him who becomes overly holy, and owing to his holiness ignores the needs of his wife for sex. At the same time that Miriam is being condemned by the biblical text and by the midrash for her untoward accusation against Moses, the text ventriloquizes the voice of the woman whose husband devotes himself excessively to the study of Torah and refrains from intercourse. The midrash goes on to emphasize the good intentions of Miriam, while still recognizing that the Torah narrates her punishment for this act:

> Behold, the matter is suitable for an argument from the mild case to the severe: Since Miriam did not complain to her brother for blame but for praise, and not to decrease procreation but to increase it and only in private, and thus was punished, all the more so one who speaks against his fellow for blame and not for praise, to decrease procreation and not to increase it, in public and not in private.

Many who commit the sin of slander do so in order to decrease procreation, either by preventing marriages from taking place or by promoting disharmony between husband and wife. Miriam did the opposite. Her intention was to promote the good by restoring harmony between Moses and Tzipporah, and the proof of this is that she made her charge in private. The midrash here goes out of its way to reduce the culpability of Miriam, in spite of the severe punishment which she is given in the Torah narrative, temporary leprosy (following conventional, if inaccurate translations), precisely the normal punishment for slander in the rabbinic moral system. Her sin was only in being overly and inappropriately zealous for the performance of the commandment. By thus minimizing the disapproval of Miriam's speech against Moses and making its intentions entirely praiseworthy, the midrash is already expressing a negative attitude toward married celibacy, within the confines of a possible reading of the biblical text.

The midrash goes on to explain the rest of the story. Miriam and Aaron's complaint had to do with the way that Moses was holding himself above them—holier than thou—in his celibate behavior:

> And they said, "Did God speak only to Moses?": did He not speak with the Fathers, and they did not withdraw [from sex]? Did the Holiness not speak also with us, yet we did not withdraw?

To which comes God's reply to them:

> If there will be for you a prophet: Perhaps just as I speak with the prophets in dreams and visions, so I speak with Moses, therefore Scripture tells us, "Not so is my servant Moses" except for the ministering angels. Rabbi Yose says, even than the ministering angels.
> Mouth to mouth do I speak with him: Mouth to mouth I told him to withdraw from his wife.

At first blush, this midrash seems to be an approbation of the holiness of celibacy and even of celibate marriage, a practice well known in certain early Christian circles (Brown 1988). After all, Moses is the very highest model of what a human being can achieve in religious life. He chose to be celibate at a certain point in his life and is approbated for this very strongly by God Himself. This would seemingly then be an exemplum, as it were, to the rabbis themselves. And so, indeed, Finkelstein interprets it (Finkelstein 1964, 80; as does Biale 1989), arguing that the midrash is a support for the practice of extended postmarital separations.

In fact, I would claim that not only does this text not promote the ideal of celibacy or celibate marriage for the rabbis, it constitutes a very strong polemic against such a practice or ideal. To see why this is so, we shall need to read the text a little more closely. First of all, we must realize that the midrash is explicitly and formally citing the received tradition of Moses' celibacy. Note that it does not ask how we know that Moses had withdrawn from his wife after Sinai, only how Miriam came to know. The midrash thus conveys (and we know for a fact) that the motif of Moses' marriage blanc was current in earlier Jewish tradition. In Philo, for example, Moses is the very type of the highly regarded Therapeutae who renounce sex entirely (Fraade 1986, 264). My thesis is that the midrash cites this authoritative and widespread tradition here in order to counter it. By introducing this traditional theme precisely at this point in the midrashic text and not, for example, in the context of accounts of Moses' piety, the midrash has found a means of neutralizing and opposing the ideology of the tradition, without, however, denying its validity entirely (something that they apparently could not have accomplished given its widespread authority).

God's condemnation of Miriam and Aaron is explicitly put into terms that emphasize the exceptional nature of the relationship between Moses and God. Miriam and Aaron seem to be proposing that since they have the same status as Moses, having also spoken with God, either they should be refraining from sex also or he shouldn't be. God's rebuke to them consists of a very strong statement that Moses is special, indeed, unique. There will be other prophets, just like Miriam and Aaron, but to them God will speak in dreams and visions. They, accordingly, are not required to refrain from sexual intercourse. Even the patriarchs, Abraham, Isaac, and Jacob, were not expected or allowed to be celibate. Only Moses, with whom God spoke "mouth to mouth" (in itself a highly erotic attribute), was required to withdraw from marital life. He is either only slightly below the angels or even more spiritual than they, and no other human being was ever like him.

It would follow, of course, a fortiori, that all lesser mortals than the patriarchs, prophets, and Moses' siblings, whatever the degree of holiness to which they aspire, are not expected to be celibate. I read the midrashic text, then, as a form of opposition to the received tradition that Moses was a celibate husband. In order to neutralize the force of this authoritative motif, the midrash cites it and contests it at the same time by marginalizing it as the practice expected of and permitted only to Moses. Thus the midrash manages both to remain faithful to a powerful received tradition and at the same time to counter it. When this point is combined with the vivid expression of empathy with the neglected wife of the "prophet" who opts for celibacy, we have a robust polemical statement against the sort of practice that the Babylonian rabbis engaged in (or at any rate, say they engaged in) of leaving their wives for years on end without sexual companionship—a practice which they supported by referring to the example of Rabbi Akiva and Rachel.[22]

Once more, comparing the Talmudic version of this tradition with the midrashic text just read will reinforce this point. In the Babylonian Talmud, the story is cited thus:

> Moses separated himself from his wife. What did he reason? He reasoned for himself by a syllogism (Qal wehomer). He said: If Israel, with whom the Shekina only spoke for a short time, and only for a set time, the Torah said, "For three days do not approach woman," I with whom the Shekina speaks at every moment and without a set time, a fortiori. And how do we know that God agreed with him, for it says, "Go tell them, return to your tents" and right after that, "But you stay here with me." And there are those who say [that we learn it] from "Mouth to mouth will I speak with him." [Shabbat 67a]

This Talmudic retelling of the story is conspicuous for its absences and by its absences makes the presences of the midrashic version all the more prominent. There is no representation here, whatsoever, of the feelings of the wife, indeed no recognition that she is, in any way, an interested party in the decision. Moreover, although the difference between Moses and the ordinary people is adduced here as well, it is not done in such a way that we clearly understand that for all others renunciation of marital sex is excluded and regarded as arrogance and wrong, as it is in the midrash. One could easily read this text as a further authorization for the apparent Babylonian practice of long postmarital separations for the study of Torah, while the Palestinian version above strongly opposes the practice. Although the version that promotes the practice of extended sexual deprivation became dominant within Ashkenazi Jewish culture, up until and including the early twentieth century, the oppositional voice was allowed to remain in the traditional texts as well, and it is in that oppositional voice that we can find our allies.

"A Rigorously Unsentimental Nostalgia"[23]

I want, at this point, to point to a difference between the critical operation in which I am engaged and some other discursive practices with which it might be confused. I am not arguing that, because there was a Beruria, women were not excluded from studying Torah. I am also not arguing that because there is an aggadic passage which stands in opposition to disturbing gender practices or because there is a single voice in the Talmud which recognizes women's parity with men in the expression of sexual desire that there is not a problem with Talmudic gender practice. Undoubtedly women did not often study Torah in the Talmudic period, and this manifests a set of role definitions that reinforce gender asymmetry and hierarchy. Many husbands then, and even more later, did, indeed, leave their wives for years on end to pursue intellectual and religious aims, and women were trained to be modest and silent about their sexuality. The exceptions, as it were, only prove the rule. But—and this is the crux of my argument—on the margins of that dominant and hegemonic discourse, something else was happening. There were some women who were breaking the mold, and also some men who were uncomfortable with and who even opposed the dominant ideology. Those, perhaps, marginal men and women can become for us prototypes in a reformation of traditional Jewish gender practices that nevertheless find themselves rooted firmly in the Talmudic text and tradition.

The "payoff" of this research seems to me to be the discovery that even the androcentrism of rabbinic culture was not entirely successful or monolithic. (I suspect that this is true for virtually any culture.) I have argued that there were significant oppositional practices to the very hegemony of the dominant discourse preserved in the canonical texts. At least at the margins of social practice, and maybe even more than that, there were important ways in which women were autonomous or participated in highly valued cultural activities, such as studying Torah. Since such participation would have been threatening to the dominant male ideology, there was a determined attempt to suppress its memory. This brings my analysis in line with the conclusions of the late John Winkler, who, in his work on classical Greece, has constructed a happier situation for women than the male texts would have us believe:

> The more we learn about comparable gender-segregated, pre-industrial societies, particularly in the Mediterranean area, the more it seems that most of men's observations and moral judgments about women and sex and so forth have minimal descriptive validity and are best understood as coffeehouse talk, addressed to

men themselves. Women, we should emphasize, in all their separate groupings by age, neighborhood, and class, may differ widely from each other and from community to community in the degree to which they obey, resist, or even notice the existence of such palaver as men indulge in when going through their bonding rituals. To know when any such male law-givers—medical, moral, or marital, whether smart or stupid—are (to put it bluntly) bluffing or spinning fantasies or justifying their 'druthers is so hard that most historians of ideas—Foucault, for all that he is exceptional is no exception here—never try. (Winkler 1989, 6)

The interests of the masculinist hegemony were not served by preserving records of female autonomy. Discovery, or rather, reconstruction, of such female autonomy constitutes a point of resistance to the dominant, present hegemonies as well, in this case the ones of many segments of rabbinic orthodoxy (not all) that still wish to exclude women from full cultural participation. However, another point needs to be made as well. The very discordant or antithetical memories were also produced and preserved in the androcentric, male-authored texts. They represent, therefore, a voice of male struggle (however nascent and inadequate from our perspective) against the ideology of gender asymmetry, "a breaking of [cultural] context," to use Rachel Adler's evocative terms (1988). It is this very rudimentary oppositional practice in the early culture that gives us the power now to redeem and reclaim a usable past. I have tried to show that there was significant male opposition to the institution of a practice that erases recognition of female subjectivity and desire almost entirely, and that this opposition was grounded in an empathetic thinking beyond male cultural power or even rigid gender-based hierarchy. The opposition did not succeed in dislodging the hierarchy, nor, realistically, did it even truly imagine an alternative, but it did suggest internal sub-versions.[24] Once more, the dominant hegemony seeks to strike such cracks and fissures, to erase the sub-versions from the cultural record, but is unsuccessful, leaving us a place to creep back into.[25]

NOTES

1. This has been realized generally by many feminist critics and historians who have begun searching out in the Bible and in other ancient literature and cultural remains for whatever evidence there is or might

be found or reread for women's creativity and cultural power. Some feminist scholars have been pursuing this line of research with regard to late antique Judaism, notably Bernadette Brooten, Ross Kraemer, and Amy-Jill Levine. This kind of work can be and has to be pursued for the Talmud as well, although, to be sure, with regard to the Talmudic literature and period the evidence will be sparse indeed.

2. One still finds such methods being employed occasionally, as in, e.g., McArthur 1987.

3. In the American sense. Itamar Even-Zohar has shown that "Russian formalism" hardly remained "formalist" in this sense (Even-Zohar 1990). The greatest practitioner of this practice of reading is certainly Yonah Frankel (Frankel 1981) of the Hebrew University, to whose work I shall have occasion to refer below.

4. Jacob Neusner's solution of regarding all texts as the products of their final redactors does not solve this problem either, simply because we know equally as little about the redactors as we do about the rabbis quoted.

5. Thus even Weller (1989), who attempts to read the whole series of stories in Ketubboth as an ideological production (and does so with a fair degree of success), effectively ignores the halakhic context, seeing the stories as placed here only by "association" and not as an effort to work out the same cultural dynamic and problem that the halakhic text encodes.

6. Below, however, I will propose that this appellation be abandoned.

7. Specifically, of course, I am referring to Walter Benn Michaels, one of the authors of the original "Against Theory" essay. For more information, see Thomas 1991.

8. Both the English and American Renaissances are particularly rich in that sort of documentation, and it is hardly surprising, therefore, that they have been the privileged sites of "New Historicism."

9. Fineman 1989 is an important and serious investigation of the status of the anecdote in "New Historicist" writing.

10. In that sense, "New Historicism" has sometimes appeared to be only a much more sophisticated version of the old historical type of literary criticism that reduced the text to being an expression of the "reality" in which it was produced.

11. I have discussed a similar example at length in a paper specifically on the martyrdom stories about Rabbi Akiva (Boyarin 1989).

12. For fuller documentation, see Boyarin 1991a and 1991b.

13. Variant: Yonathan.

14. "Two or three" is a conventional Semitic expression for "several."

15. The difference in Hebrew is but one letter. Not surprisingly, the glossator could not stand to leave the text as it was.

16. The word "Ethiopian" is explained as a metaphor:

The Ethiopian woman: But was she indeed Ethiopian, she was Midianite, as it says, "And the Priest of Midian had seven daughters" (Exod. 2:16). So why does Scripture say, "Ethiopian," but to teach us that just as the Ethiopian is unusual for his skin, so was Tzipporah unusual for her beauty more than all the other women. . . . For he had married an Ethiopian woman: Why is it said again, hasn't he already said, "with regard to the Ethiopian woman," why does Scripture say, "for he had married an Ethiopian woman"? There are women who are comely in their beauty but not in their deeds, in their deeds but not in their beauty, as it says, "like a gold ring in the nose of a pig is a beautiful woman without wisdom" (Prov. 11:22). But this one was comely in her beauty and in her deeds, therefore it says, "for he had married an Ethiopian woman."

Since it is impossible to suppose that Tzipporah fits the normal denotative meaning of "Ethiopian," the term is taken as a metaphor for distinctiveness, for being somehow unusual, a fairly common midrashic move. The midrash goes out of its way to read the attribution as positive, praising Tzipporah as both attractive and righteous, thus emphasizing all the more the injustice done to her by Moses' overzealous piety. As the Talmud remarks in another context, "Rabbi Yehoshua ben Levi said, 'Anyone whose wife is a fearer of Heaven and he does not sleep with her is called a sinner, as it says, And you shall know that your tent is at peace' (Job 5:25)" (Yevamoth 62b).

17. To be sure, modern grammatical analysis of Hebrew does not recognize this as an anomaly, arguing that in Hebrew, as in other Semitic languages, when a verb appears before two coordinated subjects, it agrees with the first of them. However, as I have argued in my book (Boyarin 1990), midrashic exegesis must be understood on the basis of the rabbis' perceptions of Hebrew grammar and not ours, and the fact is that wherever this construction appears, it is treated as having special meaning by the midrash. Furthermore, the continuation of the story suggests strongly that the rabbinic reading that Miriam was the instigator of this event is not over-reading.

18. The literal translation would be from "procreation"; however, as this text indicates and others as well, this is a rabbinic term for sexual intercourse, whether or not it results in pregnancy and indeed whether or not this is its primary aim.

19. I.e., upon hearing they were prophesying she commiserated with their wives, thinking that now they would stop sleeping with them, as Moses had stopped sleeping with her.

20. I am aware, of course, that my statement here of the hermeneutics of midrash is highly oversimplified. It is dependent on my theory of midrash, as worked out in Boyarin 1990.

21. The use of the term "ventriloquy" indicates that one should not understand that there is an expression here of women's subjectivity; there is, however, a representation of an imagined women's subjectivity, an effort at empathy with women and one, moreover, with at least potential

effect in actual marriage practices. Women are often represented in rabbinic texts as subjects. Their subjectivity is, however, as here, only represented as an object of rabbinic discourse.

22. The dating of the midrash is contested. I, paradoxically, am among those who are inclined to regard it as earlier than the Babylonian Talmud, in which case it could hardly be a polemic against the practice that I am claiming was instituted by the Talmudic rabbis, but, rather, it would be against other well-attested practices of marriage blanc among Jews and non-Jews at least as early as the first century. It becomes then a polemic against the Babylonian institution *avant le lettre*.

23. This phrase is Robert Alter's (1991, xiii), used with reference to Benjamin, Kafka, and Scholem. Benjamin's notion of a redemptive critique, at least, does lie at the bottom of much of my sensibility, as I will make clear later on.

24. I owe this coinage to Chana Kronfeld.

25. The wonderful image of cultural change as a "creeping back" into history is Mieke Bal's.

REFERENCES

Adler, Rachel. "The Virgin in the Brothel and Other Anomalies: Character and Context in the Legend of Beruriah." *Tikkun* 3, 6 (1988).

Alter, Robert. *Necessary Angels: Tradition and Modernity in Kafka, Benjamin, and Scholem.* Cambridge, Mass.: Harvard University Press, 1991.

Biale, David. *From Intercourse to Discourse: Control of Sexuality in Rabbinic Literature.* Paper presented at Center for Hermeneutical Studies Coll. 60, Berkeley, 1989.

Boyarin, Daniel. "Language Inscribed by History on the Bodies of Living Beings: Midrash and Martyrdom." *Representations* 25 (1989): 139–51.

———. *Intertextuality and the Reading of Midrash.* Bloomington: Indiana University Press, 1990.

———. "Internal Opposition in the Talmudic Literature: The Case of the Married Monk." *Representations* 36 (1991a): 87–113.

———. "Reading Androcentrism against the Grain: Women, Sex, and the Study of Torah." *Poetics Today* 12 (Spring 1991b): 29–54.

Brown, Peter. *The Body and Society: Men, Women, and Sexual Renunciation in Early Christianity.* Vol. 13 of *Lectures on the History of Religions.* New York: Columbia University Press, 1988.

Even-Zohar, Itamar. "Polysystem Studies." *Poetics Today* 11, 1 (Spring 1990): 1–253.

Fineman, Joel. "The History of the Anecdote: Fiction and Fiction." In *The New Historicism*, ed. H. Aram Veeser. New York: Routledge, 1989.

Finkelstein, Louis. *Akiba: Scholar, Saint, and Martyr.* Antheneum, 1936; New York: Macmillan, 1964.

Fraade, Steven D. "Ascetical Aspects of Ancient Judaism." In *Jewish Spirituality from the Bible through the Middle Ages*, ed. Arthur Green. World Spirituality: An Encyclopedic History of the Religious Quest. New York: Crossroad, 1986.

Frankel, Yonah. *Readings in the Spiritual World of the Stories of the Aggada.* Tel Aviv: United Kibbutz Press, 1981.

Hodge, Robert. *Literature as Discourse: Textual Strategies in English and History.* Baltimore: Johns Hopkins University Press, 1990.

McArthur, Harvey. "Celibacy in Judaism at the Time of Christian Beginnings." *Andrews University Seminary Studies* 25 (Summer 1987): 163–81.

Sawicki, Jana. *Disciplining Foucault: Feminism, Power, and the Body: Thinking Gender.* New York: Routledge, 1991.

Thomas, Brook. *The New Historicism and Other Old-Fashioned Topics.* Princeton, N.J.: Princeton University Press, 1991.

Weller, Shulamit. "The Collection of Stories in the Passages of Ketubot 62B–63A" (Hebrew). *Tura* 1 (1989): 96–102.

Winkler, John. *The Constraints of Desire: The Anthropology of Sex and Gender in Ancient Greece.* London: Routledge, 1989.

Kabbalah

Chapter 5

From Sealed Book to Open Text: Time, Memory, and Narrativity in Kabbalistic Hermeneutics

Elliot R. Wolfson

The following tradition is reported by the Hasidic master, R. Zadoq ha-Kohen of Lublin: *we-khakh qibbalti ki ha-'olam kulo hu sefer she'asah ha-shem yitbarakh we-sheha-torah hu perush she'asah we-hibber 'al 'oto ha-sefer*, "Thus I have received that the world in its entirety is a book that God, blessed be He, made, and the Torah is the commentary that He composed on that book" (Zadoq ha-Kohen 1912, 44b). One is immediately struck by the almost childlike simplicity of this statement, on the one hand, and its spiritual profundity, on the other. The Hasidic tradition articulated by R. Zadoq is rooted deeply in the Jewish idea that God's creative act is essentially linguistic, in fact that divine creativity is an act of written composition. The first book that God writes is the world and the second the Torah. This statement implies, in a quintessentially Jewish manner, that God's first book, the text of the cosmos, requires a commentary, Scripture, and that commentary, we can well imagine, engenders other commentaries that not God but human beings create in a seemingly endless effort to reveal the hidden depths concealed in the original traces of God's writing that make up the universe.[1] R. Zadoq's comment, while perhaps not consciously intended in this manner, subverts any hermeneutical theory that posits a final truth, a foundation that ends all play of meaning. In perfectly good Derridean fashion we may say that the way back leads not to an original truth, but rather to an origin that is a text that needs to be interpreted by another text.[2] In the beginning there is interpretation.[3] The necessity of commentary thus constitutes the very texture of existence from the vantage point of the Jew. There is nothing that is not inscribed within the book and therefore open to interpretation, not even God's being.[4] One is here reminded of the provocative observation of Jacques Derrida: *il n'y pas de hors-texte*, "there is nothing outside of the text" (Derrida 1976, 158). All transcendence is reduced to textuality.[5]

Basic to classical Jewish belief is the view that the fabric of the world and human existence is textual.[6] Not only is language the house of being, the clearing in which Being manifests itself by pulling away from its concealedness, as Martin Heidegger would put it, but language is the very being that is unveiled. Indeed, the unveiling itself is nothing but the time of being's becoming. Insofar as the divine language, the language of creation, is Hebrew, the language of the Jews, it follows that the latter are assigned a special role in this process of unveiling. Most specifically, the situation of the Jew is that of the writer.[7] The Jews are a people born of the book and so too is their God.[8] It is not insignificant that one of the essential motifs that has informed the religious imagination of Jews through the ages is the image of God who writes. From the perspective of one of the most influential trends of the mystical tradition within Judaism, the theosophical kabbalah, God is not only the one who writes but the one who is written.[9]

The emergence of divine textuality is portrayed in kabbalistic literature as the evolution of consciousness and the articulation of speech, that is, a progression from silence to language that is expressed graphically and phonically. While any number of sources could be cited to illustrate the linguistic process of God's self-disclosure, I will use as a basis for my reflections in this study one representative figure, the towering Lithuanian Talmudist and kabbalist, Elijah ben Solomon Zalman, the Gaon of Vilna (1720–1797),[10] who has been chosen not because of the novelty or uniqueness of his thinking with respect to these matters but rather due to his clarity of expression.[11] I will avoid in this case, as I would in all other motif studies in kabbalistic literature, the lure of generalization and oversimplification. There is hardly consensus on any of the major themes that informed this rich and variegated corpus of Jewish writing. What is most important in the study of kabbalistic texts are the details, for, as the Gaon of Vilna himself put it, "when the details are neglected the general principle disappears," *be-vittul ha-peratim nistaleq ha-kelal* (Gaon of Vilna 1975, 74b).[12] Nevertheless, with respect to the issue at hand there is a remarkable uniformity of vision that shaped the myth and ritual of kabbalists through the generations. The detailed analysis of R. Elijah's writings should yield some basic knowledge about kabbalistic hermeneutics in a more general framework.

The Gaon of Vilna's application of the process of God's linguistic unfolding to creation is presented as a commentary on the statement in the opening passage of the ancient Jewish esoteric work, *Sefer Yezirah*, to the effect that God "created the world by means of three books *(sefarim)*, the *sfr*, the *sfr*, and the *sfr*." Apparently, in its original setting each of these would have been vocalized as *sefer*, that is, book.[13] According to the Gaon of Vilna, however, the three occurrences of the word *sfr* should be vocalized as *sefer, sefer*, and *sippur*.[14] The first *sefer* is the book that is sealed *(sefer he-hatum)* or the book of concealment *(sifra di-zeni'uta)*, which corresponds to the hidden thought *(mahshavah setumah)* of God that contains the ideational forms of all existence. The second *sefer* is the book composed of the written letters by means of which heaven and earth were created and is therefore disclosed to the one who reads. The third element is the *sippur*, the oral narration that is revealed to all and that corresponds to the ten utterances *(ma'amarot)* through which the world was created. The essential task of the book, therefore, is to uncover the hidden depths of divine concealment through linguistic embellishment: "The book is the disclosure of thought *(gilluy mahshavah)* for thought is hidden in man and is not revealed except by means of his speech or writing" ([1882] 1986, 1a). God's infinite thought, paradoxically a book that cannot be narrated and hence no text at all,[15] is unveiled in the written book that is an open text,[16] but even the latter is only interpretable when it is articulated verbally. The point is reiterated in an important text of the Gaon of Vilna, the "Ten Principles" *('asarah kelalim)* on the nature of emanation, published and discussed for the first time by Joseph Avivi (1993, 107–50). The following passage is derived from the second of these principles:

> His will is revealed to us by means of three things, *sefer, sefer*, and *sippur*, for [the word] *sefer* is an expression of disclosure *(gilluy)*.[17] The will is revealed always by means of either action *(ma'aseh)* or speech *(dibbur)* which declares His will. The action is writing for He writes His will in a book, and the action reveals His will two times, once at the time of writing His will is revealed in the book, but it is not yet revealed in a complete disclosure *(gilluy gamur)*.

Rather there is the potentiality that it will be revealed to any one
who reads it, and at the time of reading it will be revealed in a
complete disclosure. Thus His will, blessed be He, is revealed in
writing two times, i.e., by means of the book *(sefer)* two times . . .
but it is still like a sealed book *(kesefer he-hatum)*, for no one
understands His glory, blessed be He, and His true will through
them except the wise sages who read them and well place the
contemplation of their intellects *('iyyun sikhlam)* upon the action of
the Lord and the work of His hands. . . . The essence [of the
disclosure] was at the venerated revelation *(ma'amad ha-nivhar)*
when they all stood on Mount Sinai and understood from all the
created entities that He created them and no other . . . and the
speech itself was at that time for they heard His holy words. (Avivi
1993, 126–28, and see discussion on 112–13)

Elsewhere the Gaon of Vilna applied this triadic structure exclusively to the Sinaitic revelation: the first stage is the *sefer* that corresponds to the ideal Torah in the mind of God that lacks semantic
manifestation; the second stage to the *sefer* that is maximally the
written Primordial Torah or minimally the Tablets of Stone upon
which were etched the ten commandments; and the third, to *sippur*
that is the articulation of the Decalogue to Israel at Sinai.[18]

The transition from sealed book to open text to oral discourse is
understood as well by the Gaon of Vilna in sexual terms:[19] the
sealed book corresponds to the father or *Hokhmah*, the *sefirah* of
Wisdom; the open text to the mother or *Binah*, the *sefirah* of
Understanding; and speech to the son or *Da'at*, divine Knowledge,
which is not an independent *sefirah* but rather the aspect of the
phallus that is hidden in *Binah*, but whose roots are in *Keter*
(Crown),[20] the first of the *sefirot*, and thus is designated by the
technical term *Yesod de-'Atiq*, the Foundation of the Ancient One.[21]

Everything was created in pairs as it is said everything that the
Holy One, blessed be He, created was created masculine and
feminine. And this is the *sefer* and the *sefer*, and so too the tablets
were five corresponding to five . . . and the speech *('amirah)* is the
Knowledge in the tongue for through it the ten commandments
were uttered, and it comprises the two books. . . . The two books
are masculine and feminine and the *sippur* is Knowledge through
which is the union and it joins them together as one. (Gaon of
Vilna 1884, 4a)

Da'at is in the position of the tongue, which corresponds to the phallus, that joins Father and Mother, *Hokhmah* and *Binah*, and thus is called *Yesod de-'Abba wa-'Imma* (Gaon of Vilna 1986, 13d). It is likely that the phallic positioning of *Da'at* also underlies the Gaon of Vilna's identification of the latter with the entity called in zoharic literature, the *bozina de-qardinuta*, the flame-of-darkness or hardened spark.[22] According to some passages *Da'at* is the *bozina de-qardinuta* that is hidden in the stomach of the Mother, that is, *Binah*,[23] or in the mouth of the Holy Ancient One, *'Atiqa Qadisha* (25d). According to an alternative set of symbols, Knowledge is the tongue that mediates between Wisdom and Understanding, which correspond either to the palate and throat (cf. 13d; 14d–15a) or to the right and left hands (1b–c, 15a; cf. 1884, 4a). Commenting on the description in *Sefer Yezirah* 1:3 of the covenant of the one *(berit yahid)* that "is set in the middle in the circumcision of the tongue *(milat ha-lashon)* and the circumcision of the foreskin *(milat ha-ma'or)*," the Gaon of Vilna remarks that the covenant of the tongue "is the third *sfr*, which is the *sippur*, i.e., the tongue that is the *Da'at* of *'Arikh 'Anpin* that mediates between *Hokhmah* and *Binah* . . . and the circumcision of the foreskin is *Yesod de-'Atiq* as mentioned above" (1884, 6c).[24] Oral discourse is thus engendered by the union of the masculine and feminine, the sealed book and the open text. Reflecting a long-standing *topos* in Jewish esotericism, the Gaon of Vilna views the tongue above as standing in the position of the phallus below.[25]

> *Da'at* mediates between *Hokhmah* and *Binah* just as *Yesod* mediates between *Ze'eir* [masculine *Tif'eret*] and *Nuqba* [feminine *Shekhinah*]. This is what is said in the first chapter of *Sefer Yezirah*, "ten *sefirot belimah*, corresponding to the number of ten fingers, five against five, and the covenant of the one set in the middle in the circumcision of the tongue and the circumcision of the foreskin," and these are the two covenants of Torah, the first is the covenant of Torah and the second the covenant of circumcision. (1986, 15a)[26]

Hence, the production of speech by the tongue (the covenant of Torah) is to be seen as a form of oral ejaculation that parallels the seminal discharge from the penis (covenant of circumcision).[27] In the Gaon's own words:

> The arousal of a person to sexual intercourse is in thought, and the
> semen is displaced from the brain, which is in the thought that is
> concealed from everything.[28] Afterwards is the sexual intercourse,
> which corresponds to speech that is between man and his colleague.
> Thus the union is in the covenant of the tongue and the covenant
> of the foreskin. They are parallel in all matters. (1867, 156a)[29]

It must be noted, however, that on occasion the Gaon of Vilna
reverses the order of God's linguistic disclosure such that the proper
alignment is *sefer, sippur,* and *sefer,* that is, the concealed book,
which is divine thought *(mahshavah),* followed by oral narration,
which is divine speech *(dibbur),* and then the open or written text,
which is the final action *(ma'aseh).*[30]

> *Sefer* in [the word of] Creation, *sefer* in [the world of] Making . . .
> *sippur* in [the world of] Formation, which correspond to thought
> *(mahshavah),* speech *(dibbur)* and action *(ma'aseh).* The first book
> is in thought *(mahshavah),* and the second in writing *(ketivat yad),*
> which is the action [related in the expression] "His powerful works"
> (Ps. 111:6) by means of the twenty-eight joints [of the hands][31] . . .
> and the explicit name of twenty-eight letters.[32] Speech is by
> means of the ten vowel-points, for writing involves letters just as
> one actually writes a Torah scroll. Speech is only possible through
> vowels, and this [vocalization] concerns speech and not writing.
> The cantillation notes are for the sake of comprehending the
> meaning of Scripture in thought.[33] Therefore, in the writing of a
> Torah scroll there must be the three *sefarim* [i.e., *sefer, sefer,* and
> *sippur*] mentioned above. As it is said,[34] one must write [the
> scroll] from a written text *(ha-ketav),* and that is the first book
> wherein there is no speech of the writer nor [the state of] "His
> powerful works." Afterwards he speaks and writes, *sippur* and
> *sefer,* speech *('amirah)* and action *(ma'aseh).* Even with respect to
> Moses the speech of God, may He be blessed, was in place of the
> first book. (1867, 156a)

According to this passage, then, the correct order is *sefer, sippur,*
and *sefer,* corresponding in turn to *mahshavah, dibbur,* and *ma'aseh,*
that is, thought, speech, and action.[35] The first stage is the concealed book of divine thought, the second is speech, and the third the
written text that is the most revealing of all linguistic disclosures.
The written text would therefore be in the position of the son who
comes forth from the union of the first book and speech.

Despite the discrepancies regarding some of the finer details of the symbolic correspondences, the Gaon of Vilna consistently maintains that the process of divine autogenesis is linguistic in nature. Moreover, the primordial linguistic act is graphic. Thus, commenting on the image employed in the *'Idra Rabba* section of the *Zohar* of the white skull shining in thirteen engraved aspects or sides (*Zohar* 3:128b),[36] the Gaon of Vilna notes that "these are the root of all engravings *(gilufin)*, and this is the beginning of all emanation. Therefore the beginning of everything is the engraving *(ha-gelifah)*" (1986, 11b).[37] In support of his view the Gaon of Vilna cites both the beginning of *Sefer Yezirah*, wherein the verb *haqaq* is used to describe God's creative act, and the passage that has been placed at the beginning of the *Zohar*, which uses the Aramaic equivalent *galif*, ultimately traceable to the Greek *glyphō*, to carve or to engrave. That the emergence of Wisdom or divine thought should also be seen as an act of writing is evident from the fact that the Gaon of Vilna refers to it as a book. This book, as I have already noted above, is the Primordial Torah, symbolized as *Hokh-mah* or the first point of emanation that breaks through the divine concealment. Thus the Gaon of Vilna comments on the zoharic expression, the "concealed of the concealed" *(setima di-setimin)*:

> That is to say, *Keter*, which is more concealed than *Hokhmah* or *Binah* and all the grades that are in them, and it is the end of the worlds of the Infinite *(sof 'olamot 'Ein-Sof)*. The beginning of disclosure *(tehilat ha-gilluy)* is the point, for the point is the beginning of the Torah prior to all the letters. It is in everything in actuality and all things are in it in potentiality. (1882, 2a; cf. 1867, 139b)

To be sure, the Primordial Torah is a sealed book, the book of concealment, that is, a book that cannot be read, or, alternatively expressed, the book of nonfigurative writing, a writing that does not employ figures or representations. Nevertheless, it is significant that this emanation is characterized as a book rather than oral discourse. Writing and not speaking stands at the beginning of God's way.[38] The elaborate theosophic myth of God's unveiling privileges the graphic over the phonic, the written over the oral.

> Just as thought is not comprehended except in speech, so too *Keter* [is only comprehended] in *Hokhmah* and so in sexual union what is in the brain is made known, and thus it is in all matters. The

beginning of all reality is the *yod*, the point that precedes everything, for all writing *(ha-ketav)* comes from the point that is the
beginning of everything. (Gaon of Vilna 1867, 156b)

This orientation informed the symbolic and religious world of the
kabbalists for whom the writing of books, especially books that deal
with esoteric matters, represents in the most fundamental sense an
attempt to speak the unspeakable, to visualize the invisible, to name
the unnamable. The purpose of the book, as Jabès put it, is "[t]o
ratify the Divine absence. To write the text of this absence as we
read it" (1989, 24). Yet, by inscribing this absence the unveiled is
veiled in the mask of a transparent face.   Herein consists the
paradox of writing: that which lies hidden and withdrawn in the
dark is brought to light but only in such a manner that it is concealed in its revelation. Disclosure is of necessity dissimulation.[39]

    To appreciate the kabbalistic perspective on the nature of
writing adopted by the Gaon of Vilna, it would be worthwhile to
reflect momentarily on the Derridean notion of the trace as "the
absolute origin of sense in general. Which amounts to saying once
again that there is no absolute origin of sense in general. The trace
is the differance which opens appearance and signification" (Derrida
1976, 65). The trace, therefore, "is not absence instead of presence,"
but rather that "which replaces a presence which has never been
present, an origin by means of which nothing has begun" (Derrida
1978, 295). One might argue that it is inappropriate to apply the
Derridean notion of the trace to a traditional kabbalist like the Gaon
of Vilna insofar as the latter, unlike the former, still assumes the
existence of a transcendental signified outside the text, a metaphysical referent whose presence is apprehended by human consciousness. Whereas the Derridean notion of trace precludes the possibility of origin—hence we can only speak of the trace inasmuch as
there is no origin—the Gaon's idea of trace, reflecting the *reshimu* of
Lurianic mythology, that is, the residual trace of divine light that
remains after the Infinite paradoxically withdraws itself from itself
into itself,[40] is predicated precisely on the presumption of such an
origin. Thus in a text to which I have referred above, the "Ten
Principles," the Gaon of Vilna discusses the trace *(reshimah)* left
after the Wisdom and Providence of God withdraw from the place to
which they were attached. The withdrawal or regression *(histalqut)*
is not complete, however, for a small trace is left behind so that the
matter can be sustained and serve as a sign to indicate the presence

of God's Wisdom and Providence. Utilizing further technical Lurianic terminology, the Gaon of Vilna refers to the withdrawal of Providence and Wisdom *(silluq ha-hashgahah weha-hokhmah)* as shattering *(shevirah)* and death *(mitah)*.[41] The trace supplies the possibility of retracing the origin (Avivi 1993, 131–32). In a second passage from this work the dialectic of regression *(histalqut)* and egression *(hitpashtut)*[42] is connected to the two lights, the inner *(penimi)* and the encompassing *(maqif)*.

> There are two lights, the inner and encompassing . . . the secret of the light that remains in the vessel in the secret of the inner [light] and that is the trace *(reshimu)*, and the encompassing is the light that is hidden, it could not enter the vessel and it withdrew. Thus the inner light derives from the egression *(hitpashtut)* and the encompassing from the regression *(histalqut)*. (Scholem 1954, 136)

It would appear, then, that there is a fundamental difference between the kabbalistic and deconstructionist viewpoints, a difference based on opposing ontological assumptions regarding the possibility of positing an origin as a transcendental signified. Yet, the question that must be posed is: Can one speak of a transcendental signified in the thought of the Gaon of Vilna? Is there any origin before the trace of which one can ever speak in positive, kataphatic terms?

The reality beyond the first book, according to R. Elijah Gaon, is the hidden concealment of *Ein-Sof*, which he calls by various zoharic expressions including, most frequently, the Head that is not known, *reisha de-lo 'ityeda*,[43] that defies signification. All signification occurs within the textual boundaries of the first book, which is the book of concealment. The negative theology implied by the Gaon of Vilna is not radically different from what is suggested by the Derridean notion of the trace,[44] for the origin to which the book of concealment points is not an origin that can ever be known or demarcated. The *Ein-Sof* cannot properly be referred to as a transcendental signified, for it forever eludes signification. "Know that one should not think at all about the *Ein-Sof*, blessed be He, for it is even forbidden to designate it the necessary of existence . . . it is even forbidden to call it *Ein-Sof*" (Gaon of Vilna 1986, 38b).[45] "The Cause of all Causes *('illat 'al kol ha-'illot sibbat kol ha-sibbot)* is garbed in the Primordial Anthropos *('adam qadmon)* for we do not know how to name it at all. Thus the first three *[sefirot]* of the

Head that is not known are divided into three aspects. The first is the Supernal Crown *(keter 'elyon)* and that is the aspect of the Primordial Anthropos *('adam qadmon)*, and here we do not even say that it is not known for we are not permitted to speak of it at all" (Gaon of Vilna 1882, 23b). The idea of a traceable origin that is more than a trace must therefore be erased, indeed origin is nothing but erasure. Thus, reflecting on the divine name *Ehyeh*, "I will be," derived from Exod. 3:14 and applied to the beginning of God's will, the Gaon writes: "The name *Ehyeh* is the name of impregnation *(shem ha-'ibbur)*, for it has not yet been revealed, but rather [it signifies that] I will be revealed in the future . . . this is the secret of the withdrawal and the impregnation *(sod ha-silluq weha-'ibbur)*" (Avivi 1993, 145).

The primary divine name is, technically speaking, no name at all, for it does not designate anything that is, but rather connotes that which will be in the future. Hence, this name denotes the secret of impregnation, the pure potentiality of the future, which is at the same time the secret of withdrawal inasmuch as it is no definite characteristic. Following the zoharic interpretation, the Gaon asserts that the name *Ehyeh* signifies that "I will be revealed in the future" *(Zohar* 3:11a). This name is employed to designate the beginning of reality for it "reveals that He will be revealed in the future, even though now He is hidden and cannot be comprehended at all" (Avivi 1993, 144). The very name of the beginning of God's will indicates that it cannot be known, that it is no beginning at all for it is always that which will be revealed. The name *Ehyeh* conveys the idea that the beginning is regression, *histalqut*; this does not, however, imply the sense of going back to an earlier place or state, but rather that the beginning is always and forever reversion, a drawing away, a concealing that is yet to be manifest.

In another context the Gaon of Vilna remarks that the word *'atiq*, the name of the first configuration of the divine, has a double connotation: it means the ancient one *(zaqen)* but also regression *(silluq)*.

> Since the elder is from ancient times, and this withdrawal *(zimzum)* is the most ancient of everything, it was therefore called by the name *'atiq*; and also on account of the fact that this withdrawal *(zimzum)* is the regression *(silluq)*, it is another reason for its name being called *'atiq*. Since there are other withdrawals after this first

withdrawal, this aspect was called the '*atiq de-'atiqin* (the Ancient of Ancients). (Avivi 1993, 126)[46]

The name '*atiq* has the same semantic signification as *Ehyeh*, that is, the primary aspect of divinity is nothing but concealment, regression, absence that can never be presence. The point is underscored as well in the critical zoharic context whence is derived the terminology of the Head that is not known, which, as I noted above, is the expression utilized by the Gaon of Vilna to refer to *Ein-Sof* or the aspect of *Keter* that is connected to *Ein-Sof*. In that passage it is said of this Head that it is "the Head of all heads, the Head that is no head, it is not known what is in that Head, for it is not comprehended by wisdom or understanding" (*Zohar* 2:288a–b, *'Idra Zuta*). Commenting on this, the Gaon writes that "in its place it is no head at all" (Gaon of Vilna 1882, 23b). Language here is pushed to its limit, summoned to say that which cannot be said: the origin of all is characterized as the Head that is no head. To be the Head that is no head that Head must both be and not be a head. If one were to translate this into a form utilized by Heidegger and Derrida, the infinite origin of all being would be depicted graphically by the word "head" with an X crossing it out. What one is left with, then, are the textual markings of the book, the emanation of Wisdom or the Primordial Torah, that reveal that which remains concealed, indeed, concealment as such.[47] The beginning of that book is concretized in the point, the first graphic (and, we might add, phallic) stroke that extends into all letters.

Hence, the paradox that marks the nature of writing is evident in the first book that God writes, indeed the book in which God is first written, the book of concealment which is the Primordial Torah comprised in the point of Wisdom.[48] Here again one would do well to heed carefully the reflections of the Gaon of Vilna on the expression, *sifra di-zeni'uta*, the book of concealment,[49] an independent unit incorporated in the zoharic corpus: the word *sifra*, the book, refers to Wisdom, while the word *zeni'uta*, concealment, alludes to the infinite aspect of the Godhead called by the zoharic expression *reisha de-lo 'ityeda* (the Head that is not known). The *sifra di-zeni'uta* thus is about the "concealment that is the *Ein-Sof*, the Head that is not known that is called the concealment, and Wisdom, which is called the beginning *(re'shit)*, is its book and its disclosure" (Gaon of Vilna 1986, 17a). The conjunction of the two terms "book" (*sifra*) and "concealment" (*zeni'uta*) forges a synthesis that uncovers the paradox of writing: the book is the "disclosure and the attire of the Head that is not known so that it may be revealed below" (Gaon of Vilna 1986, 1a). Divine Wisdom is described concomitantly by the terms "disclosure" *(gilluy)* and "attire" *(levush)*, terms that have diametrically opposing significations. To be disclosed is not to be attired, to be attired is not to be disclosed. Yet they are here joined together in this most pregnant expression: what is revealed is revealed through the garment, the *gilluy* is the *levush*.[50] The primary function of the book, as may be gleaned from the description of the first book, is to uncover, to reveal, but this unveiling is achieved through the assumption of veils, the text disrobes by putting on clothes. The absent face of the Head that is not known, the primordial concealment, is adorned by the masks of Wisdom. Language, and in particular writing, strips the Infinite naked by covering it with the apparel of symbolic images and forms.

> All of the emanation is to clothe within it that Head that is the totality of the emanation. . . . It is clothed in all the emanation by means of Wisdom . . . and this is the book of concealment *(sifra di-zeni'uta)*. Therefore this wisdom is revealed only to those who are humble *(zenu'in)*,[51] as it is said (Babylonian Talmud, Qiddushin 71a), "[The name of forty-two letters] is only transmitted to one who is humble," and it says (Babylonian Talmud, Qiddushin 71a), "since the [number of the] insolent increased [the twelve-letter name was only transmitted to humble priests]," and it says, "But wisdom is with those who are humble" (Prov. 11:2).[52] The essence of this wisdom is to conceal *(lehazni'a)*, as it says (Babylonian Talmud, Hagigah 13a), "The lambs will provide you with clothing" *[kevasim li-levushekha]* (Prov. 27:26)—matters that are the mysteries of the world *(kivshono shel 'olam)* [should be under your garment]. "Honey and milk are under your tongue" (Song of Songs 4:11).[53] Accordingly, this too is called the book of concealment *(sifra di-zeni'uta)*. The beginning of emanation is hidden, the Head that is not known, and the beginning of disclosure is in Wisdom. Thus the two of them are the principle of all emanation, the one in conceal-ment and the other the beginning of disclosure. The essence of its being clothed is through Wisdom. (Gaon of Vilna 1986, 1b)

The unfolding of consciousness from silent thought/concealed book to written and oral text is thus the enfolding of divine concealment in the veil of Wisdom, a process that is referred to as *hitlabshut*, dressing (cf. Gaon of Vilna 1884, 9b–c) or *tiqqun*, adornment.[54] It is evident, moreover, that in the teaching of the Gaon of Vilna, again reflecting a much older structure of thought expressed in Jewish esotericism,[55] the dialectic of disclosure and concealment is localized in the phallus or an aspect of the Godhead that corresponds ontically and functionally to the phallus. Consider, for example, the following passage:

> The disclosure *(gilluy)* begins from *Yesod* of the supernal configuration *(parzuf 'elyon)*, and it becomes *Keter* and *Da'at* in the lower one, and it is *Yesod de-Binah* (Foundation of Understanding). Within *Keter* of *'Arikh 'Anpin* is revealed *Yesod de-Binah* of the Head that is not known, and there is the *bozina de-qardinuta* in the dew of the precious stone, and its Ether, which is called *Ein-Sof*, is never grasped. What is named here [*Zohar* 1:65a] *Ein-Sof* is in *Yesod de-Hokhmah* (Foundation of Wisdom) of the Head that is not known. There is the beginning of that concealment *(zeni'u)* that is not comprehended or known. (Gaon of Vilna 1882, 23a)

Without deciphering all of the technical jargon employed in this text, suffice it to say that the primordial concealment of God is linked to the phallic aspect of the Infinite, *Yesod de-Hokhmah* of the Head that is not known, which is designated as *Ein-Sof*. On the other hand, the beginning of disclosure of that concealment is also linked to a phallic aspect, *Yesod de-Binah* of the Head that is not known. It is the second phallic aspect that facilitates the manifestation of what is concealed in the first phallic aspect insofar as in *Yesod de-Binah* there is an element of divine judgment *(din)* or strength *(gevurah)* that provides the limitation necessary for the infinitely expanding light to be revealed in a condensed and constricted form. In the complex symbolism of theosophic kabbalah, both expansion and limitation, mercy and judgment, are qualities of the phallus that is the locus of the divine androgyne.[56] The Gaon's insight that concealment and revelation are associated with the phallus is another way of articulating this basic belief of a one-sex theory (both masculinity and femininity have their ground in the phallus) that has informed kabbalistic myth and ritual. It is also the conceptual underpinning of the link that he makes between modesty and mystery:[57] the concealment *(zeni'uta)* may be revealed only to the humble *(zenu'in)*. The nature of the former illuminates that of the latter, that is, the modesty required here is of a sexual nature.[58] Only to the one who acts with the proper sexual conduct, especially related to the phallus, are the secrets manifest.

In great measure, this dialectic of concealment and manifestation underlies the Gaon of Vilna's understanding of *zimzum*, the contraction and withdrawal of divine light. That is, the purpose of the diminution of light is to allow for its reception by other beings. The act of diminishing and reduction is the flip side of the process of adornment *(hitlabshut)* and egression *(hitpashtut)*. "Every spark," writes the Gaon of Vilna, "is the source of the measure" (1882, 23a), that is, every manifestation of light derives from an act of limitation imposed by the measure that is an instrument of the attribute of judgment. The contraction of light, therefore, does not imply distancing God from the concatenation of worlds but rather the condensation of God within those worlds. Hence, when viewed dialectically, the concealment of the divine light that ensues from the *zimzum* is a form of revelation.[59] As R. Elijah expressed it: "This is the essence of the *tiqqun*, to diminish the light so that the lower entities could receive the light. This too was the initial intention in the withdrawal of the light *(zimzum ha-'or)*" (Gaon of Vilna 1986, 2c).[60] In another context the Gaon elaborates on this theme:

> The essence of the creation of the world was to reveal the glory of His kingship *(lehitgalot kevod malkhuto)*. . . . Therefore it was necessary for Him to withdraw *(lezamzem)* His good will so that there would be a boundary and limit, and that is the beginning of His existence, the absence *(he'der)* of His will, blessed be He. This is the secret of *zimzum* for He withdrew His will, blessed be He, so that the creatures could receive His good will even though they have boundaries and are finite. . . . The matter of *zimzum* was at the time of creation when it arose in His will to create so that they would be in this image *(temunah)*, and this image actually clove to His will after He diminished His will so that the reality of the created entities could receive and comprehend His will, for this is the purpose of the intention of His creation. The Creator made this image in Wisdom, Understanding, and Knowledge. (Avivi 1993, 125–26, 129; and see discussion, 122)

In other passages it is especially the manifestation of *Malkhut*, divine kingship, that is underscored as the purpose of the *zimzum*.[61] I will cite one representative text wherein the dialectic of concealment and manifestation is highlighted as the ultimate purpose of *zimzum*:

Thus you will understand that there are several worlds prior to the *zimzum*, but permission is not given to contemplate and discern what is before the *zimzum*. The secret of *zimzum* is here from *Ze'eir 'Anpin* and below, which consists of the six extremities [from *Hesed* to *Yesod*], "the world is built from mercy" (Ps. 89:3).[62] Therefore it is forbidden to inquire, as it is written, "You have but to inquire about bygone ages *(yamim rishonim)*" (Deut. 4:32), which are the six days of creation *(sheshet yeme bereshit)*, the six extremities. But you cannot ask about "what is above [and what below, what is before and what after"] [Mishnah Hagigah 2:1] for that is prior to the *zimzum*, and "anyone who gazes [at four things it would be fitting for him if he had not come into the world]." The matter of the curtain, the *zimzum*, and the withdrawal of the light is for the sake of *Ze'eir 'Anpin* and *Nuqba*, for they could not receive the light of *'Atiqa Qadisha*. Therefore there was the death of the [Edomite] kings and the nullification of the land, and the curtain so that *[Ze'eir 'Anpin]* would not receive light that is above his navel wherein is the Holy of Holies [cf. Gaon of Vilna 1986, 9d]. . . . This is the *tiqqun* of *Ze'eir 'Anpin*, but for the sake of the *Nuqba* . . . the *zimzum* was necessary . . . and this is the import of what is said that the *Ein-Sof* constricts itself for the sake of its kingdom *(malkhuto)*. Through the *zimzum*, which is the secret of judgment, there is a thickening of the vessels of *Malkhut* for by means of them she can be revealed. (Gaon of Vilna 1986, 26a)

Again we confront the conjunction of disclosure *(gilluy)* and garbing *(levush)*, although in this case the latter is referred to as the thickening of the vessels. The withdrawal of light, designated by the Gaon of Vilna by both Lurianic terms, *zimzum* and *shevirah*, is a manifestation of divine judgment insofar as a limitation is imposed upon the infinitely expanding effluence of divine mercy. The connection of this process to the linguistic activity described above, especially the act of writing, emerges from the following passage:

The withdrawal *(silluq)* and shattering *(shevirah)* is in the aspect of the points *(nequddim)*, which is in the pattern of an actual point *(dugmat ha-nequddah mamash)*, the general matter *(davar kelali)* that cannot be grasped nor anything spoken of it except that its number is ten. This is the root of all letters, for there is no letter that does not have a point. Similarly, there is no created entity that does not have a point, which is the thing that is first grasped. That which has no point is not a thing. So too His providence, blessed be He, and His primordial will, which is the source of all providence, is not grasped at all except that its number is ten, which is the principle and root of everything. This is withdrawn *(nistaleq)* from the vessels like points from the letters, and these are the vitality of the worlds *(hiyyut ha-'olamot)* like the vowels are the vitality of the letters. . . . They are in the secret of the eyes, for the eye is in the pattern of an actual point . . . and from there is the providence and vitality of everything, and it is in the secret of emanation . . . i.e., this is a portion of His unlimited will, blessed be He. . . . The contraction *(zimzum)* and boundaries *(gevulin)* of this [divine mercy] are the secret of judgments *(sod ha-dinin)*, and they are the principle of creation, for the creation was for this reason. By means of this His hidden will, blessed be He, and concealed goodness are revealed, for everything is one. (Avivi 1993, 138–40)

From this citation it follows that the dialectic underlying the myth of *zimzum* is identical with the Gaon of Vilna's understanding of divine writing. The first book, Wisdom, is the book of concealment for it clothes and thereby reveals the primordial concealment of the Godhead. The second book, which corresponds to *Binah*, the emanation of Understanding, is referred to as the "book that is weighed on the scales," *sifra de-shaqil be-matqela*. Although in the original zoharic context the expression *sifra de-shaqil be-matqela* is simply another designation for the *sifra di-zeni'uta*, the Gaon of Vilna distinguishes the two. The latter may be designated the book within the book, that is, the text that opens from the closure of the book.

The image of the scale is used to depict the harmony of opposites, the basic dialectic in the sefirotic pleroma, the opposing right and left sides balanced by the central pillar that is a synthesis of the two extremes. More specifically, the Gaon of Vilna relates the image of the scale to the triadic structure of *Hokhmah*, *Binah*, and *Da'at*, the *sefer*, *sefer*, and *sippur* of *Sefer Yezirah*, which are the three states of consciousness *(mohin)* in the upper aspect of the Godhead, the Head that is not known, represented by the letters YHW (Gaon of Vilna 1986, 4c, 13c), or the lower manifestation of this triad in the attributes of *Hesed*, *Din*, and *Rahamim*, love, judgment, and mercy, which constitute the three lines of the emanative order (cf. Gaon of Vilna 1986, 1d, 4b, 14b; and 1882, 32c–33a).

It is in this light that one must understand the statement of the Gaon of Vilna that "all of the emanation is called *matqela*, for all of them are in the secret of one scale alone" (1882, 32d). The *matqela* serves as an obvious phallic symbol, the tongue in the middle corresponding to the penis and the weights on either side to the testicles. Insofar as that is the case, the *matqela* conveys the idea of sexual unity or balance between male and female,[63] the aspect of expansion and that of limitation.[64] Thus, while the word *matqela* itself designates the upper phallus or the tongue, that is, *Da'at* (cf. Gaon of Vilna 1986, 1c, 14b), the entire image of the scale, and even more specifically the activity of being weighed on the scale, signifies the unity of masculine and feminine, mercy and judgment (cf. Gaon of Vilna 1986, 1d–2b). Hence, the phrase "the book that is weighed on the scales" refers to the second book, the emanation of *Binah* or the state of consciousness *(mohin)* that corresponds thereto, which expresses the union of the male and female, *Ze'eir 'Anpin*, the six lower *sefirot* from *Hesed* to *Yesod*, and *Nuqba*, the *Shekhinah*.

> The essence of Wisdom is to clothe the concealment and to reveal it, and that of the Mother is to emanate *Ze'eir 'Anpin* and *Nuqba*. That is why the word *sifra* (book) is mentioned twice, the first one is the book of concealment, which refers to Wisdom on account of the concealment, and the second book is the book that is weighed on the scales on account of the scales. It does not say "the book of the scales" *(sifra de-matqela)* as it says "the book of concealment" *(sifra di-zeni'uta)*, which would have implied that it is the disclosure of the scales *(gilluy ha-matqela)*. Rather it is the book that is weighed and revealed on the scales. (Gaon of Vilna 1986, 2a)

To transpose the language of the Gaon of Vilna into a contemporary key: the first book reveals the fundamental paradox of writing, the concealed is uncovered by means of veiling, and thus it is a sealed book, a book of sealing, secrecy, enclosure. The second book moves us beyond the closure of the first book to the open text that, according to the symbolism of the theosophic kabbalists, embraces the union of masculine and feminine depicted as the balance of the scales. The second book is fully expressed in the third cipher, the *sfr* vocalized as *sippur*, that is, narrative discourse. At this stage of unfolding, the written and oral modes of discourse converge.

> The secret of the *sippur* that calls out and unifies [male and female] . . . and this is the secret of the scale, for before there was a scale they did not look at one another face-to-face, that is, in the world of chaos before there was the secret of Knowledge, the holy sign *(mazzla qadisha)*, the dissemination *(hitpashtut)* of the Crown. (Gaon of Vilna 1884, 4b)

The secret of the *sippur*, which corresponds to *Da'at*, is the Torah[65] that is given after two thousand years of chaos,[66] which is interpreted by the Gaon of Vilna in light of the zoharic imagery at the beginning of the *Sifra di-Zeni'uta*, that is, the state before there was balance of male and female characterized as the face-to-face gaze.

In another passage the Gaon of Vilna reiterates the paradoxical nature implied in the book of concealment, but in that context he introduces another element that is a significant feature of kabbalistic hermeneutics, viz., the correlation of temporality and textuality.

> Wisdom is the disclosure of the concealment *(gilluy shel ha-zeni'uta)* . . . for within it is clothed the concealment that is called *Ein-Sof*, as it is said, "In wisdom You made everything" (Ps. 104:24). It is known that the *Ein-Sof* was clothed in Wisdom and by means of it everything was made. From here and onward the *Ein-Sof* is clothed by means of Wisdom, and this is the meaning of what is written, "But wisdom is with those who are humble" (Prov. 11:2). The humble *(zenu'im)* were mentioned for they are the seven days of creation, the seven *sefirot* through which He was clothed in the emanation. (Gaon of Vilna 1986, 7d)

According to the Gaon of Vilna, the unfolding/enfolding of divine concealment in the book embraces the transition from eternity to time. The structure of temporality, therefore, is one with that of consciousness.[67] The humble, *zenu'im*, to whom wisdom is given, are the seven lower *sefirot* of the Head that is not known that correspond to the seven days of creation for through them the concealment, *zeni'uta*, was revealed.[68]

> The seven days of creation are themselves the seven adornments of the skull, and they are the dimensions and boundaries for the light to be revealed and the creation to come to be, and everything is in the aspect of adornment *(tiqqun)* and shattering *(shevirah)*. In truth they are the *tiqqun* for all garbing *(hitlabshut)* so that the light that is good will be revealed and the will that is called *tiqqun*, and the cause of the *tiqqun* is in those seven days, as is known. (Avivi 1993, 142)

These seven stand in marked contrast to the first three *sefirot* (the *mohin* of *Hokhmah*, *Binah*, and *Da'at*) that remain hidden and beyond the order of time. The adornment of the concealment in the book only takes place with respect to the seven lower emanations that are the ideal paradigms of time.

These six days of creation are the six lower *[sefirot]* of the Head that is not known, for from them the emanation begins. This is the meaning of "You have but to inquire about bygone ages" (Deut. 4:32), for these are the first days *(yamim rishonim)*, the primordial days *(yamim qadmoniyyot)* as is known, and from them the emanation begins, and something of a disclosure *(gilluy)*, which is not the case with respect to the first three *[sefirot]* of the Head that is not known, for there is nothing that is known or comprehended. (Gaon of Vilna 1986, 33d)

From the continuation of the above passage it is clear that Sabbath comprises the first three *sefirot* (or *mohin*) of the Head that is not known, *Hokhmah*, *Binah*, and *Da'at*, and that the seventh day corresponds to the messianic era inasmuch as the six days are the six millennia of history.[69] The coming of the Messiah represents not the cessation of time but its fullest realization, which the Gaon of Vilna depicts in some contexts as the stage wherein the mercy of God, *Hesed*, fills the "mouth of the penis," that is, the *sefirah* of *Yesod* (1986, 17a, 19a). Bracketing the messianic dimension of this intriguing nexus of symbols, I wish to focus on the connection between time, represented ideally by the six sefirotic archetypes that are the beginning of the emanation of the concealed aspects of the divine, and the primary book that likewise was characterized as the manifestation of that which is concealed. "His simple will, blessed be He, in the secret of unity withdrew and there remained only the aspect of the point, and the aspect that was in an aspect of the general point from the outset became the aspect of the *waw*, a line *(qav)* by means of the six days of creation" (Avivi 1993, 144). There is an essential connection between the book and time, textuality and temporality, as both betray the fundamental dialectic of hiddenness and manifestation. This dialectic imparts to temporality the same erotic nature that we have seen characterizes textuality and the transition from sealed book to open text.[70] The essential feature of time, as Emmanuel Levinas has written, is the not yet, the openness of the future that shapes past and present.

A *not yet* more remote than a future, a temporal *not yet*, evincing degrees in nothingness. Hence *Eros* is a ravishing beyond every project . . . and not disclosure of what *already exists* as radiance

> and signification. . . . The hidden, and not a hidden existent or a
> possibility for an existent; the hidden, and what is not yet and what
> consequently lacks quiddity totally. (Levinas 1969, 264)

As we have seen above, the Gaon of Vilna appropriates the zoharic
understanding of the name *Ehyeh* as "I will be revealed in the
future" and thereby suggests that the beginning of emanation, the
simple and infinite divine will, is characterized by an essential
deferment. It is precisely this deferment, the not yet, that is the
essence of time. This not yet, the possibility of the hidden being
revealed, constitutes the texture of textuality as well. From the
vantage point of the mythic structures that inform the theosophic
system articulated by R. Elijah Gaon, the ontic ground of both
temporality and textuality is the phallic aspect of divinity.

The ever-flowing stream of time is not simply a continuous
duration of the same, a closed cycle of eternal recurrence, but it is
rather that which welcomes the novel future by retrieving the past
in the present. Time is marked, again to utilize the language of
Levinas, by fecundity, which is the characteristic of difference,
change, otherness, novelty, the "rupture of the continuity and
continuation across this rupture" (Levinas 1969, 284). This notion
of fecundity, linked to the aspect of paternity,[71] is especially ger-
mane to this discussion insofar as the Gaon of Vilna affirms that
time in its infinity is a quality of the masculine, indeed the male
potency par excellence, the *membrum virile*. The term fecundity is
a perfect parallel to the Gaon of Vilna's use of the expression *shem
ha-'ibbur*, the name of impregnation, to designate the beginning of
existence, that is, the beginning is characterized only by the possibility to become, the pure potentiality of engenderment that is the
secret of concealment and impregnation. Time is constituted not by
finitude but rather infinite progression. What is to become is of the
essence of time, a future marked by discontinuity that can retrieve
the past only by its reshaping, its reconfiguration. Time always is
to be and never was, for to speak of time that was is to be no longer
in time. The being of temporality is radical becoming. "Hebrew
time," wrote André Neher, "does not start over again like Greek
time; it engenders." Nowhere is this insight more validated than in
the classical texts of theosophic kabbalah, for from the vantage point
of this complex symbolism time is never of the past nor even of the
present but rather the perpetual extending forward.

Symbolically, the time of creation corresponds to the lower six emanations, from *Hesed*, divine love, to *Yesod*, the phallic foundation of the world. Such a notion is expressed in early kabbalistic literature, especially in commentaries on the first chapter of Genesis, and endures through many generations of kabbalistic writing. Yet, collectively time is best characterized as the male potency, and indeed these six emanations together constitute the masculine persona of the divine anthropos. It follows, therefore, that temporality as such is localized in *Yesod*, the *membrum virile*. The temporal character of this attribute of God is underscored by its designation as the "righteous, foundation of the world," *zaddiq yesod 'olam* (Prov. 10:25). *Yesod* is truly the *axis mundi* but not because the phallus is sacred space. On the contrary, this divine gradation is given this name because it is the temporal basis for the spatial coordinate, alluded to in the word *'olam*, which is the feminine quality. In other words, the expression *zaddiq yesod 'olam* signifies the androgynous unity of the divine, the *zaddiq* (Righteous) is the *yesod* (Foundation) of the *'olam* (World); this can be translated into time (correlated with the masculine) grounding space (the feminine).[72] Time is not for the kabbalist dependent upon physical space, but is in fact the phenomenal and ontic ground of space. In the messianic era there is an overcoming of space by time, a reconstituted temporality that is the eternity of Sabbath.

It is appropriate, moreover, to view the infinite temporality that engenders consciousness in terms of the structure of narrative. In his groundbreaking work, *Time and Narrative*, Paul Ricoeur developed at length what he referred to as "the circle of narrative and temporality" that he explains in one context as follows: "Time becomes human to the extent that it is articulated through a narrative mode, and narrative attains its full meaning when it becomes a condition of temporal existence" (1984, 52). Ricoeur demonstrates the necessary correlation between the activity of narrating a story and the temporal character of human experience. It seems to me that precisely such an understanding of time is implied in the aggadic orientation that reaches full development in kabbalistic writings.[73] Insofar as creation arises through divine language, it follows that the nature of time is determined by narration of a story; God's story is human history as humanity's story is God's history. Temporality is linked to narrativity, and just as the former is characterized by the erotic play of hiddenness and disclosure, so too the latter. That narrativity, aggadah, is depicted in this way is illustrated by a passage in the *Zohar* wherein the word *higgid*, to speak, tell, narrate, is said to allude to a "secret of wisdom" insofar as the letters *gimmel* and *dalet* are contiguous. That is, the letter *gimmel* symbolizes the male and the *dalet* the female, and their juxtaposition indicates that there is no barrier separating the two. The masculine *gimmel* and the feminine *dalet* are joined by the phallus, represented by the *yod*, thus spelling the word *gid*, which can signify the male reproductive organ. From the union of the *gimmel* and *dalet* through the *yod* the narrative discourse *(aggadah)* proceeds (cf. *Zohar* 1:234b).[74] The zoharic idea is elaborated by the Gaon of Vilna:

> [The masculine] *Yesod* has thirteen *(yod-gimmel)* adornments *(tiqqunin)* in the secret of [circumcision] being covenanted in thirteen covenants (Babylonian Talmud, Nedarim 31b) [which correspond to] the thirteen attributes [of mercy], and [the feminine] *'Ateret* is the *dalet* . . . this is the secret of the *gid* [comprising the letters] *yod gimmel dalet.* (1882, 12a)

The power of speech ensues from the joining of the masculine and feminine attributes of God, both localized in the androgynous phallus. One can, therefore, speak of the common structure of temporality and narrativity. In its extensionality time indeed is the masculine potency par excellence.

This dynamic, moreover, underlies the conception of memory and covenant implicit in theosophical kabbalah. One of the functions of language, whether written or spoken, is to extend recollection over time.[75] As noted above, the essential feature of time is infinite extension; the latter is the mark of memory as well. From the kabbalistic perspective memory is not, as Proust put it, in "search of lost time," but is rather the engenderment of the past to the future through the present. Memory is as much the construction of the future as it is the retrieval of the past.[76] This quality of memory follows from the kabbalists locating it in the aspect of the divine that corresponds to the phallus. Already from the earliest kabbalistic texts the word *zekhirah*, remembrance, is linked to *zakhrut*, masculinity.[77] This aspect of the divine is also identified as the covenant. Indeed, the covenant is the seal that beckons memory and overflows in the infinite succession of time. By heeding the covenant one participates in the past and engenders the future. The covenantal relationship is not a static recall of the closed past, but rather the opening of the past through the present to the indeterminate future. Memory betokens not only Jewish survival but identity as well insofar as it is localized in the attribute that corresponds to the phallus, the covenant of circumcision.[78]

From a structural perspective, an intrinsic connection pertains between textuality and temporality, narrativity and memory. All of these participate in the activity of writing that embraces the erotic dialectic of concealment and disclosure characteristic of the phallus.[79] The nature of the scripted book, like its divine paradigm, is to reveal the hidden trace through dissimulation. As such, writing has its ontic ground in the phallus. In the final analysis, for the Jewish male the unveiling of the sealed book is a recollection of the flesh, a participation in the textual memory that is incised upon the circumcised penis. The repetition of this covenant occurs through the writing of the eternal concealment that has not yet been manifest. Just as the phallus is the locus of the divine androgyne, and hence the rite of circumcision is a ritual of symbolic androgynization, so too every act of writing. Reflecting on the expression, *sefer zikkaron*, a "book of remembrance," the Gaon of Vilna observes that the "book is [the feminine] *Malkhut* and memory is [the masculine] *Yesod*, in the secret of 'all Your males' (Exod. 23:17, 34:23; Deut. 16:16) as is known, and they are in one bond" (1882, pt. 2, 18c). The open text, it will be recalled, is the "book that is weighed in the balance," that is, the book that expresses the union of masculine and feminine. To write is to record one's memory in the text, to seal one's fate in the engraving of time that ensues from the veiled disclosure of the exposed concealment.

NOTES

1. "The divine book embraces all the unfinished books of man. Hence, thinking we read God, we only read ourselves" (Jabès 1989, 86).
2. See Derrida 1976, 18–26 and 92–93; and 1978, 67 and 278–93.
3. "The beginning of the book is a beginning for being and things. All writing invites to an anterior reading of the world which the word urges and which we pursue to the limits of faded memory" (Jabès 1984, 150). "There is no truth but interrogative, no reality but interpretation" (Jabès 1992, 85).
4. "Judaism cannot be conceived or justified outside the book" (Jabès 1992, 57). See Stamelman 1985.
5. For a different interpretation of Derrida's statement, see Hart 1989, 165: "Accordingly, when Derrida claims that there is nothing outside

the text, he is making a remark concerning constitution, not concerning what *is*. In other words, he does not say that everything is *only* a text but that everything is *also* a text" (author's emphasis). On the presentation of Derrida as an example of a "Jewish heretic hermeneutics," see Handelman 1982, 163–78.

6. This aspect of the Jewish tradition has been emphasized in the post-modern writing of Edmond Jabès. See, e.g., Jabès 1977, 31–32; 1989, 70. It is possible that with respect to this issue Jabès indeed was influenced by the kabbalistic tradition. See Laifer 1986, 91–106.

7. This too has been emphasized time and again in Jabès's writings. See, e.g., 1977, 122; 1984, 12 and 27; and 1992, 69. See Derrida 1978, 64–78; and Handelman 1982, 175–76.

8. See Jabès 1989, 5. For discussion of this thematic in the writings of Jabès, see Derrida 1978, 64–78; Handelman 1985; and Laifer 1986, 107–25.

9. For an extensive discussion of this motif, see Wolfson 1995.

10. Recently, two studies on the kabbalah of the Gaon of Vilna have appeared. See Avivi 1993 and Brill 1993.

11. Some of the relevant texts of the Gaon of Vilna have been cited and discussed in Avivi 1993, 32–36.

12. On the priority given to the particular in the cosmological scheme, see the comment of the Gaon of Vilna in *'Asarah Kelalim*, §7, in Avivi 1993, 138.

13. I have followed the suggestion of Gruenwald 1973, 483, that this probably represents the original reading of the text.

14. See, by contrast, Avivi 1993, 32, who suggests that, according to the Gaon of Vilna, the first *sfr* should be vocalized as *sefar*, i.e., counting, calculation, or reckoning, in contrast to the second, which is *sefer*, i.e., book. See Avivi 1993, 62. I see no justification for that suggestion in the writings of the Gaon. On the contrary, it seems evident that for him there are two books *(sefarim)*, the first sealed and the second opened. Even the latter is fully unveiled only through recitation *(sippur)*. The necessity to vocalize the first occurrence of *sfr* as *sefer* is underscored as well by the Gaon's attribution of the zoharic term *sifra di-zeni'uta*, the book of concealment, to divine Wisdom *(Hokhmah)*. See also Gaon of Vilna 1986, 1a–b and 15b: "Wisdom is called *sefer* on account of the writing." To vocalize the first *sfr* as *sefar* thus misses the whole point of the Vilna Gaon's hermeneutic. It is likely that the vocalization suggested by the Gaon reflects the influence of *Zohar* 2:137b. Cf. Moses Cordovero, 1962, 12:1, 65b–66a; 1989, 60; 1976, 65.

15. Compare to the words of Jabès 1992, 83: "'The book of God is read in the open air,' Reb Argi had written. And Reb Sadda: 'Thought has God's lightness. The book of Thought is a celestial book. There is no unknown but is infinite.'"

16. On the transition from closed book to open text, see Derrida 1978, 294,

who describes writing as "a nonsymmetrical division designated on the one hand the closure of the book, and on the other the opening of the text. . . . The question of writing could be opened only if the book was closed."

17. Cf. the passage in the commentary on *Sifra di-Zeni'uta* by Yizhaq Isaac Safrin of Komarno (1878, 94a): "The secret is that it is called book when the light of *Ein-Sof*, *'Adam Qadmon*, *'Atiq*, *'Arikh* and *'Abba* is drawn from concealment to disclosure through His people, Israel."

18. See Gaon of Vilna 1884, 2b, 4a. These texts were discussed by Avivi 1993, 33–35. See also *Tiqqune ha-Zohar* (1867, 120a) cited by Avivi 1993, 62.

19. Cf. the supercommentary of Yizhaq Isaac, *Be'er Yizhaq* (1988, 20–21), on the commentary on the Torah of the Gaon of Vilna, *'Aderet 'Eliyahu.*

20. Cf. Gaon of Vilna 1986, 13c: "*Da'at* is contained in *Binah*, even though it has not yet emerged it is contained in her secretly. Yet it is known that *Keter* is the root of *Da'at* and *Da'at* is in his place." On *Keter* as the place of *Da'at*, see also the Gaon of Vilna's commentary on *Zohar* 1:3b in *Yahel 'Or* (Gaon of Vilna 1882), 2b; *Sefer Yezirah 'im Persuh ha-Gra*, 4a–b: "The secret of *Da'at* is in the place of *Keter*, for the world was created by means of *Hokhmah* and *Binah*, and all the unity is in *Keter* and its dissemination below which is the secret of *Da'at*."

21. Cf. Gaon of Vilna 1884, 6c. See text printed in Avivi 1993, 141, where *Yesod de-'Atiq* is said to be hidden in the forehead of the will, i.e., in the uppermost manifestation of the Godhead.

22. On this zoharic concept, see Tishby 1989, 276–77, and Liebes 1976, 145–51 and 161–64. I have emphasized the phallic nature of this entity, especially connected with the function of inscribing or engraving, in several studies. See Wolfson 1990, 233 n. 140; 1994; and 1995.

23. See Gaon of Vilna 1986, 6a; 1867, 19b; 1884, 3c, 7b. Cf. 1882, 6a–b, where the *bozina de-qardinuta* is identified as *Yesod ha-Binah*, i.e., the phallic aspect of the feminine attribute of Understanding. See ibid., 23a. This identification is occasioned by the association (already attested in the *Zohar*) of this spark with activities of *gevurah*, strength, or *din*, judgment, which are usually valorized in kabbalistic literature as feminine traits. See esp. 1986, 5c.

24. See Gaon of Vilna 1884, 7a.

25. Based on *Sefer Yezirah* 1:3; see Gruenwald 1973, 488; Wolfson 1987a, 207 n. 57, and 211 n. 79.

26. See Avivi 1993, 50–52. It should be noted that the Gaon on occasion actually distinguishes three forms of union in the sefirotic realm: kissing *(nishuq)* of *Hokhmah* and *Binah* in the mouth of *'Arikh 'Anpin*; hugging *(hibbuq)* of *Hokhmah* and *Binah* by the hands of *'Arikh 'Anpin*; and copulation *(ziwwug)* of *Ze'eir 'Anpin* and *Nuqba* by means of the phallus. See Gaon of Vilna 1986, 14c–d, and discussion in Avivi 1993, 36–42, 54–57.

27. From this it follows that study, and in particular study of kabbalistic secrets, is a sexual act, the mouth taking the place of the active male principle and the ear the passive female principle. See Gaon of Vilna 1986, 16d–17a; and 1882, 16c, where the teaching of kabbalah to someone unworthy is compared to the sin of spilling semen in vain.

28. This, of course, reflects the Galenic view, widespread in medieval medical, philosophical, and mystical literature, that the semen originates in the brain. This view was also quite influential in kabbalistic sources, beginning with *Sefer ha-Bahir*.

29. Cf. Gaon of Vilna 1986, 14b, 14d–15a, 22d.

30. See Avivi 1993, 34–35.

31. There is a play here between the word *koah* in the biblical expression, *koah ma'asav*, "His powerful works" (Ps. 111:6), and the twenty-eight joints of the hands based on the fact that the consonants of the word *koah*, *kaf* and *het*, numerically equal twenty-eight.

32. Cf. Gaon of Vilna 1867, 39a. The power *(koah)* of God's creative act is related to the twenty-eight letters in the first verse of Genesis, which is also connected to *Hokhmah* by breaking that word into *koah mah*, i.e., the power of the Tetragrammaton, which equals forty-five (the numerical value of the word *mah*) when written out in full. The number twenty-eight is also related to the expression YHWH Elohenu YHWH (Deut. 6:4) and its permutation (derived by writing the consonant that immediately follows each letter, e.g., the *kaf* for a *yod*, *mem* for a *lamed*, and so on) KWZW BMWKSZ KWZW, i.e., the phrase and its permutation add up to a sum of twenty-eight, cf. 1884, 3c. On this technique of letter permutation, *'alef-bet gimmel-dalet*, employed in Jewish mystical literature, see Wolfson 1990, 206–7.

33. For a study of this theme, see Wolfson 1988–89; 1989–90.

34. Babylonian Talmud, Megillah 18b; Menahot 32b; Maimonides, *Mishneh Torah*, Hilkhot Tefillin 1:12; *Tur*, Yoreh De'ah 274.

35. Cf. Gaon of Vilna 1884, 3b, where the letters *'alef*, *mem*, *shin* are said to correspond to the triad *Hokhmah*, *Binah*, and *Da'at*, which, in turn, correspond to *mahshavah*, *dibbur*, and *ma'aseh*. Especially significant is the testimony of the Gaon of Vilna's student, Moses Solomon Toltuchin, in his notes to *Sefer Yezirah 'im Persuh ha-Gra*, 2d, which he received orally from his teacher, that the correct order is *sefer*, *sippur*, and *sefer* corresponding to *mahshavah*, *dibbur*, and *ma'aseh*. See Avivi 1993, 35, who cites this reference.

36. It is evident that, according to the Gaon of Vilna, these thirteen markings within *Keter*, which are also depicted as the upper thirteen attributes of mercy, correspond to thirteen covenants that are ontically grounded in *Yesod*. See, e.g., Gaon of Vilna 1986, 26b.

37. See also Gaon of Vilna 1882, 6a.

38. It is worthwhile in this context to recall the view expressed by Gershom Scholem: "For the Kabbalists, linguistic mysticism is at the same time

a mysticism of writing. Every act of speaking . . . is at once an act of writing and every writing is potential speech" (Scholem 1972, 67). See Biale 1979, 99–100. I have argued in a different way that it is writing, or more specifically engraving and inscription, that is the primordial linguistic act of God that must be distinguished thematically from speaking. To collapse every act of writing into speech and vice versa is to miss the significantly nuanced attitude expressed in many kabbalistic texts. For further discussion, see Wolfson 1995, where I explore in great detail the grammatological as opposed to logocentric orientation of various kabbalistic texts.

39. See Levinas 1987, 102–7.
40. See Tishby 1942, 24–28; and Scholem 1954, 264; 1974, 130–35.
41. See Tishby 1942, 52–61; and Scholem 1954, 265–68; 1974, 135–40.
42. See Scholem 1954, 263, and sources cited on 411 n. 56.
43. This technical term is based on a passage in *Zohar* 3:288a–b (*'Idra Zuta*), where the third of three heads, the uppermost aspect of the divine, is referred to as the "Head of every head," the "Head that is no head and which is not known." See *Zohar* 3:289b. Avivi 1993, 36, claims that the "Head that is not known" for the Gaon of Vilna designates the first emanation or *Keter*. While this interpretation is certainly borne out by various passages in the Gaon's writings (see, e.g., 1884, 8d), it must be noted that in some contexts the Head that is not known is either explicitly or implicitly identified as the *Ein-Sof*. See 1986 4c, 13d, 17a; 1882, 16c, and compare 1882, 2a, cited above. See especially *'Asarah Kelalim*, §9, in Avivi 1993, 140: "The first light is called the Head that is not known for it is hidden, and since it is hidden and not revealed to us it is in relation to us in the aspect of *Ein-Sof* from the perspective of the concealment. Therefore they said that the *Ein-Sof* is hidden in it insofar as it too is not revealed to us except through the cause of existence." See the *Sod ha-Zimzum* printed in 1986, 38c (concerning this text, see Avivi 1993, 27; to the manuscripts he mentions there one could add MS New York, Jewish Theological Seminary of America Mic. 1952, fols. 1a–3a), where the Head that is not known is identified as the end that is prior to the supernal will. For discussion of the divine will in the Gaon of Vilna's kabbalah, see Avivi 1993, 90–101. Elsewhere *Keter* is described as the ether that comes forth from the *Ein-Sof*; see ibid., 14a. It seems that, according to the Gaon of Vilna, *Keter* is coeternal with the *Ein-Sof* although in some sense ontically distinguishable. See, e.g., 1986, 38c, where *Ein-Sof* is said to cleave always to the beginning of the line which is the Supernal Crown, the divine will; and 1884, 3b: "Before the Holy One, blessed He, created the world He and His name were one in *Keter* for there the entire name is comprised in the tittle of the *yod* in complete unity, and from *Hokhmah* and downwards it divides into four letters and four configurations." See 1884, 8a, where it is stated explicitly that *Keter* is to be counted as one

of the ten *sefirot* even though it is the source of them. See also 1884, 9d, where the Gaon writes that the *"Ein-Sof* by means of its being clothed in the Wisdom of the Primordial Anthropos *(hokhmah de-'adam qadmon)* emanated the ten *sefirot* that are in [the world of] emanation. Therefore all of them are within Thought." Cf. 1882, 24a. On the image of the *'adam qadmon* in the Gaon's writings as contrasted with Lurianic kabbalah, see Avivi 1993, 90–91.

44. See Derrida 1989.

45. Cf. Gaon of Vilna 1882, 23a; 1975, 74b. For a classical formulation of apophatic theology influenced by the kabbalah of the Gaon of Vilna, see Eliashov [1909] 1976, 5a.

46. For this etymology of the word *'atiq* as concealment, see the disciple of the Gaon of Vilna, Menahem Mendel of Shklov, 1987, 4, 6, passim. See Avivi 1993, 110, who already referred to this reference.

47. See the important note of Moses Solomon Toltuchin printed in Gaon of Vilna 1882, 6d, which deals with an explanation of the *sefirot* that he received from the Gaon of Vilna. The term is related to the word *mispar* because the unity of substance of the emanations breaks down into multiplicity only within human thought and intellect. In and of themselves these emanations are unknowable or, in the language of *Sefer Yezirah*, they are *belimah*, i.e., *beli mahut*, without substance.

48. That the book of concealment corresponds to the Torah is evident in the Gaon of Vilna's remark that this zoharic section has five chapters that correspond to the five books of the Torah. See 1986, 1a.

49. See Brill 1993, 136 n. 18, who uses the example of the Gaon of Vilna's interpretation of the expression *sifra di-zeni'uta* to illustrate the point that for him kabbalistic terms are used functionally. Brill did not, however, pay attention to the ontic nature of the Gaon of Vilna's remarks, let alone to their applicability to a more general hermeneutic of writing and textuality.

50. See text printed in Avivi 1993, 140, where it is said that the Creator is revealed through His existence, which is a garment. On the dual nature of God as hidden *(nistar)* and revealed *(nigleh)*, see the commentary of the Gaon of Vilna to Song of Songs 5:10 in *Sifre ha-Gra* (Jerusalem, 1982), 30c–d. See, however, Gaon of Vilna, *Sefer Mishle 'im Be'ur ha-Gra*, ed. M. Phillip, 1985, 50, cited by Avivi 1993, 65 n. 5, whence it is clear that the esoteric meaning is disclosed through the exoteric, the hidden through that which is revealed. On this theme in thirteenth-century kabbalistic hermeneutics, especially the *Zohar*, see Wolfson 1993. The dialectic of concealment and disclosure is one of the cornerstones of kabbalistic theosophy affirmed by much earlier texts. A particularly important source for the Gaon of Vilna was the writings of Moses Cordovero and the Lurianic material. See, in particular, the formulation of Luria 1898, 22c: "He arranges these garments in which to be garbed, and the concealment *(he'elem)* is the cause of the revela-

tion *(gilluy)*, for He is not comprehended nor is pleasure derived from His light except by means of these garments."

51. The connection between *zeni'uta* as concealment and those who are humble, *zenu'im*, especially related to Prov. 11:2, is made already in Isaac Luria's commentary on this zoharic unit. See Luria 1898, 22a.

52. See Gaon of Vilna 1985, 134, where a connection is likewise made between modesty and silence, i.e., the *zenu'im* mentioned in Prov. 11:2 are those who are silent so that they may learn from their masters. In that context the silence occasioned by humility has nothing to do with esoteric knowledge.

53. The Talmudic passage (see Babylonian Talmud, Hagigah 13a) continues "matters [or words] that are sweeter than honey and milk should be under your tongue," i.e., they should not be spoken or revealed.

54. On the virtual synonymity of *levush* and *tiqqun*, see Gaon of Vilna 1986, 3c. See also Menahem Mendel of Shklov 1987, 7: "The *tiqqun* is called what His light is garbed in *(mah shenitlabesh 'oro)*, for it is His will, blessed be He, that it will be received and comprehended that everything comes from one root."

55. See Wolfson 1987a, 207–13; and Liebes 1993, 26–30.

56. For full discussion of this motif, see Wolfson 1994.

57. On the link between mystery and modesty, see Levinas 1987, 87: "Hiding is the way of existing of the feminine, and this fact of hiding is precisely modesty." See also Levinas 1969, 264. For Levinas the mystery is connected to alterity, otherness, which he sees as distinctively feminine. While the feminine is sometimes portrayed in kabbalistic literature in terms of the dialectic of hiding and revealing, the principle locus of this dialectic is the masculine and, in particular, the phallus.

58. The use of the word *zan'ua* to refer to sexual modesty is found already in classical rabbinic sources. See, e.g., Palestinian Talmud, Pesahim 4:4; Ketuvot 5:8; Babylonian Talmud, Shabbat 53b; Yoma 54a; Sotah 10b.

59. This is not the place to enter into a lengthy discussion on the topic of *zimzum* in the Gaon of Vilna's thought, a pivotal issue that was part of the critique of Shneur Zalman of Lyady, who accused R. Elijah of a literalist interpretation of this concept based on a faulty idea of absolute transcendence creating an unbridgeable abyss between God and world. See Scholem 1954, 348; 1974, 135; and recent discussion in Brill 1993. Ironically enough, the doctrine of *zimzum* in the writings of the Gaon, when understood properly, comes very close to Habad doctrine in particular and Hasidic thought in general. See discussion of the former in Elior 1992, 79–91; and compare especially the description of *zimzum* in Yizhaq Isaac Safrin of Komarno 1878, 93d. The dialectical rhythm of manifestation and concealment implied in the notion of *zimzum* may in the case of both the Gaon of Vilna and Hasidism go back to a common

source in the kabbalah of Moses Cordovero. See Ben-Shlomo 1965, 95–100; Scholem 1974, 134; and Sack 1989. For recent review of earlier kabbalistic sources for the doctrine of *zimzum*, see Idel 1992.

60. See Menahem Mendel of Shklov 1987, 4, 6, passim. See Avivi 1993, 110, cf. the passage from Menahem Mendel of Shklov referred to in n. 46.
61. For relevant passages and analysis, see Avivi 1993, 93–95.
62. I have rendered the verse in accordance with the Gaon's reading and not according to its plain sense.
63. On the development of this motif in earlier kabbalistic, especially zoharic, literature and its rabbinic precedents, see Liebes 1976, 146 and 329–30. I have also recently discussed this image; see Wolfson 1995. For discussion of this symbol in the kabbalistic writings of the Gaon of Vilna, see Avivi 1993, 50–51, and 82–86.
64. Cf. Gaon of Vilna 1882, 23a: "The matter is that the quality of mercy *(behinat ha-hasadim)* is to expand infinitely and without limit, and the quality of strength *(behinat ha-gevurot)* is to give measure and balance."
65. Compare text in Avivi 1993, 130.
66. Based on the rabbinic tradition that the world is divided into three periods—two thousand years of chaos, two thousand years of Torah, and two thousand years of Messiah. See Babylonian Talmud, Sanhedrin 97a. This schema corresponds to the *tria tempora* of Christian apocalypticism reflected in the Pauline division of history: *ante legem, sub lege,* and *sub gratia.* See Funkenstein 1982, 132 and 146 n. 14.
67. This insight is basic to phenomenological studies on time that have influenced my thinking. As representative studies, see Husserl 1964; Heidegger 1962, 349–488; and Heidegger 1985.
68. Compare text in Avivi 1993, 128, where the technical name of God in Dan. 7:9, *'atiq yomin,* the "Ancient of Days," is transformed into a designation of these potencies that are the primordial days of creation, *ha-yamim ha-qodmin la-kol.*
69. The view of the Gaon of Vilna thus reflects Nahmanides' messianic conviction which was buttressed by his acceptance of the eschatological scheme of Abraham bar Hiyya, apparently borrowed from Christian sources, understood in kabbalistic terms, i.e., the days of creation typologically correspond to the periods of history and symbolically correspond to the divine emanations. See Funkenstein 1982, 139–41.
70. On the erotic nature of textuality, see Barthes 1975.
71. See Critchley 1991, 179–81; and Handelman 1991, 205–8, 254–55, and 324. I have deliberately ignored an essential element of Levinas's notion of fecundity, which involves the ethical demand of the other-in-the-same. See Gibbs 1992, 28–29, 237–38.
72. On the feminine as space or habitation, see Levinas 1969, 154–56.
73. On the role of time in rabbinic aggadah, see Fraenkel 1989.
74. For citation and further discussion of this text, see Wolfson 1987a, 213.

75. See the extraordinary analysis of Krell 1990.
76. See Jabès 1992, 79.
77. On the connection of memory and the phallus and the (philologically mistaken) supposition that the two terms derive from the same Hebrew root, see Kristeva 1987, 87.
78. See Jabès 1989, 72.
79. On circumcision as the inscription of the divine name, see Wolfson 1987b. See also Levin 1985, 202–4, and Derrida 1986.

REFERENCES

Avivi, Joseph. *The Kabbalah of the Gra* (Hebrew). Jerusalem: Kerem Eliyahu, 1993.

Barthes, Roland. *The Pleasure of the Text*. Trans. Richard Miller. New York: Hill and Wang, 1975.

Ben-Shlomo, Joseph. *The Mystical Theology of Moses Cordovero* (Hebrew). Jerusalem: Bialik Institute, 1965.

Biale, David. *Gershom Scholem Kabbalah and Counter-History*. Cambridge, Mass., and London: Harvard University Press, 1979.

Brill, Alan. "The Mystical Path of the Vilna Gaon." *Journal of Jewish Thought and Philosophy* 3 (1993): 131–51.

Cordovero, Moses. *Pardes Rimmonim*. Jerusalem: N.P., 1962.

———. *Zohar 'im Perush 'Or Yaqar me-ha-Ramaq*. Vol. 9. Jerusalem: Mif'al Yaqar, 1976.

———. *Sefer Yezirah 'im Perush 'Or Yaqar me-ha-Ramaq*. Jerusalem: Mif'al Yaqar, 1989.

Critchley, Simon. "'Bois'—Derrida's Final Word on Levinas." In *Re-Reading Levinas*, ed. Robert Bernasconi and Simon Critchley. Bloomington and Indianapolis: Indiana University Press, 1991.

Derrida, Jacques. *Of Grammatology*. Trans. Gayatri Chakravorty Spivak. Baltimore and London: Johns Hopkins University Press, 1976.

———. *Writing and Difference*. Translated with introduction and additional notes by Alan Bass. Chicago: University of Chicago Press, 1978.

———. "Shibboleth." In *Midrash and Literature*, ed. Geoffrey H. Hartman and Sanford Budick. New Haven and London: Yale University Press, 1986.

———. "How To Avoid Speaking: Denials." In *Languages of the Unsayable: The Play of Negativity in Literature and Literary Theory*, ed. Sanford Budick and Wolfgang Iser, trans. Ken Friedan. New York: Columbia University Press, 1989.

Eliashov, Solomon. *Leshem Shevo we-Ahlamah*. Piotrkow: 1909; Jerusalem: Yeshivat ha-Hayyim we-ha-Shalom, 1976.

Elior, Rachel. *The Paradoxical Ascent to God: The Kabbalistic Theosophy of Habad Hasidism.* Trans. Jeffrey M. Green. Albany: State University of New York Press, 1992.

Fraenkel, Jonah. "Time and Its Role in the Aggadic Story." In *Binah: Studies in Jewish History, Thought, and Culture.* Vol. 2, ed. Joseph Dan. New York; Westport, Conn.; and London: Praeger, 1989.

Funkenstein, Amos. "Nahmanides' Symbolical Reading of History." In *Studies in Jewish Mysticism,* ed. Joseph Dan and Frank Talmage. Cambridge, Mass.: Association for Jewish Studies, 1982.

Gaon of Vilna (Elijah ben Solomon Zalman). *Tiqqune ha-Zohar we-Tiqqunim me-Zohar Hadash 'im Be'ur ha-Gra.* Vilna: S. J. Fine and A. Z. Rosenkranz, 1867.

———. *Yahel 'Or.* Vilna: Rom Publishers, 1882.

———. *Sefer Yezirah 'im Perush ha-Gra.* Warsaw: Isaac Goldman, 1884.

———. *Be'ur 'al ha-Ra'aya Mehemna me-Rabbenu Eliyahu me-Vilna.* Jerusalem: Rare Judaica Publishing House, 1975.

———. *Sifre ha-Gra.* Jerusalem, 1982.

———. *Sefer Mishle 'im Be'ur ha-Gra.* Ed. M. Phillip. Petah Tiqvah: Yeshiva 'Ohel Yosef, 1985.

———. *Sifra di-Zeni'uta 'im Be'ur ha-Gra.* Vilna, 1882; Jerusalem: Hamesora, 1986.

———. *'Asarah Kelalim.* In *The Kabbalah of the Gra* (Hebrew), ed. Joseph Avivi. Jerusalem: Kerem Eliyahu, 1993.

Gibbs, Robert. *Correlations in Rosenzweig and Levinas.* Princeton, N.J.: Princeton University Press, 1992.

Gould, Eric, ed. *The Sin of the Book: Edmond Jabès.* Lincoln: University of Nebraska Press, 1985.

Gruenwald, Ithamar. "Some Critical Notes on the First Part of *Sefer Yezira.*" *Revue des études juives* 132 (1973): 475–512.

Handelman, Susan. *The Slayers of Moses: The Emergence of Rabbinic Interpretation in Modern Literary Theory.* Albany: State University of New York Press, 1982.

———. "'Torments of an Ancient World': Edmond Jabès and the Rabbinic Tradition." In *The Sin of the Book: Edmond Jabès,* ed. E. Gould. Lincoln: University of Nebraska Press, 1985.

———. *Fragments of Redemption: Jewish Thought and Literary Theory in Benjamin, Scholem, and Levinas.* Bloomington: Indiana University Press, 1991.

Hart, Kevin. *The Trespass of the Sign: Deconstruction, Theology, and Philosophy.* Cambridge: Cambridge University Press, 1989.

Heidegger, Martin. *Being and Time.* Trans. John Macquarrie and Edward Robinson. New York and San Francisco: Harper and Row, 1962.

———. *History of the Concept of Time.* Trans. Theodore Kisiel. Bloomington and Indianapolis: Indiana University Press, 1985.

Husserl, Edmund. *The Phenomenology of Internal Time-Consciousness.* Ed. Martin Heidegger, trans. James S. Churchill, with an introduction by Calvin O. Schrag. Bloomington and London: Indiana University Press, 1964.

Idel, Moshe. "On the Concept of *Zimzum* in Kabbalah and Research" (Hebrew). In *Jerusalem Studies in Jewish Thought* 10 (1992): 59–112.

Isaac, Yizhaq. *Be'er Yizhaq: Commentary on Elijah ben Solomon 'Aderet 'Eliyahu.* Jerusalem: N.P., 1988.

Jabès, Edmond. *The Book of Questions.* Vol. 1. Trans. Rosmarie Waldrop. Middletown, Conn.: Wesleyan University Press, 1977.

———. *The Book of Questions.* Vol. 2. Trans. Rosmarie Waldrop. Middletown, Conn.: Wesleyan University Press, 1984.

———. *The Book of Resemblances.* Vol. 3, *The Ineffaceable, The Unperceived.* Trans. Rosmarie Waldrop. Hanover and London: University Press of New England, 1992.

———. *The Book of Shares.* Trans. Rosmarie Waldrop. Chicago: University of Chicago Press, 1989.

Krell, David F. *Of Memory, Reminiscence, and Writing: On the Verge.* Bloomington and Indianapolis: Indiana University Press, 1990.

Kristeva, Julia. *Tales of Love.* Trans. Leon S. Roudiez. New York: Columbia University Press, 1987.

Laifer, Miryam. *Edmond Jabès un judaïsme après Dieu.* New York, Berne, and Frankfurt am Main: Peter Lang, 1986.

Levin, David M. *The Body's Recollection of Being: Phenomenological Psychology and the Deconstruction of Nihilism.* London, Boston, Melbourne, and Henley: Routledge and Kegan Paul, 1985.

Levinas, Emmanuel. *Totality and Infinity.* Trans. Alphonso Lingis. Pittsburgh: Duquesne University Press, 1969.

———. *Collected Philosophical Papers.* Trans. Alphonso Lingis. Dordrecht, Boston, and Lancaster: Martinus Nijhoff, 1987.

Liebes, Yehuda. "Sections of the Zohar Lexicon" (Hebrew). Ph.D. diss., Hebrew University, Jerusalem, 1976.

———. *Studies in the Zohar.* Trans. Arnold Schwartz, Stephanie Nakache, and Penina Peli. Albany: State University of New York Press, 1993.

Luria, Isaac. *Sha'ar Ma'amere Rashbi.* Jerusalem: Bet El, 1898.

Mendel, Menahem of Shklov. *Mayyim 'Adirim.* Jerusalem: Hamesorah, 1987.

Ricoeur, Paul. *Time and Narrative.* Vol. 1. Trans. Kathleen McLaughlin and David Pellauer. Chicago: University of Chicago Press, 1984.

Sack, Bracha. "The Doctrine of *Zimzum* of Moses Cordovero" (Hebrew). *Tarbiz* 58 (1989): 207–37.

Safrin, Yizhaq Isaac. *Zohar Hai.* Vol. 2. Przemysl: Druck von A. Zupnisk and Knoller, 1878.

Scholem, Gershom. *Major Trends in Jewish Mysticism.* 3d ed. New York: Schocken, 1954.

————. "The Name of God and the Linguistic Theory of the Kabbala." *Diogenes* 79 (1972): 59–80.

————. *Kabbalah*. Jerusalem: Keter, 1974.

Stamelman, Richard. "Nomadic Writing: The Poetics of Exile." In *The Sin of the Book: Edmond Jabès*, ed. Eric Gould. Lincoln: University of Nebraska Press, 1985.

Tishby, Isaiah. *The Doctrine of Evil and the "Kelippah" in Lurianic Kabbalah* (Hebrew). Jerusalem: Schocken, 1942.

————. *The Wisdom of the Zohar: An Anthology of Texts*. Trans. David Goldstein. Oxford, U.K.: Oxford University Press, 1989.

Wolfson, Elliot R. "Circumcision, Vision of God, and Textual Interpretation: From Midrashic Trope to Mystical Symbol." *History of Religions* 27 (1987a): 189–215.

————. "Circumcision and the Divine Name: A Study in the Transmission of Esoteric Doctrine." *Jewish Quarterly Review* 78 (1987b): 77–112.

————. "Biblical Accentuation in a Mystical Key: Kabbalistic Interpretations of the Te'amim—Part I." *Journal of Jewish Music and Liturgy* 11 (1988–89): 1–16.

————. "Biblical Accentuation in a Mystical Key: Kabbalistic Interpretations of the Te'amim—Part II." *Journal of Jewish Music and Liturgy* 12 (1989–90): 1–13.

————. "Letter Symbolism and Merkavah Imagery in the Zohar." In *'Alei Shefer: Studies in the Literature of Jewish Thought Presented to Rabbi Dr. Alexandre Safran*, ed. Moshe Hallamish. Bar-Ilan: Bar-Ilan University Press, 1990.

————. "Beautiful Maiden without Eyes: Peshat and Sod in Zoharic Hermeneutics." In *The Midrashic Imagination*, ed. Michael Fishbane. Albany: State University of New York Press, 1993.

————. "Woman—The Feminine as Other in Theosophic Kabbalah: Some Philosophical Reflections on the Divine Androgyne." In *The Other in Jewish Thought and History*, ed. L. Silberstein and R. Cohn. New York: New York University Press, 1994.

————. "Erasing the Erasure: Gender and the Writing of God's Body in Kabbalistic Symbolism." In *Circle in the Square: Studies in the Use of Gender in Kabbalistic Symbolism*. Albany: State University of New York Press, 1995.

Zadoq ha-Kohen of Lublin. *Mahshevot Haruz*. Piotrkow: N.P., 1912.

Liturgy

Chapter 6

The Poor in Deed Facing the Lord of All Deeds: A Postmodern Reading of the Yom Kippur Mahzor

Adi Ophir

I. A Critique of the *Mahzor*: Context and Method

For most secular Jews in Israel, there is still an aura of sanctity about the High Holy Days, and Yom Kippur in particular. On that day the synagogues are full of people who do not visit synagogues any other day of the year. People who do not believe in sin and repentance go to the synagogue as a thing that is done, out of respect for their grandfather or because they follow their father's custom, and are reluctant to abandon a tradition they have followed for years. For others, the service is a way of participating in a particular Jewish community and a way of belonging to the Jewish people as a whole. Many worshippers come to the synagogue because they still feel a sense of dread, the last trace of respect for a god whose decrees they do not follow any longer. They feel a troublesome sense of guilt that whispers to them: "It mightn't help, but it can't do any harm." Whatever the reasons, multitudes of secular Jews fill the benches of the synagogues (and are therefore often labeled "*masorti'im*," that is, traditionalist Jews) and mix with their religious brethren. They sit or stand cramped beside one another, and with some help from the more habituated Jews they leaf through the Yom Kippur *Mahzor* ("Cycle") or book of prayers. Because of the high proportion of secular Jews who visit the synagogue on this day, the *Mahzor* is the most read and most known Jewish religious text, apart from the Passover Haggadah.[1] Furthermore, most of the Israeli secular Jews who participate in the prayer ritual of Yom Kippur fulfill—even if only for a brief period of time—the role of the worshipper as dictated by the *Mahzor* and join the congregation of learned and experienced worshippers. When this is the case, there is no difference between the secular worshipper and the religious one: they both practice the ritual as dictated by the text and by the customs of their congregation.

Thus, the Yom Kippur prayer ritual is a cultural arena that a broad secular public shares with the entire religious population. In this arena, each worshipper takes up a preordained position, that of the sinner who repents for his sins, asks for atonement, and stands, as if alone yet always together with the entire congregation, facing the Almighty. The worshipper's position has a more or less fixed form, and his liturgic practice follows rules that are relatively independent of the beliefs or attitudes he happens to have regarding theological or ethical questions. These practices, which the secular and the religious Jew share, pertain to relations between the individual and the community and the nation, and relations between the latter three entities and the Creator. These practices also pertain to the differentiation between the private and public spheres and the demarcation between the sacred and the profane. True, after the concluding *Neilah* service, secular and religious Jews return to quite different worlds. And the manner of return, too, is quite different. But for a brief while a partnership exists, at least a partial one. The gathering around a common text and the performance of the common rite for which the text is a *partitur* blurs the distinction between religious and secular Jews, separated as they are, even in the synagogue, by different life-worlds and belief systems.

The fascinating ability of secular and religious Jews to sit together on Yom Kippur will be a focus of this essay. And what makes this topic so fascinating, of course, is the bitter and painful separation of secular and religious Jews at all other times during the year. This separation is what meets the eye of any keen political or social observer of Israeli-Jewish society. Not only political rivalry and conflicting interests split the two groups apart, but they are split by social and cultural isolation in institutions from schools to the judiciary. And they differ not only in their worldviews but also in everyday practices from modes of consumption to habits of leisure. There are also sometimes open, even violent, expressions of hatred, xenophobia, and resentment on both sides, and no less importantly and certainly related to these phenomena, there is also a steadily growing gap of mutual ignorance (cf. Gotkind-Golan 1990; Levi 1988; Oron 1993).

Of course, this picture is oversimplified. Neither the "secular" nor the "religious" form monolithic groups. It is questionable if there is any significant overlapping between that segment of the secular population that crowds the synagogues on the High Holidays and those who are quick to become militant in matters of coexistence between the two communities. But despite all of this, lines of intensive interaction and successful cooperation may be delineated no less than lines of confrontation and strife, for example, in the army, in the great endeavor of colonization of and quarrel over the occupied territories, in certain sectors of the economy, and, to a lesser extent, in the academy (cf., e.g., Liebman 1990; Friedman 1991, chaps. 10–11).

However, what is perhaps most significant about the partnership between secular and religious Jews during the Yom Kippur ritual is that it is the only one enacted entirely on a religious terrain. In the army, in politics and State ceremonies, in the economy, the religious Jew meets the secular Jew in a world that has been thoroughly secularized, even if there are ongoing attempts to endow portions of these with new religious meanings. Even on Passover night, when most Israeli Jews read the Haggadah at the Seder table, the common ground is not a religious public sphere but the private sphere of the family. On Yom Kippur, at the synagogue, the common ground is religious from beginning to end and there is a reversal of movement, even though a temporary one, from the secular back to the religious sphere. In Israeli-Jewish culture, changes of terrain and a partnership of this sort are quite unique.

My hypothesis is that what allows the secular and the religious Jew a common ground during the High Holidays[2] is precisely what makes their continuous strife bearable and their ongoing cooperation through the rest of the year possible. This may be so not because of any secret spiritual quality of the Holy Days, and it certainly does not imply any causal link between the social time and space of the synagogue and other social spheres. My claim is rather that looking at the synagogue may be worthwhile for economic reasons, the economy of observation and analysis: it is there that whatever has survived secularization in the secular Israeli Jew may become visible and readily given to articulation. Not merely the effective accommo-dations of religious Jews to modern life in a secularized, albeit

Jewish society,[3] this element that has survived secularization is constitutive of the uneasy but nonetheless successful coexistence between secular and religious Jews in Israel.

I will not be able to make good on this sociological claim in this essay. It is presented here as a context and suggestive motivation for the analysis that follows. This analysis has a much more limited scope: it is an attempt to use the main liturgic text of the Yom Kippur ritual in order to articulate that "unsecularized common ground" between secular and religious Jews. The *Mahzor* is conceived here as the script and framework for the ritual of repentance, but my critical reading of it does not pretend to consist of a comprehensive interpretation of the ritual. Rather, I intend to bring about an understanding of how that unique partnership in the ritual between religious and secular Jews is made possible and shaped by the prayer book itself.

The major hermeneutical questions stemming from the above socio-political context are: How does the text constrain its possible uses by so diverse readers? and, vice versa, How do different users, with different, sometimes conflicting purposes, manage to maneuver so diversely within the framework of the same text? And the brief answer is, I think, that it is not meanings and interpretations but practices that are at stake here, not expressions of Jewish "mentality" or "worldview" but expressions of the rules that regulate behavior in a single, relatively isolated arena of the life-world. Once the hermeneutical questions are set in these terms and the text is conceived as an aggregate of discursive practices and a set of rules for ritualistic practices, it is only natural to approach both the questions and the text by way of some kind of deconstructive reading.

Another hermeneutic presupposition may be drawn from a further examination of the context of reading. It is a context of seemingly deep divisions between two parties; the opposition seems clear and the evidence for it quite compelling. Therefore, so as not to beg the question, so as not to impose upon the text a preconceived cluster of opposing meanings, that opposition must be avoided as much as possible in the context of interpretation. Once again, there is an appeal here for a deconstructive or, more widely, postmodern approach.

Finally, "the text itself"[4]—if I may still be allowed to use the term, provisionally, at least—gives some directions for its critical reading. The *Mahzor* is a hybrid of texts composed in different periods, arranged, so it seems, in a quite haphazard way, except for the skeleton of the *Amidah* (eighteen prayer) and the standard confession *("we have trespassed . . .")* at each of the five services. It is neither a work of art nor a collective oeuvre but an amalgam of prayers, hymns, and supplications that lacks coherency and systematicity. Such a text calls for a reading that looks neither for origin nor for an author, a reading that can ignore the myriad strands of the text's genealogy in favor of its present playfulness. This playfulness is enabled yet constrained by the procession of the ritual. The ritual may be looked at like a game whose rules it is the interpreters' task to discern and articulate. If the secular and the religious Jew find there a certain common ground, they must be able to play in the same field by the same rules. This is, of course, already the language of a postmodern reading.

The discussion that follows is part of a fragmentary series in six sections.[5] Each section articulates, interprets, and critiques a different aspect in the repentance game, a different phase in the position that the *Mahzor* guides the worshipper to adopt. It does so with a conscious attempt to explicitly relate the text-object and the technique of its objectification. The point of departure for each section is a thesis familiar to readers of postmodern theory, one of the tenets of the postmodernist point of view. In each section, one such tenet—or its very negation—is exemplified and demonstrated by certain discursive practices in the *Mahzor*. The interpretation of these practices is then further developed, applying that same postmodernist tenet.[6]

Now these postmodern readings are articulated on the background of an alternative approach, a typically "modernist" one that negates or ignores the said postmodernist tenet. Two divergent forms of this kind of modernist reading are discerned and very briefly examined: an "intrinsic" reading that usually produces the ideology of the religious practice and an "extrinsic" reading that may be conceived in terms of a critique of ideology. The advantage of a postmodern reading would consist in showing both the ideology of the ritual and its critique to be options opened by the very same text.[7] Thus, the dialogue of the deaf between the modernist secular critic and the believer who defends himself in modernist or premodernist terms may be avoided. In fact, both directions of modernist reading are never engaged in order to be refuted; they are bypassed. No attempt is made to disprove the explicit content of the religious "worldview" embodied in the prayer, to justify or delegitimize the prayer's "deep intention" or to expose its "hidden" motivations in the depths of the individual's soul or its "disguised" function at the basis of social existence.

Postmodern reading (mine, at least)[8] stays close to the surface of the text; it hardly asks what one means by a phrase but rather how one can play, act, cope, and compete by phrasing. Not only is use preferred over meaning, and the reader has become a user, but also the question of use is reversed: How does a text use its own users, manipulate them, prepare, in advance, the scope of their strategic moves in the game it constitutes? Thus, postmodern reading does not grant its object the unity of an artifact. Rather, it exposes through it the texture of a landscape, a cultural field that runs further, but not deeper, than what first meets the eye. And postmodern reading never forgets that the landscape it exposes is not given to it from high and above, through observation alone, for it too traverses the landscape it delineates, it too is affected by it.

II. A Transcendent Point of View

> The God of the universe is omnipotent! His word is established for ever, but he is invisible to all. . . . He knows all things eternally; he writeth and numbereth what hath ever been done. . . He beareth rule over his work . . . tremendous in his habitation . . . [He] expandeth the earth on a vacuum, yet shall its inhabitants not be destroyed. (*Musaph* Service, 325–27)[9]

Both modernists and postmodernists know that no transcendent, disinterested point of view is available for humans, that the totality of nature or history is beyond humans' grasp. They both assume that an omniscient God, who "*knowest . . . all the secret things, as well as the revealed*" (33) and "*callest to mind all things long forgotten*" (337), is a construct of religious discourse. But whereas modernists who have killed God sought to replace Him, postmodernists look calmly at the corpse and care little about what is done with it. They are free of bad conscience and of the anxiety for finding substitutes. These, however, are not statements about the possibility of faith in God, only of His representation in human language.

An omniscient God is represented in the Yom Kippur prayer and addressed by it. Many of the phrases in the *Mahzor* have a fixed reference and most have a fixed addressee: an all-knowing God Who remembers all things long forgotten and before Whom nothing is concealed. This is a God who is exalted and transcendent; the distance between Him and the individual worshipper is infinite. But the *Mahzor* does not attempt to represent the totality of that which the Omnipotent God knows and upon which He acts; the text only specifies the kinds of things supposedly contained in this totality and the point of view from which it is apprehended. God is present in the text in the multiplicity of His praises, superlative descriptions, the garments of His glory, and the dread of His power and verdict. In contrast to what might be implied by the austere demands of rational speech about a transcendent god *("there is no possible estimation of the innumerable attendants of thy glory nor any explication of thy holy name"* [339]), the Almighty of the *Mahzor* is neither unknowable nor indescribable. He is represented to His believers in a rich and many-layered language.

A critical modernist reader may ask, of course, if it is really the same God who is both *"merciful and gracious, long-suffering, and abundant in beneficence"* (49) and at the same time *"delighted in the affliction of the soul of his pious people"* (149), and, on the other hand, how it is possible that *"He who calleth forth the generations . . . foretelling the end from the beginning"* (221) is also the one who needs to *"searcheth all the hearts on the day of judgment"* (223). And one can reply, with both the medieval philosophers and with Yeshayahu Leibovitch, that the Holy One Blessed be His Name is beyond all description, that any description is an unjustified limitation of His essence, and that any attempt to describe Him is fundamentally false testimony to the mental and spiritual incapacity of the person who intends Him, an empty and poetic expression of reverence and no more (and this answer would still be a modern one [Leibovitch 1979, chap. 1]). And from here one can conclude that true statements about the Almighty are only those sentences that negate the descriptions existent in religious discourse. The object being described is so perfect, the descriptive language is so inadequate, and the gap is unbridgeable in principle.[10]

Other modernist readers have tried to defend the language of the prayer by arguing that it does not "seriously" intend to describe the God it addresses. The object of the prayer is not to be sought between or beyond heaven and earth, not even in the fictive world that the prayer itself creates, because this is a language whose function it is to direct the mind and arouse the emotions, to ease communication among the worshippers and between each individual and the divine addressee, an empty hole that the prayer both creates and fills. In other words, the prayer is meant to enact, not to represent (e.g., Phillips 1968; Lawson and McCauley 1990, chap. 3).

Two assumptions are common to these modern approaches to the language of the prayer: (a) there is a sharp division between representation and action, and hence the represented content does not depend on the character of the act of representation and is capable of being examined apart from it (this division is what finally leaves the epithets of God in the prayer with only an emotive or performative function); and (b) the phrases addressed to God have a signified that is absent in principle, an absence so extreme that it obliges an eschewal of any pretension to refer or to mean adequately. From a postmodern perspective, which conceives representation itself as a mode of action and the absence of the signified as an effect of certain strategies of representation, both assumptions are flatly denied.

Hence, for a postmodernist reading, God is no longer the absolute, always absent referent; descriptions of God are no longer taken as linguistic faults or as performatives disguised as descriptions. From a postmodernist viewpoint, the God of the *Mahzor* is an addressee of a special sort, a pole of intentions, flexible and not uniform, created by the ensemble of representations that describe Him, that is, the entire series of phrases and subphrases that refer to Him. Conceived as an addressee, not merely as a referent of the liturgic discourse, God's existence or essence is not a basic assumption necessary for "making sense" of (or endowing) each of His diverse representations.[11] "God," the referent, is an accompanying implication and a late effect of several discursive genres or language-games in the prayer, and this referent takes a specific form only when there is a demand or a quest for meaning of particular phrases or of the entire series of phrases. Usually, such a quest is external to the ritual, to the event in which the text is actually used (cf. Lawson and McCauley 1990, chap. 3).

In the ritual, by virtue of the descriptions those phrases contain, God becomes transformed from the object of reverence and dread into the addressee of confession and repentance. It is impossible to understand the prayer without understanding the way in which it produces God as an absolute pole of address and concern, and the function of God as an absolute addressee cannot be understood without grasping the game of labels, epithets, and predicates that represent Him.

Of course, it would be a mistake, a false move in the game, to understand any of God's numerous epithets and labels that fill the *Mahzor* as an adequate representation of any single aspect of the perfect One. Yet the epithets, labels, and predicates follow upon each other with a seeming compulsiveness *("Excellence and faithfulness . . . understanding and blessing . . . ornament and decency . . . unity and reverence . . . crown and glory . . . good doctrine and sensibility . . ."* [209]), as if they sought to replace the Unique One with their variegated, restless multiplicity. As though the only way to represent the unrepresentable in principle is by multiplying epithets to infinity, thus denying any of them an independent viability, letting them cancel each other out in the way they follow upon each other, replacing each other, diverting the gaze, sending it off around the whole breadth of the earth, across all times, to all the spheres of existence. Together they combine into a description of what is beyond all description, of God "in-itself," but also, and perhaps mainly, of God's relation with all His creatures and with His chosen nation in particular.

There is no point in seeking out contradictions between the various descriptions or in trying to extract from them a coherent picture of God as it is formed in the worshipper's mind. The descriptive language has one referent and an infinity of predicates, which are almost always differentiated from each other not due to the differing meanings (their signifieds) but by the first letters of their signifiers *(aleph, beth, gimel, dalet* or the reverse, *taf, shin, resh, kuf* is generally the order of the titles in most of the *piyyutim* or versified prayers). Such principle of difference is arbitrary, of course, but with a few simple rules (e.g., the alphabetical order), it creates numerous possibilities of play among the epithets. Playing consists here of employing irregular disparities and difference of tension among the various epithets, transforming the order of their sequences. Apparent contradictions[12] are blurred in this abundance, silenced by the intensity of these sequences. Series of epithets follow one another, borrow from one another, inverse or even explode one another, yet all the while adding glory to the Name, being always short of expressing its infinite meanings but never short of expressing the infinite distance of its omnipresent referent.

This is a distance that must be bridged without being denied or eliminated. Each one of the manifold epithets and predicates is but one of the small paving blocks that cover the solid structure—the interplay of epithets' sequences—of a bridge to infinity. Through acts of naming, labeling, and predicating, repeated ad nauseam, the prayer turns the transcendent and sublime One into an accessible interlocutor and at the same time reaffirms His status as the source of all speech and its absolute end. Thus it becomes possible to live a human life suffused with sin in the shade of an omniscient God Who grasps all sins at once, without being terrified to death, without losing hope, without even ceasing the round of daily life or making any change in the habits, customs, or tradition in the milieu where sins pile up and darken as crimson.

This kind of intentionality that the Yom Kippur *Mahzor* produces is part of a conspiracy behind which there is no planning mind. The conspiracy has a clear function: to confuse the Omniscient, without for a moment ceasing to acknowledge His authority as the Judge of all the earth. The entire community of worshippers is party to it, as if trying to evade, through sophistry abundant in verbiage, the risks of speaking blasphemy or slander. And at the same time, it is a conspiracy that joins the community and enjoins it against the individual, to alarm him, to domesticate him, to empty him of deeds, to posit him as a nihil in the face of the One before Whom all things are annihilated.

Yet this conspiracy, one must remember, is but a game, a game whose arch-rule (and also one of whose main stakes) is to include the absolute source of all rules as a participant in the game. He can become a participant precisely because His image is so full with gaps and contradictions that allow the maneuvers of the game. Thus, for example, the one who remembers everything is asked to forget (the sins, e.g., 59); the one who never forgets is reminded of what he might have forgotten (the covenant and the *zhut*, the merits, of the forefathers). The God of the *Mahzor* is a player with a defined position, against Whom one may mobilize the best devices, to mislead Him (without ever defying His will) to combine against Him in changing alliances (while seeking reassurances for His Own alliance, the covenant), and in the end, to subsist in the shade of His presence.

It is possible, for example, to multiply His epithets and predicates extensively so as to include all kinds of attitudes with regard to all possible kinds of sin: *"Answer us, thou who are good and beneficent one, answer us, thou who knoweth the inclination of man . . . thou who suppresseth anger . . . who are clothed with righteousness . . . who art near to those who worship thee"* (71). One can negate oneself before Him completely, beg mercy like a leaf in the wind: *"O my God, before I was formed, I was unworthy and now that I have been formed I am as though I have not been formed. Dust am I in my lifetime, how much more at my decease"* (39). And even though the Almighty is omniscient it is worthwhile to remind Him of His covenant (e.g., *"look therefore to the covenant, and regard not at the impulse [Yetzer]"* [55]) and point to a selection of the deeds of salvation He has performed in the past.[13] But in every case one must always preserve the double status enjoyed by the Judge of all the earth, Who is both the source of the rules *("And with love hath thou given us, O Lord our God this Day of Atonement, for pardon, and forgiveness and atonement"* [27]) and also the chief player on the court of the game of forgiveness *("Verily it is thou who art Judge and Arbitrator, who knowest all, and art witness, writer, sigillator, recorder, and teller"* [337]).

This game of repentance, it must be reemphasized now, is kept open for any Jew, the most secular included, who can join the game without committing himself to any specific command or defined contents of belief. All he needs to do is to accord God His double role as an arch-source of and arch-player in the game. And this he does by his very speech acts, by the almost mechanical way he joins the crowd in uttering the hymns of the prayer, being carried away by their consoling, unchanging rhythm. Neither his sins as a Jew who does not observe the Halakhic law nor any other particular sin calls for any special attention. For in any case, all possible sins have been written down in advance and none of his sins excludes him from the community of worshippers who are seeking repentance and atonement.[14] His almost natural integration into the congregation of the more orthodox worshippers[15] is an important mechanism for the reaffirmation of Jewish solidarity and of the secular Jews' partnership in a national-religious community. Thus the primacy of religious practices that claim to determine the limits and force of this partnership is also reaffirmed.

The secular Jew who participates in the prayer activates this mechanism—whether unknowingly or in complete agreement—thus endowing the entire ritual with a surplus national value. For on Yom Kippur, on each Yom Kippur, secular Jews who take part in the ritual reaffirm that they are still playing that old game that goes on forever, until the Messiah comes, on that same court handed down by tradition, together with God and the community of His believers. This is a game in which all rules have been fixed in advance, never to be replaced or transformed and in which there are two kinds of stakes: an explicit one, to survive harsh judgment until next year's round, and an implicit one, to remain part of the team. The secular Jew does not really play for the first kind of stakes, for he has lost faith; he is playing in order to belong. But he can belong only according to the rules of the game. Thus, together with the religious Jew, he reaffirms every year his uncompromising differentiation from the Gentile, the source of his afflictions,[16] the nonerasable, painful presence of his desires *(Yetzer)*—the source of his sins,[17] and the presence of God in his life-world as an absolute absence.

The attempt to belong, so it seems, opens an enormous gap between the secular life-world and the ritual of repentance. In the life-world of most secular Israeli Jews, God is not absent (but signified), He is simply irrelevant (hardly has any signifiers). The *Yetzer* is cultivated, desires are welcome, and their satisfaction are intensively pursued in many sinful ways. But there remains the Gentile, blessed be he; being repeatedly negated, he maintains the necessary continuity with everyday secular life (but no more than the necessary; see below, 206 ff.) that enables the relation of the sacred ritual to the secular life-world. He thus saves the secular Jew from a complete inversion of the basic values and norms of his life-world and the ritual of repentance from becoming a carnival of secular life.

III. A Single Metanarrative

> All vows, obligations, oaths or anathemas . . . which we shall have vowed, sworn, devoted, . . . or bound ourselves to, from this day of atonement until the next day of atonement (whose arrival we hope for in happiness). . . . Blessed art thou, O Lord, the King who pardoneth and forgiveth the iniquities of his people . . . and causeth our trespasses to pass away annually. (Evening Service, 15, 29)

From a postmodern perspective, the pursuit of principles for comprehensive, everlasting forms of representations is a vanity fair. This is the case not necessarily because reality is inherently chaotic or infinitely prolific and not only because there is no final ground or procedure to judge among conflicting representations of "the same" but because representation takes part in the proliferation of the represented and in the production, as well as in the transgression, of its assumed order. Narratives take part in the formation and transformation of that which they narrate. The memory of the past is actively present in the present in an inevitable manifold of fragments; metanarratives are blueprints for syntheses of these fragments that wish, and fail, to escape the fate of the fragmentary manifold. The attempt to reconcile or decide among competing narratives always necessitates the telling of more narratives. No claim to present one unifying metanarrative that encompasses the life of mankind, or universal history, or even the life of one nation or one individual can be redeemed.

The Yom Kippur *Mahzor* assumes as self-evident the complete opposite of this postmodern theme. The text implies and gives partial expression to a diasporic *(galuti)* metanarrative that frames Jewish history, encompassing the whole of time, from the creation of the world to the messianic culmination of God's presence in history. At several moments during the ritual the text narrates decisive moments from a historical, biblical past. This past consists of a series of specific events that may but do not always yield a chronological order, from the covenant with Abraham to the destruction of the Second Temple. In common, fixed patterns, the *Mahzor* portrays a posthistorical future, God's return to Zion, and the restoration of the Kingdom of David.[18] In the posthistorical future of promised redemption, the past will be restored in some undecided sense (political? spiritual?) of restoration.

But these two temporal axes are but background to a continuous diasporic present. This present is enclosed in a cyclic pattern of cosmic temporality that robs it of all historicity and annihilates—retroactively and in advance—any possible effect of human action on the course of affairs. This ahistorical present stretches from the destruction through the present moment of enunciation (in the prayer or otherwise) and further into the entire foreseeable future.

To this threefold temporality there roughly corresponds a triple classification of sins. In the first group of sins (mentioned only once in the text, in the *Musaph* service) there are sins that are considered to be the origin and cause of exile (291; Goldschmidt 1970, 766). Another cluster of sins consists of those reproduced in each generation and that, together with their accompanying afflictions, are the very essence of exile (those are mentioned ad nauseam). In this group some sins are privileged: they postpone redemption and prevent the end of exile.[19] In any case, the exilic mode of existence is not represented as a special, "abnormal" historical condition but a metaphysical one, not merely something that happens in time, but rather that which gives time its form, investing all meaning in a remote past and an even further remote future and emptying the present of meaning in the meantime.

Whatever the details of such a diasporic metanarrative are, it is immediately called into question by both kinds of modernist readings. The modernist may cast doubt on the historical rupture that runs through this metanarrative—before and after the Temple's destruction—and question the undifferentiated present lasting ever since. These two points, however, are but two aspects of the same fault: lack of historicity. The modernist rejects the notion of a cyclical, repetitious present upon which the diasporic metanarrative is based and calls for an alternative metanarrative that gives a historical account of the continuous existence of the Nation, against all odds, and for the conditions of its exile.

Modernists do not differ in their search for an alternative metanarrative, only in the kind of alternatives they propose. The first intrinsic modernist readings must work within the main tenets of Jewish religion and, at most, transform the basic structure of the diasporic metanarrative.[20] Free of religious tenets, the second extrinsic modernist readings may try to include the diasporic metanarrative as an expression of diasporic conditions of existence, or, perhaps, even as a factor in their reproduction. But in any case, this diasporic narrative is seen as a phenomenon to be accounted for in the framework of an alternative metanarrative. However, the wide differences between these two positions need not occupy us any further in this context, for it is their basic similarity—the fact that they both presuppose an alternative metanarrative—that is crucial in the present discussion. Most important among these metanarratives, in the Israeli context at least, is the Zionist one, which has, as is well known, both intrinsic (religious) and extrinsic (secular) forms.

From a modernist point of view, Jewish history must be conceived historically, that is, as the story of a single entity, the Jewish People, that has emerged at a certain historical moment, and later evolved and developed gradually through time, revealing different, changing aspects of its "nature" in different times and places and due to changing historical circumstances, yet maintaining a solid continuity of some primordial element: "spirit," "faith," "culture," or "fate." "Diaspora" is the general term for these changing historical circumstances, and the modernist metanarrative must pretend that they too have maintained a basic unity and continuity. It must also frame the explanations for the fact that the Nation has survived all challenges to it and that in this century, at the eve of its almost total destruction, it chose the route of political emancipation.

Of course, one does not read all this directly into or out of the *Mahzor*; but if one holds a modernist position, this is what frames one's reading of the text. The way biblical stories are mentioned thus becomes a pretext for the main plot, the relation between God and his people in exile.[21] Redemption becomes a telos of the historical process, a false one according to the extrinsic reading, or a real one to be achieved with some help from the faithful pioneers of Jewish history, according to the intrinsic reading.[22] And most importantly, the cycle of sins and repentance is reincorporated into the history of the Nation. It is presented either as that which has produced false consciousness and obscured the way for Jewish political emancipation,[23] or as that which, because still unbalanced, prevents the realization of the telos of Jewish history.[24]

A postmodern reader does not believe in metanarratives. In contrast to the attempt to see various expressions of the state of the Nation in various moments of its history in the *Mahzor*, she looks there for the textual means that create the Jewish diasporic metanarrative and stabilize its temporal organization. Without begging the question of the role of these textual means in the preservation of a diasporic "mentality" or the formation of a modern Israeli one, she may seek to understand them as a factor that is still shaping Jewish forms of diasporic existence. In particular, she may look for the possibilities these textual strategies have opened since they have become a main scene for interaction and cooperation between secular and religious Jews.

First, it must be noted that the unfolding of the history of the Nation and the formation of the ritual's temporality take place in the course of intense negotiation. On the one side stands—or is posited—the divine partner who creates the opportunity. In an attempt to restore a cosmic equilibrium repeatedly violated, He offers the sinners—each individual and the entire Nation—a mechanism of self-purging and confession: for He *"desire[s] not the death of the sinner, but that he return from his evil way and live"* (337). On the other side stand the worshippers; they try to join the process of repair in relatively comfortable conditions and propose the terms of the deal: *"And the sins that I have committed against thee, blot out through thy mercy, but not by means of severe bodily sufferings and malignant diseases*" (39). These terms are repeated several times during the holy day and later the Almighty is even pressed to act accordingly: *"O Lord, we have done what you dictated to us, you too do with us what you have promised"* (347).

What this positioning of the two partners establishes, in fact, is an annual (cyclic) rhythm of sin and repentance (as the opening *Kol Nidrei* clearly expresses it: *"From this day of atonement until the next day of atonement"*). But the annual rhythm is also a rhythm of annulment. As sins meet their judgment, destined to be punished or forgiven, they are erased from divine memory. And after the last service, *Neilla*, a new list of sins to be confessed next year is opened at once. Through all of the years the individual and the community can become neither more sinful nor purer. There are no means for comparison; all social or historical differentiations that might have been relevant (for example, that this generation is inferior to the one before it, or that the sins of a particular section in the community are greater than those of other sections) are removed in advance: accumulation, progress, or decline are out of the question.

The worshipper makes his confession and awaits his forgiveness this year exactly as he did last year and will in the next. Atonement, so it seems, is designed to ensure peaceful coexistence between a fragile creature with a propensity to sin and his perfect Creator, who has made everything in wisdom—the evil impulse, the disaster of the destruction of the Temple, and the distress of exile included. The worshipper asks his Creator to forgive him for being driven too often by that evil impulse and calls upon Him to put an end to the shame of destruction and the suffering of exile. But, in fact, he makes it known that he is guilty, no matter what, and therefore unworthy of redemption, and also that he still has faith in that God who has made his situation so miserable. He expresses this faith, or simply consoles himself, through the story of redemption in some unforeseeable future. Then, at the end of the day, everything returns peacefully to its place, the shofar is blown, everyone says, with relief and new hope, "Next year in Jerusalem," and they all run home to revive their hungry bodies.

Between that present moment of temporary relief and the unforeseeable future of final redemption, a foreseen future has been anticipated, of next-year prayer, when the ritual will be repeated. This future is not posthistorical but ahistorical, a repetitious present or a future of repetitions, and not only of the same ritual but also a repetition of the same kind of relations between the individual and his God, between God and His Nation, and between the Nation and any of its members, a repetition of the same kinds of behaviors, sins, and repentance and the same kind of withdrawal from action in history (more adequately, withdrawal from giving an account for such acting). The confession, the repentance, the whole ritual of atonement, was not designed to diminish sin, let alone to eradicate it or change the conditions generating it. If there is a narrative here, a plot, a drama, it does not lie in the seemingly volatile relations between God and his worshippers, for on this scene everything is foretold and no authority is given. The diasporic metanarrative preempts any attempt to speak about the life of individuals, the community of worshippers, or the Nation as a whole in the language of the drama or of historical narrative.

Despite the obvious fact that sin relates to action, and diverse, detailed tables of sinful actions are represented repeatedly,[25] the ritual (in sharp distinction from the Catholic confession) does not refer to any particular—past or future—act of the individual or the community. Sins are actually inevitable, because *"no living creature can be just in thy presence"* (53), and one need not look for any particular act to determine their source. Human action seems but a dull decor in the ritual of atonement that clearly divides the sphere of action in two: divine acts that determine the fate of humans, human acts that hardly affect anything but divine judgment. The ritual is persistently arranged so as to neutralize, in advance, any attempt to act in history or even to conceive of sin, evil, and suffering in terms of actual social reality and its possible transformation.

However, the cycle of sin and repentance is not a nonmediated relation between the sinner and his God but a mediated one, the mediator being the People of Israel.[26] Being a member of the Nation means having a special spectrum of sins, options of repentance, and chances for being forgiven that no gentile has. The cycle of sins and repentance is incorporated into the history of the Nation and it functions there as that which bends the axis of time and forces it to go in circles, with neither memory nor progress, except for preexilic memories and postexilic hopes.

Sin and exile seem perpetually linked: *"We have acted wickedly, and have transgressed, we, therefore, have not been relieved"* (63). But only at a few, quite exceptional points does the *Mahzor* state this explicitly: *"Because of our sins we have been exiled from our native country"* (291; Goldschmidt 1970, 766). Sins come first; they

are exile's moving cause, what gives it substance and form, what
defers its coming to its end. Whereas the Nation mediates between
the sinner and his God, sins mediate between the individual and the
Nation. Sinning individuals keep the Nation in exile and preserve
exile as the mode of existence of the Nation. At the same time, a
Nation in exile is the framework of and scene for the perpetual sins
of individuals.

Sins come first and yet no sin is original. Sins originate in
individuals, they belong to them by right; responsibility for sinning
is never transferred to an Other, another time, place, or cause: *"We
are not shameless of face . . . to declare that we are righteous . . . we
have sinned. We have trespassed, we have dealt treacherously, we
have . . ."* (33). In contrast to the original sin of Christianity, which
preceded human history and constituted its very possibility, the
principal form of the original Israelite sin is fixed within history and
accompanied the Nation from the exodus from Egypt until the
destruction of the Temple. Before that destruction, in historical
past, sin had a history of its own—the Golden Calf, Korah, Achan,
Bathsheba on the roof, Naboth's vineyard—each sin with its unique
character and its crisis and tragedy, its price and moral. But of this
history there is no mention in the *Mahzor*. Instead there is a short
list, not really a history but a chronicle, of events in which God
answered famous pious men in trouble. This list is revealing for its
acute historical sensibility: it runs from Abraham on Mount Moria
to Ezra in exile, with whom historical time ends and the long
ahistorical present begins. As the list concludes: *"May he who
answered the virtuous, pious, perfect, and upright, answer us"* (73).
No particular events are recorded any longer, let alone their sequence, only their general kinds. There is no longer any connection
between particular acts (sins or supplications) and their consequences (punishment or relief), only a general, continuous punishment: exile forever accompanied with the never-ending murmur of
its supplication.

Both sin and salvation are subsumed under the most general
pattern of the Jewish metanarrative, summarized in a common
formula that is not unique to Yom Kippur alone: *"Thou have chosen
us of all people . . . and brought us near . . . unto thy service"* (27).
The addition to the *Musaph* prayer makes explicit what the formulation in the rest of the prayers implies: *"But because of our sins, we
have been exiled from our native country and removed from our land"*

(291). Framed with a diasporic narrative, individual sins are shaped as contingent but anticipated expressions of the national sin.

The history of the nation in exile is a monolithic block of time that contains only two fundamental situations that frequently alternate with each other: persecution and salvation. There is no generation in which one cannot say, with a sense of self-recognition: *"I will give vent to my soul, and recite how the presumptuous have eagerly swallowed us up; for in the reign of a certain Emperor, no remedy was found"* (383); there is no generation about which one cannot say *"for we have strayed from thee, we have erred from thy precepts"* (383); and there is no generation for which one cannot wish for the day when *"all manners of wickedness vanish as smoke, when though shall remove the dominion of wickedness from the earth"* (27). The individual bewails the general disaster, confesses the sins of the whole community, and reaffirms, on every Yom Kippur, the most basic pattern of the Nation's history.

This is a very flexible metanarrative indeed. Precisely because it is indifferent to action in history—it does not record any particular postbiblical event and erases the memory of outstanding individuals—it opens the way to a myriad of approaches to history for both the individual and the collective. The dehistoricization of action and the deconstruction of particular and individual cases of sin and punishment make drama and history irrelevant for rc[27] behavior, for the purity and purification of everyday life. By the same token it makes rc behavior, sin, and punishment irrelevant for action in history. Therefore, the modernist metanarratives alluded to above are not so much competitors of and substitutes for the diasporic one, but possible options contained within it (toward which it is equally indifferent). The ultra-orthodox objections to Jewish action in history come from elsewhere, they have no roots at the Yom Kippur ritual and its accompanying literature, and they find no support in its temporality. Whether one works for a messianic redemption or for more earthly, political forms of relief from suffering, one is placed outside the cycle of sins and repentance. The ritual bears very little on the world of everyday practice, of politics and social action, no matter what position one holds. It is precisely for this reason that secular and religious Jews can overcome their differences in the framework of the ritual and share, with ease, the open structure of its metanarrative.

IV. The Status of the Individual

On the authority of the Makom and on the authority of the commu-
nity [Kahal], in heavenly gathering and in earthly gartering, we
hereby permit to pray with the delinquents. (Beginning of Evening
Service, 15)

We have trespassed, we have dealt treacherously, we have stolen, we
have spoken slander. . . . For the sin which we have committed
against thee, either by compulsion or voluntarily, and for the sin
which we have committed before thee with a stubborn heart . . . and
for the sin which we have committed . . . and for the sin which we
. . . and for the sin. (Standard prayer in all services; e.g., 33)

Postmodern discourses deconstruct the subject. The subject is not
the origin of its unity and identity; these are never stable and
always in need of being recaptured and reasserted. Subjectivity is
not a structure that can ground judgments of any sort, be they
cognitive, moral, aesthetic, or, least of all, personal-introspective.
Subjectivization, not subjectivity, is what is at stake in the way a
historically determined culture and society shapes individuals. To
be a subject means to *occupy* or *hold* a pregiven position in a
discourse, a cultural field, a social system. To be a subject means to
be caught in an intricate, fluid field of power relations and to be
always in need of taking certain positions with respect to these
relations. Like the "emissary of the community,"[28] the postmodern
individual is "poor in deeds": she may excel or fail in her performance, but she is neither the proper author nor the proper end of
the deeds she would like to claim her own as well as those ascribed
to her by others.

Anachronistic as it may sound, the subject is indeed deconstructed in the Yom Kippur ritual (perhaps in Jewish liturgy in
general). Most of the confessions are written in the first person
plural. The worshipper does not stand alone opposite his Creator or
opposite his impulses, limitations, fragility, sins. Like the entire
prayer, the confession, too, is a collective one. There is no correspondence between the individual's deeds and the nature of his repentance. The confession, the forgiveness, and the atonement are
arranged in a fixed format: private sin is always already part of the
condition of the collective. The worshipper faces his God through
the mediation of the entire nation or in its name and always as its
member. As the directions of the popular commentator on Jewish

liturgy, Eliyahu Kitov, suggest, the penitent "should say the entire text of the confession without skipping even those sins that he knows in the depth of his heart that he never committed. For all Israel are accountable/responsible [*arevim*] for each other" (Kitov 1972, I, 53). Even "the emissary of the community" who stands in front of the Ark is not really individuated; any male with a clear voice who knows the melodies can become the emissary [*Shliach Tzibur*] and sing the hymns that are written for him in advance.

God, Lord of all Deeds, is the only subject in the full sense of the word. Except that His subjectivity is a projection of the religious discourse that, in this ritual at least, constitutes God as the eternal addressee whose own words are always anticipated, uttered, and reiterated by others, the worshippers. About themselves, the worshippers admit that they are "lacking in deeds."[29] The emissary of the community opens his prayer before the additional service with a complete abnegation of his selfhood: *"Here I am the poor in deeds"* (Goldschmidt 1970, 325). In the final analysis, no deed can originate with the individual. This is a problematic statement, for the notion of repentance requires that individuals would be the authors of their sins. Forgiveness presupposes responsibility, intention, choice, and resolute decision—in short, personal sovereignty and autonomy of some kind. But such moments of subjectivity are excluded from the regular order of the ritual or relegated to some prayers that precede it.[30]

One of these prayers is *Tffila Zakka* (pure prayer), composed in Hungary in the eighteenth century. Though not very popular anymore, it is still said in some communities before *Kol Nidrei* "with wailing and with great intending." It deals with the sovereign subject as if it were a kind of necessary nuisance that one cannot manage with and cannot manage without. One cannot do without choice between good and evil, otherwise the whole notion of providence would collapse; but one cannot bear the consequences of this choice, for the evil impulse is so tempting and the reasoned will so weak. So instead of taking direct responsibility for his sins, the worshipper asks for the permission to take responsibility for the holiness of the day and for its five kinds of tortures that would purify him of his mistaken choices. The confessor thus acknowledges individual responsibility and at the same time rids himself of it. And even before the prayer is halfway done the plural voice takes over from the language of the first person singular: *"And we knew that we are committed to suffer the tortures . . . and torment our body"* (H33). The Zakeh is but a tuning of an instrument.[31] From here on only the entire orchestra is heard: *"And it shall be forgiven to the whole congregation of the children of Israel, and to the stranger who sojourneth among them; for all the people act ignorantly"* (15).

From the outset, the authority of the community *("daat ha'kahal")* presides over the individual and allots him a range of possible actions and attitudes. The individual is not totally exempt from a private confrontation with his sins, but this privacy has a limited force, which originates in the public sphere *(rshut harabim)*, and a limited, defined time before and outside the official prayer. When sin has been driven out of the individual's private sphere, the entire world of practice has become a public matter: the extent of the various practices is prescribed by the law (that endlessly extensive network of precepts and prescriptions) and the ultimate end of these practices is eternally fixed by the spiritual survival of the Nation and its redemption at the end of time. Private experience and instrumental reason have no place in this religious public sphere. These two outcasts, privacy and instrumental reason, will continue to play side by side in close affinity: there will be no privacy other than that which has been exteriorized in everyday instrumental actions and there will be no social actions that have any value or significance except for a transient, private meaning for those involved in them. Above all, the individual cannot construct his image and identity out of the splendor of his deeds, even if these are pure and innocent, nor can the world of practice be measured according to the splendor or innocence of those who take part in it.

The prayer constitutes for each (adult male) individual in the community the same position of a participant-performer. There is no mechanism for expressing private feeling, not even for making social distinctions according to moral or religious standards. Yet the individual's private sphere, his existential experience and social distinctiveness, is not eliminated; it is ignored. The individual is thus allowed to keep his privacy uninjured, for the prayer neither calls it by name nor gives it any existence in the official language of religious discourse. With the blowing of the shofar after the *Neilah* prayer, the individual remains within his own realm exactly as he was at the beginning of *Kol Nidrei*—desiring, dreaming, and suffering, devoid of meaning. Any attempt by a particularly impudent privacy to overrun its bounds is stifled at its inception; and, vice versa, no attempt is made to reshape the private realm. Prayer, like Wittgenstein's philosophy, leaves everything as it is.

The first person singular has not been entirely erased from the *Mahzor*, but in what remains of it there is nothing to attest to the traces of the individual as a subject or to offer him a crevice through which he might save a lost "authenticity." On the contrary, the use of the singular is part of the mechanism that negates the individuality of the individual worshipper. In the section that closes the silent prayer *(Amidah)*, after the confession, "We have sinned," in which all the kinds of sins have been mentioned and classified, the worshipper says, *"O My God, before I was formed, I was unworthy, and now that I have been formed I am as though I have not been formed"* (39). By this he accepts the fact of his nullification in the face of his Creator and reaffirms the equality, in principle, of all worshippers, each one of whom is nothing but *"dust in [his] lifetime, how much more at [his] decease, a vessel full of shame and disgrace"* (39). And in the same breath he asks to be given atonement without too much *"bodily sufferings and malignant diseases"* (39). Of the entire process of repentance, only the anticipated suffering obliges a shift to the singular. Even this suffering, however, is apprehended in its universal dimension only, as future suffering that equally threatens every single individual.[32]

The most distinctive use of the first person singular is found in the *Musaph* service, in the words of the High Priest in the Temple at the moment of his entrance into the Holy of Holies: *"O God! I now acknowledge that I have sinned. I have committed iniquity; I have transgressed against thee; even I and my household"* (359). There is a distant echo here of the special emotional state of the individual standing before his Creator and of the experience that happened, in Maimonides' words, "at the height of the day." The text becomes intense, highly poetic, sensual, openly celebrating appearances *("how glorious was the appearance of the high priest when he came forth safe from the holy sanctuary"* [367]). But then too, we must recall, the priest was the only one who confessed; the entire nation looked on from afar and he alone, stripped of his privacy, in a well-staged moment of the ceremony at the Temple, embodied the way the nation stands before its God.[33] The *Mahzor* reconstructs that moment in several passages that break the continuity of the *piyyutim* and attest to the distance between worship at the Temple and in the synagogue, between sovereignty and exile, and between the biblical ritual as a mechanism of social distinction and social hierarchy and the diasporic ritual with its tendency to level hierarchies and erase social differences.

At this point, the critique of ideology might emphasize the substitution of a national subject for an authentic individual one. It might point to a double process of projection of individual sin and punishment onto the nation and of the moment of individual choice onto God. This type of external reading might seek to disclose the illusion of repression and fraud involved in shifting the focus of responsibility for the sin from the individual to the collective. It would stress the manner in which the language of the prayer gives expression to the identity and unity of the collective subject.

The ideology of the prayer, on the other hand, might try to balance the effects of deindividuation and deprivatization by presenting the existential force of the prayer and the resultant act of repentance. It might seek to restore an irreducible status to the individual and to make the success of the entire process of repentance dependent on his inner, most private *kavanah* (intention). The text may tolerate this extrapolation, as much as it can bear the extrapolation of an extrinsic, "psychologized" reading. In the first case, one's *kavanah* is taken seriously, as an authentic expression of an inner self; in the second, it is interpreted as an expression, a symptom, of a deluded self, of the work of false consciousness. But in both cases the individual is assumed to be an active agent who controls, to a certain extent at least, the meaning of the ritual, and this assumption is maintained without any evidence on the surface of the text or the course of the ritual. Which is to say, the individual, as a source or a victim, is interpreted as a hidden, "deep" structure of the religious phenomenon and his subjectivity is constructed without adequate textual evidence.

Free of that supposedly inner depth that the text expresses and activates, a postmodern reading of the same sections looks at the same textual practices not as expressions of subjectivity but as a mechanism for its construction and deconstruction. Such a reading seeks to articulate a network of connections and differences between the various occurrences of the first person singular in the *Mahzor* and the plural language generally adopted by it and considers the effects of these connections and differences. The analysis of the worshipper's position presented above is a partial example of such an approach.

The subject, both the private and the national one, is grasped not as the foundation of liturgic discourse but as its construct, a position defined from within the liturgy. In the *Mahzor*, this position is produced by the systematic "we," the pole around which the entire text is woven. The addressor designated by this "we" is never the source of the speech that flows from him, but always only a performer of a text that was there before him. This text is an aggregate of quotations, where quotations of quotations are heaped up on top of one another and interlaced within one another, lacking a clear source, or any trace for the context of composition. Everything there has always already been said more than once, in other times and places, by different speakers to different addressees, but now all these phrases are gathered and directed to one pole, to the absolute addressee of the discourse. The position of the subject-speaker is defined by the mode of presence of this absent addressee and by the mode of intentionality toward Him. The *Mahzor* contains instructions for performing discourse in the absence of a source and in the presence of an absent addressee.

Postmodern reading thus reveals here—in clear opposition to what the ideology of the prayer wishes to praise and its critique wishes to dismiss—a game of gestures and positionings free of any authorial presence. The absence of both source and addressee liberates the ritual from any fixed authority and opens before the individual speaker a horizon of nonhierarchical relations with all other worshippers, those co-present at the site, or performing the ritual in other sites at the same time, but also all those who have performed the ritual in the past.[34] The worshipper's relation with the collective is unmediated, and the collective itself is unbounded by spatio-temporal boundaries. A national subject and a way to take part in it emerge here, and they are both concrete in the infinity of their expressions, but abstract in their conceptualization.

In the *Mahzorim* that were prevalent in Eastern Europe and are still widely used in many ultra-orthodox congregations in the United States and in Israel, there appear some additional prayers and hymns (some of them only in Yiddish) in which the singular is used consistently and without reservations.[35] Yiddish is a channel by which the worshipper can relate an alienated, sublime, and ornate rhetoric to his everyday life, the privacy of his experiences, and, ultimately, to his actual sins. But this is a one-way channel. Yiddish, the *"mame loshen"* (mother-tongue) and language of everyday life, allows the individual to come to terms with the intellectual expectations of the prayer at his own level of understanding, but not to take full part in it. Yiddish creates a special route of prayer for people with "linguistic handicap," dividing the prayer into two levels of performance, one more private, the other wholly public, but also one more historically embedded and dependent, the other disembodied and historically independent.

This distinction only emphasizes the disparity between text and performance, between the text as a sacred source that is beyond time and place, and a performance that is dependent on a profane context and dictated by the limitations of a particular congregation of worshippers. Ultimately, the limitations of performance derive from the arbitrary and accidental everyday world, and they give expression to differences between different congregations within the ahistorical totality of the nation—a totality that erases all differences. The connection that Yiddish creates between the sacred and the profane and between the ahistorical and the historical marks a boundary between the two realms, but at the same time makes possible a certain coexistence between them. The linguistic disparity is a disparity between an earthly world in which the individual can actualize both his existence as a separate person and his affiliation to a concrete community and a world in which the ahistorical idea of the nation exists and provides the individual with both the basis of his affiliation to the whole and the meaning of his existence. In both cases, the presence of the Yiddish beside the Hebrew makes possible a hierarchical coexistence of the sacred with the profane and of the collective with the individual.

On the face of it, the hierarchical difference between the languages protects the sanctity of the ritual and the purity of the prayer. In fact, it protects the life-world and its experiences from the incursion of the sacred dimension. The differentiation in the modes of performance preserves the experience of *tshuva*, of repair and conversion, which the ritual shapes, from bursting uncontrollably beyond the bounds of the Holy Day and instigating an unbridled process of conversion in everyday life. But this differentiation also makes it possible to channel something from the sacred into the profane world.[36]

When Hebrew is both the profane language and the sacred language,[37] the barriers are removed, eliminating the hierarchy, reducing the distance between text and performance, between sacred and profane, and between the sense of privacy and the sense of belonging to the collective. Orthodox and secular Jews tend to react to this in different ways. On the one hand, among the Orthodox there is an expansion of the sacred into the distinctly profane realms, and the institution of *tshuva*[38] has begun to flourish in many contexts beyond that of the High Holidays. On the other hand, in the absence of faith, the secular Jew, even when he is a "traditionalist," is not a partner to the fundamentally religious intentionality that turns the ritual into a ceremony of conversion. In the absence of mechanisms of mediation between the sacred and the profane, more and more parts and aspects of the ritual are becoming obscure to him. He thus remains alienated from the "deep meanings" of his prayer, whatever these may be. He plays the ritual and he plays with the text; he follows some of the rules, more or less mechanically, and evades other rules. But he still plays on the same court with the Orthodox worshipper, and he accepts in fact, unknowingly or clear-mindedly and gladly, the slide of the sacred into the profane world. Indirectly he collaborates with the increasing process of colonization of the life-world and of the private realm by a transcendental collective, that same collective that pretends to bridge the gap between the individual who has no deeds and the Sovereign of All Deeds.

For the religious Jew, the ritual of repentance starts long before the Day of Atonement. *Slichot,* penitential prayers, are said through the month of Elul preceding Yom Kippur, during the two days of prayer of Rosh Hashanah, and throughout the week of the "ten days of repentance." On Yom Kippur eve itself the religious Jew comes to the synagogue after a whole day of preparation and sanctification that includes a private ritual of confession in the afternoon or after the meal. For him repentance is clearly a kind of work, in the psychoanalytical sense, in which his entire personality is involved. When the ritual finally erases most traces of individuality and molds the many singular voices into the singular voice of the nation of Israel, the individual is prepared and ready for the transforming experience. Not so with the secular Jew.

The secular Jew comes to the synagogue right after the meal, which is an event in itself, usually a delight for the senses and a very earthly pleasure. He may have spent Rosh Hashanah on the beach (the lake of Galilee is especially popular at that time) and has not changed his routine of life during the following week, except perhaps for some additional shopping in packed stores. For him, Yom Kippur can never function as a rite of passage and when he comes to the synagogue he can hardly understand the ritual as a possible rite of passage for others. He is usually quite ignorant of most of the context of the ritual as experienced by the religious Jew.

He participates in it in a very selective way, yet this selection is quite brutal, an outcome of neglect, ignorance, and cultural distance; it is not deliberate and it is executed with little awareness. The secular Jew who comes to the synagogue on Yom Kippur, to the extent that he uses the *Mahzor* at all, is left with the skeleton of the ritual, devoid of those mechanisms—textual and social—that balance or resist the forces of dehistoricization and collectivization and compensate for the process of deindividuation that the worshipper undergoes during the ritual.

The secular Jew is welcome into an extremely flexible text that contains no prerequisites for participation in the ritual it sustains. Relatively easily he is drawn into the world of the exilic, powerless Jew, for whom the present resembles the past. This congregation of believers resembles any other and all sinners resemble each other. Relatively easily he is *mitmaser* to the forces of collectivization and dehistoricization. He has come there in the first place because he wants to belong and partnership is what he gets. It is a partnership in an ideal, idealized community, whose locality and historicity—the power relations that pervade it and the desires that motivate it—have all been effaced, or blurred, or brought to a common, undifferentiated denominator. The more one belongs to this community, the less one can be aware or give an account of the real forms of partnership(s) maintained within the concrete religious community and the real relations between this community and other communities and other social structures, from the state to the family, and from the Jewish to the non-Jewish population. The distinction between the ideal and the real here is not metaphysical; it is a socially and culturally embodied distinction between the world of the synagogue and everything that takes place outside of its spatial domain and the sacred time demarcated by the religious ritual. For the secular Jew this distinction is quite clearcut. In other words, for the secular Jew, the *Mahzor* is an ideological text, pure and simple, in the old, good Marxist sense of the term. But it takes a post-Marxist, poststructuralist, postmodern reading and analysis to realize this.

NOTES

I am indebted to Shlomo Fischer, Amos Funkenstein, and Amnon Raz-Krakotzkin, who read earlier versions of this paper and gave me invaluable comments. When writing the final version, I benefited from the generous support of the Shalom Hartmann Institute in Jerusalem and from helpful conversations with members of the seminar on prayer held there during 1993–94.

1. In the last decade there has been a remarkable change in patterns of behavior of secular Israelis during Yom Kippur, especially in highly secularized areas like downtown Tel Aviv and some of the city's more affluent suburbs. More people in more places dare to drive their cars during the Holy Day, fewer people visit the synagogue, and if they do they stay there for shorter periods of time. Most interesting is the new habit of many to gather outdoors on Yom Kippur evening and walk along the empty streets, turning them, for one night, into a truly public space. Still, synagogues are full with worshippers for whom Yom Kippur is the only time that they visit the synagogue throughout the year. As to the central role of the Haggadah in Israeli life, see Ophir 1994.

2. And in Passover too, yet in a different form. See Ophir 1994.

3. Many social, political, and cultural phenomena in contemporary religious communities in Israel may be ascribed and interpreted as responses to modernization and accelerated secularization of the Israeli-Jewish environment. See, e.g., Eisenstadt 1985; Fischer 1991 and forthcoming.

4. Apart from the theoretical objections to the idea of "the text," the mere diversity of versions among the various communities and their transformations along the years do not permit one to deal with the *Mahzor* as a single text; at most the *Mahzor* is a family, or rather a tribe, of texts, the reconstruction of whose genealogy can be only partially accomplished. For such a reconstruction, cf. Elbogen 1972, 24, 33; Goldschmidt 1970. Nevertheless, in what follows I hardly refer to any textual modification or transformation and concentrate mainly on the more or less fixed liturgic structures and on those passages that appear in most versions of the *Mahzor* in use today in Israeli synagogues. Therefore, I keep referring to the *Mahzor* conveniently and inaccurately as "a text."

5. Three sections appear below; the three others deal with the representation of divine judgment, the representation of power, and the semiotics of sin in the *Mahzor*. The unpublished sections roughly correspond to three main presuppositions of postmodern discourse: there is no final grounding for cognitive, ethical, and aesthetic judgments; discourse is a scene of rivalry and competition and is always pervaded by power relations; what matters in discourse is not the meaning of the signified but the play of the signifier. An earlier version of these fragments appeared in Hebrew (Ophir 1991).

6. No attempt is made here to give an exhaustive description of a "post-

modern point of view"; neither the possibility of such a description nor the unity of that point of view are presupposed. And yet the tenets or themes used here as points of departure and perspectives of interpretation are characteristically postmodern.

7. More generally, and more accurately, an "extrinsic" reading takes discursive and nondiscursive religious practices as its object, without ever holding a position in a religious discourse or becoming a participant in a religious language game. An "intrinsic" reading engages itself with the interpretation and critique of religious practices from within a certain religious discourse and takes seriously the validity claims of such discourse, seeking to reaffirm or refute them with reasons. I am speaking here about two kinds of approaches, without any claim to do justice to the enormous bodies of literature that embody, qualify, and differentiate them. Extrinsic critique of Jewish religious discourse may be traced back to the writers of the Haskalah. Max Nordau and Yoseph Haim Brenner are two of the most prominent critics in the earlier years of the Zionist movement (e.g., Nordau 1936, vol. 2; Brenner 1985a; cf. Cnaani 1976, 36–55, 71–81). A contemporary critic is Boaz Evron (1988, 21–127). It is worth noting that the critique of religion is a marginal issue in contemporary Israeli public life; its place has been taken long ago by political criticism of the policies of the religious parties. As for a contemporary, modern, intrinsic reading of Jewish religious discourse, see Leibovitch 1979; Hartman 1985. Levinas or Soloveitchik may supply more prominent examples for intrinsic reading, perhaps, but I have mainly the former thinkers in mind, for they have a much wider Hebrew readership.

8. I am writing under the influence of Wittgenstein's later philosophy of language (especially as developed by Lyotard 1988), the Foucauldian conception of discourse (especially Foucault 1972, 1981), and more generally the philosophical "mood" known as deconstructionism, but I am not following or applying any of these systematically.

9. Most references to the *Mahzor* are to the *Form of Prayers for the Day of Atonement* (no date). A few passages are translated from Goldschmidt's critical edition (1970) or from a popular Hebrew edition, *Mahzor Knesset Israel* (Jerusalem: Eshkol, n.d.). References to this text are marked with "H."

10. Medieval negative theology is "modern," at least in the sense that it limits what can be said and claimed to be known about the divine Being in rational discourse. For a consistent and more radical Israeli version of negative theology that follows Leibovitch, see Kasher 1977.

11. As the long tradition of negative theology has made clear, God cannot become a referent for "rational" discourse without running into difficulties of predicating an unbounded, unlimited being, which is actually not "a being" but Being-itself (e.g., Tillich 1951, vol. 1, 237). However, whatever the theological difficulties, in the language of the ritual God

is clearly posited as a referent, and repeatedly so. Conceived as a referent of a believer's or an atheist's utterance, God's existence must be one of His predicates, a necessary one. God is not a Centaur, or Kant's coin, that may or may not exist, without affecting the meaning of all other phrases that refer to Him. Existence is part of what Heschel calls "the minimum of meaning" of God (Heschel 1955, 125–28; cf. Adams 1987, chaps. 13, 14; Alston 1989, chap. 5).

12. For example, the contradictions between *"He dwelleth in secret"* (183), *"hidden from all"* (210), and *"He covereth himself with light, as with a garment . . . the resplendence of his throne is radiant fire"* (197), or between a *merciful Father* whose *"garment [is] righteousness"* and *"He has girt himself around with zeal and revenge"* (183).

13. There are at least two lists of famous supplications and divine answers, a short one that includes Micha, Daniel, and Ezra (67), and a longer one that runs from Abraham on Mount Moria to Ezra in exile (71). On the latter, see below, 198.

14. Even Elisha Ben Avoia, *"Acher"* (Other), was given, according to one tradition at least, a last occasion to repent (Babylonian Talmud, *Hagiga* 15a).

15. If during the ritual there are social forces at work that undermine this integration, they cannot use the *Mahzor*; they rather circumscribe it, for no hierarchy among different ranks of worshippers is inscribed in the text or can be extracted from it.

16. This, despite the fact that in the *Mahzor* the separation between Jew and Gentile is relatively marginal and expressed almost only in the language of everyday prayer *("Thou hast chosen us from all people")*. The blurring of the separation between Jew and Gentile is expressed most typically in *Maftir Jonah*, the Book of Jonah, read in the afternoon service. God, so the Book ends, has pity even on a corrupted Gentile city like Ninevah, whose dwellers "cannot discern between their right hand and their left hand." The universal moment, however, is immediately placed in a proper particularized context, in the way the *Maftir* is concluded and its lesson is drawn. An appeal is made to God to pardon his people, for as everyone has just learned, He is known as One *"who keepeth not his anger forever"* (411).

    Some hymns included in older versions of the prayer, which emphasize the separation and call upon God to take revenge on the Gentiles, were mostly excluded in recent times and are hardly ever sung. Thus, for example, there is the hymn of the morning service in the Ashkenazic version *"Mi Lo Yiraacha Melech Ha'goyym"* (Who does not fear you, King of Nations) that presents a series of differences between Israel and the Gentiles in a simple form of opposition and uses the same form to call for divine revenge (Goldschmidt 1970, 186–201). Another example is a hymn from the Additional Service, *"Adonai Melech avdo Goyym / bala batei goyym"* (God has reigned as a king, the gentiles have perished/He swallowed gentiles' houses) (380–81). See also Goldschmidt 1978, 363–68.

17. In some hymns and prayers, e.g., in the prayer *Zakka* that precedes the Evening Service, the *Yetzer* (impulse) is presented as the "internal Other" of the practicing Jew (see below). Sometimes the soul-body opposition is expressed in an almost Platonic-Christian fashion, e.g.: *"Guf u'neshama yarivu/ze el ze ammarim yashivu"* (body and soul quarrel, answer back each other) (Goldschmidt 1970, 296–97).

18. According to one outstanding passage only, the third benediction added to the Eighteen Benedictions in the Morning Service (242).

19. One may say that sins postpone redemption and no sin is an exception to this rule. The fact remains, however, that only a few sins are mentioned explicitly in this context.

20. The most famous representative of this kind of reading in this context is that of Gush Emunim, of Rabbi Kook and his disciples. In their hands, the diasporic metanarrative has been historicized and politicized. The destruction of the Temple is still a main turning point, but now the loss of political sovereignty is foregrounded, overshadowing the loss of a whole system of religious practices. Exile has become a story of continuous heroic attempts to maintain the link between the Nation and the Land of Israel, and redemption has become the telos and coming end of a long historical process, among whose discernible stages are the main events of our time: the slaughter of European Jewry, the establishment of the State of Israel, and the "liberation" of Western Eretz-Israel in June 1967.

21. The most impressive story is that of the ritual at the Temple. It is pervaded with yearning and nostalgia, a mixture of a sense of awe and deep loss: "How glorious was the appearance of the High Priest when he came forth safe from the holy sanctuary" (367). The apotheosis of the preexilic relation between God and His people is also what best describes what is now (ever since the destruction of the Temple) absent. The loss is immediately interpreted in the following *Techinot* that continue the narrative: "But our ancestor's sins destroyed the House . . . and as a result of *our* sins we have no *Ishim* and no *Asham* [kinds of sacrifices]" (368).

22. The most prominent modern teleological interpretation of repentance (in general, not necessarily that of Yom Kippur) is that of Rav Kook (Kook 1985). For the relation between cosmic, cyclical time, repentance, and historical progress in Kook's thought, see Arieli 1980.

23. This is the main argument in the secular Zionist critique of religion. See, for example, Brenner 1985b; Sirkin 1929; Tavenkin 1972.

24. In a standard orthodox textbook on Yom Kippur, in the context of interpreting the phrase *"Al daat ha'kahal ve'al daat ha'makom"* (on the authority of the public and on the authority of God), one finds the following typical statement: "And now, that it is permitted for them

[the criminals] to pray with all of Israel, for all of them are descendants of Abrahm, Issak and Jacob, and the will of them all is to do the will of God. And who retards [the harmony between God and his nation]? Exile retards and the temptations of evil impulse" (Kitov 1972, I, 51–52). Exile is both the cause and effect of the retarded salvation, and also both the cause and effect of the prolongation of sinful behavior.

25. I have elaborated on these tables in the unpublished section of this essay on the semiotics of the *Mahzor*.

26. For the trinity individual-God-Nation in the prayer, see, e.g., Soloveit-chik 1968, 33–41. The diasporic mode of existence of the Nation gives sin and repentance their special, cyclic form. At the same time, the nation also provides a shelter against the ire of God: being part of the Nation is reassuring (the worshipper reassures himself time and again) for the promise of the covenant is always present, never to be broken, yet the fulfillment of this promise is always postponed and so can be repeatedly invoked.

27. I.e., religiously correct.

28. "Emissary of the Community" is the title given to the person who leads the prayer and recites those passages for "solo voice" to which the congregation responds.

29. In Hebrew, *ein banu maasim*. The edition I am using here renders the phrase "destitute of good works," whereas "good" is certainly an addition of the translator.

30. Ancient and recent thinkers alike have noticed this tension without necessarily resolving it. Thus, for example, Maimonides, in his "Codes of Tshuva" (1961, chap. 1:1), when talking about confession in general, emphasizes the first person singular. But he makes it clear that in Yom Kippur both confession and forgiveness are collective matters (chap. 2:7–8). Even Rav Soloveitchik follows Maimonides here, despite his characteristic existentialist sensibilities, and excludes the first person singular from the ritual of atonement. He accepts the common rule that makes a special room for a private confession in the afternoon service at the eve of the Holy Day (in Peli 1984, 97–125). And there are more simplistic explanations that take the confession in the plural voice as "but a framework fixed for those who do not know to express themselves, so they too will be able to confess" (Falk 1980, 17).

31. In the Sephardic *Mahzor* there is a parallel hymn of a different kind, *"Lecha El Teshukati"* (To you, God, my desire), that sticks to the singular language throughout. It is said to be "a kind of confession" and is sung before *Kol Nidrei* (Kitov 1972, I, 50–51). In general, I assume that a careful comparison between the Ashkenazic and Sephardic prayer books (which I have not done) will point to a greater degree of expression to the personal voice in the Sephardic *Mahzor*.

32. The next appeal to God is still in the singular, in the form common to every Amidah prayer *("My God! preserve my tongue from wicked*

calumny"), and it is transformed immediately into the second person *("O do it for the sake of thy name")* and then is sealed in the plural, in an utterance about all of Israel *("He may give peace to us and also to the whole People of Israel")* and its redemption (38).

33. In a parallel passage of the *Birkat Cohanim* (Priests' Benediction), in a section that has been omitted from the most versions of the text in Eretz-Israel, the common worshipper says: *"Sovereign of the Universe! I am thine and my dreams are thine; I have dreamt a dream, but know not what it portends"* (Goldschmidt 1970, 597). The privacy of the dream, itself a threatening locus of intimacy, is erased; its interpretation, which might have been of special significance to the individual, is something he gives up from the outset; and finally, in a last act of repression, it becomes the dream of all the people of Israel.

34. There is no trace of authorship in any of the *piyyutim.* No particular contribution to the ritual is recorded in the framework of the ritual itself, and the difference between author and performer has been erased.

35. Examples may be found in ordinary American editions of the *mahzor* with Yiddish translation and commentaries; e.g., *Mahzor Kol Bo with Hebrew Taytsch [Yiddish] Interpretation in the Name of Beit Israel.* The book contains additional prayers in Yiddish in the first singular (e.g., before *Zakeh,* "Tchina far licht baantshtein" for Yom Kippur eve [15–17]; two *tchinot* before *Kol Nidrei* [33]; "Request after the Prayer," said after the evening service [88]), as well as additional prayers in the first person singular in both Hebrew and Yiddish (e.g., a hymn sung at the end of the morning service, while taking the Torah scrolls from the arc ["Lord of the world, fulfill the requests of my heart"] [175] and a prayer during the afternoon service while taking the Torah scrolls out of the arc ["Lord of pity and forgiveness, listen to me and answer me"] [286–87]).

36. In a later section of the unpublished part of this essay, I try to show how this tension between the sublime and the everyday is elaborated so as neither to desecrate the sanctity of the former nor violate the routine of the latter.

37. This is the case in most of the communities in Israel today, except for the ultra-orthodox. But here, too, Hebrew penetrates into some realms of social reality, especially when dealing with politics and the economy. Among Sephardic ultra-orthodox Jews there is no equivalence to Yiddish.

38. *Tshuvah,* "repentance," also means "return" or "conversion" of secular Jews to Orthodoxy.

REFERENCES

Adams, Robert M. *The Virtue of Faith*. Oxford: Oxford University Press, 1987.

Alston, William P. *Divine Nature and Human Language: Essays in Philosophical Theology*. Ithaca, N.Y., and London: Cornell University Press, 1989.

Arieli, Nachum. "Tshuva in the Thought of Rav Kook." In *Hagut: An Anthology for Jewish Thought* (Hebrew) (no editor given). Jerusalem: Ministry of Education, Department of Rabbinic Culture, 1980.

Brenner, Yoseph Haim. "In Journalism and Literature" *[Ba'Ittonut u'BaSifrut: Al Hezion Ha'shmad]*. In *Ktavim*, vol. 3. Tel Aviv: Hakkibutz Hameuchad and Sifriat Hapoalim, 1985a.

———. "Self-Appraisal in the Three Volumes" *[Haarachat Azmenu Be'Sholoshet Hakrachim]*. In *Ktavim*, vol. 3, 1985b.

Cnaani, David. *The Proletarian Second Aliyah and Its Relation to Religion and Tradition* (Hebrew). Tel Aviv: Sifriat Poalim, 1976.

Don Yehiya, Eliezer. *Cooperation and Conflict between Political Parties: The Religious Community, the Labor Movement, and the Israeli Ministry of Education* (Hebrew). Dissertation thesis, Hebrew University of Jerusalem, 1978.

Eisenstadt, Shmuel Noah. *The Transformation of Israeli Society*. Boulder, Colo.: Westview, 1985.

Elbogen, Ismar. *Der jüdische Gottesdienst in seiner geschichtlichen Entwicklung*. Leipzig [1913]; Hebrew edition, Tel Aviv: Dvir, 1972.

Evron, Boaz. *A National Reckoning* (Hebrew). Tel Aviv: Dvir, 1988.

Falk, Zeev. "The Contemplative Foundations of Hilchot Tshuva." In *Hagut: An Anthology for Jewish Thought* (Hebrew) (no editor given). Jerusalem: Ministry of Education, Department of Rabbinic Culture, 1980.

Fischer, Shlomo. "Two Patterns of Modernization: On the Ethnic Problem in Israel." *Theory and Criticism* 1 (1991): 1–19.

———. "Talmudic Games: Orthodox Communities in Israel." Forthcoming.

Form of Prayers for the Day of Atonement. Rev. ed. New York: Hebrew Publishing Company, n.d.

Foucault, Michel. *The Archaeology of Knowledge*. Trans. A. M. Sheridan-Smith. New York: Pantheon, 1972. (*L'Archaeologie du savoir*. Paris: Gallimard, 1969.)

———. "The Order of Discourse." In *Untying the Text*, ed. R. Young. London: Routledge and Kegan Paul, 1981. (*L'Ordre du discurs*. Paris: Gallimard, 1971.)

Friedman, Menachem. *The Haredi (Ultra-Orthodox) Society: Sources, Trends, and Processes*. Jerusalem Institute for Israeli Studies Research Series No. 41, 1991.

Goldschmidt, Daniel. *Mahzor for Yamim Noraim (including all Ashkenazic versions), vol. 2, Yom Kippur, Proofread and Annotated* (Hebrew). New York: Leo Baeck Institute; Jerusalem: Koren, 1970.

———. *On Jewish Liturgy: Essays on Prayer and Religious Poetry.* Jerusalem: Magnes, 1978.

Gotkind-Golan, Noami. "The *'Heichal'* Cinema as a Symptom for the Relations between Religious and Secular Jews in Israel in the Eighties." In *Religious and Secular: Conflict and Accommodation between Jews in Israel* (Hebrew), ed. Charles Liebman. Jerusalem: Keter, 1990.

Hartman, David. *A Living Covenant: The Innovative Spirit in Traditional Judaism.* New York: Free Press, 1985.

Heschel, Abraham J. *God in Search of Man.* New York: Harper Torch Books, 1955.

Kasher, Asa. "Theological Shadows." In *Sefer Yeshayahu Leibovitch* (Hebrew), ed. A. Kasher and J. Levinger. Tel Aviv: Students Union, 1977.

Kitov, Eliyahu. *The Book of Consciousness.* [1963] Jerusalem: Yad Eliyahu Kitov Publishing House, 1967.

———. *Sefer Ha-Todaah.* Jerusalem: Alef, 1972.

Kook, Abraham Y. H. *Orot Ha'tshuva* [The Light of Repentance]. Jerusalem: Mosad Harav Kook, 1985.

Lawson, Thomas E., and Robert N. McCauley. *Rethinking Religion.* Cambridge: Cambridge University Press, 1990.

Leibovitch, Yeshayahu. *Judaism, Jewish People, and the State of Israel* (Hebrew). Tel Aviv: Schocken, 1979.

Levi, Amnon. *The Ultra-Orthodox* (Hebrew). Jerusalem: Keter, 1988.

Liebman, Charles S., ed. *Religious and Secular: Conflict and Accommodation between Jews in Israel* (Hebrew). Jerusalem: Keter, 1990.

Lyotard, Jean-Francois. *The Differend: Phrases in Dispute.* Trans. Georges Van Den Abbeele. Minneapolis: University of Minnesota Press, 1988.

Mahzor Knesset Israel. Jerusalem: Eshkol, n.d.

Mahzor Kol Bo with Hebrew Taytsch [Yiddish] Interpretation in the Name of Beit Israel. New York: Hebrew Publishing Company, n.d.

Maimonides. *The Code of Maimonides (Mishne Torah), The First Book: The Book of Science.* Trans. Solomon Gandz and Hyman Klein. New Haven: Yale University Press, 1961.

Nordau, Max. *Max Nordau El Amo: Ktavim Medinyym.* Vol. 2, ed. B. Netanyahu. Tel Aviv: Sifria Mdinit, 1936.

Ophir, Adi. "From Pharaoh to Saddam Hussein: Deconstructing the Passover Haggadah." In *The Other in Jewish Thought and History*, ed. Laurence Silberstein and Robert Cohn. New York: New York University Press, 1994.

———. "The Poor in Deed and Other Postmodernists." *Masa* (*Davar's* Literary Supplement), 13, 20, and 29 September 1991 (in three parts).

Oron, Yair. *Jewish-Israeli Identity* (Hebrew). Tel Aviv: Sifriat Poalim Publishing House, 1993.

Peli, Pinchas H. *Soloveitchik on Repentance: The Thought and Oral Discourse of Rabbi Joseph B. Soloveitchik.* Ramsey, N.J.: Paulist Press, 1984.

Phillips, Dewi Z. *The Concept of Prayer.* London: Routledge and Kegan Paul, 1968.

Sirkin, Nachman. "A Plea to Jewish Youth." In *The Writings of Nachman Sirkin* (Hebrew), ed. B. Katznelson and Y. Kaufman. Tel Aviv: Dvir, 1929.

Soloveitchik, Joseph B. *The Man of Faith.* Jerusalem: Mossad HaRav Kook, 1968.

Tavenkin, Izaack. "Toward a Portrait of the Labor Movement in Eretz Israel" (Hebrew). In *Dvarim.* Tel Aviv: HaKibbutz Hameuchad, 1972.

Tillich, Paul. *Systematic Theology.* Chicago: University of Chicago Press, 1951.

Pedagogy

Chapter 7

The "Torah" of Criticism
and the Criticism of Torah:
Recuperating the Pedagogical Moment

Susan Handelman

> Literature is written for the sake only of those who are in the
> process of development, and of that in each of us which is still
> developing. Hebrew, knowing no word for "reading" that does not
> mean "learning" as well, has given this, the secret of all literature
> away. For it is a secret, though a quite open one, to these times of
> ours—obsessed and suffocated as they are by education—that books
> exist only to transmit that which has been achieved to those who
> are still developing. (Rosenzweig 1965, 216)

> Over facile opinion notwithstanding, teaching is not primarily an
> intersubjective relationship between people but a cognitive process
> in which self and other are only tangentially and contiguously
> involved. The only teaching worthy of the name is scholarly, not
> personal. (de Man 1986, 4)

These statements represent two fundamentally different notions of
"literature," "teaching," and "knowing"—terms that are central for
both literary and religious studies. In Judaism especially, the notion
of "teaching" is intimately bound up with the meaning of "Text": the
very word "Torah," often mistranslated as "Law," comes from the
Hebrew root *yud, reish, hey [yarah]* and means "instruction" or
"teaching." But epistemology and hermeneutics—not pedagogy—
have been the primary loci for recent interdisciplinary work in
literature and religion. I would like in this essay, however, to begin
to recuperate for the study of "Literature and Religion," and for the

dialogue of Jewish tradition and literary theory, the notion of texts as "teachings."

The recent turn of much poststructuralist thought to politics has influenced many critics to assert that every interpretive position, every mode of knowing, rests on an implicit ideology. But we also need to ask: Doesn't every theory or account of knowing also have an implied pedagogy—which is often unconscious or covert? Could we speak, then, of a pedagogical epistemology, or of a way in which teaching talks back to theory? Or, put still another way, is teaching not only the conveying of knowledge, but itself a way of knowing in excess of whatever it conveys? And don't these questions need to be asked of the literary text as well: What does it mean to say a text "teaches us something"? Can the idea of the "literary" incorporate the notion of "teaching"? Does a text "teach" us how to teach it?

The central idea I want to try to work out here might be phrased as follows: *epistemology is itself produced out of the teaching relation*. Now, at first glance this may sound like a truism, but I mean to examine it on a deeper level—not to look at teaching or pedagogy as a set of devices, or the handmaiden to theory, but as itself a way of knowing. This is a different focus from many of the books published in the last several years that conceive the relation of literary theory to pedagogy as either ideological or pragmatic. In most of those volumes, the main issue is how to "apply" literary theory to the classroom, or open the canon, or change the curriculum. In these works epistemology precedes pedagogy, whereas I want to look at it from the reverse perspective.[1]

I. The Student/Teacher/Text Relation

There have been a few contemporary literary and cultural theorists who have looked at pedagogy epistemologically and vice versa. Among the most interesting are Pierre Bourdieu and Shoshana Felman. Bourdieu, in his *Reproduction in Education*, writes that "no one acquires a language without thereby acquiring a *relation to language*" [italics his] (1990, 116), and that "pedagogy involves the entire relation to language and culture" (127). Bordieu's analysis of pedagogy focuses on a cultural critique of the institution of learning in France, and he well demonstrates the "symbolic violence" involved in specific teaching practices. While I admire many of his insights, my purpose here is not to elaborate a sociology of knowledge, or ideology critique, or quest for the "political unconscious." Rather, my interest is in a kind of "pedagogical unconscious."

Bourdieu, however, has some very incisive words about the way teachers operate: "Teachers are themselves former model pupils who would like to have no pupils except future teachers. Teachers are predisposed by their whole training and all their education and experience to play the game of the institution" (1990, 135). The "teacher," moreover, "is able to maintain within his own discourse, his pupil's discourse, and his pupil's relation to his own discourse" (126). Bordieu means this in a negative sense—the teacher's discourse limits and constrains even as it constructs the student's discourse. Yet it seems to me that there is an additional lesson here, that the common characterization of the interpretive process as something that occurs between a "reader" and a "text" is inadequate. This notion of a dialogue, or the duality of text and reader, comes out of a tradition of epistemology that considers knowledge to be a bilateral relation between a subject and an object. If the relation of the student to the teacher is also the relation to language and culture itself, then *the "subject position" of the "student" is not equivalent or reducible to that of the "reader."* (Perhaps Wolfgang Iser's idea of an "implied reader" needs to be revised to incorporate the notion of the "implied student.")

If we ask about the teaching relation, the model would need to be changed to a trilogical one—"teacher-student-text" instead of "reader-text" (or "subject-object" or "knower-known"). In other words, the relation to the teacher is the relation to the text (teacher could be defined here both as person and/or the text in its teaching person or function). And no text is independent of its teacher or its teaching function.

Shoshana Felman has a remarkable essay on pedagogy entitled "Psychoanalysis and Education." The essay is essentially a deconstructive analysis of teaching and knowledge in which she argues that "every true pedagogue is an anti-pedagogue" confronted with the impossibility of teaching. Or, as Freud once wryly remarked, education—like psychoanalysis—is an "impossible profession." Just as the unconscious conditions consciousness, ignorance, Felman asserts, would be a radical condition of the very structure of knowledge. What Freud understood was how the patient's active resistance to knowledge can *teach us* something. And Freud, we remember, also listened to and learned from the voices of those who had been muted, such as hysterical women.

In psychoanalysis, Felman writes, the analyst becomes "the student of the patient's knowledge" (1982, 33), and it is precisely *what the patient does not know that she knows* that is crucial. The patient thinks the analyst knows, and looks to the analyst for answers, but unbeknownst to the patient, the reverse is the case: it is the patient herself who contains the answer. Roland Barthes also wrote an insightful essay on teaching, "Students, Intellectuals, Teachers," in which he compared the position of the teacher not to that of the *analyst* but to that of the *patient*. For the *patient* talks compulsively to the silent audience of the analyst, like the teacher talking compulsively to the class. Felman adds that just as the psychoanalyst becomes the student of the patient's knowledge, so, too, "the teacher is the one who learns and teaches nothing other than the way he learns. The subject of teaching is an interminable learning" (Barthes 1977, 37).

In Felman's schema, then, literary knowledge (like psychoanalytic insight) is distinguished from philosophical knowledge in that literary knowledge is "non-authoritative knowledge not-in-possession of itself," whereas philosophical knowledge presumes mastery over its own meaning. "Literature" knows it knows but does not know the meaning of its knowledge. This conclusion, of course, is vintage deconstruction and echoes a point made by Paul de Man. On the subject of teaching, however, de Man's ideas were disastrous—precisely because of his obsession with certain epistemological questions and his neglect of the relations out of which that epistemology is produced.[2] De Man's impersonal model for teaching, quoted at the beginning of this essay, is chilling. Like his theory of language, it presupposes an autonomous world of signs independent of persons. He appropriated the epistemological critique of Derrida as mainly a *cognitive* problem; the ultimate problem of interpretation then became "undecidability" and, thus, the interpreter could go no further than ironic aporias. For de Man, "rhetoric" became the "other" of philosophy as a kind of post-Cartesian epistemology, but he deprived rhetoric of its fundamental sense of language as an *action* or effect on a public audience—and, by extension, as *teaching*.

II. The Other as My Teacher

To de Man's critique of epistemology and his statement that teaching has nothing of the interpersonal about it, I would juxtapose another of Franz Rosenzweig's statements:

> But all this that can and should be known is not really knowledge. All that can and should be taught is not teaching. Teaching begins where the subject matter ceases to be subject matter and changes into inner power . . . The *way* to the teaching leads through what is "knowable"; at least that is the high road, the sole road one can in good faith recommend to every questioner." (Quoted in Glatzer [1953] 1961, 347)

When Rosenzweig talks about "*the* teaching" in the preceding quote, he is invoking, of course, a Jewish notion of Torah. Rosenzweig was an extraordinary German-Jewish philosopher, critic, theologian, and educator who lived an all-too-brief life (1886–1929). He was stricken in 1921 with amyotrophic lateral sclerosis and became completely paralyzed by 1923, losing all faculty of movement and speech. One of the most extraordinary things about Rosenzweig was that even before his illness he abandoned what promised to be a glorious career in the German University in order to found the "Lehrhaus," an Institute for Adult Jewish Education in Frankfurt. In so doing, and in the way he coped with his paralysis, he became a quite different kind of "teacher." His move out of the realm of abstract philosophy and academic life was also in accord with the critique of Hegelian thought he had worked out in *The Star of Redemption* (1921). *The Star* was also a reworking of the relations between philosophy and theology, Judaism and Christianity, religion and art.

Rosenzweig was also a major influence on a contemporary French-Jewish theorist, Emmanuel Levinas, whose work is a crossing of philosophical phenomenology with Jewish thought, and whose critique of epistemology leads in another direction than de Man's—precisely to the relation with the other as "teaching." Levinas is a fresh resource for thinking about the relation of literature and religion; his own life has been marked by theoretical and pedagogical doubleness: he was both a professor of philosophy in French universities, and teacher and director of the Paris school of the Alliance Israelite Orientale. He became well known for his lectures on Talmudic texts, and has been gratefully acknowledged by

Derrida as an important source for Derrida's own critique of Western metaphysics.[3]

Levinas's Talmudic lectures are commentaries on the Talmud, yet are subtly permeated by the philosophical themes of his work in phenomenology. His philosophical work, in turn, is permeated by Jewish ideas while not overtly mentioning Judaism. In the philosophical work, there are some extraordinary passages dealing with the nature of teaching, and these, too, are attempts to "translate" into phenomenological terms the Jewish concept of "Torah."

A brief (and crude) sketch of how this "translation" is accomplished might go as follows. Like many postmodern thinkers, Levinas offers a critique of ontology and systems of thought that attempt to grasp the totality of being. The apprehension of Being, he argues, is not reducible to representation by a consciousness grasping its objects: "The relation between same and other is not always reducible to the knowledge of the other by the same, nor even to the *revelation* of the other to the same" (Levinas [1961] 1969, 28). Levinas is interested in the "non-knowing with which philosophical knowing begins," that place where totality breaks up, but which also conditions the totality itself (24). One of those places is what he terms "the face of the other." The "face" is the way the other represents her or himself, *exceeding the idea of the other in me*. In part, Levinas is drawing on Descartes's "idea of infinity," that is, an idea that "overflows" the thought that thinks it, remains exterior to it—and in part on the biblical notion of the "face" *(panim)*.

The "face of the other" is not for him a visual image; it is, rather, a facing *relation*. The other faces my own separate and narcissistic ego, interrupts, and shames it—a calling into question that is the call of conscience as both an appeal and an order. The connotations of the Hebrew word for face in biblical and rabbinic tradition are all-important here. The verbal root *panah* in Hebrew connotes a "turning" toward something, and also a kind of personal presence.[4] In Levinas, facing is being confronted with, turned toward, facing up to, being judged and called to by the other. Facing is a disruption of that free, autonomous self that through its reasoning and consciousness thinks it can construct the world out *of* itself, or know the world *from* itself.

The "other," then, disturbs my being at home with myself. This other, though, is neutralized when s/he becomes a theme or object of knowledge because that reduces her or him to the same. And that reduction reflects the project of reason to be autonomous (Levinas

1969, 44), a knowledge of-and-for-itself versus a knowledge for-the-other. Socratic truth exemplifies this kind of self-sufficiency, and so Levinas critiques the Socratic notion of truth and Socratic pedagogy as an "ego-logy" because Socrates claimed to be only a midwife, eliciting from his interlocutor what the interlocutor *already* knows. Nothing new, nothing other, can break in—nothing from the outside.

For Levinas, "the condition for theoretical truth and error is the word of the other," and to approach the other in conversation is to welcome the expression of the other, "in which at each instant he overflows the idea a thought would carry away from it. It is therefore to *receive* from the other beyond the capacity of the I." Here are the key sentences:

> But this also means: "to be taught." The relation with the other, or conversation, is a non-allergic relation, an ethical relation; but inasmuch as it is welcomed this conversation is a teaching *[enseignement]*. Teaching is not reducible to maieutics; it comes from the exterior and brings me more than I can contain. (Levinas 1969, 51)

Epistemology would then be produced out of the teaching relation. As Levinas writes:

> The objectification and theme upon which objective knowledge opens already rests on teaching. The calling into question of things in a dialectic is not a modifying of the perception of them; it coincides with their *objectification*. The object is *presented* when we have welcomed an interlocutor. The master, the coincidence of the teaching and the teacher, is not in turn a fact among others. (1969, 69–70)

From this point of view, the other who disrupts the knowing subject becomes the "teacher," and the knowledge the knowing subject grasps is a *relation to the other*. For Levinas, this is exemplified in language because "language maintains the other—*to whom* it is addressed, whom it calls upon and *invokes*" (Levinas 1969, 73). In other words, language institutes a relation irreducible to the subject-object relation; the revealing function of language is not limited to its coherence, or to conveying the coherence of concepts.

> The calling in question of the I, coextensive with the manifestation of the other in the face, we call language. The height from which language comes we designate with the term teaching. . . . This voice

coming from another shore teaches transcendence itself. Teaching
signifies the whole infinity of exteriority. And the whole infinity of
exteriority is not first produced, to then teach: teaching is its very
production. The first teaching teaches this very height, tantamount
to its exteriority, the ethical. (Levinas 1969, 171)

Now this redefinition of knowledge as always a relation to the other,
not a reflection of some essential independent substance, accords
with much postmodern thought (i.e., meaning is always a function of
relation rather than the identification of any independent essence).
For postmodern theology, such a position has led in many directions:
to a God defined as the "play of signs," or "name of the Abyss," or to
a "God beyond/otherwise than Being."[5]   For Levinas, a God otherwise than Being is traced in the relation to the human other, and
the other's calling me to accountability and responsibility. He then
redefines ethics as the primary relation and binding to the other
that precedes and conditions any epistemology—and any politics if
that politics is not to revert to violence.

III. Midrash as Pedagogy

To this point, I have been working out some of the relations of
pedagogy and epistemology in postmodern theory and Jewish
thought, but have not applied any of this to Jewish texts. It is now
time to look at some rabbinic texts and some current attempts to
understand them in light of literary theory.   Deconstruction,
semiotics, cultural poetics, anthropology, and hermeneutic theory
have all recently been applied to the rabbinic genre of midrash with
interesting results, but the intense pedagogical self-consciousness of
midrashic texts has been little discussed.[6]   The relation of the
midrashic hermeneutic to the midrashic pedagogy needs much more
examination.

Judah Goldin has perceptively written, "Midrash is not just
device. It is pedagogy. Pedagogy makes use of devices, devices do
not make pedagogy" (1988, 280).   Now the pedagogical self-consciousness of midrash is due in part to its origins in orally delivered
sermons. And further, as George Steiner has pointed out, rabbinic
interpretation does not have textual explication as its ultimate goal;
it has a strong moral-pedagogical thrust: "The rabbinic answer to
the dilemma of unending commentary is one of moral action and

enlightened conduct. The hermeneutic exposition is not an end in itself. It aims to translate into normative instruction meanings indwelling in the manifold previsions of the sacred message" (Steiner 1989, 30). I would even venture to say that hermeneutics and homiletics cannot be separated and that they are brought together under the category of the pedagogical. Again, I am trying to shift the ground to ask: What if we took the social relation of teaching or preaching as a ground for epistemology rather than the reverse? (Even the most avowedly secular and materialist literary theories contain exhortations about the need to battle political oppression. Ideological and cultural criticism is intensely homiletic.)

Of course, the meaning of the word "Talmud"—the name given to the major corpus of Jewish exegesis, commentary and law—is "study" or "learning"—from the Hebrew root *lamed, mem, dalet [lamad]*. The very form of the Talmud makes it indeed difficult for someone who has never learned a page of it to pick it up and just start "reading." It is not only that the Talmud assumes all kinds of background knowledge, or that it speaks in a kind of shorthand code to the already initiated, or that it has a particular kind of redaction history. The key issue here is the relation of rabbinic hermeneutics to rabbinic pedagogy. What is the relation between the rabbis as "readers" of revelation and the rabbis as its "teachers"? For the relation of teacher and student is not the same thing as the relation of text and reader.

The Talmud presents itself as the dialogue and debate of teachers, and it indeed is a "knowledge produced out of the teaching relation." As Steven Fraade emphasizes in his excellent recent book on Midrash, *From Tradition to Commentary: Torah and Its Interpretation in the Midrash Sifre to Deuteronomy*, "Ancient scriptural commentary is not simply a series of *declarative* assertions about the meanings of words . . . but an attempt to effect a relation between that text overall and those for whom it is 'scripture.'" In other words, these commentaries "are not simply constative conduits of meaning, but also performative media, by which the polymorphic 'World' of the text and its students are transformatively brought towards each other" (Fraade 1991, 13). Fraade is taking the idea of performative versus constative utterances from J. L. Austin and speech-act theory. Fraade's argument, though, is that it is the *redactor* of the midrashic collections who sets up what I would call a "pedagogical hermeneutic": the redactor juxtaposes and arranges the multiple interpretations to "draw and direct the text's students into a dialogical engagement with these voices" (1991, 125). That is, the very genre of the anthology that constitutes the redacted midrashic collections subtly directs the student to sort, reshape, and transmit the heterogeneous interpretations and traditions through continuous study and teaching.

As Fraade notes, in the rabbinic perspective, the word of God is itself polyphonous, filled with multiple meanings, and the task of Israel is to continue Sinai, to reenact the revelation by uncovering those meanings. So the divine-human dialogue is reenacted in the very *structure* of midrashic anthologies; the "dialogical struggle of interpretation becomes a continual reenactment of the original struggle of revelation at Sinai" (1991, 124). The students "socially enact the text" through their study of it and "advance its unfinished work by filling out the anonymous narrative voice" (18). Moreover, "as they work through the commentary, the commentary works through them." In the process, the disciples become sages, who teach the broader Jewish society as well (19), for the "sages knew their success or failure . . . depended not so much on their own exegetical genius as on their ability to raise the next generation of sages that would continue their exegetical work" (120).

Taken together, all of this means that the "literary form" of the midrash (and the Talmud) teaches us how it must be taught. This is a knowledge that requires a teacher, which is produced out of the very teaching relation that it itself often thematizes. The content of its teaching is inseparable from the form of its teaching. This absolute necessity for a teacher also preserves the tradition, even as the Written Torah is being transformed by the interpretations of the Oral Torah; and it also makes learning personal and links the student with the teachers and students whose debates and doings are described within its pages.

As Fraade puts it, "The *Sifre* in describing the study activity of the sages and their disciples also describes how its own text of Torah teaching ought to be studied by its students." If that is true, "then we cannot understand the social work of that commentary without attempting to pose ourselves in the place of such students, even as we employ the distancing tools" (1991, 20). Yet what does it mean to "pose ourselves in the place of such students"? And is there a way even more deeply to connect Austin's notion of "performative speech-acts" with the pedagogical moment in midrash and in the teacher-student situation?

In a penetrating study of the relation of postmodern theory to the classroom, Mary Alice Delia has written that the "performative" in the pedagogical moment might be better described (and enacted) as a "staging" (1991, 124).[7] "Staging" is not repeating what "is there," but generating, enacting, and embodying living relations between a text and its audience or actors. When something is staged, it is put into motion, re-created, transformed. To return to the psychoanalytic model, the cure comes about through a "staging" that Freud called "transference." Transference is the unconscious "transfer" onto the analyst of effects directed at key figures in the patient's early life. The analyst becomes a screen onto which are projected the patient's unconscious conflicts, and these are then *reenacted* in the relation with the analyst. When this unconscious "staging" is brought to light and interpreted, the conflicts "play out" and can be resolved.

So perhaps we could further say that the knowledge produced out of the teaching relation is a knowledge that is "staged." And further, that *knowledge itself is that which can be staged between teacher and student.* There, in that relationship, it is given life, and it comes to be knowledge. Indeed, many midrashim teach, preach, and interpret by "staging" the scene, dramatizing it. Midrashic hermeneutics "stage" the Bible and beckon the students onto the stage, which is also the scene of revelation and its unfolding history. This hermeneutic calls us to participate in that unfolding, not only to intellectually interpret a text, but also to perform it, to practice it in the stages of our own lives.

IV. The Teacher-Student Bond

A special bond is created between student and teacher in this mutual staging and engendering of knowledge. There is an intriguing text on this relation in the Talmudic tractate *Makkot 10a*. The context of the passage is a discussion of the three "cities of refuge" to which persons guilty of involuntary manslaughter could flee for asylum from the revenge of the blood relatives (Deut. 19:214, 4:42). The text discusses the case of a student who must go into exile to one of these cities:

> A Tanna taught: A student who is exiled—his teacher is exiled with him in accordance with the text, "and that fleeing . . . he

might live" [Deut. 4:42] which means—provide him with whatever he needs to live. R. Zeira remarked that this is the basis for the saying, "Let no one teach Mishnah to a student who is unworthy." R. Yochanan said: "A teacher who goes into exile—his students are exiled with him." But this cannot be correct, since R. Yochanan also said: "Where do we derive from Scripture that the study of the Torah itself affords asylum? From the verse 'Then Moses separated three cities . . . Bezer in the wilderness . . . Ramoth . . . and Golan . . .' which is immediately followed by the verse 'and this is the Torah which Moses set before the children of Israel'" [Deut. 4:42]. This discrepancy is not difficult to explain. One of his sayings applies to the scholar who maintains his learning in practice, while the other applies to one who does not maintain it in practice.

Maimonides, the great medieval philosopher and Talmudist then codifies as law this mutual exile of student and teacher in his classic Jewish legal code, the *Mishneh Torah*, where he writes: "A student who goes into exile into a city of refuge—his teacher is exiled with him, as it is said 'that he might live,' which means—provide him with whatever he needs to live." Maimonides then adds, "For without the study of Torah, those who possess wisdom and those who seek after it are considered as dead. And thus the teacher who goes into exile—his students are exiled with him" (*Hilkhot Rotzeakh,* beginning of chap. 7 [my translation]). He is alluding here to a verse in Eccles. 7:12: "The excellence of knowledge is that *wisdom gives life* to those who have it." In other words, the teacher-student relation is not simply a matter of conveying knowledge, but of life itself; and they are so interdependent that one's teacher must join one in exile.

In his philosophical masterwork, the *Guide for the Perplexed* (1956), Maimonides also refers to this teacher-student relation in discussing the meaning of the word *yalad*, "to bear" or "give birth" (Part 1, chap. 7). One of its figurative uses is "the formation of thoughts and ideas" and, says Maimonides, "one who has instructed another in any subject, and has improved his knowledge, may be regarded as the parent of the person taught." Jose Faur interprets this comment of Maimonides and this generative metaphor for teaching Torah (that the teacher is as if he gives birth to the student) to mean that knowledge is generative, not static, and that Torah itself is not "knowledge" but what *produces* knowledge.[8]

V. Teaching as Creative Withdrawal

In the Jewish mystical tradition, there are other interesting analogies between the act of teaching and that of creative birth. And in some hasidic sources, the process of teaching is used to explain the kabbalistic concept of the creation of the universe through divine "self-contraction," known as the *tzimtzum.* The basic idea is that infinite God had to "contract" himself, so to speak, in order to allow a "space" for finite creation to occur. A teacher, the analogy goes, must perform the same kind of act. If a teacher tries to transmit an idea with all the complexity of her or his own understanding of it, the student will be overwhelmed and confused. The teacher needs to take her or his knowledge and "contract" or condense it so that the student, after intensely studying the condensed points, can eventually grasp the teacher's idea in its original depth and detail.[9] Furthermore, only *by virtue of* the condensation and concealment can the idea be transmitted to and eventually unfolded by the student.

It indeed seems that all the great teachers have taught in parables—forms in which meaning is highly condensed and contracted—and that the deepest knowledge can *only* be conveyed in that indirect way. And perhaps that also is what constitutes "literary knowledge": it, too, is knowledge teachable only through condensation, story, and parable.

Perhaps one could also use the kabbalistic model to say further that just as the act of *tzimtzum* precedes and makes possible any specific finite creation, so too the teaching relation is the possibility of any specific knowledge. In the kabbalistic model, the condensation is a *self-contraction* that creates an "empty space" for the creation of the universe. And to return to the notion of staging —the "empty space" necessary for creation, is in a sense, like the space of a stage, which is itself an "empty space" to be filled by the interactions of the performers. The foundational pedagogical act, similarly, would also be an act of creative self-limitation (in Levinas's terms, an openness to the other), not an act of self-expansion and assertion of mastery of teacher over the student. In a way, Shoshana Felman's definition of literary knowledge as "non-authoritative knowledge not-in-possession of itself" also reflects a type of "self-contraction." But the kabbalistic model takes it further: for the *purpose* of this self-contraction is to give birth to the other—that is, to "make a space" for the reader/interpreter/student. This would make literary knowledge not a paralytic aporia but a positive pedagogy.

VI. The Teacher-Student Relation as Messianic

If the student-teacher relation reflects the principle of creation, there is also a sense in which it embodies revelation and redemption.   Levinas, in his role of rabbinic commentator and Jewish pedagogue, notes this in one of his earliest Talmudic lectures that deals with comments at the end of the tractate *Sanhedrin* on the nature of the Messiah.   I can only discuss here a fragment of his analysis, and the Talmudic text he analyzes.   Says the Talmud,

> Rav said: The world was created only on David's account. Shmuel said: On Moses' account; R. Yochanan said: For the sake of the Messiah. What is his [the Messiah's] name? The School of R. Shila said: His name is Shiloh, for it is written, "until Shiloh come" [Gen. 49:10]. The School of R. Yannai said: His name is Yinnon, for it is written, "May his name endure for ever: as long as the sun may his name be perpetuated *[yinnon]*" [Ps. 72:17]. The School of R. Haninah maintained: His name is Haninah, as it is written, "for I will show you no favor *[haninah]*" [Jer. 16:13]. Others say: His name is Menahem the son of Hezekiah, for it is written, "Because Menahem ["the comforter"], that would relieve my soul, is far" [Lam. 1:16]. The Rabbis said: His name is "the leper scholar," as it is written, "Surely he has borne our griefs, and carried our sorrows: yet we did esteem him a leper, smitten of God, and afflicted" [Isa. 53:4].

The question concerns the identity of the Messiah, and the sages are offering different possible names: Shilo, Yinnon, Haninah, Menachem.   Levinas astutely points out that the names the students ascribe to the Messiah are the names of their *teachers*, the heads of the rabbinical schools, and Levinas finds an extraordinary implication here:

> The experience in which the messianic personality is revealed . . . comes back to the relationship between student and teacher. The student-teacher relationship, which seemingly remains rigorously intellectual, contains all the riches of a meeting with the Messiah. This is the truly remarkable thing: the fact that the relationship between student and teacher can confirm the promises made by the

prophetic texts in all their grandeur and tenderness is perhaps the
most surprising novelty in this passage. (Levinas 1990, 85)

He adds that the plays on words each school uses to name the
Messiah are themselves significant. It is not just a matter of finding
a resemblance in the sound of the teacher's name to the prooftext,
but each prooftext characterizes something about the teaching
relation. "Shiloh," for example, from *shalvah* meaning "peace,"
indicates "the presence in the teacher's lessons of peace and abundance." Psalm 72, the prooftext for "*Yinnon*," speaks of justice and
aid for the downtrodden, and of a king who gives to the poor and
whose dominion covers the earth. This, indeed, is a "messianic
vision." "The teacher-pupil relationship does not consist in commu-
nicating ideas to one another. It is the first radiant sign of messianism itself" (Levinas 1990, 86).

Now this is a view of the teacher-student relation in its most
ideal sense, a view in opposition to Bourdieu's elaboration of the
symbolic violence in academic institutional life. But it well accords
with Levinas's notion of the other as teacher, and of ethics as a
"non-allergic relation to the other," an "eschatology of peace" prior to
epistemology, and prior to politics. Without this prior possibility (or
eschatology) of a nonviolent relation to the other, Levinas argues,
even the most idealistic politics will degenerate into violence to the
other.

VII. The Student as Teacher

Since the Talmud also declares that "one should always teach one's
students in a concise manner" *(Pesachim* 3b), it is more than time to
conclude. The final words belong to a midrash that beautifully
embodies the Levinasian idea that the "other" is my teacher, down
to even the least learned person. The *Sifre* (Piska 41) is commenting
on Deut. 11:13, "And it shall come to pass, if you hearken diligently
to my commandments which I command you this day."

> "Which I command you this day" (11:13): Whence do you learn that
> even if one learns an interpretation from the least learned of the
> Israelites, he should consider it as if he had learned it from a Sage?
> From the verse, "Which I command you." . . . And furthermore, as
> if he had learned it not from [many ordinary] Sages but from the
> [most learned seventy members of the] Sanhedrin, as it is said,
> "Masters of assemblies *[asufot*; Eccl. 12:11], "assemblies" meaning

the Sanhedrin, as it said, "Gather *[esfah]* unto Me seventy men of the elders of Israel" [Num. 11:16]. And still further, as if he had learned it not from the Sanhedrin but from Moses, as it is said, "They are given from one shepherd" [Eccl. 12:11]. . . . And finally, as if he had learned it not from Moses but from the Almighty One, as it is said, "They are given from one shepherd," and "Give ear, O shepherd of Israel, you that lead Joseph like a flock [Ps. 80:2], and "Hear, O Israel, the Lord our God, the Lord is one" [6:4].[10]

NOTES

1. For more information, see, for example, Gless and Smith 1992, Cahalan and Downing 1991, Moran and Penfield 1990, Nelson 1986, Gabriel and Smithson 1990, Scholes 1985, Graff 1987, Henrickson and Morgan 1990, Zavarzadeh and Morton 1991, and Kecht 1991. The bibliography and bibliographic essay in Cahalan and Downing are especially comprehensive.

2. Where Felman differs from de Man is in her affirmation that "pedagogy in psychoanalysis is not just a theme, but a rhetoric; not just a meaning but an action which may belie the stated meaning, the didactic thesis" (1982, 26). Using Austin's speech-act theory, she adds that in looking for the pedagogical moment, one should not necessarily look to statements about pedagogy but rather to the illocutionary force of their utterance. There are pedagogical speech-acts and ways in which statements perform certain gestures often in spite of themselves. Now this framework, while better than de Man's, still subordinates the pedagogical to another category—speech-act theory.

    I would not want to subsume the teaching relation purely under the category of rhetorical analysis. For it seems to me that even though the rhetor must adapt herself or himself to the audience in order to persuade, this model lacks the reciprocity of the teaching relation and the solicitation of the "otherness" of the student—and the way in which the student is also outside the teacher's frames of reference, "other," "disruptive."

3. I have elaborated on these issues in my *Fragments of Redemption: Jewish Thought and Literary Theory in Benjamin, Scholem, and Levinas* (Handelman 1991).

4. See, for example, Maimonides' discussion of the meaning of the trope "face" in *The Guide for the Perplexed* (1956), part I, section 37. Among the biblical significations Maimonides enumerates for "face" *(panim)* are "the presence and existence of a person"; "the hearing of a voice without seeing any similitude," i.e., the inability to comprehend God's true existence as such; and "attention or regard" for the other person.

5. For more information, see, for example, the work of the theologian Mark C. Taylor, especially 1984, 1987, and 1982.

6. See, for example, the work of Michael Fishbane (1985 and 1989), Daniel Boyarin (1990), Jose Faur (1986), David Stern (1991), Susan Handelman (1982), Geoffrey Hartman and Sanford Budick (1986), and Howard Eilberg Schwartz (1990).

7. "Stagings [are not] attempts to manipulate or control students. By 'stage' or 'staging' I mean the act of displaying or exhibiting an idea, setting it up (in the stage sense) for examination, raising the idea or concept for *trial*. Teachers, of course, put ideas on trial as a matter of course, but without recourse to the full apparatus and machinery of the stage. . . . A good staging makes a spectacle of itself. Like any production, it makes dramatic use of props, machinery, movement, scenes, action. A good staging by grammatological definition, is the work, edifice, achievement of the *bricoleur*, tinkering, thinking. . . ." (Delia 1991, 124–25)

   Delia also notes the relation between the "stages" adolescents go through, the staging of ideas in a drama, and the stages of knowledge in pedagogical action: "But to 'stage' means also, according to the Oxford Dictionary, 'to cause a (a person) to pass through stages; to bring about (something) in stages'" (1991, 125; see also 161, 164). She also acknowledges her debt (164) to and differences from Gregory Ulmer's *Applied Grammatology: Post(e) Pedagogy from Jacques Derrida to Joseph Beuys* (1985). Ulmer's is one of the few books to examine pedagogy epistemologically.

8. Comments made in personal conversation, April 1992. I also thank Professor Faur for highlighting these references.

9. In order to enable a student to receive, appreciate, and internalize the teacher's idea, the teacher has first to "entirely remove the light of his intellect and conceive an intellectual light that is on the receiver's level. [Therefore, he will make] a number of *Tzimtzumim* and will conceal [his own thought process] in order that it be appreciated by the receiver. But this *Tzimtzum* does not affect the teacher, for he sees the depth and breadth of the idea even in its limited form. Therefore, for him, the *Tzimtzum* does not conceal at all" (Schneerson 1989, 65).

10. I wish to thank several friends and colleagues for helping me think through the ideas in this essay: Ellen Spolsky for inviting me to a conference at Bar-Ilan University in Israel on "Literature and Epistemology," for which an early draft of this piece was written as a lecture; Marc Bregman, Barry Holtz, William Cutter, and Jose Faur for help and encouragement in thinking about the rabbinic materials; and Mary Alice Delia, whose many years as a superb high school teacher and many years as a student of literary theory have resulted in abundant wisdom about pedagogy and epistemology.

REFERENCES

Bourdieu, Pierre, and Jean-Claude Passeron. *Reproduction in Education, Society, and Culture.* London: Sage, [1970] 1990.

Barthes, Roland. "Writers, Intellectuals, Teachers." In *Image / Music / Text,* trans. Stephen Heath. New York: Hill and Wang, 1977.

Boyarin, Daniel. *Intertextuality and Midrash.* Bloomington: University of Indiana Press, 1990.

Cahalan, James, and David Downing, eds. *Practicing Theory in Introductory Literature Courses.* Urbana: NCTE, 1991.

Delia, Mary Alice. "Killer English: Postmodern Theory and the High School Classroom." Ph.D. diss., University of Maryland, College Park, 1991.

de Man, Paul. *The Resistance to Theory.* Minneapolis: University of Minnesota Press, 1986.

Faur, Jose. *Golden Dots with Silver Doves.* Bloomington: University of Indiana Press, 1986.

Felman, Shoshana. "Psychoanalysis and Education: Teaching Terminable and Interminable." *Yale French Studies* 63 (1982): 21–44.

Fishbane, Michael. *Biblical Interpretation in Ancient Israel.* Oxford: Clarendon Press, 1985.

————. *The Garments of Torah.* Bloomington: University of Indiana Press, 1989.

Fraade, Steven. *From Tradition to Commentary: Torah and Its Interpretation in the Midrash Sifre to Deuteronomy.* Albany: State University of New York Press, 1991.

Gabriel, Susan, and Isaiah Smithson, eds. *Gender in the Classroom: Power and Pedagogy.* Urbana: University of Illinois Press, 1990.

Glatzer, Nahum. *Franz Rosenzweig: His Life and Thought.* 2d rev. ed. New York: Schocken, [1953] 1961.

Gless, Darryl, and Barbara Hernstein Smith, eds. *The Politics of Liberal Education.* Durham: Duke University Press, 1992.

Goldin, Judah. *Studies in Midrash and Related Literature.* Ed. Barry Eichler and Jeffry Tigay. Philadelphia: Jewish Publication Society, 1988.

Graff, Gerald. *Professing Literature: An Institutional History.* Chicago: University of Chicago Press, 1987.

Handelman, Susan. *The Slayers of Moses.* Albany: State University of New York Press, 1982.

————. *Fragments of Redemption: Jewish Thought and Literary Theory in Benjamin, Scholem, and Levinas.* Bloomington: Indiana University Press, 1991

Hartman, Geoffrey, and Sanford Budick. *Midrash and Literature.* New Haven: Yale University Press, 1986.

Henrickson, Bruce, and Thais Morgan, eds. *Reorientations: Critical Theories and Pedagogies*. Urbana: University of Illinois Press, 1990.

Kecht, Maria-Regina. *Pedagogy Is Politics: Literary Theory and Critical Thinking*. Urbana: University of Illinois Press, 1991.

Levinas, Emmanuel. *Totality and Infinity: An Essay on Exteriority*. Trans. Alphonoso Lingis. Pittsburgh: Duquesne University Press, [1961] 1969.

———. *Difficult Freedom: Essays on Judaism*. Trans. Sean Hand. Baltimore: Johns Hopkins University Press, 1990.

Maimonides, Moses. *The Guide for the Perplexed*. Trans. M. Friedlander. 2d ed. New York: Dover, 1956.

———. *Mishneh Torah*.

Moran, Charles, and Elizabeth Penfield, eds. *Conversations: Contemporary Critical Theory and the Teaching of Literature*. Urbana: NCTE, 1990.

Nelson, Cary, ed. *Theory in the Classroom*. Urbana: University of Illinois Press, 1986.

Rosenzweig, Franz. 1955. *On Jewish Learning*. Ed. Nahum Glatzer. New York: Schocken, 1965.

———. *The Star of Redemption*. 2d ed., 1930. Trans. William Hallo. New York: Holt Rinehart, 1970; Notre Dame: Notre Dame University Press, 1985.

Schneerson, Joseph Issac. *Bosi L'Gani-5710*. Brooklyn: Sichos in English, 1989.

Scholes, Robert. *Textual Power*. New Haven: Yale University Press, 1985.

Schwartz, Howard Eilberg. *The Savage in Judaism*. Bloomington: Indiana University Press, 1990.

Steiner, George. *Real Presences*. Chicago: University of Chicago Press, 1989.

Stern, David. *Parables in Midrash*. Cambridge, Mass.: Harvard University Press, 1991.

Taylor, Mark C. *Deconstruction and Theology*. Ed. Carl Raschke. New York: Crossroad, 1982.

———. *Erring: A Postmodern A/theology*. Chicago: University of Chicago Press, 1984.

———. *Altarity*. Chicago: University of Chicago Press, 1987.

Ulmer, Gregory. *Applied Grammatology: Post(e) Pedagogy from Jacques Derrida to Joseph Beuys*. Baltimore: Johns Hopkins University Press, 1985.

Zavarzadeh, Mas'ud, and Donald Morton. *Theory/Pedagogy/Politics*. Urbana: University of Illinois Press, 1991.

Hebrew Literature

Chapter 8

The Struggle over the Canon of Early-Twentieth-Century Hebrew Literature: The Case of Galicia

Hannan Hever

(Translated by Sonia Leiden)

1. The "Culture Debate" in the Zionist Movement

The aesthetic discourse in and through which the Hebrew literary canon was constructed embodied power struggles that were taking place in the cultural and political arenas of the early twentieth century. The rise of the Zionist movement as a modern political movement was inextricably bound up with modern Jewish national culture. Questions concerning the role of culture in the emerging Zionist nationalism were regularly addressed and deliberated from the very inception of the movement. Debates focused on the extent to which Zionist culture should be based on tenets central to orthodox Judaism, the maskilic enlightenment tradition, or a new form of secular Jewish modernist culture. Another version of the new Jewish cultural nationalism saw Zionism as linked to the internal dynamics of Jewish daily life in specific diaspora communities and developed a conception of "labor culture" as a way of grounding Zionist ideals (Almog 1982, 129–61).

The discussions within the Zionist movement about cultural affairs, known at the time as the "Culture Debate," became a major political issue among Zionists at the turn of the century. Many regarded the instruction of Jewish history and the expansion of the Hebrew language and literature as the foundation of a national Zionist education (Luz 1985, 187–213). Indeed, in these fields of cultural activity, political dissension was rife, yet it was precisely this dissension that ultimately fashioned the face of the Zionist movement, for it shaped the inventory of new national symbols and the newly emergent national literature. The cultural significance attributed to this emerging national literature lay in the aesthetic presuppositions that informed Zionist thinking. The call for a national revolution was frequently postulated as the need to transform the dismal drabness of diaspora life into ideals of beauty, zest for life, and national pride. Beauty, it was believed, was crucial to the formation of the new national culture coming-into-being at the time. Martin Buber perceived the nationalist movement as heralding a "new culture of beauty" among the Jews, while Mordechai Ehrenfraiz noted that a cultural revival occurred as a result of "our revived desire to release beauty incarnate, our own self-beauty, which was imprisoned for thousands of years, and let it soar to previously inconceivable heights" (as quoted in Almog 1982, 83–84).

What precisely was the nature of this beauty? How can it be gauged and in what ways was it woven into, and reflected in, the newly forming national literature? These questions will be addressed as we outline the emerging literary canon whose very selection reflected a new concept of national beauty. The formation of the literary canon will be described as the result of political struggle, at times fierce and violent, between different concepts of literary practice. The literary struggle over the construction of modern Jewish Hebrew subjectivity was, thus, part of larger cultural ideological struggle. This may be observed in the confrontation that took place at the end of the nineteenth century between Ahad Ha'am and Micha Yosef Berdichevsky concerning the future of modern Hebrew literature. This ideological debate, which determined the outline of the entire debate about the canon of modern national Hebrew literature at the time, came about following the publication of "Teudat HaShiloah," the manifesto, or statement of purpose, which opened the first issue of *HaShiloah* (1896) edited by Ahad Ha'am. Following the debate, two categories of literature can be seen. On the one hand, we have the literature of the center, the "major literature," which posits itself at the core of national culture. On the other hand, we have the "minor literature," the subversive literature, which undermines the values and concepts of the center. After reviewing the Ahad Ha'am–Berdichevsky debate, we will turn to Galician literature as one case in which the dynamics of culture and political ideology can be clearly seen.

2. The Ideological Debate between Ahad Ha'am and Berdichevsky

In Ahad Ha'am's manifesto, "Teudat HaShiloah," his primary claim was that modern Hebrew literature must "instruct us in the ways of the inner world" (Ahad Ha'am 1943, 126) of the people. Ahad Ha'am wanted to publish only material with explicitly Jewish content. Anything accepted for publication had to be directly relevant to the Jewish experience and concerned with the Jewish "national will for survival" and ways to secure it: "Knowing ourselves, understanding our lives and wisely molding our future" (Ahad Ha'am 1943, 127). Ahad Ha'am had no doubts whatsoever about what the moral purpose of modern Hebrew literature should be; his positivist views led him to believe that its most significant contribution lay in "arousing our national considerations and expanding our knowledge thereof" (127). Worthwhile literary work was expected to extend the knowledge and understanding of the Jewish people. What we want are "good stories from the past or present of our people that provide a faithful portrait of our conditions in various times and places" (127). Accordingly, Ahad Ha'am had little regard for belletristic writing, although he did not categorically reject belletristic writing—he only set it aside until the plight of the nation had been adequately settled.

> Yet even a work of art conveying nothing but its own beauty, arousing emotions for the sake of pleasure only, even such works of art must be valued alongside the intellectual things in life; but in *our present circumstances*, we feel that our feeble literature should not disperse its limited strength on such works, lest there be more urgent matters that require attention. For this very reason you will not find many poems in this issue. After all, most poets no longer follow in the footsteps of Yehuda Leib Gordon, who tried to combine in his poetry reflections on our various needs in life. And leave poesy per se, that overflow of emotions about the wonder of nature and the pleasures of love, etc., to those pursuing the languages of the world, for they will surely find enough of it. (Ahad Ha'am 1943, 127–28, my emphases)

Addressing his readers in the first person plural, Ahad Ha'am represents the collective community, and exploits the literary and editorial options open to him accordingly. Firmly embedded in a positivist concept of the nation as a historically conditioned biological entity,

Ahad Ha'am believed that the national spirit prevails throughout history and that its lasting manifestations assume the form of a "national will for survival." As a biological phenomenon, he believed the national spirit would guarantee Jewish survival, in much the same way as religion had in the past. Given the large-scale historical changes in Europe, it was now up to the national will or spirit to ensure the survival of the Jews by establishing a contemporary, secular national culture and introducing it into Jewish-Palestine via a spiritual center that would both create a new sense of cultural cohesion and meet the spiritual requirements of the emergent national culture. In the shift from the notion of a shared territory to that of a spiritual center as the prerequisite for the Jewish nation, some of the deep conceptual differences between Ahad Ha'am's cultural nationalism and Berdichevsky's more radical Zionist stand can be seen.

These differences were clearly expressed in the second issue of *HaShiloah*, which contained a response by Berdichevsky (who was then coeditor with Ahad Ha'am) to Ahad Ha'am's manifesto. Most pointedly, he protested against Ahad Ha'am's distinction between Jewish and universal values and against the singularity ascribed to the Jewish diaspora, which subjugated, he believed, aesthetic norms to pragmatic moral and social collective norms. Against Ahad Ha'am's collectivist approach, Berdichevsky regarded the individual as a universal entity. He wished to replace Ahad Ha'am's positivism about the Jewish national spirit with the vigor of romantic vitalism. Berdichevsky chided Ahad Ha'am, "You are, indeed, a serious thinker, Mr. Ahad Ha'am! Which is precisely why you make light of poesy, for you fail to discern its value to man or nation, just as you fail to note that a nation's survival is grounded in its poetry more than in its thinking" (Berdichevsky 1960, 155).

Ahad Ha'am believed that the "national will for survival" was a hard fact, given in history, while Berdichevsky clearly distinguished between historical events and their subsequent reconstruction: "Our heritage is a burden and we, the last of the Jews and the first of the new Hebrews, must now construct a new nationhood for ourselves." Thus, when Ahad Ha'am declared that *HaShiloah* would steer clear of aesthetic tenor, he was conveying the desire to conserve Jewish intellectual energies rather than squander them on belletristic. Berdichevsky, on the other hand, believed that the fact that Jews had failed to master belletristic writing did not necessarily justify ignoring this mode of writing, neither did it condone distinguishing so unequivocally between Jewish requirements and universal needs: "Indeed, we have too few literary works! And the few there is should no longer be attributed to our founding writers exclusively, so do not force us to place Judaism on one side and humankind on the other!" (Berdichevsky 1960, 127).

Reassessing the polemic in terms of representations of power reveals that Ahad Ha'am believed that will and desire were closely linked to the practical availability of options and to the nation's ability. Berdichevsky, however, keenly distinguished between the capacity to do something and the desire and need to do so. To him, as an antipositivist, these were distinct conceptual categories. Hence, he was able to reverse the hierarchy proposed by Ahad Ha'am and subordinate ability to need: "When people feel a need for something, it means they have the ability to obtain it, now or in the future" (Berdichevsky 1960, 157). Nonetheless, in a response to Berdichevsky, Ahad Ha'am reiterated the positivist subordination of "need" to "ability": "There is little doubt that our people, like all others, has the need for all sorts of science and writing, even if these have nothing to do with Judaism. But as for the ability to nurture this need, we know that our literature comprises only lean ears of corn" (Ahad Ha'am 1943, 130–31). In response to charges by "*HaTze'irim*," a group of young intellectuals led by Berdichevsky who were attempting to redefine the future of modern Hebrew literature, Ahad Ha'am called for legitimizing the collectivist national stand, which for all intents and purposes reflected his own view as a member of a national minority. In the following statements Ahad Ha'am links the weakness of national minorities to the need for a collective discourse.

> It appears that what I first conveyed in "Teudat HaShiloah" failed in its mission, for the younger generation perceives it as total "heresy" as far as "humanity" is concerned. "We *wish* immediately to belong to the Hebrew people, in one fell swoop, to share genesis." "We *need* to site human enlightenment and its needs on a par with our own history." "There is not enough room!"
> We want to! We need to!—but *are we able to*? Unfortunately this question is not being addressed by the younger generation, and cannot be asked, for it is not the kind of question our people generally ask about national matters (indeed, the people of Israel *do know how* to inquire into their ability when it comes to private affairs), which is why everything is about face, we are panic stricken, our aspirations coming and going, our work bearing no

fruit, for the road between the lofty objective and limited action is always extremely long. (Ahad Ha'am 1943, 131, my emphases)

Whatever led Ahad Ha'am to protest, "We need to!—but are we able to?" led Berdichevsky similarly to conclude that while "we *expect* the Hebrews to surpass everyone else, yet our *capacity* to do so is limited" (1960, 41, my emphasis). However, both Ahad Ha'am and Berdichevsky accepted that in the context of the nationalist debate at the time, "need" and "desire" were no substitutes for "capacity" and "ability." But Ahad Ha'am sought the harmonious survival of a nation, while Berdichevsky was fueled by the apparently paradoxical historical circumstances of the Jews at the time. It was within the overall attempt to balance the "need" of the Jews with their "ability" that Ahad Ha'am saw fit to banish belletristic writing from the emerging Hebrew national canon, for he was convinced that such works could always be read in other languages. Berdichevsky, however, felt that the newly emerging national canon should be grounded in emotive, belletristic writing. In the midst of this debate about national needs and ability, Berdichevsky postulated an aesthetic concept that cast aspersions on the naturalism (which he refers to as realism) prevalent in Hebrew literature at the time. "Realistic writers are convinced that poetry is meant to reflect life and to present its overt or blatant appearance; they forget, however, that the very core of poetry lies in revealing the hidden" (Berdichevsky 1960, 154).

In an alternative to the naturalistic approach, Berdichevsky (and as we will see, Yosef Haim Brenner) favored highlighting the plausible in realistic representation, for he believed that precisely the tension between the overt and the hidden would provide the political basis for their aesthetic perceptions. Further, according to Berdichevsky, the apparent disparity between a nation's need for fictional representation and its ability to produce such writing did not have to be resolved immediately. The "torn heart" phase was thus perceived as a natural and necessary, if not vital, phase to be experienced by most young Jews. For realism, as already mentioned, itself embodied hidden forces of utopianism. In taking his antipositivistic approach, Berdichevsky believed that the discrepancy between "need" and "ability" would not lead to abandoning hopes for a national utopia. What could not be attained collectively could be accomplished, briefly, by the individual. In effect, it is the tenuousness of the national collective that imposes upon the intellectual avant-garde, especially on a few individual writers, the central function of sustaining hope for the collective national objective.

> When it is asked: "Why doesn't our artistic writing include praiseworthy works of excellence?" The answer is: "Because in our lives we are misbegotten; yet life itself is misbegotten, for we have raised some pitiful writers. The shepherds are not without sheep, it is the sheep who are without shepherds." (Berdichevsky 1960, 155)

Relating solely to the yardstick of romantic vitalism, Berdichevsky was not really concerned with the potential benefits of realizing a national utopia. He was content with the very presence of the ideal itself and with rigorous plentiful allusions to its desirability. Any resolution of the discrepancy between "need" and "ability" was thus contingent on his universalist concept of individuality:

> Is it any wonder that things seem so disrupted? Is it any wonder that we bemoan our sons who "tend other vineyards," finally leaving us one by one? . . . The existence of our nation, the very possibility of creating a nation must be based on encompassing a unity of individuals within an overall social framework and their ability to merge into a common receptacle to be sustained throughout the ages. The nation will only become a reality when we cultivate an adequate spiritual and material climate for its artists and makers.
>
> Let us mold the life of a single individual, and the rest will follow suit. (Berdichevsky 1960, 41)

The construction of a national Subject was hence viewed as contingent on the sovereignty of the single individual. This was illustrated most clearly in Berdichevsky's offensive on Ahad Ha'am, whereby he paradoxically formulated his idea of national identity, itself based, finally, on the individual's exclusive authority. Indeed, in an essay entitled "Contradiction and Construction," Berdichevsky stated that "there is no Israeli thinking, there are only thinking Israelis." The historical consciousness underlying Berdichevsky's conception is that of an ambiguous, undecisive, historical moment marking concurrently the end of one era and the beginning of another. At any rate, as the historical moment itself cannot determine how it should best be understood, it is up to the individual human beings inhabiting it to do so.

All basic conditions, both internal and external, which have
determined our existence to date, have disintegrated. . . . And the
fear in our hearts is real, for we are not on firm footing regarding
our next move—and we are now facing two worlds in collision: to
be or to no longer be! To be the last of the Jews or the first of the
new Hebrews. (Berdichevsky 1960, 29)

In another essay he added: "If I might say something about the
beliefs and values handed down to me by my forefathers, I must be
free to choose to appropriate or entirely reject them, without
severing ties between myself and my people" (1960, 38).   This
paradoxicality also underlies the national identity dilemma signified
by the doctrine of the "torn heart," another reference to the opposition between universalism and national particularism.   The per-
suasiveness of this dilemma and its implicit authority are grounded
in the fundamental ambivalence embodied in the notion of "internal
rupture," which both merges, even as it distinguishes between,
notions such as apportionment and fusion, the particular and the
general, the Jew and the Gentile.   However, even as he is positioned
within this ambivalence, Berdichevsky repeatedly undermines the
collectivist identity of the national Subject.   Instead of a collective
authority that typically signifies that a minority national consciousness has come to terms with its marginality and other limitations,
the national Subject Berdichevsky chose to construct subjugated the
general to the private, and in so doing, accorded universal authority
to a particular form of nationalism.

3.   Jewish Writers in Galicia—The Dispute

Toward the end of 1908, Yosef Haim Brenner left London and made
his way to Galicia.   By then a well-known writer throughout the
Jewish Hebrew-speaking world, Brenner had just ended a brief yet
significant chapter in his career during which he set up an extensive
program of literary activities in London (see Bakun 1975, 1990).
Returning to the Galician capital Lvov early in February 1908,
where he remained for about a year before setting out for Eretz-
Israel, Brenner soon became involved in the local literary scene.
Before long, local Galician writers sought his comments and views,
which were subsequently published in the local literary periodicals.

The Hebrew-speaking Jewish center in Galicia was at that time at the beginning of a revitalization. Throughout the Jewish Enlightenment, Galicia was an important center of Hebrew literary activity, yet a significant decline in its cultural and literary practices took place toward the end of the period, relegating Galicia to the cultural periphery, especially with regard to the emergent corpus of Hebrew literature. Galician writers had often since been treated with scorn and derision, and Galicia's cultural production throughout most of the nineteenth century was generally regarded as inferior. However, toward the end of the nineteenth century and early into the twentieth, Galicia began to show signs of being revived and was once more reinstated as an operative center of Jewish culture. The rise of Zionism and its attendant Hebrew culture began to restimulate cultural life in Galicia, especially in the realm of literary activity. Veteran and young writers alike, including Yitzhak Fernhoff, Reuven Fahan, Avraham Lebensrat, Asher Barash, and the early S. Y. Agnon, had published their works in local Galician literary journals, especially in *HaMitzpheh*, under the editorship of S. M. Lazar. Occasionally some of these writers were lucky enough to have their works printed in major Hebrew monthly journals published in other, more prominent centers. "Beware the Galicians," cautioned Galician critic Rabbi Benyamin in an essay published in 1909 (Rabbi Benyamin 1909), foreshadowing the success of such reputable writers as S. Y. Agnon, master of modernist prose fiction, and Avraham Ben-Yitzhak (Sonne), master of modernist poetry.

All things being equal, a writer of Brenner's caliber was bound to make waves in Galicia, and indeed before very long he became embroiled in a bitter literary dispute in which he launched a frontal attack on the entire body of Hebrew literature being produced in Galicia at the time. Focusing especially on works by Reuven Fahan and Yitzhak Fernhoff, Brenner ruthlessly denounced them. "Heaven protect our literature!" he cried. "This is nothing but idle banter and rubbish!" Brenner stated that "many Jews in Galicia have a command of the Hebrew language (in its practical sense); Galician Jews still seem to be strongly affiliated with Hebrew works from the past, . . . nevertheless, no literary work has been produced here for many years, and there is, for all intents and purposes, no Hebrew literature in Galicia at all!" (Brenner 1985a, III, 250–51).

While this diatribe attests to Brenner's contentiousness, it also urges us to inquire why he would take it upon himself, being, after all, just a passing visitor, to so viciously attack writers whom he regarded as nonentities as far as literary competence was concerned. Moreover, Brenner was not the only literary figure to voice his criticisms, making one wonder why a group of reputable literary critics should bother to attack the Galician writers and their works if they considered the quality of the writing to be so unquestionably inferior.

What I will try to show is that, despite their negligibility in the eyes of the critics, the political stances and corresponding poetic resolutions manifest in the literary texts produced by the young Galicians genuinely jeopardized the hegemony of the emerging national modern Hebrew literature. Regional Hebrew literature in Galicia at the time was thus significantly molded against the existing literary canon, that is, the corpus of new national literary works that comprised the standard literary yardstick for all modern Hebrew literature at the end of the nineteenth and the beginning of the twentieth centuries.

4.   "Before the Elections" by Yitzhak Fernhoff

Among those works produced in Galicia that were attacked because, I believe, they formed the beginnings of an alternative literary canon was a collection of stories entitled *MeAggadot HaHaim* (From the Legends of the Living) by Yitzhak Fernhoff (1908). Fernhoff was a prominent Hebrew writer active in Galicia toward the end of the nineteenth and early twentieth centuries, who spent most of his time editing and publishing local literary publications. These included a series of *Sifrei Sha'ashuim* (Books of Amusements) followed by *HaIvri HaHadash* (The New Hebrew) and *HaYarden* (The Jordan).

Generally speaking, universal suffrage had led to stormy debates within the Jewish community, as illustrated in Fernhoff's story entitled "Lifnei HaBehirot" (Before the Elections) (Fernhoff 1908) written against the backdrop of the 1907 Austro-Hungarian general elections. The questions that arose related to the very participation of Jews in the political arena, and the modes of such possible participation. An extremely important political issue for Jews in Galicia at the time was whether they should be represented as part of a unified national party of the Jews of the Hapsburg Empire or as a separate political entity of Galician Jews. "Before the Elections" represents and juxtaposes a number of Jewish characters signifying a variety of political views. Fernhoff presents a debate in which we can find one character who represents the radical Jewish nationalist position and argues for unconditional civil rights for the Jews, and another who is doubtful about how the Jews will conduct themselves as a national minority during the course of the elections. On the one hand, there is an air of apprehension regarding any form of Jewish political activism that might increase the political weight of the assimilationists, while on the other hand there is the Orthodox position favoring a Christian candidate over an assimilationist or a Zionist one. Yet toward the end of the debate an "extremely skeptical pessimist" voices his opinion:

> Whom the Jews will vote for in heterogeneously populated areas I have no idea. They may vote for the nationalist [that is, for the Zionist—H.H.], for the assimilationist, or for the Christian. Anything can happen. But as for the other county, in town W.—I have no doubts whatsoever that an antisemitic candidate will be elected. (Fernhoff 1908, 32)

And when asked what this view is grounded in, the pessimist replies: "Because *all* those living in this quarter are Jewish" (32). The point of this story clarifies the author's position: the pessimist is convinced that the Jews will inevitably act against their own interests. The underlying political assumption concerning this irony is unequivocal: the author dismisses the idea of rejecting the diaspora, and urges the Jews to take full advantage of their civil rights in the diaspora. The question raised by the pessimist is structural rather than quantitative, that is, it has little to do with whether the Jews, wherever they might be, statistically constitute a minority or majority. It pertains rather to the idea of Jewish political consciousness and how it may be structured. Is this the same consciousness generally ascribed to national minorities, who, fully aware of their political weaknesses, are yet intent on fully realizing their civil political rights? Or is it the consciousness of a statistical minority that has already relinquished its political potential either out of sheer indifference or as a result of a radical Zionist stance that calls for the rejection of the diaspora? The paradoxical formulation of this last point underscores that the political dilemma facing Galician Jews at the time was more a matter of political structure than a matter of numbers and percentages of Jews in different districts.

In this story Fernhoff grants political legitimacy to Jewish political activism that extends beyond the act of a single individual in the name of collective rights for a national minority in the diaspora. For Brenner and his fellow critics who totally rejected a Jewish presence in the diaspora, the subversive component in Fernhoff's position was contained precisely in its potential relevance for Zionists and had little to do with the anti-Zionists or a-Zionists. Pointedly addressing the cultural and political implications of Zionist participation in the general elections for the Austro-Hungarian parliament, "Before the Elections" implies a relatively low commitment to the radical, anti-diaspora Zionist position. This suggests that, in Galicia, the more extreme version of Zionism was gradually becoming incorporated into what was becoming known as "Laboring for the Present." Laboring for the Present stressed an evolutionary process of bringing Zionism to fruition, acknowledging that nothing was expected to be resolved immediately or cataclysmically.

Brenner and Berdichevsky's political critique of the Galician option of Jews surviving by fashioning themselves into a "national minority" paved the way for their cultural critique. Following the well-known formulation of Herder, the essential prerequisite for all modern discourse on national identity became the relation between a national language and a national territory. According to Berdichevsky, "A spiritual and material culture, nationally independent, cannot exist without the fundamental national territorial claim to land, or without a socially and historically material reservoir from which both spirit and matter can be refreshed" (Berdichevsky 1960, 62). Similarly, Brenner pointed out that the inadequacy of Galician literature stemmed primarily from its lack of territory, its "landlessness," as he put it. Nonetheless, Brenner and Berdichevsky present their political critique largely as an aesthetic critique, in which their aesthetic standards are determined a priori. They thus *appear* to be divorced from any political interests that may have been predicated on the historically specific political struggle they were fighting. However, by historically relocating these aesthetic standards we may be able to uncover some of their implicit political uses at the time.

5. "From the Karaites' Lives" by Reuven Fahan

A stance similar to Fernhoff's may be noted in several narrative texts written by Reuven Fahan and appearing in *MeHayei HaKaraim* (From the Karaites' Lives) (1908), a form of ethnographic prose. These stories address the lifestyles of the Karaite community in

Galicia. Having lived in Galicia ever since the sixteenth century, toward the middle of the nineteenth century the Karaites obtained full civil rights throughout Russia. Yet Fahan refers to the Karaites in these narratives primarily by evoking a sense of their frailty as a disappearing ethnic minority. For instance, one story entitled "Ever Meduldal" (Limp Organ) (48–51) focuses on Kazimir Shmuelowitz, a Karaite who converts to Christianity and rises to prominence in Polish society. Oscillating between both worlds, Kazimir Shmuelowitz appears to be completely at home among the Poles, yet never seems to feel that he has betrayed his own people. He is thus able to maintain ties with his family by purchasing a house for his father "so that he himself would always be one of them, part owner of the property along Karaite Road, and so his mother would know that the ties between him and her could never really be severed" (50). Interestingly, this "territorial" solution to Kazimir's ambivalent standing is textualized in standard Zionist terminology, as the house, for instance, is referred to as "*Nahalat Avot*" (the land of the forefathers) (51).

The Karaites themselves view his move favorably; and, as the narrator adds when reporting the news, they "display feelings generally articulated by a relatively 'powerless' community observing one of its proselytized members with pride—for he does not bear signs of being a traitor" (51). The Karaites thereby seem to have come to terms with their vulnerability as an ethnic minority.

Fahan's decision to recount this tale of the Karaite "Other" from a distinctly Jewish perspective reveals something of the Jews' sense of their own patronage (see Feitelson 1970, 156) and represents the Jewish minority as the more powerful of the two minority communities. At the same time, if this portrayal is in any way indicative of the Jews' attitude toward the Karaites, it probably suggests Fahan's acceptance of a Jewish national minority in the diaspora. By way of deduction, then, the text urges the historical Hebrew reader to come to terms with the historical reality of the Jews, whose existence as a national minority in the diaspora is presented here as a feasible option for Jews at the turn of the century. Fahan's view, in a nutshell, is not far removed from those who believed in "Laboring for the Present."

"*She'ifa La-Hutz*" (Reaching for the Outside) (Fahan 1908, 52–57), another story in Fahan's collection, presents a rather different Karaite case. Here we have a protagonist who betrays his original Karaite identity. His childhood suffering because of lack of identity—being neither Jewish nor Christian—is later replaced by the abuse of his Karaite origins in order to secure a legal career. Given the prevalence of Polish anti-Semitism, not admitting one's Jewish descent was an advantage, and the said protagonist was finally able to secure a court position. Unlike the empathy evoked in "Limp Organ" toward the Karaite who chose to withdraw from his own community, this story criticizes the way this Karaite used his ethnic identity for personal gain, yet renounced his immediate family and community at large. The author seems to be implying here that despite the Karaite community's ostensible powerlessness, the Karaite protagonist in question should not have forsaken his birthright. Adopting an ambivalent stand, the author suggests that even if exploiting one's status as an outsider can be excused, disregarding one's commitment to his/her powerless minority community cannot equally be excused. Displaying different attitudes toward each respective Karaite, the author seems to be urging them to come to terms with their own positions as members of disadvantaged minorities in alien surroundings.

6. Zionism and the Canonization of a National Literature

Literary canonization was integral to the establishment of the ideological consensus of modern Jewish nationalism (Parush 1992, 110–11). Constructing a national literary consciousness among the Jews took place concurrently on several different fronts. In the overall endeavor Haim Nahman Bialik was to play a major role, yet perhaps no less central were Brenner and Berdichevsky, who systematically precipitated the construction of a Hebrew literature as a corpus of modern national literature. In the early years of the twentieth century, Brenner and Berdichevsky, renowned writers, critics, and "publicists," had come to function as standard-bearers of literary taste. Once their position as key cultural agents was acknowledged, both their professional and personal relationships were enhanced. The affinity between the two writer-cum-critics was reflected in their compliance regarding the boundaries determining the emergent literary canon.

Viewing Galicia's marginal writers from today's perspective allows us to reassess the cultural significance of writers and literary works that have been excluded from the canon of modern Hebrew literature and relegated to its edges. This act can be perceived as an attempted redress for the historical process of marginalization and a recuperation of the texts within the dynamics of modern Hebrew literature that at the time was in the process of shaping a new Jewish national identity. By reinterpreting formerly suppressed literary practices, we hope to extend the range of past literary options. We also hope to describe what the texts that remained part of the canon have imparted to us as a range of historically determined and politically selected literary products and not as an accumulation of selected and given authorized texts. Pointing out what mechanisms led certain leading agents to exclude particular texts from the canon entails uncovering the cultural and material circumstances in which these texts were produced and is bound to expose clashes of interests and power struggles between the parties involved. This form of criticism was advocated by Walter Benjamin when he described the task of the critical materialist historian as "brushing history against the grain" of official historical writing (1969, 259–62), which, by its very nature, reduces and limits the possibilities available and constricts them within a constructed linear and unified official historical progression from the national past to the present (see Anderson 1991, 161–62).

The primary issue on the agenda of those who constructed the emergent modern Hebrew canon was which Hebrew narrative would a wide public regard as paradigmatic and "naturally" true. As noted by the feminist critic Lillian Robinson, the issue of literary canon, in general, was considered a gentleman's agreement secured by an elite to whom it was valuable and it was not actually perceived as a vehicle of oppression (Robinson 1989, 572). Accordingly, many cultural practices within the hegemonic culture shape standard national Subjects, which are perceived as perfectly natural, commonplace products of literary writing. The practice of historiography, for instance, is central to constructing the canon of a national literature. Throughout the "revival" era, Hebrew literary historiography maintained a systematic linearity that over the years coincided with a more or less stable image of the standard national Subject. At the same time, historical writing removed from its index those who tried to undermine the hegemonic version of the Zionist canon. Yet, as we hope to show, this does not imply that the criteria determining the inclusion or exclusion of an author in the canon is contingent on a writer's overt political stance. Constructing a standard Subject has more to do with the representation of a desirable image for human existence that prescribes guidelines and values within the context of the hegemonic culture.

The linear progression of modern Hebrew literary historiography is predominantly grounded in the concept of *"Sifrut HaTehiya,"* Revival Literature, which integrates the idea of a literary revival with a national renaissance. The reversal within Hebrew culture that took place at the advent of modern Jewish nationalism is almost always marked by the historical writing known as "Storms in the Negev" that followed the 1883 pogroms in Russia that so abruptly dashed the maskilic hopes of eastern European Jewish intellectuals for a Jewish existence in the diaspora (e.g., Katz 1979, 3–12). The shift from *"Sifrut HaHaskala,"* Enlightenment Literature, to Modern Hebrew Literature is thus located around the end of the 1880s and the beginning of the 1890s, and modern Hebrew literature is considered, often by some of its own producers, to have been contingent on the historical events of the 1880s (Shaked 1977, 25).

7. A Universalist Canon vs. Regional Literature

As we have previously suggested, the conception of a national literature is generally based on the presupposed yet constructed desirable "national Subject." If we perceive a national literature as a form of historical representation based on a constructed image of subjectivity and reality, rather than as a natural, inherent narrative, we can "isolate" the components of the historiographical description and examine its delimiting power structures. The aesthetic notion underpinning most Western hegemonic views of a national literature can be referred to as universalistic. And this universalism locates the point of departure for the construction of the national collective in the free individual. According to the universalistic representation, the free individual is bound to undergo the experience of a national Subject during the course of building a new nation. The Western nationalist ideology on which this view is based evolved in the wake of the Western Enlightenment. Relocating the modern national Subject within a new national framework, Western national ideology highlights the individual's constituency as a free and equal individual within the national collective. This collective is perceived as a "typical," national collective, no different from any other (Talmon 1982, 14). "The nationalist idea," claimed Brenner at the time, "is only important insofar as it renders us free, proud, sure, rich in spirit, and creative" ([1908] 1985a, III, 234). However, the literary representation of universality must be realized by representing single individuals: "Precisely those who experienced 'nationalism,'" wrote Brenner, distinguishing between maskilic literature and that of the era of national revival, "who did not pay any attention to their own personal career, but pooled all their resources for the building of the nation—they will sing unto their people the song of the Hebrew 'individual,' praise and protect the individual" (Brenner 1985a, IV, 1403–4).

Hence it is clear, for example, why David Frishman's political, anti-Zionist stance did not exclude his literary production from the national canon, but functioned centrally in his own realm of activity, thereby contributing to shaping the canon of modern Hebrew literature (Parush 1992, 10–11). To be sure, Frishman was extremely negative about the prospects of the Zionist movement as a political movement that would cure the Jewish people's afflictions. Yet at the same time, where the standard Subject was concerned, his position was not very far removed from that of Berdichevsky and Brenner; for he too held collective Jewish redemption to be contingent upon the spiritual redemption of the single Jewish individual (Parush 1992, 11–12, 17–43 passim).

The sort of universality mentioned above, which is embodied in the concept of a national Subject, occurs regularly in the rhetoric of what Antonio Gramsci (1971) has identified as the "ethical state." The idea of the ethical state is represented, first and foremost, in a cultural consensus regarding the universal status of hegemonic institutions that are perceived as natural and universal bodies through which mutually exclusive interests are reconciled. Issuing from these hegemonic institutions is a "moral gaze" that claims the right to judge, as it were, from the standpoint of "archetypal man." Literary products were a critical component of Western national consciousness because the aesthetic experience authorizes us to control the archetypal standpoint almost as though it were unmediated. Authors, then, come to be considered as representative and literary works are read as testimonials of typical human experiences. These authors, generally, do not regard this type of ethical universalism as personal, biographical experience, but rather as a manifestation of basic human desires and values. The authors are hence perceived as both representative and canonical (Lloyd 1987, 20). In this way, a historically determined approach to nationalist ideologies is shaped by a range of universal values linking the particular to a transcendental aesthetic reality. To this end, a range of attributes, traditionally shared in standard nationalist reality, is evoked whose very authority derives from its universality. These shared attributes provide the spectator/reader with a fixed range of metahistorical criteria by means of which specific moments within reality can be evaluated (Gramsci 1971, 240–41, 258–59, 261–63; Forgacs 1993, 177–90; Hall 1986, 5–25; Lloyd 1993, 9).

It is the spectator/reader's vision of the "ethical state" that enables us to posit the opposition between canonical and noncanonical literature as a struggle between what Gilles Deleuze and Felix Guattari have named "major" and "minor" literature (1986, 16–27). The power of "major literature" is grounded in the ambivalence of "common property" representing shared human possessions that effectively embody essential human desires and the universality of human nature. Because the representation of common human nature is implicitly "moral," major literary works belonging to the national majority claim that they are "disinterested." As David Lloyd (1987) has shown, the realm of the aesthetic in which a "major literature" is sited is thereby linked to the moral transcendence of political, racial, and class differences. It should, however, be noted that the major literary work derived its hegemony from this very disinterestedness: grounded in the concept of universality, "major literature" acquires its own moral legitimacy while imposing a dominant ethnocentric ideology (imperialism in Western history).

Typically, "minor literature" is conceived as a literature seeking to contest and overthrow the canon and its values. However, despite its attempts to violate the canon, "minor literature" can never fully appropriate features that are central to canonical literature; it thus always remains on the edges or margins (Lloyd 1987, 20).

Literary works produced by a minority, especially by a national minority, can purport to be "minor literature" even while they pose as a majority literature seeking to obscure group differences of race, nationality, and gender. As "minor literature" it also seeks to undermine prevailing aesthetic criteria and to propose an alternative aesthetic. Thus, at times, "minor literature" will find itself in a condition that the literary critic Myra Jehlen, in speaking about women's literature, calls the paradox of women writers—being "torn between defending the quality of their discoveries and radically redefining literary quality itself" (Jehlen 1981, 592). This paradox may ultimately be resolved only if it is perceived in terms of a historically determined power struggle.

In our case of Galician literature, it would appear that Fahan and Fernhoff's valorous attempt to propose an alternative to the mainstream Zionist canon was not followed up by a revision of mainstream aesthetic criteria, but rather by the unequivocal denial of most of the Galicians of a place in the canon. Only years later, after Reuven Fahan died in the Holocaust (Fernhoff having died even before), did they become symbols of a Judaism destroyed and were reassessed by proponents of the canon. Yet for all the compassion they eventually evoked (Sadan 1964, 118–29) as tokens of a forgotten culture (see Fernhoff 1952), they were finally excluded from the aesthetic arena, and the mainstream canon was reenforced.

Unlike "major literature," which strives to construct a Subject in possession of autonomous moral identity, "minor literature" is typically faced with the ongoing task of negation. Whereas in a novel embedded in "major literature" the narrative continuum will peak when a plot is realized or destroyed by desire, in minor literary works such as Kafka's "The Castle" the consummation of desire is always deferred. K.'s identity as a surveyor is always cast in question and he is never really equal to the other characters in the Castle. Subsequently, he unremittingly, yet to no avail, strives for recognition that he hopes might grant him a clear-cut role in society (Lloyd 1987).

The "minor literature" of Fahan, too, addresses the social and national identities of the Karaites, yet finally never clearly delineates or accounts for these identities. Writers and readers of "major literature" consider the narrative of "minor literature" to be unproductive, for it does not bring to fruition the desired collective objective. Indeed, radical Zionist criticism views the Karaites as laboriously striving toward a purposeless and unethical end. And yet we may see this as a function of Fahan being charged with having "sinned" simply because he dared to empathize with the Karaites and because he tried to represent their collective narrative in the same terms as the Jewish national one. Fahan's narrator is careful not to abrogate fully the frailty of the Karaite presence in the diaspora; he thus authorizes Jewish survival in the diaspora, and so undermines the privileged status of radical Zionists. In contradistinction, Berdichevsky and Brenner formulate narratives that climax with the construction of the individual Subject as a force to be reckoned with. "What struck me more than anything," Berdichevsky wrote to Brenner in February of 1908 after reading his play *"Meever Lagvulin"* (Beyond the Crossroad), "was that your hero's sorrow is not what humbles him, nor does his cry for pity following his distress and suffering, but rather the pride he manages to muster" (Berdichevsky and Brenner 1984, 38).

8. The Majority as a National Minority

The radical tendency toward obliterating Jewish existence in the diaspora led to reconceptualizing the most desirable future for Jewish survival. The mode of Jewish existence in the early twentieth century, as a national minority in the diaspora, was formulated in standard utopian terms of a national majority. This thrust, which presents a *minority as a national majority*, led to the representation of Zionism as the political avant-garde of the Jewish people. The concept of a national minority nestled within the nations of the world, crystallizing its political thinking and strategies in terms of a national majority, became part of the internal politics of Jewish life. The concept evolved as part of a broader internal-nationalist avant-garde thrust, which awarded the Zionists, a statistical minority among the Jews of Europe, the unusual status of the trailblazing wedge for the entire Jewish population of Europe solely on the strength of the inner convictions of its members. In effect, one might be expected to view the entire concept of "Zionism as avant-garde" as totally opposed to notions of Jews as minority communities remaining in Europe and "laboring for the present" (Almog 1982, 151).

Indeed, the perception of Zionism as an avant-garde movement proved greatly advantageous to Herzl and other adherents of political Zionism, who sought to reconcile the enormity of the movement's transnational mission, soon to be realized, with the fact that only a minority of Jews were Zionist flag-bearers. "Zionism," claimed Herzl, "is not a party. Its followers will come from many parties, just as it encompasses all parties in the life of a people. Zionism is the Jewish people-in-the-making" (Herzl 1897 in Almog 1982, 145). Zionists frequently attempted to ground the avant-garde position in history, as in the case of Max Nordau, who presented himself as one of Gideon's three hundred warriors (Almog 1982, 145).

In both direct and indirect modes, Brenner and Berdichevsky embraced the avant-garde approach to Zionism, and by the end of the century they had provided a canonical framework for several versions of a universally normative national literature. Brenner perceived the utopian slant of modern Hebrew literary production as essential to its future development. Moreover, he noted in an article written during his stay in Galicia that there is no Hebrew literature that can be perceived

> in the sense of an everlasting building, assembled brick by brick over generations, a self-generative entity progressing of its own accord, drawing new, revitalizing strength from its many readers. . . . But here are a number of gifted Hebrew writers who carry the light of the Lord in their hearts, and simply write in spite of everything . . . deeply-spirited writers, who seek to state their views regardless, and whose literary circumstances make them appear like flies trying to climb up a flat, slippery pane of glass—there have always been precious few such writers among us, yet there are still some! (Brenner 1985a, III, 237)

Opposing this model of heroic literature ("in spite of everything"), a literary model that became the basic foundation of Gershon Shaked's project of the history of modern Hebrew literature (see Shaked 1977, 32–34), a rather different attitude was adopted by Reuven Fahan, Yitzhak Fernhoff, and their young Galician colleagues, who sanctioned the idea of a local rather than a universal literature and preferred not to take a clear-cut stand on the diaspora dilemma and the demand for a Jewish nation with its own history, language, and territory.   Against the universalist views of the canonizers who sought to ground nationalist norms in individual rights, those in favor of regional or national autonomy and some of those who privileged "laboring for the present" wished to secure the political rights of the Jewish community and its status as a national minority.

9. The Politics of "Laboring for the Present"

Fernhoff's and Fahan's works entered an arena fraught with dissension about the future of modern Hebrew literature. Within the overall context of Zionist politics at the time, some of the most heated debates on this matter took place shortly after the "Helsingfors Conference" (1906), which legitimated the Zionist policy of "laboring for the present" and extended the concept of national responsibility to include the right to a Jewish life in the diaspora alongside demands for "laboring for the future" of Eretz-Israel (see Almog 1982 130–73).   While the "catastrophic" view of Zionism regarded a one-time, permanent solution as mandatory, the view promoting "Laboring for the Present" sought a gradual series of evolutionary steps toward Zionist goals.

From the year 1900, Zionist "political strategy" began to be more sensitive to the position that the dissolution of the diaspora was contingent on other major historical constraints. Members of the Zionist movement were urged to reconsider their objectives in view of the movement's newly conceived transitional role, which would eventually bring about the dispersion of the diaspora. Aware that this might be a rather lengthy process, certain parties began to consider the strategy of Zionists becoming politically active in their respective countries of residence. Galicia, which at the time belonged to the multinational Hapsburg Empire, had an extremely pluralistic population comprised of people with many different national identities. Jews in the Hapsburg Empire were awarded civil rights in 1868 and subsequently were allowed to vote. While this move led to an increased number of assimilated Jews, it also strengthened support for the Zionist movement.

The new Austrian government, which was founded in 1906, elicited hopes for democratization and inspired new directions within the existing framework of the Zionist organization. For example, Jews who were stuck between the Poles and the Ukrainians were forced to attempt to acquire some kind of political autonomy. At the Zionist conference held in Crakow in July 1906, there were demands for a party that would pursue "political structures for the Jews within the Austrian monarchy which would protect their national, cultural, and political rights" (Gelber 1958, 526). Those Zionists who countered this initiative grounded their views in the overall rejection of the diaspora as even a partial solution for the Jews. Assimilationists, too, were highly critical of the demand for regional autonomy, choosing rather to fight it to the death. Yet unlike the 1906 Helsingfors conference held by the Russian Zionists, where similar decisions were taken on rights for Jews as a national minority and where the importance of "Laboring for the Present" while living in the diaspora was weakly acknowledged, the conference in Crakow had some real political consequences, as support for the regional autonomy of the Jewish national minority was established and continued to grow (522–28). And to the dismay of the Zionist Executive (under president David Wolfson), Galician Zionism, which had never really enjoyed much attention, began to flourish independently of the Vienna Zionist center (530–40).

Brenner arrived in Galicia shortly before a struggle between the Zionists and the assimilationists took place, in which the former gained the upper hand. For example, in numerous communities the Zionists obtained the decisive vote on issues of Jewish education. This followed a disagreement between the two camps concerning the marked wave of anti-Semitism in the educational system at the time and the assimilationists' refusal to take a definitive stand on Jewish education (Gelber 1985, 165). This struggle peaked during the 1907 general elections when the Zionists won a most impressive number of electoral votes among the Jews.

Works by Fernhoff and Fahan were thus produced within a specific context of Austrian-Zionist culture, which had a firm tradition of "Laboring for the Present" (Almog 1982, 159). Austrian Zionism was concerned with the economic prosperity of the Jews in the diaspora and a desire to prepare them, culturally and mentally, for life in Jewish-Palestine. Some of these Zionists were not merely committed to recruiting economical, cultural, and political resources for future immigration to Eretz-Israel, but sought to buttress Jewish life in the diaspora and secure political rights for the diaspora Jews as well. Thus "Laboring for the Present" had practical consequences in the form of programs designed to ensure autonomous Jewish life in the diaspora (see Dubnov 1937, 52–82). These programs, of course, rested on the assumption that Jewish existence in the diaspora as a national minority was wholly legitimate. This is why the Jews could not be satisfied with equal civil rights as individual citizens in their host countries, but sought to further secure their identities as distinctive groups. The Austro-Hungarian electorate, especially the Austrian Socialists, supported the idea of national autonomy for communities sharing a common cultural identity (Talmon 1982, 173–212). Their support was based on the prevalent notion that the multinational population of the Hapsburg Empire could exist if the single individual could be perceived as part of a national minority, rather than as a member of a national territory.

10. Berdichevsky on Fahan

Berdichevsky's response to Fahan's book *MeHayei HaKaraim* (From the Karaites' Lives) was published in 1908 in *HaOlam*, the organ of the Zionist movement (Berdichevsky 1960, 172–73). Berdichevsky had a particular aversion to the book, due to the way it endorsed

"Laboring for the Present" by acknowledging and legitimating Jewish existence in the diaspora. Berdichevsky commented that Fahan's patronizing tone toward the Karaites in this collection of stories was a form of self-glorification characteristic of diaspora Jews, intended to distract them from the deep despair in which they were engulfed. The narrator, according to Berdichevsky,

> is introduced as a winner Rabbinite [Orthodox Jew] to the Karaite temple and proceeds to moan, moan more than narrate, forgetting that we ourselves are not firmly situated, and that we ourselves are people of a diaspora. . . . The types the narrator presents to us, with their miserable minds and experiences, may as well be affiliated to Rav Ashi . . . rather than to Anan [founding Karaite—H.H.]. (1960, 173)

Berdichevsky indicts Fahan for setting up a false opposition between Rabbinite and Karaite Jews. Because he sees Jewish life in the diaspora as quite undesirable, Berdichevsky believes that the Galician Jews have chosen to construct this fictional opposition as a means of displacement. Instead of facing their own bitter plight and admitting their own position of weakness, they have projected their own misery onto the Karaites' even more miserable predicament, thereby softening the harshness of their own fate. Elsewhere, in his article "*Adama*" (Territory), Berdichevsky alludes directly to supporters of Jewish autonomy in the diaspora. Just as he regarded the literary and political output of Galician Jewry as flawed, he is critical of the Austro-Hungarian supporters of autonomy. He faults them for having relinquished the territorial imperative he feels is mandatory for establishing a national identity (Berdichevsky 1960, 62–63).

Berdichevsky's rather too conspicuous bias reveals, however, that Fahan and Fernhoff are actually proposing an alternative Zionist vision that includes an acceptance of the diaspora. As the leading voices of modern Hebrew literature at the time, Brenner and Berdichevsky, were, it seems, prescriptive spokesmen for the canonical literary center, which itself represented a national community modeled largely on the modern sovereign nation and autonomous moral Subject. This fully rounded character was designed to arouse in its readers, themselves members of an "imagined" nation, feelings of identification based on universal attributes presumably shared by themselves and the character(s) portrayed.

Within the historical context of early-twentieth-century Hebrew culture, this notion of a minority as a national majority functioned in a very important way. On the one hand, modern Hebrew literature was grappling at the time with a self-image that reflected its own frailty (Miron 1987, 23–56). Yet at the same time there evolved, alongside the Zionist movement, a flurry of cultural and literary activity that had a powerful imaginative, utopic dimension. For instance, the leading Hebrew literary journal, *HaShiloah,* was founded in 1896, one year before the establishment of the Zionist Organization and the first Zionist Congress in Basel. As mentioned earlier, the alternative proposed by Galician writers was altogether more compatible with the emergent standpoint of the national Jewish minority in the diaspora. This Jewish ethnic minority was busy fighting for its own autonomy against the multinational backdrop of the Hapsburg Empire and staunchly opposed the Zionist demand for a sovereign, territorial nationalist entity (Talmon 1982, 173–77). The rift between local Galician writers and leading literary figures such as Brenner and his colleagues began to grow, and their political differences were finally manifested in aesthetic and poetical terms. The writers Brenner accused of having produced noncanonical, unaesthetic texts were in fact following the rules of an alternative aesthetic, which, under the historical circumstances of Hebrew literature at the beginning of the twentieth century, could be described as subversive, seeking, as it did, to undermine the hegemony of the emerging national culture.

11. Majority vs. Minority and Fictionality vs. Documentation

From the outset, Brenner considered the local version of Galician Zionism to be provincial (see also Sadan 1967, 133). He perceived it as limited in Zionist conviction and as a consequence of the Galicians' constricted mental and spiritual abilities. Brenner also believed that the Galicians had little, if any, capacity for literary writing. And what little they had was flawed, for it was shaped by inadequate Jewish social structures (Brenner 1985b, 275–76; 1985a I, 251).

When Brenner addressed Fahan's "From the Karaites' Lives," he expressed rage at Fahan's artistic presumptuousness, that is, at his "very pretension of being an artist." Brenner does not deem Fahan's text worthy of being called "literature," and suggests that it should rather be relegated to newspaper publications and placed alongside journalistic correspondence. Brenner stresses the problematic status of Fahan's book as a work of art and in effect works to remove it from the canon of Hebrew literature. The main reason for exclusion is found in its apparently dubious generic affiliation, implied by the book's subtitle, "Types and Illustrations."

> It may indeed have been inconsequential for our writer here to pen lengthy correspondence to *HaOlam* [The World] about the way he sees life in the Karaite quarter, which was no doubt extremely interesting: Laws of purity and profanity, sitting in the dark on the Sabbath, etc., etc.,—No! Of all [subtitles] "Types and Illustrations." . . . And did not Zangwill describe the lives of children in the Ghetto, London Jews, so why shouldn't Reuven Fahan compose "Types and Illustrations" from lives of the Karaites? And lest you ask: where are the "Lives of Karaites"—do the Karaites live a secluded existence, a distinct economic life, a life in which they construct spiritual categories of their own, a life which can determine its own value and significance? (Brenner 1985a, III, 253)

Brenner thus delegitimizes Fahan's canonical status, stipulating that in order for a text to be incorporated into the literary canon it must portray a complete lifestyle experience possessing a distinctiveness of its own. More aptly, Brenner's nationalist patterns of thinking called for a distinctive lifestyle whose particular attributes could readily be represented in universalist terms. Thus we see here how the success or failure of the work to transform the particular into universal human traits becomes the criterion through which Brenner distinguishes between documentary representation, journalistic writing, and literary fictional representation.

The distinction between realistic fiction and documentation is often a matter of interpretation. For, as noted by Roland Barthes, realism is not a window looking out onto reality, but the outcome of symbolic processes. Reading a text containing representations of objects as they exist "out there" in the world as realistic fiction—in our case, "types and illustrations"—basically amounts to interpreting the textual representation of other texts. Hence, the "realistic" effect is achieved primarily by identifying represented elements as familiar textual products, rather than as objects that actually exist in the world. In this sense, these elements are believed to possess universally omnipresent powers (Barthes 1970, 20–23, 122–28).

In regard to the "types" indicated in Fahan's subtitle, Brenner, Berdichevsky, and M. M. Feitelson all specify that they have no "individual mental attributes" (Feitelson 1970, 156). What they mean, most likely, is that Fahan's characters do not have attributes that make it easy for us to perceive them as individuals in their own right. Yet "individuality" is by no means a singular, one-time occurrence. Indeed, the single individual stands in binary opposition to the collective, and as such is grounded on the representation of the human being by and through an accepted universal, rather than by forming particular identities. A critical interpretation based on Fahan's text thus presumes the existence of a desirable extraliterary world juxtaposed to the alternative "reality" constructed within the literary text. Thus, the critical claim concerning the absence of individual characters in Fahan's text is based on a normative concept of reality that is diametrically opposed to the literary text. It is this normative concept that underlies Brenner, Berdichevsky, and Feitelson's canonical criticism and poses the individual character as a universal category that is first and foremost universally human and only secondarily ethnically or nationally specific (Feitelson 1970, 255). The primary function of this normative representation of reality is to outline the future utopic dimension of national survival for members of the contemporary national community. This normative view advanced by the critic-cum-interpreter does not claim to represent reality as it is, but rather seeks to construct a desirable version of reality; it thus plays a crucial role in constructing the imagined national community (Anderson 1991).

Distinguishing between the fictional and the documentary or historical is basically synonymous with distinguishing between a truthful claim and a fictional claim. Hence, the distinction between reading a text as fictional or reading it as documentary has nothing to do with the reader's degree of success or failure, but rather with distinguishing between a range of different reading aesthetics that may all be applicable to one and the same text (see Stierle 1980, 83–105). Documentary representation calls for truth validity, for it applies to representations that have a concrete status in time and space. On the other hand, realistic or plausible fiction establishes generalizations that demand recognition as truth that may not be concretely valid, but would ring conceivably true in a range of possible instances. What determines whether a particular fictional character meets the required standards of realistic fiction? First and foremost, the appraisal of the critic-cum-interpreter. Critical sensibilities concerning the extent to which a fictional character is universal or typically human will be shaped by a critical assessment of the text's target readership. When the critic-cum-interpreter discerns a readership that is likely to perceive a character as "representative," he or she will accordingly introduce this character as a product of realistic fictional representation. But if the critic-cum-interpreter is unable to discern whether a readership would identify a character as the overall generalization, as representative representation, he or she will not be able to cite the said character(s) as the product(s) of realistic fictional representation. When the critic-cum-interpreter decides that a readership is unlikely to attribute universal traits to the fictional character in question, he or she thereby precludes the possibility of identifying the text as fiction and will thus classify the text as nonfiction or documentary and identify its textual components and embodied characters accordingly.

The fictional-documentary opposition often proves to be an application of two possible critical strategies. Inability to adduce one option will promptly lead to application of the other, and vice versa. This dichotomy also pertains to the political implications that followed the critical appraisal of Galician literature: interpretations of literature as fiction are committed to national utopia and the rejection of the existence of the diaspora in the present. For Brenner and Berdichevsky, standards of realistic fiction functioned as aesthetic guidelines in the formation of the national literary canon.

12. Fiction by Brenner and Berdichevsky

Brenner wrote prolifically during his sojourn in Galicia, where his works were also published. Alongside critical works and public debates he also penned two of his more celebrated works there, "*Shana Ahat*" (One Year) and "*Min HaMeitzar*" (From Wretchedness). Both works adhere to literary standards authorized by Brenner himself. Brenner sought to create an effect of fictionality in a most radical mode. As Menahem Brinker (1990) has shown, he used the nonfictional illusion of autobiography to enhance the authority of his fictional writing. Brenner used what Brinker calls the "rhetorics of honesty" to mold personal data into fictional types. These types had the power to represent an era and a national community. Thus, although in his critical essays Brenner demanded a clear distinction between fiction and nonfiction, in his literature he liked to employ nonfictional illusions and thus he contributed to the transformation of documentary, autobiographical (i.e., minor) representation into universal (major) representation.

At the center of his Galician and other works, Brenner locates a Subject, the young Jewish recluse, often featured in other Hebrew literary works written toward the end of the nineteenth century and early into the twentieth (Halkin 1958, 339–71; Bakun 1978). Most conspicuous examples of this character were Dr. Vynik, the protagonist of *"HaTalush"* (The Detached) by Y. D. Berkowitz (1904), and Michael, protagonist of Berdichevsky's *"Mahanaim"* (1900). The biographies of the central characters in these texts represent, as it were, the collective biographies of the younger generation who on the one hand renounced their parents' orthodox way of life, yet on the other were frustrated by the fact that Enlightenment values could not reconcile the unmistakable contradictions in their lives. Having experienced profound spiritual and mental crises, members of this generation returned to the fold of the national collective, more often than not as single individuals taking comfort in their own inner worlds.

Such a process of individuation is undergone, for instance, by Menahem, Berdichevsky's protagonist in *"Menahem"* (1900), and by other characters in such works as *"HaZar"* (The Foreigner) and *"Mahanaim."* This duplicitous process of negative universalization entails, on the one hand, the characters' differentiation from configurations of social identity such as the family, the community, and the nation, while at the same time accumulating great personal strength, grounded in the characters' withdrawal from the constraints of social identity and their increased resilience as single individuals. The basic structure of character representation in Berdichevsky's fiction is a conflictual one that evolves into an oxymoronic situation.

In *"Menahem,"* for example, the character's name is grounded in an oppositional allegory comprising light and darkness: "Menahem of the Meir [Illuminating—H.H.] Family," while "his forefathers went about in the dark, and his townspeople went about in the darkness" (Berdichevsky 1991, 19). Menahem, who had renounced his life as a Jew among his own people and gone to a foreign land to acquire knowledge, focused on erudition and the sciences. Depending on secular Enlightenment was represented as rife with inner contradictions, which included the radical elimination of Menahem's traditional Jewish past and the construction of a new lifestyle: "Everything he had had before was taken away and given to him anew . . . he lost everything yet he found everything . . . having rejected everything, he rebuilt everything by himself" (Berdichevsky 1991, 19). The central conflict in this narrative is revealed when Menahem realizes that his quest is in vain, for wisdom and science will get him nowhere. The rational maskilic resolution gives way to a vitalistic one: "His soul is devoid of vital substance, his life depleted of the ability to live, his heart bears no love or kinship" (20). Menahem relinquishes all former social bonds and dispositions ("He has neither a people nor the need(s) for a people, no parents nor kinfolk, he cries out for love and the sorrow of love"), and turns to the only possible resolution, a universality realizable only by way of the isolated individual.

> At last he found everything by losing everything . . . his soul is now steered by his head, for he is master of all his own thoughts and visions. All the riches in the whole world are now being kept for him, for he has had none of this happiness yet, that is, he is master *of everything* because he has not mastered but a single corner. (Berdichevsky 1991, 21; my emphasis)

In this way Berdichevsky's texts construct autonomous ethico-moral Subjects, "rounded" individuals who persuasively impress their readers as truly representative, in light of their claim for universal attributes that can be shared by characters and readers alike. Unlike the documentary text that bases its rapport with the reader on uniquely specific, familial, and tribal features appearing at given moments in time and space, the fictional text establishes an affiliation on the basis of plausible universal attributes in a familiar historical situation. Hence, it is apt that the modern nationalists who perceived the concept of the nation to be vital and all-encompassing placed the single Hebrew individual at the center of the nation. Hence, the national literature seeking canonization molded a hegemonic world picture authorized by its very claim to the creation of compelling forms of generalizing representation.

The canonical writers functioned on behalf of a "major literature" in the throes of a power struggle with the Galician "minor literature," which comprised marginal and secondary literary works (Deleuze and Guattari 1986). Indeed, in order to bar the minor Galician writers from the emergent national canon, Brenner bombarded them with propositions authorizing the aesthetic standards of the "major literature." Trying, by way of aesthetic statements, to delegitimize the Galicians, Brenner masked his political interests through aesthetic claims. Like other members of the critical coterie of "major literature," he also referred to Fahan's book as an ethnographic documentary, that is, a work comprised of elements that may be significant in their own right but are ultimately lacking because they cannot be generalized. The book's shortcoming, in Brenner's eyes, lay in the very presumption of it being a work of literary fiction. Brenner believed that Fahan's text lacked the universal features required to generate the normative, universalistic empathy in its readers. Thus, Fahan's writing lacked the features required to help its audience construct a notion of modern nationalism.

13. Originality vs. Collectivism in "Minor Literature"

Unlike Brenner and Berdichevsky's commitment to individuals, minor Galician texts foregrounded collectivist discourse, primarily through the construction of characters. Feitelson (1970, 157) and Berdichevsky criticized the monotony of the Karaite characters in Fahan's book—their similarity to one another, and the superficial differences between them. Unlike major literary texts, Fahan's minor texts do not specify private life experiences that represent via universalization the national community. Hence, noted Feitelson, "the human being within the Karaites is not well portrayed." He also pointed out that the stories do not really portray people who are Karaites (as one would portray them in belletristic writing), but he portrays rather male and female Karaites (Feitelson 1970, 157).

A common manifestation of Galician cultural collectivism is the blurring between the private and the public realms. Thus Brenner, in his critical diatribe on literary and publicistic writing in Galicia, ridiculed the way Galician writer Gershon Baader failed to distinguish between his own private affairs in his public writing (Brenner 1985b, 271). The minor text's collectivism is measured, among other things, by its tendency to obscure its own artistic origins. Unlike "major literature," which seeks to highlight the originality of the literary text and the fact that it is produced by an individual artist's imagination, "minor literature" introduces the text as the product of a collaborative effort. It was common in Galician cultural arts to obscure and blur the boundaries between the original work, the professional artist, and readers who were themselves often writers (see Kleinman 1908).

Fahan and Fernhoff's "minor literature" refuses to report how autonomous Subjectivity is acquired and in this they deny the task of a "major literature." This refusal on the level of the represented world embodies another refusal on the level of the mode of representation. Instead of appearing as an original and autonomous text, which has explicitly artistic roots, the minor text adopts strategies that are contingent, as it were, on previous texts. Brenner was indignant about the fact that half the stories in Fernhoff's book were adaptations and translations, and that in the subtitle the author made no attempt to be original. Elsewhere, Brenner criticized a almanac edited by Gershon Baader at Lvov for incorporating the reprinted works of well-known authors (Brenner 1985b, 275). A text signed by Adondon (1908), apparently a pseudonym used by S. Y. Agnon in his youth (see Kressel 1968; compare Bakan 1982, 98–122), after he immigrated from Galicia to Eretz-Israel, harshly criticized Fahan's *From the Karaites' Lives*, stating that the book represents all that is deficient in Galician literature and that no one has been able to find in it "anything original, everything is always 'about something or other' that already exists" (Adondon 1908, 72).

We are just one step away from more detailed claims against the poetics of "minor literature," such as, for instance, Berdichevsky's critique of the rhetoric of Fahan's narrators, whereby "he generally *informs* rather than *composes*, and when he does compose, *he repeats the same tune over and over*, till we know it from beginning to end" (Berdichevsky 1960, 273, my emphasis; see also Feitelson 1970, 256). Berdichevsky bemoans the narrator's privileging of telling over showing; telling leads to indirect, mediated speech and obscures the autonomic effect of the major Subject. The height of "telling" takes place when there is what Berdichevsky called a lapse from fictional narrative into documentary reporting and from original utterances to imitation and simulation: "the narrator copies into the stories *complete prayers* from the Siddur; often completely forgetting that he is a narrator, he reads the inscriptions on the graves of the deceased heroes, row by row" (Berdichevsky 1960, 273).

The stories' predictable and schematic plots undermine the autonomy of the represented Subjects. The canonical hegemonic Subject constructed by Berdichevsky and Brenner rejected the social context in which the diaspora existed, and it is this total rejection that led to the establishment of the radical Zionist alternative option. But when rejection of the diaspora is only partial, as in Galician texts, the alternative option proposed is not mandatory. Hence, compromise led to the collapse of the universalistic grounding of the national Subject. In addition, the critical advocates for the "major literature" could not come to terms with the lack of originality or autonomy of the Subjects constructed in Galician literature and therefore did their best to exclude this literature from the canon of modern Hebrew literature.

REFERENCES

Adondon (Agnon, S. Y.). "Bibliography." *HaPoel HaTzair.* Tamuz-Av, 1908.

Agnon, S. Y. *Me-Azmi el Azmi* (From Me to Myself). Tel Aviv: Schocken, 1976.

Ahad Ha'am. *Kol Kitvei Ahad Ha'am* (The Collected Writings of Ahad Ha'am). Tel Aviv: Dvir, 1943.

Almog, Shmuel. *Zionut VeHistoria* (Zionism and History). Jerusalem: Magnes, 1982.

Anderson, Benedict. *Imagined Communities.* London and New York: Verso, 1991.

Bakun, Itzhak. "Introduction." In *Y. H. Brenner—Mivhar Mamarim al Yezirato HaSipurit* (Y. H. Brenner—Selected Essays on His Fiction), ed. I. Bakun. Tel Aviv: Am-Oved, 1972.

———. *Brenner HaTzair* (The Young Brenner). Vols. 1, 2. Tel Aviv: Ha-Kibbutz HaMeuhad, 1975.

———. *HaTzair HaBoded BaSiporet HaIvrit 1899-1908* (The Young Solitary in Hebrew Fiction). Tel Aviv: Agudat HaStudentim, 1978.

———. *Mitoch HaHavura* (From within Community). Tel Aviv: Papyrus, 1982.

———. *Brenner BeLondon* (Brenner in London). Beer Sheva: Ben-Gurion University, 1990.

Barthes, Roland. *S/Z.* Trans. R. Miller. New York: Oxford University Press, 1970.

Benjamin, Walter. "Theses on the Philosophy of History." In *Illuminations,* ed. Hannah Arendt, trans. Harry Zohn. New York: Schocken, 1969.

Berdichevsky, Micha Yosef. *Kitvei Micha Yosef Berdichevski* (Ben-Gurion) (The Writings of Micha Yosef Berdichevsky). Tel Aviv: Dvir, 1960.

———. *Sippurei 1900* (The Stories of 1900). Tel Aviv: Iriat Hulon and Reshafim, 1991.

Berdichevsky, Micha Yosef, and Yosef Haim Brenner. *Halifat Igrot* (Correspondence). Tel Aviv: Beit Dvora VeImanuel, 1984.

Brenner, Yosef Haim. *Yosef Haim Brenner Ktavim* (The Writings of Yosef Haim Brenner). 4 vols. Tel Aviv: HaKibbutz HaMeuhad and Sifriat Poalim, 1985a.

———. *HaKtavim HaYidiim Shell Y. H. Brenner* (The Yiddish Writings of Y. H. Brenner). Ed. Yitzhak Bakun. Beer Sheva: HaKatedra Le-Yiddish, Ben-Gurion University, 1985b.

Brinker, Menahem. *Ad HaSimta HaTeverianit* (Until the Tiberian Lane). Tel Aviv: Am-Oved, 1990.

Deleuze, Gilles, and Felix Guattari. *Kafka, Toward a Minor Literature.* Trans. Dona Polan. Minneapolis: University of Minnesota Press, 1986.

Dubnov, Shimon. *MiKtavim Al HaYahadut HaYeshana VeHaHadasha* (Letters about Old and New Judaism). Tel Aviv: Dvir, 1937.

Fahan, Reuven. *MeHayei HaKaraim: Tziyurim VeTipusim* (From the Karaites' Lives: Types and Illustrations). Halich: Akselrod, 1908.

Feitelson, Menahem Mendel. "MeHayei HaKaraim" (From the Karaites' Lives). In *BeHinot VeHaarahot* (Inspections and Evaluations), ed. A. B. Yaffe. Ramat-Gan: Masada, 1970.

Fernhoff, Yitzhak. *Sefer HaMitnagdim,* ed. Israel Cohen. Tel Aviv: Dvir, 1952.

———. *MeAggadot HaHaim* (From the Legends of the Living). Podgorzje: Hanizpe, 1908.

Forgacs, David. "National-Popular: Genealogy of a Concept." In *The Cultural Studies Reader,* ed. Simon During. London and New York: Routledge, 1993.

Gelber, Michael Natan. *Toldot HaTnuah HaZionit BeGalizia 1875–1918* (The History of the Zionist Movement in Galicia). Vol. 2. Jerusalem: HaSifria HaZionit and Reuven Mas, 1958.

Gramsci, Antonio. *Selections from the Prison Notebooks.* Ed. and trans. Quintin Hoare and Geoffrey Nowell-Smith. London: Lawrence and Wishart, 1971.

Halkin, Shimon. *Mavo LaSiporet HaIvrit* (Introduction to the Hebrew Fiction). Jerusalem: Mifal HaShichpul, 1958.

Hall, Stuart. "Gramsci's Relevance for the Study of Race and Ethnicity." *Journal of Communication Inquiry* 10 (1986).

Jehlen, Myra. "Archimedes and the Paradox of Feminist Criticism." *Signs* 6 (Summer 1981).

Katz, Yaakov. *Leumiyut Yehudit: Masot VeMehkarim* (Jewish Nationalism: Essays and Studies). Jerusalem: HaSifria HaZionit, 1979.

Kleinman, Moshe. "MeZakei HaRabim" (They Who Justify the Many). *HaMitzpeh,* 29 Tevet 1908.

Kressel, Getzel. "Reshito shel Agnon Be'HaPoel-HaTzair" (Agnon's Beginnings in the Young Worker). *HaPoel HaTzair,* 1968.

Lloyd, David. *Nationalism and Minor Literature.* Berkeley: University of California Press, 1987.

———. *Anomalous States.* Durham: Duke University Press, 1993.

Luz, Ehud. *Makbilim Nifgashim* (Parallels Meet). Tel Aviv: Am-Oved, 1985.

Miron, Dan. *Bodedim BeMoadam* (Singular in Their Time). Tel Aviv: Am-Oved, 1987.

Parush, Iris. *Kanon Sifruti VeIdeologia Leumit* (Literary Canon and National Ideology). Jerusalem: Mosad Bialik, 1992.

Rabbi Benyamin. "BeToch HaEreg: Dor Shileshim—Dor Tzanua" (Woven into the Fabric: The Third Generation, The Humble Generation). *HaPoel HaTzair*, 3 June 1909.

Robinson, Lillian. "Treason our Text: Feminist Challenges to the Literary Canon." *Critical Theory since 1965*, ed. H. Adams and L. Searle. Tallahassee: Florida State University Press, 1989.

Sadan, Dov. *Avnei Gvul* [Border Stones]. Ramat-Gan: Masada, 1964.

———. *Kvuzot Ilit Ushchavot Manhigut BeToldot Israel UbeToldot HeAmim* (Elite Groups and Leading Classes in the History of Israel and Its People). Jerusalem: Magnes, 1967.

Shaked, Gershon. *HaSiporet HaIvrit, 1880–1970* (Hebrew Fiction). Tel Aviv: Keter and HaKibbutz HaMeuhad, 1977.

Stierle, Karl. *The Reader in the Text*. Princeton, N.J.: Princeton University Press, 1980.

Talmon, Yaakov. *Mitos HaUmma VeHazon HaMhapecha* (The Myth of the Nation and the Vision of Revolution). Tel Aviv: Am-Oved, 1982.

Jewish Thought

Chapter 9

The Hermeneutic Turn in Franz Rosenzweig's Theory of Revelation

Yudit Kornberg Greenberg

Rosenzweig's theological construction in *The Star of Redemption* offers a new thinking not only on creation, revelation, and redemption, but also on language, textuality, the question of self and other, and the production of meaning. His notion that revelation is a privileged linguistic moment has fruitful implications for the philosophical debate on the hierarchical order of speech and writing, and for the religious debate on the relationship between revelation and tradition.[1]

There is a fundamental tension between Rosenzweig's claim for the privileged status of audible speech as an experience of Presence, and his simultaneous claim for texts that can bring about such an experience. The priviliging of speech in Western philosophy has produced a hierarchical order with which some contemporary thinkers vehemently disagree. If speech is a primary and immediate experience, and thus can be identified with an experience of Presence, then writing or reading are secondary or inferior activities.[2] While on the one hand, Rosenzweig exhibits such logocentric tendencies in the second part of *The Star of Redemption*, his method of reference to biblical text and his reliance on its relational powers ignores or perhaps intentionally dissolves the boundaries of audible and written speech (Rosenzweig 1972, 1976).[3]

The focus of this essay will be an explication of Rosenzweig's notion of speech and its relationship to the textual dimension of his concept of revelation.[4] My aim is to go beyond a logocentric reading of Rosenzweig's speech thinking in an effort to show the depth of the dialectic of speech and text that permeates his concept of revelation. Underscoring a significant methodological and conceptual shift in his discussion, I will expose Rosenzweig's hermeneutic turn, from the notion of *speech as revelatory* to the notion of a *revelatory text*. More than merely accounting for the relevance of metaphors from the Song of Songs, I will scrutinize Rosenzweig's conviction that this text is pivotal to his theory of revelation, and by extension that texts can be revelatory and transformative. I will examine his midrash on the Song and focus on key phrases that convey that the Song was a revelation to him. I will suggest that recent hermeneutic theories such as "reader response" are helpful in unpacking the import of textuality in Rosenzweig's concept of revelation.

Finally, I will show that Rosenzweig's ontology of speech as revelation, with its subsequent tension between audible and written speech, represents an effort to translate a religious dynamic into philosophical theology. This is the dynamic between living experience and tradition, to which rabbinic and kabbalistic hermeneutics attest.[5] This characteristic trend in Jewish thought further illuminates the hermeneutic dimension of Rosenzweig's concept of revelation.

The Logocentric View of Revelation

In order to understand the nexus of speech and the experience of revelation, it is necessary to introduce several claims that Rosenzweig makes regarding language in general and speech in particular. He rejects traditional philosophical assumptions of cognition that have perpetuated the subservience of language to ideas and reality, and that have repressed time and history. He terms traditional philosophical treatment of language and time as the "old thinking" and launches a massive attack on Idealism in particular.

In turn, we find in *The Star* an account of the primordial or transcendental origins and dimensions of language.[6] Rosenzweig explicates the possibility of a speech prior to speech, distinguishing between the potential for speech and the exteriorization of such a possibility in the encounter with the other (Rosenzweig 1972, 108–11; 1976, 120–23). An original blueprint of language precedes the occurrence of speech and is manifested in the act of speech. Exhibiting primordial origins and reality itself, language is "the original symbolism of reality itself and accordingly in the closest sense of identity with this reality" (1972, 150; 1976, 167). Language in Rosenzweig appears to be identical with reality. Moreover, its recurrence parallels the daily renewal of the universe. Rosenzweig explicates this parallel between the transcendent dimension of language and the miracle of the world's recreation as follows:

> The human word is a symbol; with every moment it is newly created in the mouth of the speaker, but only because it is from the beginning and because it already bears in its womb every speaker who will one day effect the miracle of renewing it. (1972, 111; 1976, 123)

The above claim underscores the transcendent properties of speech that render it a continual manifestation of the Eternal. Rosenzweig distinguishes between human speech and divine speech as follows: Human speech is not *created* by human beings for it has primordial origins. God's speech is by far more creative, for it is through the divine word that the world came into being. At the same time, human speech is *symbolically* creative by re-creating itself out of its primordial blueprint. Additionally, speech *demands* that it would be *continuously* re-created for it is "the thread running through everything human that steps into its miraculous splendor and into that of its ever renewed presentness of experience" (1972, 111; 1976, 123).

Thus, speech and transcendence are linked. Because of its primordial origins, language is both immanent and transcendent. If language enables us to communicate with others, Rosenzweig would contend that it is due not only to our conventional system of linguistic signs, but also to the otherness of language. Such otherness reverberates in our speaking and renders our speech a miraculous occurrence.

It is therefore pertinent to note that Rosenzweig juxtaposes his claim of the transcendence of speech with his theory of "speech thinking" (Glatzer 1961, 199; Rosenzweig 1937).[7] Speech thinking sees language itself as a form of thinking, in contrast to discursive philosophical thinking that relies completely on logic. Speech thinking's main characteristic is that it is time-bound. "It does not know in advance just where it will end."

> Speech thinking needs another person and takes time seriously. Actually, these two things are identical. In the old philosophy, 'thinking' means thinking for no one else and speaking to no one else (and here, if you prefer, you may substitute 'everyone' or the

well known 'all the world' for 'no one'). But 'speaking' means speaking to someone and thinking for someone. And this someone is always a quite definite someone, and he has not merely ears, like 'all the world,' but also a mouth. (Glatzer 1961, 200)

This concept of speech refers to the phenomenon of living speech and its everyday occurrence. But, as we saw earlier, speech in *The Star* is not only ordinary utterances but also an experience of transcendence. In other words, Rosenzweig treats language phenomenologically and metaphysically. At the same time, a significant qualification must be made; namely, that while not all *Sprache* is necessarily revelatory, revelation must be linguistic and occupy the space of the word. It should also be noted here that the former is implicit in *The Star*, whereas the latter, the belief that revelation is always linguistic, is quite explicit, as the following statement conveys: "In the world of revelation everything becomes word" (1972, 178; 1976, 199).

Textuality and Revelation

Rosenzweig's discourse on revelation proceeds to take a hermeneutic turn from discursive thought to thought shaped by text. Once he establishes that revelation is a speech act, he demonstrates it by turning to biblical text whose "speech" he believes manifests divine-human encounter. We might say here that he retextualizes his truth claims in the space of the biblical word and its web of belief. But rather than employing biblical speech as an *example* of *Sprache*, one expression among a multitude of culturally produced linguistic creations, he makes a normative Jewish claim: namely, that biblical speech is not merely an example or a description of revelatory speech but rather that it is itself *paradigmatic* of such speech.

The claim that biblical speech *is* revelatory raises the main problematic of this essay. It is the issue of reconciling Rosenzweig's logocentric view with a textually based view of revelation. How can the language of the Bible be as alive as our living speech in the present? Or to put it differently, why wouldn't the Bible according to Rosenzweig be subject to the hierarchy of speech thinking, where living speech is a primary and immediate experience and writing is a secondary and mediated act? While it seems that, hierarchically speaking, logocentrism and textuality could not be reconciled, it is our aim to show the suppleness of these categories in *The Star of Redemption*. In light of postmodernist theories such as "reader response," we believe that Rosenzweig offers very suggestive notions on textual hermeneutics and the question of the other.

Revelatory Speech and Its Auditory Dimension

Our objective to clarify the dynamism of speech and text leads us to question the phenomena of speech as revelation: Is it speaking, hearing, or perhaps both? Who and what initiates this phenomenon? Must revelatory speech be *given* to us and only then demand our response, or can we initiate the revelatory moment, making demands on it as mutual partners in this enterprise of exalted speech and therefore creating and re-creating it?

Rosenzweig proceeds to delineate what is unique about the speech of revelation. Revelatory speech is fluid and can never be fixed, reduced, and/or measured, unlike the speech of law, mathematics, or art. Rather, it is the spontaneous speech of love. "God's first word to the soul that unlocks itself to him is 'love me!' *(Liebe mich)*" (1972, 177; 1976, 198). As a commandment of love, God's word is "the immediate presentness and unity of consciousness, expression, and expectation of fulfillment" (1972, 177; 1976, 197). Moreover, revelatory speech is dialogical. The reciprocity between two speakers is essential to this moment: "If you acknowledge me, then I am."[8]   Even where we can find "something spoken" in a painting or in a book, we cannot find "speaking itself," for such speaking needs a real other, another speaker, whose presence alone dictates and demands a response, a new speech.

Yet this position that only in spontaneous and dialogical speech can we locate revelation raises the problem of the properties of such speech. While any tangible artifact can stand on its own and be considered independently of its creator, in speech, according to Rosenzweig, the presence of the speakers is essential. The presence of the speakers must apparently produce, over and against their linguistic signs and their significations, an excess, or "otherness." As revelation takes place between God and human, it is *their* presence that produces this otherness.

Rosenzweig alludes to a notion of presence as characterizing revelation. He describes the notion of divine manifestation *after* the process of creation, when God became concealed again. He states,

"The manifestation which we seek here must be such a one as is wholly and essentially revelation, and nothing else. . . . The power to change the color of created being, which is illuminated by such a moment . . . resides in the effulgence of this *coup d'oeil*" (1972, 161).

Initially Rosenzweig describes *love* as the revelatory realm between God and humanity. But later, the effulgence of love is transposed into the speech of love, the poetic dialogue of lover and beloved. Finally, it is the juxtaposition of love and speech along with the Presence of lover and beloved that satisfy the requirements for revelation. But if speech is an embodied entity, how do we distinguish revelatory speech from other embodiments of speech and form, and from other experiences and forms that are subject to embodiments and limits?

What is the phenomenon of speech that transcends the speaker and his/her speech? Our extrapolation of Rosenzweig's response to these questions suggests that the answer may lie within the auditory dimension of this speech phenomenon. The act of speaking consists, not only of words and their "acoustical images," but also of hearing. Rosenzweig describes this auditory dimension of speech as follows: "The ways of God are different from the ways of man, but the word of God and the word of man are the same. What man hears in his heart as his own human speech is the very word which comes out of God's mouth" (1972, 151; 1976, 167–68).

This passage invites several possible configurations of ideas. The most obvious is the indistinguishability of divine speech and human speech in the moment of revelation. This convergence of divinity and humanity in speech is unique and is unlike other human phenomena. Rosenzweig suggests that in the moment of revelatory speech there is a *proximity* of speakers where one is undifferentiated from the other. Furthermore, there is a close proximity of speakers and their speech, where hearing and speaking are simultaneous. The speakers hear their own speech as they simultaneously evoke the speech of their listeners who are other speakers.

Interestingly, Rosenzweig's description of the immediate experience of the prophet is derived from the notion of audition, yet surpasses dialogue. He refers to it quite explicitly in the following passage: "The prophet does not mediate between God and man. He does not receive revelation in order to pass it on; rather, the voice of God sounds forth directly from within him, God speaks as 'I' directly from within him" (1972, 178; 1976, 198).[9] Hearing then equals receptivity—a receptivity whereby the boundaries between speakers are temporarily and/or partially dissolved.

This twofold auditory dimension of speech plays a central role in Rosenzweig's notion of revelatory speech and is a key concept in the interface of textuality and revelation. Rosenzweig brings this auditory dimension into play by constructing a dialogical encounter that he pulls out of the biblical text. As he turns to the Bible, he finds that the human "I" is addressed by God, whose quest for his human counterpart is manifested as "Where art Thou?" The human readiness to respond, demonstrated in Abraham's *"Hineni"* (Here I am), completes the dialogic cycle of "word and response."[10] This moment of speech between God and person hinges upon *"gehörsame Hören"* (attentive hearing).

The Phenomena of Intersubjective Speech

It appears that Rosenzweig refers to two notions of speech in his concept of revelation: prophetic speech that overcomes the boundaries of speaker and listener and dialogic speech that retains intention, meaning, and mediation. About the latter Rosenzweig remarks, "Whoever speaks is translating his thoughts for the comprehension he expects from the other" (Glatzer 1988, 255; Rosenzweig 1937).[11] Such mediating features of dialogic speech distinguish it from the moment when God's call resounds *immediately* in the prophet's ear as the word of revelation.

Intersubjective speech, in accordance with Rosenzweig's own view of mediated speech (but counter to his notion of immediacy in prophetic speech) demonstrates the alterity of speakers and their speech. Rosenzweig develops dialogical speech and not prophetic speech as the *primary* experience of revelation. But even his dialogical notion of speech can be challenged as logocentric.

The challenge to logocentrism has been made convincingly by Derrida, who articulates and subsequently criticizes Husserl's concept of speech.[12] Husserl, like Rosenzweig, approximates a primary experience of presence. Derrida articulates Husserl's concept of speech as follows:

> When I speak, it belongs to the phenomenological essence of this operation that I hear myself at the same time that I speak. The signifier, animated by my breath and by the meaning-intention, is

in absolute proximity to me. The living act, the life-giving act, the *Lebendigkeit*, which animates the body of the signifier and transforms it into a meaningful expression, the soul of language, seems not to separate itself from itself, from its own self-presence. (Derrida 1973, 77)

Derrida, then, deconstructs this notion of speech that preserves the interiority of the subject even at the moment of exteriorization. It is precisely this temporality of exteriority, this interval of time outside of self that would shatter the supposed identity of the spoken with the act of speaking. The notion that speech transcends the boundaries of speakers and the boundaries between speaker and speech breaks down, and with it "any absolute inside, for the 'outside' has insinuated itself into the movement" (1973, 86).

This challenge to logocentrism presses us to consider the tension in Rosenzweig's writings between mediacy and immediacy. While speech is revelatory, so is the text to which Rosenzweig turns in order to demonstrate revelation. While Rosenzweig overcomes hierarchical thinking regarding speech and text, it remains in the Western philosophical "tradition of presence." His reading of the Song of Songs presents a dialogical encounter between God and the soul that suggests that the text is imbued with an animated but divine presence. While Rosenzweig is not explicit on the reasons for the Song's privileged status, he alludes to this and other selected biblical texts where he finds the "sensuality of the word brimful with its divine supersense" (1972, 201; 1976, 224).

Rosenzweig's Midrash on the Song of Songs

Rosenzweig's "midrash" on the Song of Songs further demonstrates his dialectic thinking that maintains a dynamic tension between speech with textuality. Rosenzweig's methodology as well as his ideas suggest the possibility of presence in the metaphors of the Song, as well as between the reader and this *embodied* speech of the Torah. The consequence of Rosenzweig's interpretation is that there is at least an essential nexus, if not an identity between this biblical text and the speech of revelation.

The embodied speech of the Song of Songs according to Rosenzweig is not a description of revelation; rather, it is *the* embodiment of revelatory speech. In his words, "It is not enough that God's relationship to man is explained by the simile of the lover and the beloved. God's word must contain the relationship of lover to beloved directly . . . and so we find it in The Song of Songs" (1972, 199; 1976, 222).

This passage suggests, in clear distinction from an allegorical hermeneutic, that the Song is *literally* the dialogue between humanity and God. It embodies the living presence between the I and the thou of the beloved, the space and time that defy mediation. This privileged text is thus key for Rosenzweig, both conceptually and methodologically. He retrieves the Song's speech as revelatory speech, for he recognizes the Song of Songs as "the focal book of revelation" (1972, 202; 1976, 225).

Rosenzweig's exegetical account of the Song brings to a close focus the *leitmotif* of love that is recurrent in his theological portrait of revelation. According to him, "Love is speech, wholly active, wholly personal, wholly living, wholly speaking" (1972, 202; 1976, 225–26). His commentary on verses from the Song such as "love is as strong as death" also retrieves his philosophical point of origin, the existential angst that characterizes the very beginning of the book and integrates it here in the poetics of biblical language (Rosenzweig 1927; Glatzer 1961, 276–82, 286–91).[13]

Rosenzweig argues that the frequency of the use of the pronoun "I" in the Song demonstrates the direct and immediate qualities of revelatory speech.[14] The verbs in the Song are almost always in the present tense. The sentences are short imperatives: "Draw me after you . . . open to me . . . arise . . . come away . . . hurry" (Rosenzweig 1972, 202). Such is the speech of love—direct, commanding. The line from the Song, "O that you were like a brother to me!" demonstrates and reinforces the uniqueness of revelatory speech. Revelatory speech expresses the yearning for fulfillment—a time that Rosenzweig recognizes as *outside* of revelation, for it points to the future and to redemption.

Rosenzweig's hermeneutics of the Song scripturally encodes a description of revelation.[15] The text becomes for him a pretext for rendering as plausible claims he regards as true. He confirms his notion of the experience of revelation in the truth of the text of the Song. As he states quite explicitly, "Once more we seek the word of man in the word of God" (1972, 198; 1976, 221, "*Wiederum suchen wir das Wort des Menschen im Wort Gottes)*." The consequences of his move from speech to love, to text, and to interpretation expose the text and Rosenzweig's response to it as satisfying his requirements for revelation.

Rosenzweig and Literary Theory

Rosenzweig underscores the auditory/response encounter that he identifies as revelation. His explication of this speech experience reminds us of Gadamer's linguistic "fusion of the horizons" of the speaker/reader and the world of the text (Gadamer 1982).[16] The most fecund elaboration of the tension between oral and written speech, and between living experience and text, is the following passage:

> If language is more than an analogy, if it is truly analogue (Gleichnis)—and therefore more than analogue—then that which we hear as a living word in our I and which livingly resounds towards us out of our Thou must also be 'as it is written' in that great historical testament of revelation whose necessity (Notwendigkeit) we recognized precisely from the presentness of our experience. (Rosenzweig 1972, 198; 1976, 221).[17]

Rosenzweig's dialectical thinking is quite evident here. Over and against the distinction between living experience and textuality, we find an identity in their difference. Our present moment that brings forth radically new speech is at the same time as ancient as the speech in our ancient texts. Despite their distinct moments, there is an active and partially reciprocal dynamic between the two speeches: we interact with the text and animate its speech that refracts its metaphors and truth claims; at the same time, our continuous engagement with the text results in our internalization of its mode of thinking: the speech of the text becomes inscribed in our hearts.

Recent development in literary criticism might shed light on Rosenzweig's assumptions in turning to the biblical text in validation of his views of revelation. Especially relevant here are certain reader-response theories, especially those of Wolfgang Iser and Stanley Fisher (Iser and Fisher 1974). For Iser, the literary work is actualized through a convergence of reader and text. The reader to him is actively participating in the production of textual meaning. He sees the reader as co-creator of the work. Stanley Fisher makes an even bolder move, where he identifies the reader's activity with the text. It is the reading process that determines the value of literature. This theory redefines literature and meaning not as objects but rather as a sequence of unfolding experiences. The reader becomes an essential source of all significations. While these are theories that on the surface have no relevance to metaphysics, they nevertheless share affinities with the notion of dialogic relation between reader and text that transforms the reader and transcends the text. While Rosenzweig does not describe reading or interpreting explicitly, he implicitly endorses the idea that the intrahuman divine speech can be received in infinite ways. His suggestion that an experience of presence is derived from the literality of a text such as the Song of Songs is very suggestive of reading and interpreting activities related to that text.

In choosing the Song of Songs as "the focal book of revelation," Rosenzweig makes a statement about the type of text that he considers privileged to be identified with the most elevated of all human experiences, namely, an encounter with the Transcendent. The Song is a dialogue, or a series of dialogues, between two lovers who speak the direct and urgent speech of love. Rosenzweig's own reading and interpreting of the Song suggests that the text was capable of arousing his response, which constitutes a new dialogue.[18] If speech is driven by relationship and exteriority, then the speech in the text, the speech that is the text, and subsequent related speech are re-created by the reader of such a text in proportion to her or his understanding and capacity to receive the miraculous.[19]

The text transmits speech and the reader of the text renews it. Rosenzweig depicts this empowering effect of (biblical) text as follows: "The divine in human inscription becomes as clear and actual to him for that one pulse beat as if—at that instant—he heard a voice calling to his heart" (Glatzer 1961, 258).[20] This new hearing of written speech corresponds in every essential way to the hearing of spoken dialogue, except for the presence of airwaves and audible vibrations. Texts can speak to us. While we do not hear "voices" coming out of texts, we nevertheless do not mean a metaphorical hearing either, except insofar as all hearing and all dialogue are in some sense metaphorical processes where the speaker transfers his meaning and the listener translates it.

Revelation and Exegesis in Emmanuel Levinas

As I have already shown, the relationship between revelation, reading, and exegesis in *The Star* is implicit. It is pertinent to note here the notion of revelation advanced by Emmanuel Levinas, a contemporary Jewish thinker who acknowledges Rosenzweig's inspiration and philosophical influence. Levinas is particularly close to Rosenzweig when he refers to the "prophetic" character of language.[21] According to Levinas, what renders language prophetic is its inherent transcendence that "commands an ontological order" (Levinas 1982, 8). He advances this view in his Jewish writings, where he speaks of the "prophetic dignity of language, always capable of meaning more than it says" (7).[22] The implication of this ontology of language is that exegesis is the act of participating in the transcendence of language.

While Rosenzweig refrains from using explicitly moral terminology (unless his notion of "response" is understood ethically), Levinas integrates the ethical command of the saying of language with the process of exegesis. Levinas also acknowledges the sacred quality of performative acts in literature outside of the Torah. Both secular and sacred literature induce a response, an interpretation, an exegesis. In the revelatory moment, the text acts on the reader, and the reader reciprocates by interpreting.

Echoing Rosenzweig's notion of audition in revelation but extending it specifically to the performance of exegesis, Levinas says, "The Talmud affirms the prophetic and verbal origin of the Revelation, but lays more emphasis on the voice of the person listening. It is as if the Revelation is a system of signs to be interpreted by the auditor and, in this sense, already handed over to him" (1993, 204). The nexus of revelation and exegesis can be seen in the following statements: "The structure of revelation is the call to exegesis" (1993, 193). And "[The] initiation to seek, to decipher, to the Midrash, already marks the reader's participation in the Revelation, in the Scripture. The reader is, in his own fashion, a scribe" (194).

Recalling here reader-response theories (Iser and Fisher 1974), we can see an important distinction between them and the hermeneutic notions of revelation found in the writings of Rosenzweig and Levinas. According to the latter, language inherently possesses an otherness that becomes manifest in the act of hearing and responding to texts. Iser and Fisher, on the other hand, have no metaphysical view of language but see language as the instrument through which the reader gives meaning to a text.

Both Rosenzweig and Levinas emphasize the uniqueness of revelation and its recurrence as a "new experience," subject to the newness of the moment and the person who receives it. Levinas states that "the Revelation has a particular way of producing meaning that lies in its calling upon the unique within me . . . as if each person, by virtue of his own uniqueness, were able to guarantee the revelation of one unique aspect of the truth" (1993, 195). And similarly Rosenzweig states, "This 'effulgence' flows, ever anew, from thing to thing in the fullness of time . . . revelation is unconditionally the product of the moment" (1972, 161).

This notion of the infinite meaning of exegesis and holy texts is characteristic of the Jewish hermeneutical tradition that has sustained the spiritual life of Jews throughout their history. Levinas was able not only to translate classical Jewish notions of revelation into philosophical language but also to reenact them through his own exegesis of Talmudic texts. Rosenzweig's translation of the Bible and the poetry of Halevi can also be seen as his participation in the spiritual reality of texts.

Jewish Hermeneutics

The fundamental question that we raised in our discussion of Rosenzweig's notions of speech and text is no different from the question of the method of and rationale for various systems of Jewish hermeneutics; it is the question of reconciling the authority of the tradition with that of revelation.[23]   Although one could put this question in terms of the relationship between the Oral and Written Torah that has continuously operated in the history of Jewish hermeneutics, my account renders this dynamic in the terms of modern continental Jewish philosophy.   If revelation is to be identified with scriptures received by Moses at Sinai, which are understood to possess positive and concrete content, how do we justify the interpretive contributions made by our sages and scholars throughout our history that represent clear distinctions from the written tradition?

While Rosenzweig never explicitly poses such a problematic, his account of the dynamic between living speech and textuality can be seen to parallel the religious dilemmas with which the kabbalists of the Zohar struggled and attempted to respond to.[24]   On the face of things, it seems that kabbalistic esotericism precludes any immediacy of Divine Presence in texts and their interpretations. Quite bold is their assertion that there is no such thing as an immediate revelation of the Divine word, not even in the Written Torah. Moreover, the Written Torah is *already* interpretation. According to this view, the notion of an immediate experience of the Word of God is not even relevant to normal persons: it belongs to prophets only. All that is accessible to us then is a mediated experience of interpretation, namely the "oral tradition."

On the other hand, according to the kabbalists, while the words of God as Torah are like "garments" that hide rather than disclose truth, they are also and paradoxically meant to be *the* object of interpretation. Moreover, they are subject to infinite interpretations. As the "great voice did not cease speaking," the Torah continues to give and receive new meanings. According to this mystical thinking, the decisive criterion of revelation is not any specific meaning but is rather in the speech itself, which is open to endless meanings. This openness to infinite and even contradictory meanings confirms the integral role that newness of experience plays in the tradition of Judaism.[25]

Our analysis of Rosenzweig's speech thinking and concept of revelation brought out once again the richness of his thought and the poetics of his writings. The dialectics of Rosenzweig's theology and philosophy, as our analysis demonstrated, renders it not only a contemporary philosophical theology but also a Jewish thinking.

Our investigation into Rosenzweig's phenomenology of speech as an experience of immediacy interrogated this claim; instead, we suggested that a more accurate portrait of revelatory speech is to account for the tension between immediacy and mediacy that exists in the realms of audible and written speech. A phenomenology of hearing bridges the boundaries between audible and written speech and is integral to the experience of textual responsiveness. Such responsiveness assumes close proximity as well as alterity of self and other. Rosenzweig's speech thinking, then, cannot simply be called logocentric; rather, overcoming the notion of hierarchy, speech thinking consists of both speech and textuality. As Rosenzweig's hermeneutic move from speech to text results in new texts such as this one, the speech of the human soul and its postmodern Jewish manifestation testify to its "ever renewed birth."

NOTES

1. This essay is part of a full-length manuscript, in progress, on hermeneutics and mysticism in the philosophy of Franz Rosenzweig.

2. Derrida calls this privileging of speech in Western philosophy "logo-centric." His critique of such tendencies is the subject of his early works: *Writing and Difference, Of Grammatology,* and *Speech and Phenomena.*

3. All references in this essay, unless otherwise indicated, are from William W. Hallo's translation *The Star of Redemption* (Rosenzweig 1972). References to the original text of *Der Stern Der Erlösung* are from *Franz Rosenzweig: Der Mensch und sein Werk, Gesammelte Schriften II* (Rosenzweig 1976).

   The retrieval of Biblical language, in an effort to reinstate the dialogical paradigm as a way of knowing the world, has been employed by other contemporary Jewish and Christian thinkers such as Martin Buber, Abraham Heschel, and Karl Barth.

4. This essay, to my knowledge, is the first attempt to bring Rosenzweig into the current debates on language and textuality. Other scholars who have written on language, speech thinking, and dialogical thinking in Rosenzweig's thought include Casper 1967, Horwitz 1981, Glatzer 1988, and Stahmer 1968.

5. Little attention has been given thus far to the Jewish and especially mystical elements in the philosophical and theological problems in Part Two of *The Star of Redemption.* Gershom Scholem had suggested long ago that a new orientation that pays close attention to the mystical undercurrents of *The Star* is in order. Indeed, Moshe Idel has made a good case for investigating this mystical angle in Rosenzweig, and his writings encourage further work in this area. See Idel 1988a, 162–71.

   Instead, much of the scholarship on Rosenzweig has placed him in the tradition of German idealism, opposing and/or establishing affinities to Hegel, Schelling, and Hermann Cohen. See, for instance, Freund 1979 and Mosès 1982. Mosès's comprehensive and most complete study of *The Star* acknowledges affinities with kabbalistic ideas.

6. There is a striking resemblance between the notions of primordial speech in Rosenzweig and Benjamin. For Benjamin's discussion on language, see Benjamin 1978.

7. Rosenzweig delineates his new thinking as "Sprachedenken," where living speech replaces solitary philosophical discourse, in his essay "Das neue Denken," as supplementary notes to *The Star of Redemption,* in *Kleinere Schriften* (Rosenzweig 1937, 377–79, quoted from Glatzer 1961, 199). Rosenzweig confirmed that it was the thought and work of his friend Eugen Rosenstock-Hussey, especially his essay "Angewandte Seelenkunde," that had a critical impact on his new philosophical direction. See Glatzer 1961, 199.

8. This is my rendition of Rosenzweig's reference to the kabbalistic notion of the reciprocity between God and person. In Rosenzweig's words: "If you testify to me, then I am God, and not otherwise—thus the master of the Kabbalah lets the God of love declare" (1972, 171).

9. This notion of a transcendent as a voice that is heard and is therefore immanent brings to mind Ricoeur's notion of "double speaking," which he too identifies with prophetic experience. Ricoeur says, "The idea of revelation appears as identical with the idea of a double author of speech and writing: Revelation is the speech of another behind the speech of the prophet" (Ricoeur 1980, 75).

10. Rosenzweig's elliptical reading of scripture posits God's call to Adam upon his transgression as the divine quest for humanity, which receives response, ten generations later, from Abraham. See Rosenzweig 1972, 175–76; 1976, 195–96.

11. From his essay "Die Schrift und Luther" (Rosenzweig 1937, 141–66).

12. I bring Derrida into this discussion for his clearly articulated critique of logocentrism and not for any other developments in his thinking.

13. Rosenzweig continued to be particularly drawn to the theme of love and dialogue as identifying characteristics of God's relationship to Israel, as is evident in his later translation and commentaries on Yehudah Halevi's poetry (Rosenzweig 1927).

14. According to Rosenzweig, the word "I" occurs more frequently in the Song than in any other book in the Tanach.

15. Hans Frei (1973) uses this phrase in his review of Eberhard Busch's *Karl Barth: His Life from Letters and Autobiographical Texts.*

16. This phrase is employed by Hans G. Gadamer in his *Truth and Method*, where he depicts the fusion of the horizon of the reader and the horizon of the text. Gadamer claims that "this dialogic relationship with the text is a transforming experience for the reader, much as is a spoken conversation between two people" (1982, 341).

17. I have modified the Hallo translation of several words in this passage.

18. The question of whether Scripture alone, or other literature as well, can evoke the speech of revelation remains unanswered in *The Star*. At the same time, Rosenzweig's passion for Goethe's work and his references to poetry in *The Star* are certainly suggestive of other privileged texts and speech.

19. Recent work in literary criticism underscores this Jewish phenomenon of reading and interpreting texts. See, for instance, Handelman 1982, and Hartman and Budick 1986. For a discussion of hermeneutics as a mystical experience, see Idel 1988b and 1989.

20. For a detailed and illuminating study of Rosenzweig's employment and interpretations of biblical and rabbinic literature, see Fishbane 1989.

21. Levinas's writings on revelation and exegesis are concentrated in his Talmudic writings, especially in Levinas 1982. My references will be based, primarily, on the English translation of his "Revelation in the Jewish Tradition" (1993).

22. For a recent interpretive discussion, see Handelman 1991, 282–90.

23. For a thought-provoking overview on the topic of revelation and tradition, see Scholem 1974, 282–303. For a fine and detailed examina-

tion of kabbalistic hermeneutics and revelation, see the work of Wolfson 1987, 189–215; and 1988, 311–45.

24. On the relation of exegesis and the revelation at Sinai, see Wolfson 1988, n. 45.

25. Scholem makes references to numerous midrashim, sayings, and explications that attest to this notion. See Scholem 1974, 291–303.

REFERENCES

Benjamin, Walter. "On Language as Such and on the Language of Man." In *Reflections: Essays, Aphorisms, Autobiographical Writings,* trans. Edmund Jephcott, ed. Peter Demetz. New York: Harcourt Brace Jovanovich, 1978.

Casper, Bernhard. *Das dialogische Denken: Eine Untersuchung der religionphilosophischen Bedeutung Franz Rosenzweigs, Ferdinand Ebners, und Martin Bubers.* Freiburg: Herder Verlag, 1967.

Derrida, Jacques. *Speech and Phenomena.* Evanston: Northwestern University Press, 1973.

———. *Of Grammatology.* Trans. Gayatri Chakravorty Spivak. Baltimore: Johns Hopkins University Press, 1976.

———. *Writing and Difference.* Trans. and introduction by Alan Bass. Chicago: University of Chicago Press, 1978.

Fishbane, Michael. "Speech and Scripture: The Grammatical Thinking and Theology of Franz Rosenzweig." In *The Garments of Torah: Essays in Biblical Hermeneutics.* Bloomington: Indiana University Press, 1989.

Frei, Hans. "Review of Eberhard Busch's *Karl Barth: His Life from Letters and Autobiographical Texts.*" *Virginia Seminary Journal* 30, 2 (July 1973): 42–46.

Freund, Else. *Franz Rosenzweig's Philosophy of Existence.* Trans. Stephen Weinstein and Robert Israel, ed. Paul Mendes-Flohr. The Hague: Martinus Nijhoff, 1979.

Gadamer, Hans G. *Truth and Method.* New York: Crossroad, 1982.

Glatzer, Nahum N. *Franz Rosenzweig: His Life and Thought.* New York: Schocken, 1961.

———. "The Concept of Language in the Thought of Franz Rosenzweig." In *The Philosophy of Franz Rosenzweig,* ed. Paul Mendes-Flohr. Hanover, N.H.: Published for Brandeis University Press by University Press of New England, 1988.

Handelman, Susan. *Fragments of Redemption: Jewish Thought and Literary Theory in Benjamin, Scholem, and Levinas.* Bloomington: Indiana University Press, 1991.

————. *The Slayers of Moses: The Emergence of Rabbinic Interpretation in Modern Literary Theory*. Albany: State University of New York Press, 1982.

Hartman, G., and S. Budick, eds. *Midrash and Literature*. New Haven: Yale University Press, 1986.

Horwitz, Rivka. "Aspects of the Problems of Language and Speech in Rosenzweig's Thought." *Daat* 6 (1981): 25–38.

Idel, Moshe. "Rosenzweig and the Kabbalah." In *The Philosophy of Franz Rosenzweig*, ed. Paul Mendes-Flohr. Hanover, N.H.: Published for Brandeis University Press by University of New England, 1988a.

————. *The Mystical Experience of Abraham Abulafia*. Trans. from the Hebrew by Jonathan Chipman. Albany: State University of New York Press, 1988b.

————. *Language, Torah, and Hermeneutics in Abraham Abulafia*. Trans. Menahem Kallus. Albany: State University of New York Press, 1989.

Ihde, Don. *Listening and Voice: A Phenomenology of Sound*. Athens: Ohio University Press, 1976.

Iser, Wolfgang, and Stanley Fisher. *The Implied Reader: Patterns of Communication in Prose Fiction from Bunyan to Beckett*. Baltimore: Johns Hopkins University Press, 1974.

Levinas, Emmanuel. *L'au-delà du verset: Lectures et discours talmudiques*. Paris: Editions de Minuit, 1982.

————. *The Levinas Reader*. Ed. Sean Hand. Oxford: Blackwells, 1993.

Mosès, Stèphane. *Systéme et Rèvèlation: La Philosophie de Franz Rosenzweig*. Paris: Les Editions du Seuil, 1982.

Ricoeur, Paul. *Essays on Biblical Interpretation*. Ed. Lewis S. Mudge. Philadelphia: Fortress, 1980.

Rosenzweig, Franz. *Kleinere Schriften*. Berlin: Schocken, 1937.

————. *The Star of Redemption*. Trans. William W. Hallo. Boston: Beacon Press, 1972.

————. *Der Stern der Erlösung* [1930]. In *Der Mensch und sein Werk, Gesammelte Schriften II*. The Hague: Martinus Nijhoff, 1976.

————, trans. *Jehuda Halevi: 92 Hymnen und Gedichte*. Berlin: Schocken, 1927.

Scholem, Gershom. *The Messianic Idea in Judaism and Other Essays on Jewish Spirituality*. New York: Schocken, 1974.

Stahmer, Harold. "F. R.: Speech Precedes Thought and Needs Time." In *Speak That I May See Thee: The Religious Significance of Language*. New York: Macmillan, 1968.

Wolfson, Elliot. "Circumcision, Vision of God, and Textual Interpretation: From Midrashic Trope to Mystical Symbol." *History of Religion* 27 (1987): 189–215.

————. "The Hermeneutics of Visionary Experience: Revelation and Interpretation in The Zohar." *Religion* 18 (1988): 311–45.

Holocaust

Chapter 10

Hasidism, Hellenism, Holocaust: A Postmodern View

Edith Wyschogrod

Hasidism was to early-twentieth-century Judaism what Hellenism was to nineteenth-century German poetry and philosophy. Both Jewish thinkers and German literati looked back from a post-Enlightenment perspective upon formative epochs of the past and saw them as transfigured by pure numinosity. Modern existence was to be repatterned by turning to what appeared to be its true foundation: for German Idealism as well as its critics, a Greek spirit that would restore human life to its aesthetic wholeness and, for modern revivers of seventeenth- and eighteenth-century Hasidism, the Judaism of the pale of settlement uncontaminated by the objectifying academicism of the *Haskalah* or Enlightenment Judaism. To be sure, the Hellenes of German imagination were long dead, whereas, at the beginning of this century, the eastern European *shtetl* was still the locus of an ongoing Hasidic life; but this later Hasidism was viewed as a dim reflection of an earlier more vital Hasidic religiosity.

In what follows I will argue that although Hellenism and Hasidism are distinctive strands, neither ran an entirely separate course, first for the obvious reason that the Jewish thinkers most influenced by Hasidism—Martin Buber and Gershom Scholem and their followers—were schooled by the German and Jewish Enlightenments as well as by the German Romantic reactions to it. But, deeper still, the basic theological concepts of the *Zohar* and Lurianic *Kabbalah* are made thematic in neo-Platonic terms. The controversies that erupt in interpreting Hasidism in the early twentieth century focus on weighing the relative importance of the intellectual neo-Platonic underpinnings embodied in its major texts against the beliefs and practices of everyday Hasidic life and the hagiographic tales about revered Zadikim. Thus, when Hasidism is invoked as a theological counterbalance against the modernity represented by the Enlightenment, its Hellenism is never far from the surface.

The disputes about the centrality of Kabbalism, the Hellenism of Hasidism, are cut short by the rise of national socialism and the virtual extermination of the Jews of Europe. Dominated by efforts to understand these events and to absorb their impact, Jewish theology in the period after World War II becomes holocaust theology. "Can one remain a believing Jew after the Holocaust?" is the question most reflective of this shift. Couched in epistemic terms, the first wave of post-Holocaust theologians seeks historical, psychological, or sociocultural explanations for the Holocaust and, generally finding none, ask, "What, if anything, follows from the Holocaust for Jewish belief and practice?" Because the issues in this polemic are relatively familiar, I shall not stress them here.

When Hasidism is displaced by Holocaust as the focus of theological speculation, Hasidism becomes an artifact for historical study while still-existing Hasidic communities become the focus of sociological analysis. I hope to show that, far from attenuating Hasidism's theological import, this new orientation with its focus on Hasidism's conceptual structure and social context, brings to the fore resources that can be exploited to develop a postmodern theology of the Holocaust, one that is best characterized as a theology of deep negation. Especially important for this task are the last phases of the Buber-Scholem debate, fresh interpretations of Jewish Kabbalism—for example, those of Moshe Idel—and recent postmodern readings of neo-Platonic metaphysics.[1]

I use the term "postmodernism" here in a methodological and in an ontological sense.[2] As a methodological term, I take postmodernism to refer to strategies for decoding the canons of reason in order to expose reason's duplicity expressed in its tactics of self-concealment. For example, Derrida exhibits the structure of Western thought as one of binary oppositions—subject/object, appearance/reality, speech/writing, and the like—in order to expose the hierarchical relations of power and value that this seemingly neutral arrangement conceals. Thus Derrida shows how one side of the dyad takes precedence over the other in the Western system of ordering.

As an ontological term, postmodernism signifies the dismantling of the understanding of being and time that has dominated Western thought from its Greek beginnings to the present. A focus upon negation is the opening move in the overturning of traditional ontology. Yet if negation is the simple obverse of being, it can still be incorporated into a system of meaning whose ontological foundations remain intact so that negation is not other than being but a property of being. A truly radical otherness would "convulsively tear apart the negative side, that which makes it the reassuring surface of the positive . . . and exhibit within the negative . . . that which can no longer be called negative" (Derrida 1978, 259), creating an unmediated heterology, an otherness, of deep negation.

The Holocaust not only lends itself to postmodern interpretation but is itself intrinsic to postmodern sensibility in that it forces thought to an impasse, into thinking a negation that cannot be thought and upon which thinking founders. It is the question that questions reason and, as such, is *constitutive* of the postmodern "ethos" so that the line between explanation and explicans, between the postmodern unmasking of rationality and the Holocaust as the event that cannot be thought, is blurred.

Hellenism and Hasidism as Romantic Theology

Before turning to my principal question—In what sense can a post-Holocaust, postmodern theology be identified with Hasidic life and thought?—it is crucial to consider first the manner in which Hasidism has been brought to light by modern interpretation. By attending to Martin Buber's reshaping of Hasidism, what is living and what is dead in the Romantic-ecstatic account of Hasidism, an account shaped in no small measure by Nietzschean philosophy, can be assessed and its usefulness for postmodernity determined.

For some Jewish thinkers at the turn of the century, Nietzschean discourse appeared as an apt model for Jewish thought. They craved a living Judaism, one conveyed in Nietzsche's contention in *Zarathustra* that "joy is deeper yet than agony" (1954, 434). Hoping to enliven Judaism as a belief and practice for their emancipated contemporaries, they were led to question the both neo-Kantianism of Hermann Cohen and the *Wissenschaft des Judentum* movement that treated Judaism as a field of scholarly study with little relevance for daily life.[3] This reaction, exemplified in the young Martin

Buber, does not take the form of a conceptual critique of Kant's philosophy of knowledge because it is concerned only with the finite determinations of the subject of knowledge, nor does Buber analyze in detail Kant's ideal of duty as exhausting the content of the moral life, both standard criticisms of Kantian philosophy. For Buber, the difficulty lies with Kant's depersonalized theology, the view that "God is an idea for Cohen, as he was for Kant . . . not a personality" (Buber 1956, 101–2).[4]

Despite his longing for a more personal relation to the divine, Buber does not endorse a fundamentalist appropriation of Hasidism's spirit. The model of scholarly objectivity present in the *Wissenschaft des Judentum* is for him too deeply bound up with the plausibility of *historical* assertions about the biblical and rabbinic worlds, so that disinterested study is not to be repudiated but harnessed to a new *theological* spirit.[5]

Buber does not brood over the specific conceptual differences between Enlightenment rationality and Romantic reason. Instead he transposes the themes of the debate into a new historical and discursive space, that of the conflict of an earlier generation between *misnagdic* Judaism, with its stress upon the legal aspects of Talmudic interpretation, and Hasidism, with its emphasis upon story, prayer, and the thaumaturgical power of ritual. Thus Buber writes that the eighteenth-century legalist and opponent of Hasidism, the Gaon of Vilna, "was responsible for the ban pronounced upon it . . . [and] wished to proceed against the Hasidim 'as Elijah proceeded against the prophets of Baal'" (Buber 1947–48, 1:14). By contrast, Buber proclaims the Hasidic masters unified in a single person, "heavenly light and earthly fire, spirit and nature" (1:14).

Central to Buber's account of Hasidism and what is most familiar to his readers is the tone of exhilaration that can take agony up into itself and transfigure it, a religious rapture that he sees as embodied in the Hasidic prayer and practice of eastern European Jews. "The core of hasidic teachings," he declares, "is the concept of a life of fervor, of exalted joy" (1:14). Like Nietzsche, Buber saw human beings as caught up in a network of social, political, economic, and cultural identities that thinned their capacities for fresh experience. Missing was a more primordial relation to world and community, one which could be activated only by reviving an *Urnatur* conceived as the primal being one already was.[6] Thus Buber writes, "Your own character, the very qualities that make you what you are, constitutes your special approach to God" (1947–48, 1:4).

Hasidism could be counted on to renew daily existence by bringing to light "the sparks of God that glimmer in all beings and all things, and [by teaching] how to approach them . . . how to 'lift' and redeem them, and reconnect them with their original root" (Buber 1947–48, 1:3). God dwells with human beings "in the midst of their uncleanness" (1:3), so that, by sanctifying the here and now, God's presence in the world, the *Shekhinah*, is free to unite with the transcendent God as bride is united with bridegroom. But this work that occurs within the divine person results not only in altering the dynamics of the divine life itself but in an affective discharge in the pious one who helps bring it about, in the liberation of holy joy. Thus Buber writes: "Everything the true hasid does or does not do mirrors his belief that in spite of the intolerable suffering, the heartbeat of life is holy joy, and that always and everywhere, one can force a way through to that joy—provided that one devotes oneself entirely to his deed" (1947–48, 1:10). The consecrated one produces a kind of alchemy of the affects, a transformation of sorrow into joy by recognizing the inseparability of the two emotions and affirming both.

It can be argued that Buber's account of redemptive joy is closer to Nietzschean world affirmation than to its putative Hasidic roots. The renewal of faith, Buber declares, depends upon one who "draws his strength from an extraordinary union between the spiritual and tellurian powers, between heavenly and earthly fire . . . [and] restores to the element of earth those whom preoccupation with thought have removed from it" (1947–48, 1:11). And this evokes Nietzsche's proclamation that all things are bound up with all things so that if "you have ever said Yes to a single joy . . . then you said yes too to all woe. All things are entangled, ensnared, enamored" (1954, 435).

However, if bliss is the condition for which latter-day quests for an aboriginal Hasidism and Hellenism yearn, the historical pasts that are imagined to generate this exaltation are worlds apart. Buber is not unaware of the loss of theological authenticity inherent in their conflation. The Romanticism that identifies Hellenism with its own rapture inspires a joyfulness of the type that Buber attributes to Hasidism, but the content of this Hellenism is treated with discretion, analyzed, and purged of what does not conform to the spirit of Hebraism as Buber sees it, the theological core of an aboriginally Jewish Hasidic piety.

It is useful to notice Buber's assessment of several strands of Hellenism that he considered significant in order to elicit his criteria for endorsing some and rejecting others. Buber is especially wary of Hellenism as a veneer that disguises Jewish roots. The first strand, that of Hellenism in Christology exemplified in Brunner and Bultmann, conceals the Hebraism of Jesus by attributing Stoic and Gnostic elements found in the letters of Paul to the teachings of Jesus (Buber 1961, 163–69). On the other hand, the second strand, the Hellenism of Plato, Buber believes, is "the most sublime instance" of the view that truth is possible and can be reached when human beings behold the ideal forms so that, with the help of the forms, justice can be established in actuality even if, in the end, justice as an ideal of the spirit is a failure (1956, 234).

I have already alluded to Buber's positive reception of Nietzschean ecstaticism. For Nietzsche (as later for Heidegger) the true provenance of this ecstaticism is to be found in a Hellenism prior to Plato, in pre-Socratic philosophy and in the tragic spirit's Dionysian passion tempered by Apollonian form where "a tempest seizes everything that is decayed, broken and withered" (Nietzsche 1967a, 123) and restores it to life. This is the Hellenism manifested nearly a century before Nietzsche in Hölderlin's elegiac "Bread and Wine" when the poet implores: "Fortunate land of Greece! You home of all the Immortals, / Is it then true indeed, all that we heard in our youth?" and issues in Hölderlin's Romantic *cri de coeur*: "Where oh where are they now . . . / Delphi slumbers, and where echoes great Destiny now?" (1954, 95).

For the early Nietzsche, Greek culture quickly lost sight of the immortals and of Hellenism's inner destiny by striving for truth rather than grandeur or "life in lavish perfection" (Nietzsche 1962, 33). At the same time Nietzsche's insistence that Socrates and Plato as moralists are Jews in spirit and not Hellenes and that moralists sap a culture's greatness goes to the heart of Nietzsche's anti-Judaism (1967b, 234), an anti-Judaism that Buber could hardly endorse. Yet Buber's account of the prophet, the ancestor of Hasidic piety, nevertheless bears the stamp of the early Nietzsche's true Hellene. For Buber the prophet is "the man of spirit . . . one whom the spirit invades and seizes, whom the spirit uses as its garment, not one who houses the spirit. Spirit is an event, it is something which happens to man. The storm of the spirit sweeps man where it will, and then storms on into the world" (Buber 1956, 235). Is this not what Nietzsche intends when he describes the Hellene as one seized by Dionysian intoxication, one whose "entire existence rested on a hidden substratum of suffering and of knowledge" (Nietzsche 1967a, 46)? To be sure, Hellenism and Hasidism go their separate ways on Buber's reading, but the Dionysian fervor of Nietzschean Hellenism penetrates Buber's account of Hasidism as a form of life.

A Theology of Absence

However insightful Nietzschean discourse as a model for Jewish thought in the early part of the twentieth century may have seemed to those who craved a living Judaism, Nietzsche's dream of ecstasy was destroyed decisively for contemporary Jewish theology in the inferno of Auschwitz. Not only had elements of Nietzsche's thinking been preempted by national socialism, but the quest for individual and collective joy seemed offensive in the eyes of a post-Holocaust community. No theology that had taken the Holocaust fully and totally into itself, Jewish or Christian, could ever again speak so unreservedly of the storm of spirit without invoking what Kabbalism called the other side, the demonic root of sacred intoxication.

In addition to the discrediting of divine enchantment the living exemplars of Hasidic spirituality in Poland, Hungary, and elsewhere were annihilated. Although Buber is keenly aware of the depredations of the Holocaust, the power of Auschwitz does not touch the core of his theological vision, perhaps because after World War II it was too late for him to create a theology as forceful as the one that had been impaired by the Holocaust. Thus Buber, in his postwar summing up of the significance of Hasidism for latter-day Judaism, continues to claim both that God helps those who wish to hallow self and world and that Hasidic eschatology posits the nondifference of this world and the other, "'that the two worlds are one in their ground and that they shall become one in their reality'" (1958, 36–37).

The invisible underpinnings of this reading of Hasidism is an inheritance of the Enlightenment's reliance on human will. Despite Buber's denial that Judaism is religious activism, he writes that it is human initiative that inaugurates the movement of divine sanctification: "Hallowing is an event that commences in the depths of man, there where choosing, deciding, beginning takes place"

(1958, 31). For him, grace is God's beneficent bringing to fruition what was begun in human effort.

For a post-Holocaust, postmodern sensibility, what is missing from Buber's understanding of the divine-human relation is the absence of absence expressed in the Holocaust as human helplessness and as God's silence. One important theological meaning of absence is to lack the power to be present—in the case of a people, the power of the collectivity to be present to its own history and that of others. Because any people can at some point become powerless, this privation of presence is, at least potentially, universal. Absence, then, as the potential draining of the power of a people to be present to its own history, is integral to every community. Correlative with this absence is the divine absence, the absence of God as an intervening power in history, not a turning away of God's face as Buber thinks, but an irremediable and irreducible absence from human affairs.

Perhaps this point can best be made by contrasting the social and theological context of the earliest recitations of a well-known Hasidic tale about the aversion of misfortune with a post-Holocaust recounting. The story, made famous by Elie Wiesel, forms the epigraph of his novel *The Gates of the Forest* (1966). An unspecified disaster that threatens the community is thwarted by the Baal Shem-Tov's retreat into the forest, where he lights a fire and recites a special prayer. Succeeding generations are similarly menaced but fewer and fewer of the salvific practices are remembered until Rabbi Israel of Rizhyn, faced with a comparable danger, realizes, "All I can do," as the epigraph concludes, "is tell the story and this must be sufficient."

Pre-Holocaust recitations of the story illustrate a yearning for the Baal Shem-Tov's meeting with the numinous that forestalls disaster and for the freshness of the first of the salvific encounters, a freshness that cannot be recovered.[7] Yet the narrative impulse is embedded in the belief that to retell is to relive, and to relive is to believe that the primal event can, in some way, be repeated. For Wiesel the tale exhibits a new narrative logic: to retell is to remember, and to remember is to relive a story that is not about a disaster averted but about an ingathering of the dead, a tale of the untellable. Such a reliving is caught up in the psychic dissonance of a remembrance that is both desired and feared.

Hasidism as Philosophy

It is worth rehearsing the content of the Buber-Scholem debate with regard to what is most primordial in Hasidism, its conceptual framework or its lived expression, in order to sift from this quarrel a post-Holocaust residue that withstands historical change. It is Gershom Scholem's contention that Buber has overlooked Hasidism's philosophical structure, that Hasidism is not only a form of life but also a conceptual matrix whose philosophical self-conscious articulation is found in the *Zohar* and the Lurianic *Kabbalah*. Scholem argues that Hasidism has been recast to suit Buber's theological ends—mystical and devotional in Buber's youth, and ethical and antignostic in his later years. It is in the latter connection, he claims, where Buber most consistently distorts Hasidism. By relying on "the legends, apothegmata and epigrams of the hasidic saints," Buber diminishes the importance of Hasidism's intellectual underpinnings (Scholem 1961, 308). Because, for Buber, all true living is meeting (the encounter with another or with God), kabbalistic theology is, for him, subordinated to the needs of a philosophy of dialogue. For Scholem, the purpose of kabbalism, appropriated unamended by Hasidism, is the attainment of communion with God and not the fleeting enjoyment of the here and now as Buber alleges. By liberating the divine sparks embedded in all things, Hasidism seeks the enjoyment of the oneness and eternity of God, the transcendence of the everyday world and not its fulfillment. Were Buber to acknowledge this, the core of Hasidism "would go against the essence of Buber's interest in [it] as an anti-Platonic, existentialist teaching" (Scholem 1961, 313).

Scholem also claims that Buber fails to report the destructive significance that some Hasidic texts attribute to the act of concentration in fervent prayer. Hasidic literature demonstrates that this type of prayer can drain the vital essence of a thing, the life principle that supports its existence. In seeking to penetrate the higher realms, such prayer lives on the vital energy of the world, leaving it depleted and without the power to sustain itself (Scholem 1961, 313). Thus the act of concentration is not only interpreted as a source of cosmic harmony but as a cause of the destruction of things and therefore as requiring special knowledge and care on the part of its practitioners.

Bound up with Buber's rejection of the destructive potential of concentration is his critique of the apocalyptic dimension of Jewish messianism. Buber draws a radical distinction between the vision of the prophets who freely intervene in history and the apocalyptic visionary who sees catastrophic events at the end of time as unalterably determined. Fearful of the gnostic element in apocalyptic writing with its hubristic stress upon the knowledge of God, Buber turns to Israelite prophecy as expressing a contrary ideal, service to God. For Buber, Hasidism is a direct descendant of Israelite prophetic activism, the intervention in historical affairs by summoning king, commoner, and priest to turn from injustice and toward God and neighbor. Scholem notices this aspect of Buber's thought when he writes. "Buber . . . Franz Rosenzweig and [other] liberal Jewish thinkers represent a tendency to remove the apocalyptic sting from Judaism" (1976, 162). By focusing upon the destructive potential of divine power and Israelite apocalypticism, it is Scholem rather than Buber who perceives the deep negation of postmodernity.

From a postmodern standpoint, it is noteworthy that Buber describes the prophet or *nabi*, the announcer, as "the one who utters the speech of heaven" (1963, 196) whereas the apocalyptic man "speaks into his notebook, he does not speak he only writes . . . he writes a book" (196). When Buber gives apocalypticism a pejorative reading and elevates speech above writing, he fails to anticipate still another crucial point of postmodern interpretation. For deconstructionist postmodernism, speech loses its theological priority and writing figures as a nihilatory and primordial power of language. Writing is not a representation of speech but always already inherent in language, not as a means subserving the ends of language and knowledge but as the very condition of the possibility of ideal objects and therefore of objectivity. The primacy of writing is already inherent in Plato's analysis of the relation between the spoken and written words. On Derrida's reading, speech is already inscription because for Plato speech is written in the soul, so that speech, the living logos, is ancillary to a more primordial writing (Derrida 1981, 109). What is more, Derrida claims, "there is an originary violence of writing because language is first writing. . . . Usurpation has already begun" (1976, 37). Speech has preempted the place of writing. Buber's disparaged apocalyptic man who writes in his notebook is a trope, as it were, for postmodern consciousness.

Equally critical for postmodernism is Scholem's analysis of Buber's view of *Yihud*, the exercise of focusing the mind on the letters of the Torah, letters that also constitute the "book of nature," in order to achieve spiritual concentration. Buber sees the practice of *Yihud* as achieving a certain wholeness or unity of life. But Scholem contends that such wholeness is not a principal interest of a world-transcending Hasidism. *Yihud*, he maintains, signifies either an exercise that unites one to some numinous source—a holy person, a divine attribute—or, if the term is used in the plural, the attainment of contemplative union with "the inwardness of the 'letters' which are imprinted in being itself" (Buber 1961, 316).

Moshe Idel's work focuses on expanding both the doctrinal understanding and the lived phenomenological context of kabbalism from the twelfth to the sixteenth centuries. He rejects Scholem's hypothesis that the expulsion from Spain raised messianic expectations that are expressed in the Lurianic *Kabbalah*, expectations that, in turn, inspired the heretical messianism of Sabbtai Zewi and the reaction to it of seventeenth-century European Hasidism. Scholem cannot be right, he contends, because the Lurianic *Kabbalah* is concerned with an intradivine drama and evinces no interest in historical phenomena such as the expulsion. It is Idel's focus upon this drama that is of interest to postmodern Jewish theology.

Idel's reading of neo-Platonism, his return to the examination of present-day kabbalistic practice in order to understand the living context of its concepts and theurgical exercises, and his remarks on the role of writing are especially useful in a postmodern context. I shall return to the last two points later. At present it suffices to note that, in his treatment of neo-Platonism, Idel states that its speculative concepts were employed to "decode" personal mystical experiences (1988, 41–42). This decoding could be achieved because the structure of the universal soul, which is open to intellectual intuition, is present in particular souls that have split off from it. This homologous structure allows the individual soul to read itself in the light of the universal soul. In addition, the ground common to both types of soul permits the individual soul to free itself through intellectual, meditational, or theurgical practice for final union with the universal soul. Although Idel stresses the Jewish symbolic rearticulation of neo-Platonic and Aristotelian ideas, these Greek motifs remain clearly visible.

What makes Idel's view interesting to postmodern Jewish theology is his insistence that the cleaving of the soul to God, *devekut*, can take the form of full union in which the soul enters the divine pleroma, there to lose itself in God or the *En-Sof*. Because this view conflicts with an essential doctrinal point in normative Judaism, that of God's total transcendence, it is anathema to both Buber and Scholem. Not only does Idel find an *unio mystico* in early kabbalistic sources but in latter-day Hasidism as well. For example, Rabbi Shneur Zalman, the founder of Habad Hasidism, writes that when a man cleaves to God he is swallowed by God (a common metaphor in the history of religions) "[and] 'this is the true cleaving, as he becomes one substance with God by whom he was swallowed, without being separate from him . . . as a distinct entity'" (Idel 1988, 41–42). Idel's thesis is important from a postmodern perspective because, when negatively reinterpreted, it renders possible the plunging of the individual soul into the abyssal, apocalyptic nonground of the divine, nonground because the abyss cannot become an ontological foundation or anchorage.

Hasidism and a Postmodern Theology of the Holocaust

In order to see how Hasidism as a conceptual matrix embodied in stories is marked by the Holocaust, I shall consider the Hellenism of the Hasidic interpretation of the divine nature to which Scholem's neo-Platonic description of Kabbalism points and shall propose a post-Holocaust, postmodern reworking of it. Unlike the philosophy of joyful affirmation, the Hellenism upon which Buber drew in his characterization of Hasidism, this postmodern reworking finds within philosophy, philosophy's other. The "mark" of this postmodernism is not sheer ineffability, but a negation that deconstructs language so that, to borrow a metaphor from the Hasidic master Nahman of Bratslav, language itself stutters (Nahman of Bratslav 1978, 270). I shall then consider a postmodern approach to the category of story that opens the way for the Hasidic tale to constitute an atheoretical mode of writing. Taken together, the philosophy of deep negation and story constitute an atheoretical mode of writing Jewish theology in a post-Holocaust age.

Consider first Plotinus's neo-Platonic prekabbalistic account of the divine life that is later, through a variety of channels, incorporated into Hasidic theology. For Plotinus, the One is the uncreated, ultimate principle of reality, autonomous, utterly without need, adequate to itself. "Think of the one as mind or as God and you think too meanly" (Plotinus 1930, 6.8.11:619), Plotinus insists. Multiplicity is the result of emanations from the uncreated One that contains within itself the will as a principle of activity. Duality begins with the nous or divine thought that thinks the eternal forms of all that exists in the lower spheres. The third hypostasis is that of the universal soul, a reflection or image of nous. The dynamics of the intradivine life consist in an upward or contemplative movement toward the next higher sphere and a downward generative movement, and in the case of the universal soul, a movement toward the material world. Not only does this scheme try to explain the generation of multiplicity, but it aims at the protection of the One that is, according to Plotinus, "generative of all, [but] none of all; neither thing nor quantity nor quality nor intellect nor soul; not in motion, not at rest, not in place not in time; it is the self-defined unique in form, or better, formless existing before Form was or Rest, all of which are attachments of Being and make Being the manifold it is" (Plotinus 1930, 6.9.3:617). If this insight is carried to its logical conclusion, the One, cordoned off from the multiplicity of nous and being, is beyond being, and this leads to the startling postmodern conclusion that the One and the nihil are nondifferent. Thus there is already deep, deep negation within the core of the divine plenitude.

In Jewish kabbalism, the place of the One is occupied by the *En-Sof*, God conceived as an infinite plenum, or as pure light. Early kabbalists interpret creation as a process of simple emanation or the progressive "coarsening" of light, and some even speak of the light as a double process of radiation and backward reflection, a movement that parallels the upward and downward dynamics of Plotinus's system (Scholem 1973, 28). The Lurianic *Kabbalah* adds the doctrine of *tsimtsum*, in which God withdraws into himself, thus forming a space or vacuum for creation *(tehiru)* through self-retraction. The *En-Sof* (like the Plotinian One) incorporates some of the functions of Plotinus's nous in that all the forces and divine attributes are incipiently contained in it but what is unique to Lurianic kabbalism is the inclusion of Mercy *(hesed)* and Stern Judgment *(din)* in the divine. Some kabbalists attribute the contraction of the divine essence that results in the creation of the *tsimtsum* to the power of *din*, an idea that leads to the theologically terrifying suggestion that "the whole process of *tsimtsum* and emanation was set in motion in order to eliminate the forces of *din*, like a sort of waste product from the essence of the Godhead" (Scholem 1973, 28).

Into the vacuum created by the *tsimtsum* God sends an illuminating ray, by means of which a primal man is fashioned through whom various divine lights break forth. This breaking forth is the central trauma of the divine life. The *sefiroth* are the emanations or spheres of divine manifestation through which God emerges from his hiddenness and are referred to as vessels *(kellim)*. According to Lurianic usage, "the sefiroth are vessels in which the substance of the *En-Sof* extends itself and through which it acts" (Scholem 1973, 32). But so powerful is the supernal light that it shatters the vessels which cannot contain it. Most of the light returns to the divine source but numerous sparks cling to the broken vessels whose defectiveness now unleashes the power of *din*. Once the vessels are broken, the biblical symbol of exile is introduced and construed cosmologically. Exile now becomes the mode of existence of all creation and the repair of the divine order, *tiqqun*, the task of human existence. For kabbalism, unlike neo-Platonism, the restorative process is not only contemplative but also bound up with observance of the Torah, thus ritual and ethical as well. In addition, catastrophic intradivine events are interpreted in terms of the historical metaphor of exile of the divine from itself (Scholem 1973, 22–44).

One further point should be stressed: for the kabbalist, the Torah is not only semantically construed as the narrative of God's relations with Israel, but as capable of being atomized into its physical letters, each one of which reflects divine power (Idel 1988, 247). Thus a Merkabah text enumerates "twelve simple letters" of the Hebrew alphabet and declares, "Their foundation is sight, hearing, smelling, speaking, tasting, sexual intercourse, work, movement, wrath, laughter, thinking, sleep" (Blumenthal 1978, 38). A cosmological foundation is attributed to the same letters as "the arms of the universe" and as the twelve signs of the zodiac (Blumenthal 1978, 38).

The catastrophic dimension within the divine life itself is played down in traditional kabbalism both because it impairs the divine nature as well as the effectiveness of Israel's redemptive role in the fallen world through obedience to the Torah. This perspective is carried over into the Hasidic tales that emphasize the constructive role of humankind in reestablishing cosmic wholeness. Postmodern thinkers who address themselves to the Holocaust in strikingly kabbalistic language are not inhibited by such melioristic theological considerations. Maurice Blanchot, a French non-Jewish novelist and critic, uses the term "disaster" to signify the negations opened up by the Holocaust. He speaks of the writing of the disaster as the disaster's scriptic annihilation of language and thought. The Holocaust, he declares, is "the absolute event of history which is a date in history—that utter burn where all history took fire" (Blanchot 1986, 47). Blanchot goes on to ask, "How can thought be made the keeper of the holocaust where all was lost, including guardian thought?" (47). Blanchot attributes the dissolution of meaning to the disaster when he avers that "it does not have the ultimate for its meaning," but rather that the ultimate is carried off in the disaster (28). To transpose Blanchot's account into neo-Platonic terms, the One, through an unthinkable negation and, *per impossibile*, is borne away by its own inner power in much the same way as black holes swallow up cosmic matter.

In traditional kabbalism, deep negation is cordoned off either as a penultimate stage or as a realm of trial that the worshipper must surmount. In the text of the *Merkabah*, for example, the initiate must face the horses of the guardians of the last gate before the divine throne, horses that "stand beside mangers of fire, full of coals of juniper and . . . eat fiery coals from the mangers of fire. There are rivers of fire beside the mangers . . . and a cloud over their heads which drips blood" (Blumenthal 1978, 64). But ultimately those who reach the *merkabah* return in peace whereas, for Blanchot, disaster, a term that he interprets etymologically as meaning deviation from the star *(astre)*, precludes cosmic or psychological rectification.

The weight of the disaster is felt not psychologically as putting the self into question but epistemically as annulling the question of self so that both question and self disappear. There is, properly speaking, no experience of the disaster, not only because the I that undergoes experience has been carried away, but because of the disaster's mode of self-temporalization (Blanchot 1986, 28). The disaster is perpetual and recurs without end, not as something positive but as a "nonevent" that never did and never will happen in any straightforward sense. The time of the disaster is a time that always already was and a time that will be in the mode of not being it and is thus the obverse of neo-Platonism's understanding of eternity as a time that always is. Thus, like the One, the disaster is beyond temporality but, unlike the One, is also inside time.

To speak of the Holocaust as a nonevent may seem a gross violation of the memory of the dead. Yet Blanchot's analysis should not be construed in a historical sense but rather as an intradivine disaster that intersects the historical one as a disruption of thought and language. Once thought and language founder, the historical itself is no longer a sequence of logically comprehensible happenings but a theologically ambiguous nonevent describable only in elliptical terms.

Derrida, in discussing Phillipe Soller's novel *Numbers,* is struck by the description of a writing that is not only self-constructing but that erases itself as it extends its space while infinitely producing itself (Derrida 1981, xxix). In his comments, Derrida calls attention to the kabbalistic structure of the work, its reference to the invisible white fire of the Torah and the black fire of the oral law that brings the invisible into visibility. The fire does not emanate from a single source but leaps from one text to another and deconstructs the already deconstructed post-Holocaust landscape, one in which there is nothing beyond "the cruel concrete work ultimately produced in the void. . . . the factories and docks [that] can be leveled, the columns of white smoke [that] cease to rise in the sky" (Derrida 1981, 345–46).

Arthur Cohen, an American Jewish novelist and theologian, does not discuss postmodern thought but nonetheless grapples with the implications of interpreting the Holocaust—the tremendum, as he calls it, following Rudolph Otto's word for the Holy—as radical negation. Cohen thus links the Holocaust to the void and describes it in postmodern neo-kabbalistic terms. Unlike the positive sacred, the Holocaust is, for Cohen, an abyss, a divide in time, caesura, that interrupts time and causality (1981, 20–21). Despite these radical claims, Cohen distinguishes what he calls the ultimacy of the Holocaust from its finality, contending:

> The tremendum is ultimate because it comprehends all negativity and contradiction but it is still not final. Finality and ultimacy differ crucially. Ultimacy entails the formal and configurational character of the real event, whereas finality describes its intention and its goal. . . . If final, everything is intended to evil and we must concede that our affairs are run, if not by blind caprice, then most surely by a malign divinity. (1981, 49)

Although Cohen is willing to attribute epistemic negativity to the Holocaust, he still seeks to salvage the traditional Jewish conceptions of divine existence and purpose. But to speak of an abyss, a tremendum, one that "comprehends all negativity and contradiction," as merely formal reflects a failure to grasp the co-implication of existence and language when an event is transhistorical in Cohen's sense. The actuality of such an event cannot be severed from its logical properties just as the formal perfections of the Plotinian One are inseparable from the One itself.

Although, from a postmodern perspective, Cohen's work is insufficiently radical, it marks a break with the familiar metaphysical frameworks that have governed theological thinking about the Holocaust. Emil Fackenheim, for example, in claiming that the Holocaust necessitates a commitment to traditional Judaism so as not to give Nazism a posthumous victory, remains bound to a Hegelian framework: the Holocaust is a negation of Judaism and must itself be negated. For Richard Rubenstein, God died at Auschwitz. Insofar as this analysis denies God's existence, Rubenstein breaks fundamentally with normative Judaism, yet, if the God whose death he has posited is the source of truth and goodness, he fails to transcend the structural articulation of traditional Jewish theology. Similarly, by assuming divine plenitude and attributing to language the failure to mirror this fullness, Rubenstein's negative theology remains within the ambit of a metaphysics that presupposes God's perfection and self-presence.

I have argued elsewhere (Wyschogrod 1985) and in agreement with the work of Emmanuel Levinas and Jean-Francois Lyotard that the Holocaust is to be interpreted in the context of an ethical metaphysics. I should like to suggest another setting for Holocaust theology—that of the deep negation incised in postmodern stories that exhibit the rents or fissures in the "normal" facades of existence. Postmodern narratives cannot re-present the disaster, because to do so would be to aim at an impossibility, to bring the disaster into full presence. How then is the story of the disaster to be told? Blanchot says of stories that they are not narrations of events but the events themselves, that in stories the event is a nodal point or lure that brings both the tale and itself into being (1981, 109). It should be remembered that bringing the event into being for Blanchot means that occurrence and interpretation are inseparable, not that events are born in interpretation but that events are as they are through the interpretation that construes them. In any case, no story can bring the disaster to the fore because the disaster is a nonevent. Only the trace of the catastrophic power that has passed like the hollow gouged by a meteor is visible through the story.

Postmodern theological stories need not unfold as a series of successive occurrences. Because postmodern narrative does not have to be synchronous with mirrored historical events, the postmodern story that is also a post-Holocaust story may be a tale whose calendar date of composition can antedate the Holocaust. As Lyotard suggests, for postmodernity, "there is no one single time; a society or a soul is not synchronous with itself" (1989, 186). (Subsequent reading may find that a story was always already postmodern in a sense that is discernible only later.) Thus it may be possible to read an eighteenth-century Hasidic story in post-Holocaust fashion as a text of deep negation. Consider, for example, the words of the Rabbi of Geras cited by Buber: "Why is a man afraid of dying? For does he not then go to his Father! What a man fears the most is that he will survey from the other world everything he has experienced on this earth" (Buber 1947–48, 2:311). A pre-Holocaust reading of this tale might call attention to the pain of a postmortem review of one's sins and sufferings, but the context of the Holocaust brings into view—from a *neo*-kabbalistic perspective, so to speak—a cosmic disarray in which the categories of experience themselves are altered. The old meaning is not excised from the story but reverberates through it, while the new meaning appears to have been always already present *in nuce*. The tales of the Hasidim and those of others who write tales that exhibit features of postmodernism (for example, Kafka, Jabès, and Borges) do not reflect or represent the disaster but forge a language of nonevent that writes the disaster. It is here, concealed in the tale, that the abyss or nonground that I have described as revealed by a certain Hellenism in kabbalism can be inscribed. It is this that is of theological interest in the Hasidic tale.

NOTES

1. Morris M. Faierstein writes that research in Hasidem has made major advances in the last decade and that "Buberian and Scholemian theories of Hasidem have been thrown into the question. . . . New directions in research show Hasidism as being a popular religious movement which nevertheless retained a place for elitist tendencies of the mystical tradition. Its ability to fuse the two he suggests may be its most significant innovation" (1991, 121). Joseph Dan contrasts historic Hasidism, the movement founded by the Besht (with the Zaddik as

intermediary between man and God and Hasidism) as it was re-created by Buber and others who were influenced by Romanticism as well as by the spiritual values of an Ur-Judaism of their own creation (1991, 180).

2. Steven Best and Douglas Kellner call attention to the diversity of postmodern positions: "There is no unified postmodern theory, or even a coherent set of positions" (Best and Kellner 1991, 2). Yet insofar as postmodernism is identified with recent French thought, it is character- ized as the "dynamic productivity of language, the instability of meaning, and a break with conventional schemes of meaning" (21).

3. Mendes-Flohr and Reinharz insist that one of the core meanings of *Wissenschaft* is science in a strict sense, "devotion to factual accuracy, normative neutrality and the quest for truth" and is central to the *Wissenschaft des Judentum's* understanding of the term (Mendes-Flohr and Reinharz 1980, 184). This reading sheds light on why Buber sees the ideal of *Wissenschaft* in Scholem as textual positivism and Scholem sees Buber as avoiding hard-nosed scientific scholarly work.

4. Steven T. Katz sees Buber's account of the twofold attitude I-Thou and I-It as parallel to Kant's distinction between the noumenal and phenom- enal worlds and therefore as evidence for the Kantian structure of Buber's thought (Katz 1983, 8–11). Lawrence Perlman rejects this view on the grounds that the noumenal world is accessible through the I- Thou relation (Perlman 1990, 104–6). Steven T. Katz replies that Perlman misunderstands Kant on God's relation to both the noumenal and phenomenal worlds (Katz 1990, 116–17).

5. Steven Kepnes calls attention to the Dilthey-inspired romantic strain in Buber's early *Tales of Rabbi Nahman* and *The Legends of the Baal Shem* but suggests that Buber's hermeneutical approach changes with the development of his dialogical philosophy with its stress upon the I- Thou encounter (Kepnes 1987, 85–86). The dialogical treatment of texts still retains a Romantic perspective but moves toward Gadamer's view of interpretation as a fusion of the horizons of the interpreter and text (93). Paul R. Mendes-Flohr (1989) develops this change in a meta- physical standpoint in connection with Buber's social philosophy.

6. Buber's early enthusiastic reception of Nietzsche is described by Gershom Scholem (1976, 131–32). Rikva Horwitz discusses Buber's rejection of Nietzsche's Dionysus as savior (1988, 140).

7. The theme of the loss of vivid religious experience with the passage of time is not new. Moshe Idel cites a comparable tale that depicts the decline of theurgy as the generations succeed one another (1988, 270). What is new is Wiesel's use of this loss to depict negative epiphany.

REFERENCES

Best, Steven, and Douglas Kellner. *Postmodern Theory*. New York: Guilford, 1991.

Blanchot, Maurice. *The Writing of the Disaster*. Trans. Ann Smock. Lincoln: University of Nebraska Press, 1981.

———. *The Gaze of Orpheus and Other Literary Essays*. Trans. Lydia Davis. Barrytown, N.Y.: Station Hill, 1986.

Blumenthal, David, R., ed. *Understanding Jewish Mysticism: The Merkabah Tradition and the Zoharic Tradition*. New York: KTAV Publishing, 1978.

Buber, Martin. *Tales of the Hasidim*. 2 vols. Trans. Olga Marx. New York: Schocken, 1947–48.

———. *The Writings of Martin Buber*. Ed. Will Herberg. New York: Meridien, 1956.

———. *Hasidism and the Modern Man*. Trans. Maurice Friedman. New York: Harper and Row, 1958.

———. *Two Types of Faith*. Trans. Norman P. Goldhawk. New York: Harper and Bros., 1961.

———. *Pointing the Way*. Trans. Norman P. Goldhawk. New York: Harper and Row, 1963.

Cohen, Arthur A. *The Tremendum: A Theological Interpretation of the Holocaust*. New York: Crossroad, 1981.

Dan, Joseph. "A Bow to Frumkinian Hasidism." *Modern Judaism* 11 (May 1991): 175–94.

Derrida, Jacques. *Of Grammatology*. Trans. by Gayatri Chakravarty Spivak. Baltimore: Johns Hopkins University Press, 1976.

———. *Writing and Difference*. Trans. Alan Bass. Chicago: University of Chicago Press, 1978.

———. *Disseminations*. Trans. Barbara Johnson. Chicago: University of Chicago Press, 1981.

Faierstein, Morris M. "Hasidism—The Last Decade in Research." *Modern Judaism* 11 (February 1991): 11–124.

Hölderlin, Friedrich. *The Selected Poems of Friedrich Hölderlin*. Trans. J. B. Leishman. London: Hogarth, 1954.

Horwitz, Rivka. *Buber's Way to "I and Thou."* Philadelphia: Jewish Publication Society, 1988.

Idel, Moshe. *Kabbalah: New Perspectives*. New Haven: Yale University Press, 1988.

Katz, Steven T. "Lawrence Perlman's 'Buber's Anti-Kantianism': A Reply." *AJS Review* 15 (Spring 1990): 109–18.

———. *Post-Holocaust Dialogues: Critical Studies in Modern Jewish Thought*. New York: New York University Press, 1983.

Kepnes, Steven. "A Hermeneutic Approach to the Buber-Scholem Controversy." *Journal of Jewish Studies* 38 (Spring 1987): 81–98.

Lyotard, Jean-Francois. *The Lyotard Reader.* Ed. Andrew Benjamin. Cambridge, Mass.: Basil Blackwell, 1989.

Mendes-Flohr, Paul R. *From Mysticism to Dialogue: Martin Buber's Transformation of German Thought.* Detroit: Wayne State University Press, 1989.

Mendes-Flohr, Paul R., and Yehuda Reinharz, eds. *The Jew in the Modern World: A Documentary History.* New York: Oxford University Press, 1980.

Nahman of Bratslav. *Tales.* Trans. Arnold Band. New York: Paulist Press, 1978.

Nietzsche, Friedrich. *The Portable Nietzsche.* Ed. Walter Kaufmann. New York: Viking Press, 1954.

———. *Philosophy in the Tragic Age of the Greeks.* Trans. Marianne Cowan. Chicago: Henry Regnery, 1962.

———. *The Birth of Tragedy.* Trans. Walter Kaufmann and R. J. Hollingdale. New York: Vintage, 1967a.

———. *The Will to Power.* Trans. Walter Kaufmann and R. J. Hollingdale. New York: Vintage, 1967b.

Perlman, Lawrence. "Buber's Anti-Kantianism." *AJS Review* 15 (Spring 1990): 95–108.

Plotinus. *The Enneads.* Trans. Stephen MacKenna. New York: Pantheon, 1930.

Scholem, Gershom. "Martin Buber's Interpretation of Hasidism." *Commentary* 22 (October 1961): 305–16.

———. *Sabbatai Zewi: The Mystical Messiah, 1626–1676.* Princeton, N.J.: Princeton University Press, 1973.

———. *On Jews and Judaism in Crisis.* Ed. Werner J. Dannhauser. New York: Schocken, 1976.

Wiesel, Elie. *The Gates of the Forest.* Trans. Frances Frenaye. New York: Avon, 1966.

Wyschogrod, Edith. *Spirit in Ashes: Hegel, Heidegger, and Man-Made Mass Death.* New Haven: Yale University Press, 1985.

Zionism

Chapter 11

Cultural Criticism, Ideology, and the Interpretation of Zionism: Toward a Post-Zionist Discourse

Laurence J. Silberstein

> Insofar as one succeeds in loosening the bland facticity of the present, contention is discerned where quiescence was supposed, and claims to authority become contentious rather than problematic. The way is then opened to inquire into the forms of power and authority that the practices of the present help to sustain.
> —Michael J. Shapiro, *Reading the Postmodern Polity* (1992)

Of the many ideological discourses to have emerged within Judaism over the past two centuries, Zionism has been the most effective in shaping contemporary interpretations of Jewish identity, Jewish culture, and Jewish history. Zionism has provided both Israeli and American Jews with basic myths, symbols, and rituals that both constitute and give expression to their self-understanding as Jews. Above all, Zionism has been highly effective in setting the discursive parameters for the ongoing struggle over Jewish identity and culture not only in Israel, but outside of Israel as well. As one observer recently commented: "Zionism, more in its contemporary Israeli incarnations than in its classical form, has become the underlying ideology of the diaspora Jews" (Biale 1986, 190).

For the most part, scholarly studies of Zionism have tended to treat the Zionist definition of reality as an accurate representation of historical processes, and the Zionist analysis of the Jewish problem as a valid description. Such studies, often written by confirmed Zionists, make no effort to critically examine Zionist discourse or question the categories through which it defines the

Jewish condition.[1] In general, the emergence of Zionism and its ascendancy to a hegemonic position is treated as a natural development in the history of the Jewish people. Rarely, if ever, do scholarly studies of Zionism consider non-Zionist or anti-Zionist discourses as viable alternatives. Moreover, little if any serious attention is given to the voices of the excluded Others, both within and without the Jewish community, Others such as Sephardic Jews, women, non- or anti-Zionist Jews, and Palestinian Arabs.

In recent years, however, the internal fissures of Zionist discourse have become increasingly evident and its hegemonic position increasingly challenged. Internal cultural, social, and political developments within Israel, the significant changes in the international balance of power, and the growing strength of American Jewry and its changing relationship with Israel have rendered problematic many of the underlying assumptions of so-called classical Zionism. Zionism, like all ideologies, provided a framework for interpreting the social-political order and legitimating specific power relations. However, historical events such as the prolonged occupation of the territories captured in the 1967 War, the invasion of Lebanon in 1982, and the Intifada that erupted in 1987 have led many to question the adequacy of that framework. This, in turn, has had the effect of significantly problematizing conventional interpretations of Jewish identity, culture, and history.

That there is a crisis in Zionist ideology is obvious from a cursory review of various writings, academic and nonacademic alike, particularly in Israel. These writings testify to the numerous fissures and contradictions that plague the discursive framework known as Zionism, through which Jews, both in Israel and the United States, endeavor to make sense of their identities, their social location in the world, their past, and their future. Writings by Israeli social and cultural critics clearly reflect the internal conflicts within Israeli society and culture.[2] Many of these critics are members of a generation socialized into the expectation that Zionism, in its classical form, provided an adequate meaning system through which to address the social, cultural, and ideological problems of Jewish life in general, and Israeli society and culture in particular. Their writings are indicative of the disillusionment that prevails among many of those raised under the banner of labor Zionism, who now find themselves confronting realities for which this Zionism had not prepared them.[3] Such works of social and political criticism highlight the basic and tragic conflicts between Jew and Arab, both within Israel and without.[4]

Recent social scientific literature offers a clear sense of the conflicts and contradictions that pervade Israeli society.[5] Challenging the dominant Zionist representation of Israel as a unified Jewish society and culture, many of these works focus on the ongoing struggle to control the prevailing discourse, the internal struggle for both cultural and political hegemony, and the ongoing conflict with Palestinian nationalism.

A growing body of writings by a younger generation of scholars, drawing upon recently released archival materials, is making it clear that many of the major problems that plague Israeli society today, rather than being historical aberrations, were inherent in the state from the outset.[6] As these studies make clear, the availability of new archival materials opened the way to a far more complex grasp of the complexities of the career of Zionism.[7] Moreover, as access to private papers, previously secret records of cabinet meetings, and other official discussions increases, scholars are becoming increasingly aware of the extent to which public discourse in Israel was limited by official versions of Israeli history. These scholars, many of them young children at the time of the emergence of the state, are not burdened with the same cultural baggage as their predecessors and do not have the same psychological investment in particular versions of Israeli history.

As historical events and scholarly studies have problematized Zionist metanarratives, far-reaching changes in social and cultural theory have rendered highly problematic the basic notions of nation, history, culture, and identity on which Zionist discourse rests.[8] However, while subverting many of the assumptions on which Zionism has been traditionally grounded, these theoretical writings help make possible a dynamic revisioning of Zionism in particular, a revisioning that opens the way for an emerging post-Zionist discourse.

Analyzing the concept of the postmodern, Barry Smart has related it to a sense that "complex transformations, questions, and problems deemed to be constitutive of the present are not adequately articulated in prevailing modern forms of theory and analysis" (Smart 1992, 182). In a similar fashion, post-Zionist discourse reflects the growing sense that the complex transformations, questions, and problems deemed to be constitutive of Israeli culture, Zionist ideology, and Judaism in general "are not adequately articulated in prevailing forms of theory and analysis." While rooted in Zionist discourse, post-Zionist discourse moves beyond it in search of more adequate ways to talk about Jewish culture, identity, and history. Thus, the emergence of post-Zionist discourse reflects a growing awareness on the part of scholars and intellectuals that the categories formulated and disseminated by Zionism no longer work to effectively illuminate the Jewish past and present.

Discourse

One of the prominent dimensions of current social and cultural theory is the emphasis on discourse. Over the past several decades, writers in such fields as philosophy, literary theory, and social theory have all emphasized, albeit in different ways, the central role of discourse in the constitution of human culture and society. In particular, these writings have emphasized the power of discourse to shape: the ways in which we conceptualize and think about reality; the ways in which communities relate to one another; the frameworks within which social and cultural activities are carried on; and the processes through which society is hierarchized and power distributed. Emphasizing the formative power of discourse, these writers stress both its socially constructed character as well as its linkage to institutionalized configurations of power.

On the simplest level, discourse refers to "a particular area of language use." Discourses differ according to concepts and categories employed, the institutional contexts in which they are used, and the "standpoint taken up by the discourse through its relation to another, ultimately an opposing discourse" (Macdonell 1986, 3).

To social and cultural theorists like Althusser, Foucault, and Hall, discourse is inexorably intertwined with the material world, inscribed in such material practices as rules, regulations, social arrangements, institutions, and cultural forms. Accordingly, discourse is taken to refer to both the social and linguistic processes by means of which we make, disseminate, legitimate, and preserve meaning (Terdiman 1985).

To highlight the intricate relationship of discourse to material forms, Foucault speaks of discursive practices: "Discursive practices are not purely and simply ways of producing discourse, they are embodied in technical processes, in institutions, in patterns of general behavior, in forms of transmission and diffusion, and in pedagogical forms which, at once, impose and maintain them" (Foucault 1977, 200). As Foucault and others have shown, discourses do much more than simply communicate meaning. Discourses and the ideologies formed from them generate, legitimate, support, and empower certain kinds of questions, debates, and conversations while suppressing, delegitimating, and disempowering others. Through discourse, we differentiate outsiders from insiders, we from them, self from other, and our community from other communities. Moreover, by means of discourse we organize, legitimate, and sustain forms of social organization and processes of social reproduction; establish and police norms; establish hierarchies of identity and difference, of subservience and authority, of taste and vulgarity (Bove 1990). Seen in this light, discourse refers to a "complex of signs and practices which organize social existence and social reproduction" (Terdiman 1985, 54).

Through discourse we establish what Foucault has called "regimes of truth," the institutional and conceptual frameworks by means of which we determine what kind of statements are true and which are false, and what kind of questions and inquiries are valid and invalid. As elaborated by Stuart Hall, a leading theorist of British cultural studies,

> Discursive formations (or ideological formations that operate through discursive regularities) "formulate" their own objects of knowledge and their own subjects; they have their own repertoire of concepts, are driven by their own logics, operate their own enunciative modality, constitute their own way of acknowledging what is true and excluding what is false within their own regime of truth. (Hall 1988, 51)

Thus, discourse is the starting point for understanding the ways in which identities are formed, conceptions of reality shaped and changed, human interactions interpreted, meaning established, institutions legitimated, and beliefs and knowledge formulated, disseminated, and perpetuated.

Foucault has convincingly demonstrated the inherent relationship of discourse to power. In a series of works, he has unraveled and depicted the complex relationship between discourse, knowledge, and power in such spheres as science, penology, education, psychiatry, and sexuality. In his view, discourse is a site of ongoing struggle. Discourse is not simply "that which translates struggles or systems of domination, but is the thing for which and by which there is struggle" (Foucault 1981, as quoted in Macdonell 1986, 97).

The focus on discourse and discursive practices produces an orientation to history that differs significantly from conventional evolutionist, progressive, or serial interpretations. Seeking to trace the emergence of conditions that made possible the social arrangements and power relations of the present, Foucault moves backward in an effort to uncover the critical disjunctures in which the dominant discourses of the present took shape, replacing those of previous eras. In Foucault's genealogical method, the focus is on discontinuity rather than continuity. When approaching human culture and society in this way, we are led to pose such questions as: What are the conditions that enable particular discourses to emerge and survive? What configurations of power sustain particular discourses and are, in turn, sustained by them? Whose interests do particular discourses serve? Who is included/excluded by particular discursive frameworks?

Ideology

The growing emphasis on discourse has had a significant effect on the interpretation of the concept of ideology, a concept particularly useful for analyzing social and political movements such as Zionism.[9] Revising earlier Marxist interpretations of ideology, theorists emphasize the discursive processes by means of which ideologies are generated, disseminated, and maintained within society.[10] Stressing, like Gramsci, the commonsensical dimension of ideology, Hall links it to such concepts as discourse, culture, and identity. On one level, ideology is taken to refer to the taken-for-granted givens, "the frameworks of thinking and calculation about the world—the 'ideas' people use to figure out how the social world works, what their place is in it, and what they ought to do" (Hall 1985, 99). As systems of representation inscribed in practices, ideologies provide members of social groups with a "bedrock of presuppositions by means of which we make sense of and organize everyday experiences" (Donald and Hall 1986, XVII).

A distinctive effect of ideological discourse is its ability to "nourish and sustain the possession and exercise of power" (Thompson 1990, 292).[11] Ideologies accomplish this by legitimating, universalizing, and naturalizing historically contingent social arrangements and hierarchies of power. Thus, ideologies "encourage men and women to 'see' their specific place in a historically peculiar social formation as inevitable, natural, a necessary function of the 'real' itself. This seeing precedes and underlies any ways in which social subjects 'think about' social reality" (Kavanaugh 1990, 310). Ideologies thus situate people in lived relations with specific socio-historical projects and political programs, enabling them "to feel at home to act (or not to act) within the limits of a given social project" (314).

Ideologies operate in discursive chains and formations in which concepts and images relate to and derive their meaning and significance from other concepts and images. Ideological formations, operating through discursive regularities, "formulate their own objects of knowledge and their own subjects, have their own repertoire of concepts, are driven by their own logics, operate their own enunciative modality, constitute their own way of acknowledging what is true and excluding what is false within their own regime of truth" (Hall 1988, 51). Accordingly, ideologies seek to set limits "to what will appear as rational, reasonable, credible, indeed sayable and thinkable" within a given social formation. To analyze ideology, therefore, entails "mapping the whole web of meanings, the discursive space, which these core ideas, working together, constitute as that ideology's 'regime of truth'—to borrow Foucault's metaphor" (Hall 1986, 38).

A distinct feature of ideologies is their effectiveness in bestowing specific identities on individuals by situating them, albeit unconsciously, in specific subject positions.

> The basic function of all ideology is to constitute individuals as subjects . . . Who is the interpellated subject? This is the key question in the analysis of ideologies . . . what constitutes the unifying principle of an ideological discourse is the "subject" interpellated and thus constituted through discourse. (Laclau 1986, 27–28)

However, these social arrangements, hierarchies of power, and subject positions that ideologies naturalize, universalize, and legitimize are never permanently fixed and, accordingly, remain objects of ongoing conflict. To Hall, the study of ideology entails the analysis of conflict-ridden processes by means of which prevailing discourses are produced, disseminated, and utilized as vehicles of control and power. Thus, to study ideology is to study the discursive processes by means of which social groups struggle for and achieve hegemony.[12]   In such struggles, groups and movements seek to induce subjects "to enunciate their relation to the world in quite different meaning or representational systems" from those they previously used (Hall 1988, 50). This focus on conflictive hegemonic processes shifts attention away from such dominant power mechanisms as the state and leads us to attend to the multiple, conflicting discourses that comprise any society.[13]

As a social force, ideology "is always materialized in concrete practices and rituals and operates through specific apparatuses" (Hall 1988, 46). For an ideology to be socially effective, it must become "inscribed in practices" (Hall 1985, 100), as Althusser has argued. Ideologies are thus disseminated through a network of social apparatuses including schools, religious institutions, family, television, films, and books.

Of particular interest for the student of Zionism is the ideology of nationalism. Like all ideologies, nationalisms provide "a powerful means of defining and locating individual selves in the world, through the prism of the collective personality and its distinctive culture" (Smith 1991, 17). In addition, national identities provide a sense of continuity, shared memory, and collective destiny (Smith 1986, 33).

Rejecting essentialistic models, scholars have, in recent years, posited antiessentialistic, historically contingent, process-oriented conceptions of both nation and nationalism:[14]   "Nations are not static targets, to be attained once and for all. They are processes, albeit long-term ones. These processes of mobilization and inclusion, territorialization, politicization and autarchy are never concluded and always subject to redefinition in each generation" (Smith 1986, 212).   Rather than viewing the elements of nationhood such as language and historical memory as givens, scholars like Smith view them as socially and culturally constructed.

Eschewing universal definitions of nation and nationalism, scholars of nationalism increasingly focus on the processes by virtue of which a nation shapes the identity of its members by means of "myths and symbols, their historical memories and central values," what Smith refers to as the "myth-symbol complex" (1986, 15). This complex, including myths of origins, ancestry, migration and liberation, golden age, and decline and rebirth, provides a group's "maps" and "moralities" (1986, 192).

Ideology and the Reconfiguration of Identity

As indicated above, along with the changing interpretations of ideology have come alternative interpretations of identity that emphasize the dynamic, discursive processes by means of which individual and group identities are constituted.[15] According to Hall, conventional interpretations view culture as comprised of shared traditions, common historical experiences, and shared cultural codes that provide "stable, unchanging and continuous frames of reference and meaning" (1990, 224). One implication of this conventional view is that we consider it possible to uncover, excavate, and bring to light the essence of cultures such as Judaism by posing such questions as: What is it to be Jewish? What is the essence/structure of Jewish culture? What is Jewishness? What are the essential teachings, values, and ideals of Judaism? How did Judaism emerge, develop, grow?

Hall, however, espouses an alternative view of culture and cultural identity, one that emphasizes movement, flux, change, and conflict:

> Cultural identity . . . is a matter of "becoming" as well as of "being."
> . . . It is not something which already exists transcending place,
> time, history, and culture. Cultural identities come from some-
> place, have histories. But, like everything else which is historical,
> they undergo constant transformation. Far from being eternally
> fixed in some essentialized past, they are subject to the continuous
> play of history, culture, and power. Far from being grounded in a
> "mere" recovery of the past, which is waiting to be found, and
> which, when found, will secure our sense of ourselves into eternity,
> identities are the names we give to different ways we are positioned
> by, and position ourselves within the narratives of past. (Hall
> 1990, 225)

Although deconstructing conventional notions of identity, Hall, it should be emphasized, does not deny that identity exists. While rejecting essentialistic conceptions of identity, Hall advocates a nonessentialistic, contingent, dynamic notion of identity that emphasizes the social and cultural processes by means of which we come to understand and preserve a sense of who we are, both individually and communally.

Hall's dynamic, conflictive view of culture and cultural identity finds support in the writings of anthropologists and ethnographers

such as James Clifford.[16] Emphasizing the processes by means of
which cultures are inscribed through writing, Clifford argues:

> Cultures are not scientific "objects" (assuming such things exist,
> even in the natural sciences). Culture, and our views of "it," are
> produced historically, and are actively contested. There is no whole
> picture that can be "filled in," since the perception and filling of a
> gap lead to the awareness of other gaps. . . . If culture is not an
> object to be described, neither is it a unified corpus of symbols and
> meanings that can be definitively interpreted. Culture is contested,
> temporal, and emergent. (Clifford 1986, 18)

Highlighting the discursive processes through which ethnographers
construct the objects of their study, Clifford emphasizes the relationship of anthropological knowledge and power: "Even the best
ethnographic texts—serious, true fictions—are systems, or econo-
mies, of truth. Power and history work through them, in ways their
authors cannot fully control. Ethnographic truths are thus inherently partial—committed and incomplete" (1986, 6–7). Clifford calls
upon his fellow ethnographers to openly confront the "contingencies
of language, rhetoric, power, and history" that infuse ethnographic
discourse. Far from being the product of detached, objective scholarship, ethnographic accounts of culture are intentional creations in
which "interpreters constantly construct themselves through the
others they study" (1986, 10). The discourse by means of which
ethnographers formulate and disseminate images of individuals and
groups of necessity excludes or marginalizes specific Others.
Consequently, to fully understand a culture or cultural identity, we
must attend not only to the dominant voices, but also to those voices
that have been silenced or excluded in conventional accounts, the
voices of the Other.[17]

The concept of the Other is basic to contemporary social and
cultural critics. According to these theorists, we form our sense of
self, our identity, in relation to Others over and against whom we
define ourselves.[18] Thus, in order to understand identity, both
individual and group, we must attend to the Others over and
against whom the self is positioned/constructed/constituted. "The
Other is, as we have seen, the medium by which we all but consciously define ourselves. Such is the identity/otherness dialectic
which must be brought into full consciousness" (Hentsch 1992, 192).

The concept of the Other, of Otherness, is particularly prominent in the writing of that family of thinkers and writers commonly identified as postmodern.

> We can, rather brutally, characterize postmodern thought (the phrase is useful rather than happy) as that thought which refuses to turn the Other into the Same. Thus it provides a theoretical space for what postmodernity denies: otherness. Postmodern thought also recognizes, however, that the Other can never speak for itself as the Other. (During 1993, 449)

Among those thinkers commonly identified with postmodern discourse, Jacques Derrida and Michel Foucault have been particularly concerned with calling our attention to the ways in which othering and exclusion are imbricated in the process of identity formation.[19] Derrida, a leading theorist of antiessentialistic discourse, argues that difference, rather than unity, simultaneity, or sameness, is the appropriate starting point for understanding Western culture in general, and the notion of identity and self in particular. Criticizing the prevailing Western views that see cultures as unified, self-contained, and autochthonous, Derrida insists that a culture can only be understood in relation to the cultural Others over and against which it defines itself:

> No culture is closed in on itself, especially in our own times when the impact of European civilization is so all-pervasive. Similarly, what we call the deconstruction of our own Western culture is aided and abetted by the fact that Europe has always registered the impact of heterogeneous, non-European influences. Because it has always been thus exposed to, and shadowed by, its other, it has been compelled to question itself. Every culture is haunted by its other. (1984, 116)

To both Derrida and Foucault, the process of identity formation is far from benign. Insofar as identity presupposes alterity, any effort by a group to establish the parameters of its own identity entails the exclusion and/or silencing of the voices of Others. Consequently, the process of identity formation entails acts of violence against the excluded Other: "The rapport of self-identity is itself always a rapport of violence with the other; so that the notions of property, appropriation and self-presence, so central to logocentric metaphysics, are essentially dependent on an oppositional relation with otherness. In this sense, identity presupposes alterity" (Derrida 1984, 117).

Derrida considers these processes of marginalization and exclusion to be endemic to Western thought and culture. The subject, argues Derrida, can only be understood in relation to the Other that calls it into being. Accordingly, as many of Derrida's interpreters have observed, the basic starting point for his deconstructive activity is the concern for the voices of alterity that have been silenced, the voices of those Others who have been marginalized, expelled, cast out, or excluded.

According to Edward Said, incorporating the voices of Others into our writing of history gives us a broader, more complex understanding. To achieve this understanding, we must engage in a contrapuntal reading of culture in which we read "with a simultaneous awareness both of the metropolitan history that is narrated and of those other histories against which (and together with) the dominating discourse acts" (Said 1993, 43).

Focusing on the knowledge-power nexus highlighted by Foucault, Said has brought to light the reifying processes by means of which Western culture has constructed images of the Other. To Said, recognizing and identifying the divisions and differences between cultures "not only allow us to discriminate one culture from another, but also enable us to see the extent to which cultures are humanly made structures of both authority and participation, benevolent in which they include, incorporate and validate, less benevolent in what they exclude and demote" (1993, 15).

Zionism

When we apply to Zionism the interpretations of discourse and ideology discussed above, we see it not as a closed, coherent, rational system of beliefs, ideas, and practices, but rather a dynamic, conflictive, discursive system that formulates, generates, disseminates, maintains, and transmits particular identities, forms of social relation, and hierarchies of power. Rather than view the basic "truths" that Zionism produces and disseminates as natural, taken-for-granted givens, we come to see them as historically contingent effects of complex, conflictive sociocultural processes.

When viewed in this light, Zionism is a socially constructed discourse, formulated and disseminated by specific groups engaged in a struggle to establish their hegemony within the Jewish world. Not only do conflicting interpretations of Zionism struggle for ascendancy within the Zionist movement, but non- or anti-Zionist Jewish ideologies are engaged in an ongoing struggle to wrest the hegemonic position from Zionism.

Like any nationalist movement struggling to establish and maintain its hegemony, Zionism seeks to establish a regime of truth in which certain statements, concepts, and claims are taken for granted as natural or givens, that is, as true reflections of social, cultural, and historical reality. In the process, Zionism, both in the pre-state period and following the establishment of the state, generated a network of institutional structures and cultural frameworks through which it sought to articulate and disseminate its ideology. These structures and frameworks, referred to earlier as social apparatuses, include educational institutions, religious institutions, family, privileged texts, a system of government, and nongovernment institutions, all of which perpetuate and reinforce Zionist hegemony. In addition, Zionist discourse is disseminated through such mechanisms as books, journals, poetry, songs, myths, symbols, rituals, textbooks, and films.

From its inception in late nineteenth-century Europe, Zionism, as both a political program and a sociocultural movement, contested existing Jewish social, cultural, and political discourses. Positing new, frequently radical alternatives to the prevailing theological and ideological conceptions of Judaism, Jewish identity, and Jewish history, Zionism sought to gain popular consent for its definitions of social and political reality. Such consent entailed accepting Zionist ideological discourse as natural, taken for granted, and commonsensical. This, in turn, required new forms of social relations and hierarchies of power through which Zionist discourse would be disseminated and established as authoritative.

Borrowing key concepts from traditional religious discourse, Zionism recast them in a secular ideological mold that rested on a network of binary oppositions through which history and social reality were interpreted. These oppositions include:

Inside/outside the homeland *(Aretz / hutz laaretz)*; Zion/Exile; *aliyah / yeridah* (immigrating/emigrating; literally, ascending/descending); *olim / yordim* (immigrants/emigrants; literally, those who ascend/descend); Hebrews/Jews; Israelis/-diaspora Jews; Jews/Gentiles *(Yehudim / Goyim)*; Jews/Arabs

(Yehudim / Aravim); Ashkenazim/Sephardim; Zionists/non-Zionists; Zionists/anti-Zionists; secular/religious; nation/-religion; nationalism/religion; Hebrew/other languages; Judaism/non-Judaism.

Far from limiting itself to political issues, Zionism, like other ideologies, redefined broad areas of social and cultural life including moral values, ethnicity, and group identity. Positioning Jews in specific relationships to reformulated narratives of the past, Zionism sought to replace Jewish religious identity with a secular, national Hebrew identity. Thus, Zionism positions Jews as members of a secular nation, deriving their historical identity and social location from the culture of that nation. In the process, Zionism marginalizes or excludes both Jews and non-Jews, relegating them to the position of the Other.

Deconstructing Zionism: An Emerging Post-Zionist Discourse

An examination of four texts drawn from three distinct discursive modes will serve to support the general theoretical argument made above. These texts, or discursive moments, each render problematic basic assumptions on which conventional views of Zionism have rested while providing support for a dynamic, antiessentialistic interpretation of Zionism. Taken together, these writings significantly problematize the prevailing interpretations of Zionism along with their accompanying views of Jewish identity and Jewish national culture. Revealing the dynamic, polyphonic, conflictive character of Zionism, each in its own way contributes to opening the space for the emerging post-Zionist discourse.

The authors of these texts include two major Israeli novelists and social critics who identify themselves as Zionists; an American anthropologist; and a Palestinian Arab who was born and raised in the State of Israel.

The first text, Virginia Dominguez's *People as Subject / People as Object*, analyzes Israeli society and culture through the discourse of cultural anthropology. Employing a antiessentialistic, deconstructionist view of culture, Dominguez critically analyzes the dynamic processes through which Jewish culture and identity are constructed, disseminated, and maintained. Like Hall and Clifford, Dominguez sees group identities as produced, revised, represented, and perpetuated through discursive practices. Drawing upon contemporary (some would say postmodern) literary, social, and anthropological theory, she uncovers the linguistic and social processes by means of which Israeli identity is created, disseminated, and sustained.

In contrast to conventional social scientists who, as Barthes cogently argued, conceal the discursive character of their interpretations, Dominguez openly acknowledges the "unnatural nature of social categories people believe to be natural" (e.g., races, ethnic groups). One of her main concerns is to "show how these categories change over time . . . how they are produced and reproduced within systems of power and inequality that they help to perpetuate" (Dominguez 1989, 5).

For Dominguez, as for Hall, identity is not a thing or object, but rather a dynamic, conflicted process. "Identities," she argues, "do not simply emerge . . . they do not derive from "natural" qualities/-divisions . . . they are constructed, through discourse, and the process of construction and dissemination is a contested one. Identity is never simply assumed . . . it is constantly being produced, disseminated, constructed, struggled over" (158).

Dominguez's analysis of Israeli culture diverges significantly from those of other social scientists. Whereas most historical and sociological studies of Judaism treat Jewish peoplehood as a given, Dominguez problematizes the concept of peoplehood. Peoplehood, she argues, is not a natural category, but must be continually constructed, disseminated, and sustained. Accordingly, to discuss Jewish peoplehood in particular is to discuss a process that entails "the objectification of specific collective identities—Israeli Jews' objectification of each other, their objectification of Jewishness, their objectification of Israeli society" (20).

Like many of the theorists discussed above, Dominguez views cultural identity as a site of conflict and struggle. The very act of constituting the identity of one's group is an act of power that privileges some while marginalizing or excluding others:

> How we conceptualize ourselves, represent ourselves, objectify ourselves, matters not just because it is an interesting example of the relationship between being, consciousness, knowledge, reference, and social action, but at least as much because it is a statement about power. They are simultaneously descriptive and prescriptive, presupposing and creative. (190)

Dominguez considers the designation of an individual or group as "the other" to be an inherent part of the process of identity construction. In the case of Israel, this process of "otherizing" is evident on two fronts. On the one hand, the hegemonic discourse of the Ashkenazic elite from eastern and central Europe has marginalized and excluded the subordinate Sephardic community comprised of immigrants from North Africa and the Middle East from positions of power. At the same time, the constitution of Jewish identity in Israel, among Ashkenazim and Sephardim alike, presumes the more "matter of fact on the surface" other, the Arab (1989, 108–9, 157).

Dominguez emphasizes the resistance of all groups, including the Jews, to being implicated in the otherizing process. On the one hand, "to see ourselves as constituting others is to acknowledge our having more power than we may wish to have or be comfortable having" (191). On the other hand, when a group acknowledges its role in constituting others, it renders suspect/vulnerable the very arguments that it uses in asserting the "'fact' and the legitimacy of [its] collective identity" (191).

In contrast to Dominguez, who employs scholarly discourse to problematize the prevailing notions of Zionism, Jewish peoplehood, Jewish culture, and Jewish identity, Amos Oz uses narrative discourse as well as social criticism.[20] Rejecting, like Dominguez, essentialistic notions of Zionism as well as Judaism, Oz graphically portrays the countervailing and conflicting voices within Zionism and within present-day Israel. To Oz, Israeli society, and the Zionist movement from which it sprung, is best viewed as a "querulous family and its trends and nuances, the panoply of love-hate relationships, the competitiveness, the use of covert influence, and the overt rivalry between its various components" (Oz 1987, 73). From the outset, Zionism has been marked by continual conflict.

In Oz's view, similar conflict between competing discourses and ideologies is inherent in the very foundations of modern Israel. Whether in the debates between Herzl and Ahad Haam concerning the essential mission of Zionism; between Ahad Haam and Berdichevski concerning the relationship of Zionism and Jewish tradition; between Ahad Haam and Brenner over the limits of Jewish discourse; between Weizmann and Jabotinsky regarding the appropriate ends and means of Zionism; between Likud and Labor concerning the occupied territories; between Gush Emunim and the peace camp concerning the relationship of Zionism and Western humanistic and democratic values; between the ultra-Orthodox and secularists over the relationship of nationalism and religion; or between Ashkenazim and Sephardim concerning the character of Israeli society and culture—Zionism has always been and will continue to be a contested discourse.

Oz is one of the keenest observers of the recurring conflicts and discursive struggles within Israeli society. In *In the Land of Israel* (1983), Oz graphically depicts the fault lines within Israeli society. Israeli society, like the Zionist movement and the pre-state Yishuv, is marked by ongoing debates over such issues as: Does Israeli society and culture represent continuity or discontinuity with the Jewish historical past formed in the diaspora? Do Jews constitute a national-ethnic group or a religious community? What is the relationship between Zionism and Judaism? between Israeli culture and traditional Jewish culture? between Israeli identity and Jewish identity? between the State of Israel and diaspora Jewry? Is Israel a Jewish state or a pluralistic, democratic, secular state?

No work more effectively depicts the multiple conflicting voices with Israeli society than *In the Land of Israel*. Narrating a series of confrontations between Jews and Palestinian Arabs, doves and hawks, religious believers and secularists, secular humanists and antihumanists, and Ashkenazim and Sephardim, Oz graphically depicts the contested character of Jewish culture and cultural identity.[21] However, far from decrying this ongoing conflict, Oz sees it as ripe with creative possibilities. In his view, Israel, like the Zionist movement as a whole, is best seen in terms of

> a drama of struggle between interpretations, outside influences, and emphases, an unrelenting struggle over what is the wheat and what is the chaff, rebellion for the sake of innovation, dismantling for the purpose of reassembling differently, and even putting things in storage to clear the stage for experiment and new creativity. (Oz 1983, 137)

To Oz, the struggle over Zionism is a struggle over Jewish culture as well as Jewish identity.[22] In *The Slopes of Lebanon* (1985), a recent volume of social and political criticism, he argues that the real dispute within Israeli society is not about territories, security, or borders, but about "differing concepts of Judaism—some of them humanitarian, others tribal and primitive, and still others midway between" (Oz 1987, 205). Largely as a consequence of the wars of 1967, 1973, and 1982, Israelis have been experiencing a severe identity crisis, continually confronted with such questions as "who we are, what we want to be, and what our source of authority should be" (Oz 1987, 75).

A third text that provides a powerful moment in the problematizing of Zionist discourse is a recent novel by the Israeli novelist and social critic, A. B. Yehoshua. Yehoshua's novel, *Mr. Mani* (1992), is an excellent example of postmodernist "historiographic metafiction,"[23] a genre that one leading theorist considers to be basic to postmodern writing in general. Notwithstanding his strongly held Zionist beliefs, Yehoshua's novel problematizes such notions as historical continuity and national identity, which are basic to Zionist discourse.

Structuring the novel around an extraordinary series of half-dialogues, conversations in which only one voice is heard, Yehoshua leaves it to the reader to imagine the unheard discourse of the Other. Throughout the work, Yehoshua confronts the reader with a polyphony of voices, positions, and perspectives, both within and outside of Judaism, that decenters any attempt at a monistic reading of Jewish history or culture. Tracing the history of Zionism through the events in the life of a Sephardic family, the Manis, Yehoshua subverts the hegemony of the Ashkenazic version of the Zionist metanarrative.[24] Joseph, the first Mani to settle in Jerusalem, came in 1846 for personal reasons unrelated to those later associated with Zionist ideology. The story of Joseph and his family, which "seethes with repeated instances of incest, both latent and manifest, and with abstinence from socially legitimated sexual relations" (Band 1992, 240), subverts the idealized images of the early Zionist settlers that form part of the Zionist mythos.

Joseph Mani (b. 1776), whose story is left for the final chapter of the book, problematizes the notion that there are clear and fixed divisions separating Jews and Arabs. This is done with particular force when he is made to say that Arabs are Jews who "did not yet know that they are Jews or had completely forgotten it" (Yehoshua 1992, 325). His namesake, Joseph Mani, preaching national awakening to Palestinian Arabs in 1918, alludes to the symbiotic relationship between Jewish and Palestinian nationalism, urging them to "Get ye an identity before it is too late. All over the world people now have identities, and we Jews are on our way, and you had better have an identity or else" (189). Taking from his pocket a copy of the Balfour declaration, which is taken by Zionists as validating their hegemony of Palestine, Joseph declares in the face of official Zionist doctrine: "This country is yours and it is ours; half for you and half for us. . . . Awake, sleep not!" (Yehoshua 1992, 189).

Yosef Mani's declaration that the Arabs are Jews who do not yet know or have forgotten that they are Jews blurs the boundaries distinguishing them one from the other. As one critic observed, "Indeed, it almost seems as if (by Yehoshua's definition) the Arab has entered into the psyche of the Israeli, and the self-definition of the Israeli is by now so intimately bound up with that of the Arab that it is impossible to say that the Arab has become a part of the Israeli" (Ramras-Rauch 1991, 12).

The Zionist metanarrative is further subverted by the stark contrast between Dr. Moses Mani, a non-Zionist Jerusalemite, the sickly, pulseless Theodor Herzl, and a young romantic Polish physician, Ephraim Shapiro, who attended the first Zionist congress only because his father had requested it. Mani runs a clinic in Jerusalem that welcomes both Jewish and Arab women. Whereas for the Hebrew-speaking Mani Jerusalem is home, the young Shapiro and his sister find it to be an exotic, almost surrealistic place.

Yehoshua also effectively subverts the sense of historical continuity on which Zionism, like all nationalist ideologies, depends. Rather than telling his story diachronically, Yehoshua, beginning with the present, moves backward through time. This has the effect of disrupting the reader's efforts to maintain a sense of historical continuity. This, in turn, subverts the Zionist metanarrative in which Israel is depicted as the inevitable outcome of a continuous course of events.

Likewise, Yehoshua problematizes the sense of cultural cohesion upon which nationalist ideologies like Zionism presume. As the book moves between different geographical and cultural spaces, the reader is struck by the complex polyphonic character of Jewish peoplehood and culture. Finally, Yehoshua's narrative is framed through the perspective of Israel's internal Other, the Sephardim, thereby subverting the hegemonic Ashkenazic interpretations of Zionism and Israel.[25]

In the words of one critic, "The whole thrust of Yehoshua's fiction is to work against totalizing concepts, which form the basis for fictions of identity that claim absolute difference between self and other" (Hoffman 1992, 247). Interweaving six different contexts (universal humanity, geography space, ethnicity, nationhood, gender, and class) within which identity is formed, Yehoshua, as the critic

Dan Meron points out, undermines any notion of a unified, cohesive group identity.[26] Whereas Zionism, like all forms of nationalism, privileges national identity over all others, Yehoshua's work has the effect of problematizing any concept of fixed identity, particularly the nationalistic concept.

In addition to providing a voice for the Sephardim, the Other within, Yehoshua also provides a voice for the Arab, the Other without. However, in Yehoshua, the voice heard speaking for the Arab is that of the Jew. In contrast, Anton Shammas, a Palestinian Arab raised and educated in Israel, provides a distinctly Arab voice.[27] In both his fiction and his nonfictional writings, Shammas repeatedly subverts the prevailing Zionist narratives of Israeli culture and identity, problematizing in the process many of the ideological assumptions upon which Zionism is based. Shammas achieves this by viewing Israeli myths, narratives, symbols, and rituals from the perspective of its Palestinian Arab citizens, thereby revealing the hegemonic processes by means of which Jewish culture has been imposed on them.

Whereas, from the Zionist perspective, the establishment of the State of Israel in 1948 was the culmination of the long struggle for nationhood and independence, Shammas, dramatically portraying the effects of statehood on the Arab population of the state, provides a powerful counternarrative:

> Since 1948, they [Palestinian Arabs living within Israel's borders] had been exposed to the state, which had defined itself, from the very beginning, as a Jewish state. This sudden exposure after 1948 knocked the ground—in the literal sense of the word—from under their cultural confidence. Those were the days of the military administration and land appropriations. (Shammas 1988c, 48).

Whereas Jews speak of the War of 1948 as the War of Liberation, Palestinian Arabs see it as a disaster that deprived them of their independence and freedom of movement. Yom HaAtzmaut (Independence Day), which to the Israeli Jew symbolizes national redemption, has an entirely other meaning for the Israeli Palestinian Arab:

> Little did we know that the state whose flags these were was not ours. Come to think of it, nobody knew, not even the young teacher who had taught us the Arabic translation of the Israeli Declaration of Independence from a brand new Reader, which also had a relatively detailed biography of Herzl. We were told, through some

outlandish reasoning, to learn those texts by heart, and to this day some sentences of the Declaration will occasionally pop up out of the blue inside my head.

So even according to the Arabic translation of the Declaration, the state was defined as a Jewish state, but nobody seemed to pay any attention to that fact. You see, we had the flags in our hands, so declarations did not matter, nor did the fact which we discovered later—that there was an utter rift between the signified and the signifier; those flags did not signify a single thing. (Shammas 1991, 220)

Thus, Shammas reveals the processes described earlier in our discussion of ideology, whereby the dominant ideology strives to position individuals as the bearers of specific identities. In this case, the dominant Zionist ideology seeks to position the Arab population in such a way that they see themselves within the framework of the Zionist historical narrative.

Shammas also represents the way in which hegemonic ideologies seek to delimit discourse, setting the parameters of what can and cannot be said. The establishment of one language as hegemonic is a key factor in this process. For Zionism, the establishment of Hebrew as the national language of Israel represented the renewal of Jewish culture in the Jews' historic homeland. To Israel's Palestinian Arabs, however, Hebrew symbolizes the cultural hegemony imposed by a conquering majority on the conquered minority:

My father, those days, was continuously and pensively struggling with the new [Hebrew] language that had invaded his small world and ours, imposing upon him confusion and a new type of illiteracy. He needed a special permit, like all the fathers of his generation, to move around in the scenes of his homeland which had turned overnight into "the homeland of the Jewish people"; but no such permits were available for moving around in the cultural scenes. (Shammas 1991, 217)

As Hannan Hever has argued, Shammas's own writing constitutes a major moment in the subverting of Jewish cultural hegemony. As Hever shows, the publication of Shammas's Hebrew novel *Arabeskot* (1986) significantly problematized the prevailing Zionist views of Hebrew as the Jewish national language. A non-Jewish, Palestinian Arab writer, demonstrating control of a rich and complex Hebrew style, turns the language of the hegemonic majority into a vehicle for the subordinated minority:

> The Hebrew culture's battery of defense mechanisms, which thwarts the development of a revolutionary consciousness, is appropriated by Shammas and used for a different purpose: to illumine the quandary of the slave forced to choose between assignment to a niche in the master culture, thereby condemning himself to imitation, assimilation, and loss of identity, and adherence to his traditional culture, thus forcing him into the position of a rejected "savage." (Hever 1990, 289)

Undermining the classical Zionist view of Hebrew literature as Jewish national literature, *Arabeskot* "forces a fundamental revision in some of the political assumptions underlying Israeli public discourse" (Hever 1990, 290).

Concluding Reflections

To conclude, I would like to review briefly some of the implications of current social and cultural theory for the interpretation of Zionism as a specific form of Jewish discourse, and, consequentially, for the interpretation of Judaism in general. As I indicated at the outset, the prevailing scholarly discourse on Zionism tends to ignore or minimize most of the issues raised by the theories discussed in this article. For example, rather than depicting Zionism as a contested ideological discourse built upon socially constructed, contingent categories, Zionism is treated as providing a lucid description of political, social, and cultural realities and the "best" or truest universal solution to the Jewish problem. Similarly, rather than situating Zionism as one among many competing Jewish discourses struggling to define Judaism, Jewish identity, and Jewish history, it is treated as the only viable option. Little, if any attention is paid in existing studies to the discursive mechanisms—social, cultural, and political, by means of which Zionism attained and seeks to preserve its hegemonizing effect. Similarly, insufficient attention is paid to the internal power struggles that characterize Zionism's achievement of hegemony and its efforts to maintain that hegemony.

Consistent with the theories discussed above, instead of reading the history of Zionism in terms of the ongoing realization of an essential vision or idea, or as a teleological process leading back to homeland, we would read it as a series of ongoing debates and struggles over who has the right to define the limits of Jewish discourse and the parameters of Jewish identity. Similarly, rather than treat oppositional or counterdiscourses as deviations or anomalies from some ideal norm, we would approach them as alternative discourses struggling to supplant the hegemonic discourse.

This approach focuses our attention on the legitimating, empowering, naturalizing, universalizing effects of Zionist discourse. Thus, we are led to ask: What are the social, cultural, and political processes by means of which certain ideological presuppositions and claims governing Zionist discourse come to be perceived as "natural," "given," "commonsensical," and "self-evident"? What hierarchies of power does Zionist discourse legitimate? What are the discursive processes by means of which Zionism constitutes objects and positions subjects, and on what subject positions does it depend for its survival? Who is included and who is excluded by various versions of Zionist discourse?

Most existing studies tend to treat Jewish or Israeli-Jewish identity in terms of essential, fixed qualities or characteristics. However, like Dominguez, we would treat this identity as the product of dynamic, complex, conflictive discursive processes. Accordingly, the success of Zionism in maintaining hegemony depends upon its effectiveness in positioning its supporters in relation to the narratives of the past and the social realities of the present and getting them to see such positions or identities as "natural" and authentic.

Many would see the critical orientation discussed in this essay as undermining the stability and continuity of Zionism and, consequently, of the Jewish people. In their view, deconstructing Zionist ideology with its essentialistic conceptions of Jewish culture, history, and identity even threatens Jewish survival. On the one hand, one could argue, the deconstructive approach herein described only serves to further the erosion of Jewish identity and culture that threatens the survival of Judaism. On the other hand, it could be claimed that subverting the foundations of Zionist discourse only feeds the argument of those who question the legitimacy of the Jewish state.

These arguments, however, rest precisely on those same givens that postmodernism problematizes, without providing an adequate response to the postmodernist critique. Thus, those who raise the question of the erosion of Jewish identity and culture presume the existence of some essential or foundational Jewish identity. Similarly, the essentialistic nationalism of those who question the legitimacy of an internationally recognized state is no less susceptible to deconstructive critique than any other form of essentialistic nationalism.

Judith Butler, among others, has effectively argued for the positive character of the deconstructive process. To Butler, deconstructive analysis can have the effect of clearing the space that then makes it possible for us to move on to the task of reformulating our discourse in a more effective way. As a feminist who does not wish to subvert the feminist enterprise by wiping away the notion of the female subject, Butler argues that one may eliminate essentialistic notions of subject and identity without surrendering the power to participate in the feminist enterprise.

> To deconstruct the subject is not to negate or throw away the concept; on the contrary, deconstruction implies only that we suspend all commitments to that to which the term "the subject" refers, and that we consider the linguistic functions it serves in the consolidation of authority. To deconstruct is not to negate or dismiss, but to call into question and, perhaps most importantly, to open up a term, like the subject, to a reusage or redeployment that previously has not been authorized. (Butler 1992, 15)

Following Butler, whose arguments in favor of the positive effects of deconstruction are among the more nuanced and more persuasive, I would argue that to engage in deconstructing the discourse of Zionism in no way precludes one from engaging in activities in behalf of the survival of the Jewish people and its culture. Rather, the deconstructive analysis of Zionist discourse may be seen as a positive process that has the effect of clearing the space necessary for new and more adequate formulations of Jewish identity and culture. Such an analysis also opens the way to a more profound understanding of the powerful social, cultural, and political effects of Zionist discourse that have not yet been adequately recognized.

Events such as the Holocaust, the establishment of the State of Israel, the emergence of a powerful and independent Jewish community in the United States, and the conflict with the Palestinians in the West Bank and Gaza following the 1967 War confront the current generation of Jews, both inside and outside of Israel, with previously unknown challenges. In the face of these challenges, many find the discourses of both religious Judaism and classical Zionism to be inadequate or simply obsolete. In the light of the realities of Jewish life in general, and Israeli society and culture in particular, how does one speak meaningfully about Judaism, Jewish history, and Jewish identity? Or, to quote one student of contemporary Jewish society, how are we to formulate "a language for understanding both the possibilities and the limitations of Jewish political [I would add social and cultural—L.J.S.] power in the modern world?" (Biale 1986, 4).

The analysis of Zionist discourse presented in this essay indicates one way to proceed in addressing these questions. Those who sense the inadequacy of Zionist discourse seek alternative means to define, articulate, and address the problems confronting Israel in particular and world Jewry in general. For them, the concepts and strategies provided by contemporary social and cultural theory provide a promising resource toward generating "a reusage or redeployment that previously has not been authorized" (Butler 1992, 15).

NOTES

Earlier versions of this article were presented at the American Academy of Religion Annual Meeting and at the Institute for Advanced Studies, Hebrew University, Jerusalem, in 1992. I am grateful to Steven Goldman, Hannan Hever, Steven Kepnes, Peter Ochs, and Adi Ophir for their helpful comments and suggestions.

1. See Lacqueur 1972; Vital 1975 and 1982; Eisenstadt 1985; Horowitz and Lissak 1978 and 1989.
2. See Oz 1987; Yehoshua 1984; S. Har Even 1987; and Evron 1988.
3. See, for example, Benvenisti 1986 and 1992. In a provocative piece entitled "Post-Revolutionary Zionism," Mordechai Bar-On (n.d.), proclaiming "I am a loyal Zionist," proceeds to describe the inadequacies of classical Zionist discourse as it relates to such issues as the attitude toward the diaspora, settlements in the occupied territories, agricultural labor, and the ingathering of the exiles. For further examples of the problematic of Zionist discourse, see Davis 1980, 235–72.
4. See, for example, A. Har Even 1983; S. Har Even 1987; Grossman 1989 and 1993; Shammas 1983, 1987, 1988b and c, and 1991.
5. See Aronoff 1989; Eisenstadt 1985; Horowitz and Lissak 1989; Kimmerling 1989; Krausz 1985; Medding 1989, 3–169; Rubinstein 1984;

Sprinzak 1991; Dominguez 1989; Smooha 1978, 1989, and 1992; Alcalay, 1993; Shohat 1988. A valuable selection from the writings of second-generation Israeli sociologists is Ram 1993. Criticizing the first-generation Israeli sociology as being infused by Zionist ideology, Ram uses the term "post-Zionistic" to describe the kind of sociology represented in the volume.

6. See Bialer 1990; Morris 1988a; Porat 1990; Silberstein 1991; and Smooha 1978. Nonacademic writers such as Elon (1971) and Segev (1986 and 1993) have contributed significantly to revealing the inherent fissures and contradictions in Zionist ideology and in Israeli society and culture.

7. See Morris 1988b. For a critique of the younger generation's approach, see Teveth 1989, and Morris's response, 1990. In the Israeli press it has become common to label the writings of the "new historians" as post-Zionist. The implication seems to be that to engage in research that leads one to call into question basic actions of the Israeli government regarding the establishment of the state is not compatible with being a Zionist, an argument that Morris, for one, would undoubtedly reject. Below I suggest a more complex conception of post-Zionism.

8. These writings are often subsumed under such labels as postmodern, post-Marxist, poststructuralist, and postfoundationalist. They share in common a skepticism of foundational claims in philosophy as well as the universal, totalistic claims of Enlightenment rationalism; assume the contingency of universal truth claims; deny the validity of metanarratives; reject totalistic social and political theories; and affirm the centrality of discourse in the construction and interpretation of human culture and society. For recent general discussions of postmodernism, see Docherty 1993; Best and Kellner 1991; Smart 1992 and 1993; and Seidman and Wagner 1992.

9. See Thompson 1984, 73–147; Gardiner 1992; Macdonell 1986, chaps. 2–3; Pecheux 1975; and Voloshinov 1973. The concept of ideology has come under serious criticism in recent years from, among others, Foucault. See Barrett 1991. While acknowledging a debt to Foucault, Hall (1985, 1987, and 1988) argues for the continuing utility of the concept of ideology, as does Thompson (1984, 1990) and Kavanaugh (1990). Following Hall and Kavanaugh, I find the concept of ideology to be useful for analyzing the social and cultural processes by means of which movements like Zionism achieve and maintain hegemony.

10. See, for example, Althusser 1971, Hall 1988, and Voloshinov 1973.

11. See also Hall 1988, Eagleton 1991.

12. In an insightful analysis of Thatcherism, Hall (1988) shows how Thatcher and her followers appropriated certain terms such as "tradition, Englishness, respectability, patriarchalism, family, and nation" and imbued them with particular meanings which, subsequently, came to be accepted as natural or commonsensical. As a result, it fell to

Thatcher's opponents to struggle to recover control over the meaning and use of these terms by setting them within a different interpretive/discursive framework. On the concept of hegemony, see Hall 1988, 60–61; Bocock 1986; Smart 1986; and Laclau and Mouffe 1985.

13. See Voloshinov 1973, 23; cited in Hall 1982, 77.

14. See Anderson 1983, Smith 1986 and 1991, Hobsbawm 1990, and Bhabha 1990.

15. For other critical discussion of identity, see Butler 1990 and Laclau 1990.

16. For recent critical discussions of culture, see Dirks et al. 1994, Grossberg et al. 1992, and Turner 1992.

17. "Cultural poesis—and politics—is the constant reconstitution of selves and others through specific exclusions, conventions, and discursive practices" (Clifford 1986, 24).

18. I have discussed the significance of the Other for the construction of Jewish cultural identity in "Others Within and Others Without" (in Silberstein and Cohn 1994). The chapters in that volume provide significant examples of the various ways in which Jews in different periods have constructed their Others and, through them, their own identity.

19. While Foucault was frequently identified as a postmodern thinker, his relationship to postmodern thought is highly complicated. See Smart 1992 and Best and Kellner 1991. In spite of Foucault's own reluctance to accept the label postmodern, there is no doubt that his writings have become appropriated as part of the discourse of postmodernism.

20. While Oz, in his fictional writings, poses countermodels and images to those of the dominant Zionist ideology of the 1940s and 1950s, this essay focuses on his nonfiction writings. For a discussion of the challenge to hegemonic notions expressed in Oz's fiction, see Shaked 1992, especially 129–39.

21. Lubin 1986 argues that Oz's narrative enables him to avoid telling the reader exactly where he, Oz, stands on political issues. However, Oz's political stance does come through to the reader, especially when the work is read in the context of Oz's other writings of social and political criticism.

22. As reflected in their emphasis on discourse, recent neo- or post-Marxist theorists such as Althusser, Williams, and Hall assign a far greater significance to the realm of culture than is traditionally assigned in Marxist thought. In these writings, culture is regarded as an independent social force rather than simply a reflection of material processes. See Williams 1977, Hall 1982, 1985, Kavanaugh 1990, and Dirks et al. 1994, Introduction.

23. See Hutcheon 1988 and 1989. For a succinct summary of her notion of historiographic metafiction, see Hutcheon 1993, 243–72.

24. Among the many articles and reviews, see in particular Band 1992,

Miron 1990, Ramras-Rauch 1991, and Ran 1990. A very useful collection of articles on *Mr. Mani*, almost all of them in Hebrew, is Ben-Dov 1991.

25. "The story is not about Sephardim. It is about Jewish history, about the problem of Jewish identity, about human beings. In that context, there is also the Sephardic perspective. What am I doing in the midst of this great controversy?" (Interview with Yaakov Beser [Yehoshua 1990a]). According to Gershon Shaked (1992, 37), Yehoshua is one of the first Israeli writers to present Sephardic protagonists as complex, independent characters. Shaked explores the way in which Hebrew fiction, beginning in the sixties, provided countermodels to those of Zionism. For recent works that directly challenge the prevailing Ashkenazic narrative, see Dominguez 1989; Shohat 1988 and 1989, chap. 3; and Alcalay 1993.

26. See Miron 1990. In an interview with Yaron London (Yehoshua 1990b), Yehoshua stated that the major theme of the book was the search for identity.

27. See Shammas 1983, 1986, 1987, 1988a, b, and c, and 1991.

REFERENCES

Alcalay, Amiel. *After Jews and Arabs: Remaking Levantine Culture.* Minneapolis: University of Minnesota Press, 1993.

Althusser, Louis. "Ideology and Ideological State Apparatuses." In *Lenin and Philosophy*, ed. Louis Althusser. New York: Monthly Review, 1971.

Anderson, Benedict. *Imagined Communities.* Verso: London and New York, 1983.

Aronoff, Myron J. *Israeli Visions and Divisions.* New Brunswick, N.J.: Transaction, 1989.

Band, Arnold J. "Mr. Mani: The Archaeology of Self-Deception." *Prooftexts: A Journal of Jewish Literary History* (September 1992): 231–44.

Bar-On, Mordechai. "Post-Revolutionary Zionism." *New Outlook* (n.d.): 1–7.

Barrett, Michele. *The Politics of Truth from Marx to Foucault.* Stanford, Calif.: Stanford University Press, 1991.

Ben-Dov, Nitza, ed. *Mr. Mani—A Novel of Conversations.* Haifa: University of Haifa, Dept. of Hebrew and Comparative Literature, 1991.

Benvenisti, Meron. *Conflicts and Contradictions.* New York: Villard, 1986.

———. *Fatal Embrace* (Hebrew). Jerusalem: Maxwell-Macmillan-Keter, 1992.

Best, Steven, and Douglas Kellner. *Postmodern Theory: Critical Interrogations.* New York: Guilford, 1991.

Bhabha, Homi K., ed. *Nation and Narration.* London and New York: Routledge, 1990.

Biale, David. *Power and Powerlessnes in Jewish History.* New York: Schocken, 1986.

Bialer, Uri. *Between East and West: Israel's Foreign Policy Orientation, 1948–1956.* Cambridge, U.K.: Cambridge University Press, 1990.

Bocock, Robert. *Hegemony.* London: Tavistock, 1986.

Bove, Paul. "Discourse." In *Critical Terms for Literary Study,* ed. Frank Lentricchia and Thomas McLaughlin. Chicago: University of Chicago Press, 1990.

Butler, Judith. *Gender Trouble: Feminism and the Subversion of Identity.* New York: Routledge, 1990.

———. "Contingent Foundations: Feminism and the Question of 'Postmodernism.'" In *Feminists Theorize the Political,* ed. J. Butler, J. and J. Scott. New York and London: Routledge, 1992.

Clifford, James, and George E. Marcus, eds. *Writing Culture: The Poetics and Politics of Ethnography.* Los Angeles: University of California Press, 1986.

Davis, Moshe, ed. *Zionism in Transition.* New York: Arno, 1980.

Derrida, Jacques. "Deconstruction and the Other" (an interview with Jacques Derrida). In *Dialogues with Contemporary Continental Thinkers,* ed. Richard Kearney. Manchester, U.K.: University of Manchester Press, 1984.

Dirks, Nicholas B., Geoff Eley, and Sherry B. Ortner, eds. *Culture, Power, History: A Reader in Contemporary Social Theory.* Princeton, N.J.: Princeton University Press, 1994.

Docherty, Thomas, ed. *Postmodernism: A Reader.* New York: Columbia University Press, 1993.

Dominguez, Virginia. *People as Subject, People as Object: Selfhood and Peoplehood in Contemporary Israel.* Madison: University of Wisconsin Press, 1989.

Donald, James, and Stuart Hall, eds. *Politics and Ideology.* Philadelphia: Open University Press, 1986.

During, Simon. "Postmodernism or Post-colonialism Today." In *Postmodernism: A Reader,* ed. Thomas Docherty. New York: Columbia University Press, 1993.

Eagleton, Terry. *Ideology: An Introduction.* London and New York: Verso, 1991.

Eisenstadt, S. M. *The Transformation of Israeli Society.* Boulder: Westview, 1985.

Elon, Amos. *The Israelis: Founders and Sons.* New York: Holt, Rinehart and Winston, 1971.

Evron, Boaz. *A National Reckoning* (Hebrew). Tel Aviv: Dvir, 1988.

Foucault, Michel. *Language, Counter-Memory, Practice: Selected Essays and Interviews*. Ed. with an Introduction by Donald F. Bouchard. Ithaca, N.Y.: Cornell University Press, 1977.

————. "The Order of Discourse" [1971], trans. Ian McLeod. In *Untying the Text: A Post-Structuralist Reader*, ed. Robert Young. London: Routledge and Kegan Paul, 1981.

Gardiner, Michael. *The Dialogics of Critique: M. M. Bakhtin and the Theory of Ideology*. London and New York: Routledge, 1992.

Grossberg, L., C. Nelson, and P. Treichler, eds. *Cultural Studies*. New York: Routledge, 1992.

Grossman, David. *The Yellow Wind*. Trans. from the Hebrew by Haim Watzman. New York: Delta, 1989.

————. *Sleeping on a Wire*. New York: Farrar, Straus and Giroux, 1993.

Hall, Stuart. "The Rediscovery of 'Ideology': Return of the Repressed in Media Studies." In *Culture, Society, and the Media,* ed. M. Gurevitch, T. Bennett, J. Curran, and J. Woollacott. New York: Methuen, 1982.

————. "Signification, Representation, Ideology: Althusser and the Post-Structuralist Debates." *Critical Studies in Mass Communication* (June 1985): 91–114.

————. "Variants of Liberalism." In *Politics and Ideology*, ed. James Donald and Stuart Hall. Philadelphia: Open University Press, 1986.

————. "The Problem of Ideology: Marxism without Guarantees." [Reprinted from *Marx—100 Years On*, ed. B. Matthews. London: Lawrence and Wishart, 1983.] *Journal of Communication Inquiry* (1987): 28–44.

————. "The Toad in the Garden: Thatcherism among the Theorists." In *Marxism and the Interpretation of Culture*, ed. Cary Nelson and Lawrence Grossberg. Urbana and Chicago: University of Illinois Press, 1988.

————. "Cultural Identity and Diaspora." In *Identity, Community, Culture, Difference*, ed. Jonathan Rutherford. London: Lawrence and Wishart, 1990.

Har Even, Alouph, ed. *Every Sixth Israeli: Relations between the Jewish Majority and the Arab Minority in Israel*. Jerusalem: Van Leer Foundation, 1983.

Har Even, Shulamit. *Messiah or Kenesset* (Hebrew). Tel Aviv: Zemora, Bitan, 1987.

Hentsch, Thierry. *Imagining the Middle East*. Montreal and New York: Black Rose Books, 1992.

Hever, Hannan. "Hebrew in an Israeli Arab Hand: Six Miniatures on Anton Shammas's *Arabesques*." In *The Nature and Context of Minority Discourse*, ed. Abdul R. JanMohamed and David Lloyd. New York: Oxford University Press, 1990.

Hobsbawm, E. J. *Nations and Nationalism since 1780: Programme, Myth, Reality*. Cambridge, U.K.: Cambridge University Press, 1990.

Hoffman, Anne Golumb. "The Womb of Culture: Fictions of Identity and Their Undoing in Yehoshua's *Mr. Mani*." *Prooftexts: A Journal of Jewish Literary History* (September 1992): 245–63.

Horowitz, Dan, and Moshe Lissak. *The Origins of the Israeli Polity.* Chicago: University of Chicago Press, 1978.

———. *Trouble in Utopia: The Overburdened Polity of Israel.* Albany: State University of New York Press, 1989.

Hutcheon, Linda. *A Poetics of Postmodernism: History, Theory, Fiction.* New York and London: Routledge, 1988.

———. *The Politics of Postmodernism.* Routledge: New York and London, 1989.

———. "Beginning to Theorize the Postmodernism." In *A Postmodern Reader,* ed. Joseph Natoli and Linda Hutcheon. Albany: State University of New York Press, 1993.

Kavanaugh, James H. "Ideology." In *Critical Terms for Literary Study,* ed. Frank Lentricchia and Thomas McLaughlan. Chicago: University of Chicago Press, 1990.

Kimmerling, Baruch, ed. *The Israeli State and Society: Boundaries and Frontiers.* Albany: State University of New York Press, 1989.

Krausz, Ernest, ed. *Politics and Society in Israel.* Studies in Israeli Society, vol. 3. New Brunswick, N.J.: Transaction, 1985.

Laclau, Ernesto. "Class Interpellations and Popular-Democratic Interpellations." In *Politics and Ideology,* ed. James Donald and Stuart Hall. Philadelphia: Open University Press, 1986.

———. *New Reflections on the Revolution of Our Time.* London and New York: Verso, 1990.

Laclau, Ernesto, and Chantal Mouffe. *Hegemony and Socialist Strategy: Towards a Radical Democratic Politics.* London: Verso, 1985.

Lacqueur, Walter. *History of Zionism.* New York: Holt, Rinehart and Winston, 1972.

Lubin, Orly. "A Poetics of Evasion in the Spring of 1982: Amos Oz's *In the Land of Israel*" (Hebrew). *Siman Keriah* 18 (May 1986): 156–62.

Macdonell, Diane. *Theories of Discourse.* Oxford: Basil Blackwell, 1986.

Medding, Peter Y., ed. *Israel: State and Society, 1948–1988.* New York and Oxford: Oxford University Press, 1989.

Miron, Dan. "Behind Every Thought There Is Another Thought Hiding: Reflections on *Mr. Mani*" (Hebrew). *Siman Keriah* 21 (December 1990): 153–77.

Morris, Benny. *The Birth of the Palestinian Refugee Problem.* Cambridge, U.K.: Cambridge University Press, 1988a.

———. The New Historiography: Israel Confronts Its Past." *Tikkun* (November/December 1988b): 19–23, 99–102.

———. "The Eel and History: A Reply to Shabtai Teveth." *Tikkun* 5, 1 (March/April 1990): 19–22, 79–86.

Oz, Amos. *In the Land of Israel.* New York: Vintage, 1983.

————. *Slopes of Lebanon.* New York: Harcourt, Brace, Jovanovich, 1987.

Pecheux, Michel. *Language, Semantics, and Ideology: Stating the Obvious.* Trans. Harbans Nagpal. London: Macmillan, 1975.

Porat, Dina. *The Blue and Yellow Stars of David: The Zionist Leadership in Palestine and the Holocaust, 1939–1945.* Cambridge, Mass.: Harvard University Press, 1990.

Ram, Uri, ed. *Israeli Society: Critical Perspectives* (Hebrew). Tel Aviv: Bereirot, 1993.

Ramras-Rauch, Gila. "A. B. Yehoshua and the Sephardic Experience." *World Literature Today: A Literary Quarterly of the University of Oklahoma* (Winter 1991): 8–13.

Ran, Tovah. "Zionism in a Sephardic Version" (Hebrew). *Al Hamishmar,* 15 June 1990, 18.

Rubinstein, Amnon. *From Herzl to Gush Emunim: The Zionist Dream Revisited.* New York: Schocken, 1984.

Said, Edward. *Culture and Imperialism.* New York: Alfred A. Knopf, 1993.

Segev, Tom. *1949—The First Israelis.* New York: Free Press, 1986.

————. *The Seventh Million: The Israelis and the Holocaust.* New York: Hill and Wang, 1993.

Seidman, Steven, and Wagner, David G., eds. *Postmodernism and Social Theory.* Cambridge, U.K.: Basil Blackwell, 1992.

Shaked, Gershon. "Light and Shadow, Unity and Plurality: Hebrew Fiction in Dialectic Relation to Changing Realities" (Hebrew). *Alpaim: A Multi-Disciplinary Journal of Contemporary Thought and Literature* (1992): 113–39.

Shammas, Anton. "Diary." In *Every Sixth Israeli: Relations between the Jewish Majority and the Arab Minority in Israel,* ed. Alouph Har Even. Jerusalem: Van Leer Foundation, 1983.

————. *Arabeskot* (Hebrew). Tel Aviv: Am-Oved, 1986.

————. "Kitsch 22: On the Problems of the Relations between Majority and Minority Cultures in Israel." *Tikkun* 2 (September/October 1987): 22–26.

————. *Arabesques: A Novel.* Trans. Vivian Eden. New York: Harper and Row, 1988a.

————. "A Stone's Throw." *New York Review of Books,* 31 March 1988b, 9–10.

————. "The Morning After." *The New York Review,* 29 September 1988c.

————. "At Half-Mast—Myths, Symbols, and Rituals of the Emerging State: A Personal Testimony of an Israeli Arab." In *New Perspectives on Israeli History: The Early Years of the State,* ed. Laurence J. Silberstein. New York and London: New York University Press, 1991.

Shapiro, Michael J. *Reading the Postmodern Polity: Political Theory as Textual Practice.* Minneapolis: University of Minnesota Press, 1992.

Shohat, Ella. "Sephardim in Israel: Zionism from the Standpoint of Its Jewish Victims." *Social Text* 19–20 (Fall 1988): 1–34.

————. *Israeli Cinema: East/West and the Politics of Representation.* Austin: University of Texas Press, 1989.

Silberstein, Laurence J., ed. *New Perspectives on Israeli History: The Early Years of the State.* New York and London: New York University Press, 1991.

Silberstein, Laurence J., and Robert L. Cohn, eds. *The Other in Jewish Thought and History: Constructions of Jewish Culture and Identity.* New York: New York University Press, 1994.

Smart, Barry. "The Politics of Truth and the Problem of Hegemony." In *Foucault: A Critical Reader*, ed. David Couzzens Hoy. Oxford and New York: Basil Blackwell, 1986.

————. *Modern Conditions: Postmodern Controversies.* London: Routledge, 1992.

————. *Postmodernity.* London: Routledge, 1993.

Smith, Anthony D. *The Ethnic Origins of Nations.* Oxford: Basil Blackwell, 1986.

————. *National Identity.* Reno: University of Nevada Press, 1991.

Smooha, Sammy. *Israel: Pluralism and Conflict.* Berkeley and Los Angeles: University of California Press, 1978.

————. *Arabs and Jews in Israel.* 2 vols. Boulder: Westview, 1989 and 1992.

Sprinzak, Ehud. *The Ascendance of Israel's Radical Right.* New York: Oxford University Press, 1991.

Terdiman, Richard. *Discourse/Counter-Discourse.* Ithaca, N.Y.: Cornell University Press, 1985.

Teveth, Shabtai. "Charging Israel with Original Sin." *Commentary* (September 1989): 24–33.

Therborn, Goran. *The Ideology of Power and the Power of Ideology.* London and New York: Verso, 1980.

Thompson, John B. *Studies in the Theory of Ideology.* Berkeley and Los Angeles: University of California Press, 1984.

————. *Ideology and Modern Culture.* Stanford, Calif.: Stanford University Press, 1990.

Turner, Graeme. *British Cultural Studies: An Introduction.* London and New York: Routledge, 1992.

Vital, David. *The Origins of Zionism.* Oxford: Oxford University Press, 1975.

————. *Zionism: The Formative Years.* Oxford: Oxford University Press, 1982.

Voloshinov, V. N. *Marxism and the Philosophy of Language.* New York: Seminar Press, 1973.

Williams, Raymond. *Marxism and Literature.* Oxford: Oxford University Press, 1977.

Yehoshua, A. B. *Between Right and Right* (Hebrew). Tel Aviv: Schocken, 1984.

————. Interview with Yaakov Beser (Hebrew) [reprinted in Ben-Dov 1991]. *Iton* 77 (May–June 1990a): 28.

————. "In the Role of a Guest: A. B. Yehoshua" (Hebrew) [reprinted in Ben-Dov 1991]. An interview with Yaron London, *Yediot Aharonot*, 4 May 1990b.

————. *Mar Mani* (Hebrew). Tel Aviv: HaKibbutz HaMeuhad, 1990c.

————. *Mr. Mani*. New York: Doubleday, 1992.

Feminism

Chapter 12

Rethinking Jewish Feminist Identity/ies: What Difference Can Feminist Theory Make?

Laura S. Levitt

> Imagine on the one hand the deconstructionist figuration of a female (reading) subject (one tends in these discussions to take the reader for the human subject) reading "as a woman"—her identity permanently deferred in the gap between her existence and the figure of woman. On the other, bodily facing this "as a woman" woman Sojourner Truth asking her famous rhetorical question "Ain't I a woman?"; the phrase, uttered as a declaration of rights, of entitlement, for a woman of color, a black woman, also to be a woman. (Miller 1991, 75)

> It could be said that the tension produced by the essentialist/-constructionist debate is responsible for some of feminist theory's greatest insights, that is, the very tension is constitutive of the field of feminist theory. (Fuss 1989, 1)

In his powerful essay on the complexities of Caribbean identity, "Cultural Identity and Diaspora," Stuart Hall argues that there are at least two different ways of thinking about what he calls "cultural identities." He writes, "The first position defines 'cultural identity' in terms of one, shared culture, a sort of collective 'one true self'. . . which people with a shared history and ancestry hold in common" (Hall 1990, 223). The second position focuses not so much on the similarities within a culture, but rather on the points of "deep and significant *difference* which constitute identity" (225). Using this second notion of cultural identity, Hall argues that "cultural identities come from somewhere, have histories. But, like everything which is historical, they undergo constant transformation. Far from being eternally fixed in some essentialized past, they are subject to the continuous 'play' of history, culture and power" (Hall 1990, 225).

In this essay I use postmodern theories of identity such as those developed by Hall to problematize what various Jewish feminists mean when we claim "Jewish feminist identities." My concern is to articulate the diversity not only among and between but even within those of us who claim these identities. It is my contention that although there has been some acknowledgment of differences among Jewish feminists, the desire to find commonality continues to erase important distinctions. In this essay I use feminist literary theory and the debates within that discourse to address this problem. I will argue that this theory can be useful in Jewish feminist efforts to appreciate and respect these differences. In order to explore how this might work, I have chosen to focus on "Dreaming Dancing and the Changing Location of Feminist Criticism, 1988," an essay by the feminist literary critic, Nancy K. Miller (1991). I choose this text because it both highlights the debates within feminist theory around "identity politics" and "critical theory" and addresses the question, "What does it mean to speak as a Jew in the context of feminist theory?"

In Part One, I will demonstrate what is at stake for discussions of identity in some of the critical debates within feminist theory. My focus will be on Miller's autobiographical anecdote of a failed attempt to use theory to talk about identity and difference. I use this account to illustrate the kinds of dangers involved in my own efforts to address this theory to talk about Jewish feminist identities. By highlighting the difficulties Miller encountered in trying to move between various notions of theory and politics, I will try not to make the same mistakes in my own attempts to bring the complexity of feminist theorizing into a discussion of postmodern Jewish feminism. But I take Miller's autobiographical move very seriously and attempt to position myself, rather contingently, at the intersection between Jewish Studies and Feminist Studies.

In Part Two, I once again ask the question, "What difference can feminist theory make in rethinking Jewish feminist identities?" Focusing on "Personal Histories, Autobiographical Locations," the final section of Miller's essay, "Dreaming Dancing," I will describe the two somewhat contradictory options Miller presents for thinking about her own identity. On the one hand, I will present Miller's attempts to problematize the category of "identity," and on the other hand I will present key passages in her text where she tries to speak "as a Jew." By juxtaposing these two acts, I will argue that Miller fails to bring the nuances of her initial discussion of identity to her attempts to speak "as a Jew." In other words, by reading Miller's text "as a Jewish feminist," I will argue for a critical consistency that appreciates the complexities and contradictions within and among Jewish feminist identities. Acknowledging my debt to Miller, I will conclude by explaining my own use of the term "identity/ies."[1]

Part One. Identity and Difference: The Problem

In order to set the stage for Miller's anecdote, let me begin by briefly positioning it within the larger context of her essay. "Dreaming Dancing" reads as a text with commentary. The text, an experimental piece entitled "Whose Dream?" is presented in its opening section. It is followed by "Personal Histories," a kind of elaborate commentary on "Whose Dream?" In brief, "Whose Dream?" addresses questions of identity and difference using a textual strategy that resists the use of a single explicit authorial voice. Instead, it weaves together a series of diverse references from feminist "identity politics" and "critical theory." In Miller's text, the voices of "identity politics" are primarily those of women of color engaged in political resistance.[2] By contrast, "critical theory" is represented by academic critics engaged in deconstructing the asymmetrical power dynamics embedded within Western discourse(s).

It might be helpful to see the connection between these two strands in Miller's text as the voices of "difference." They are similar but not the same. The former are distinctly political voices passionately committed to resisting forms of domination that oppress those defined as "different." The latter resist even the term "difference." They favor a new term altogether, *différance*. The use of this word or concept, as Derrida suggests (1982, 1–27), makes clear the differences, the gaps, the silences, that constitute discourse. Using this term, these theorists attempt to open up strategic discursive possibilities in order to resist the structure of binary oppositions. Thus the complicated relationship between these discourses, deconstruction on the one hand, and feminist "identity politics" on the other, is central to "Whose Dream?" In "Whose Dream?" Miller highlights the tensions between these discourses by juxtaposing the tropes of "dreaming" and "dancing" as used by women of color and deconstructionist critics. Suffice it to say, Miller's attempt to piece together these images is a powerful and disturbing venture, an academic tour de force. Given its critical theoretical tenor, however, "Whose Dream?" is not readily accessible. Ironically, even some of the feminists cited by Miller might find her text not only difficult to read, but politically problematic. Nevertheless, I write about this text because it illustrates what can happen when one tries to use theory to bridge distinctions between different notions of politics and difference. Miller's anecdote chronicles what happened when she presented "Whose Dream?" to a general audience. The setting for this presentation was the conference, "Feminism and the Dream of a Plural Culture," held at Queen's College in 1988. In some ways Miller's task was much like my own here. Like me, she attempted to present feminist theory to an audience that is both unfamiliar with this theory and, perhaps, hostile to it. By discussing Miller's failed attempt at bridging this gap, I want to acknowledge her difficulties as well as offer a different strategy for bringing feminist literary theory into Jewish Studies.

The Anecdote

In "Personal Histories," Miller tells us the story of her attempt to present her paper "Whose Dream?" as if it were all a big misunderstanding. She explains that she decided to present "Whose Dream?" at Queen's College because she had expected "to be speaking to a small gathering of faculty (and some of their graduate students) who had been working on problems of critical theory together" (Miller 1991, 93). Instead of finding this comfortable familiar academic audience, however, Miller writes, "I arrived to find not a small working group but an auditorium filled with people—students, members of the community, a vast heterogeneous scene" (93). Miller's initial discomfort was then exacerbated by the keynote speaker, bell hooks, the African American feminist critic,[3] who, in engaging with the audience, "expressed both her own wish as a feminist to write not in an academic voice, but a language her mother could read, and her (rhetorical?) wish for us—the speakers —to abandon the texts we had prepared, renounce academic protocol, and just talk to each other" (94).[4]

In this unlikely setting, despite feeling ill at ease, wanting to "jump ship and go home" (94),[5] Miller stayed and read her paper.

As she painstakingly recalls, the audience's response was decidedly negative; many simply got up and left the room. What is interesting about this discussion, however, is not Miller's confession, but, rather, her attempts to pinpoint what caused the failure. She argues that the problem was not only one of "context," but, rather, an example of the very real difficulties many of us in the academy experience in trying to forge a relationship between critical theory and feminist politics. In this case, using theory without explicit explanation meant that Miller could not be understood. Her good political intentions were thwarted. Miller writes,

> I felt that I had not only failed to produce a vocabulary for talking about differences (the charge of the conference agenda), but that I had somehow unwittingly violated the spirit of the occasion. Despite my attempt through the play of quotation to push at the edges of academic genre by relinquishing the authority of a critical "I" that would guide and control the reading, I had succeeded mainly, it seemed, in finding exactly the wrong tone (perhaps the marker of the very control I played at relinquishing). . . . I was left with a sense of the unbridgeability of certain differences—at least in that setting, that setup, in which I became by the structure of the event and by my own discursive position (to use the language of my paper) and style the other of oppression: the straight white woman. The effect of quotation—texts concatenated without contexts—designed to unsettle alignments through the play of language reinforced them instead. (94)

Miller powerfully and painfully illustrates precisely the kinds of tensions she and I are trying to write about. She explains how the rift between feminist politics and critical theory can actually be played out in practice. Appealing to the textual possibilities within critical theory to offer different feminist political possibilities, possibilities for talking about our differences, Miller ended up losing her own voice. To talk about "identity" without an "I" failed as a political strategy. Instead of being received as a radical innovator, a critical political ally, Miller ended up not only as the "straight white woman," an elite academic, but as "the other of oppression." In practice, her strategy failed. Given this, I want to argue for a different approach that will allow me to claim a critical voice.

In the context of a discussion of feminist literary theory within Jewish Studies, I position myself "as a Jewish feminist" and offer a particular reading of that identity. In so doing, I follow Teresa de Lauretis's suggestion:

> One's personal history . . . is interpreted or reconstructed by each of us within the horizon of meanings and knowledges available in the culture at given historical moments, a horizon that also includes modes of political commitment and struggle . . . always grasped and understood within particular discursive configurations. (1986, 8)

With this in mind, the Jewish feminist position I will offer is but one reading of what Stuart Hall might call my Jewish cultural identity. It is one of the ways I position myself within the narratives of my Jewish past.

My "I" in This Paper

By positing a specific "I" in this paper, I am claiming a subject position.[6] As Diana Fuss explains, "The essentialism in 'anti-essentialism' inheres in the notion of place or positionality. What is *essential* to social constructionism is precisely this notion of 'where I stand,' or what has come to be called, appropriately enough, 'subject-positions'" (1989, 29). Thus, in claiming the interdependency of "essentialism" and "constructionism," Fuss argues not only for a kind of risk taking, the strategic deployment of an essence, but shows how even constructionist arguments themselves are predicated on a kind of essentializing. It is in this way that I risk positing my Jewish feminist "I" in this text. The position I offer is again but one reading of the personal histories out of which I have come to read Miller's text.

I was raised in a small-town Jewish community, a community with one Jewish institution, a synagogue. It was by default Conservative. We belonged. My parents were community leaders. They were not religious. For them, Jewishness was a duty, a cultural and ethical commitment to the Jewish people. I became interested in Judaism at college through the study of religion. My interests were academic. I fell in love with "modern Judaism" and wanted to teach. I have spent most of my adult life in pursuit of this passion. My graduate studies were for me a kind of indoctrination into the world of liberal Judaism in the United States.

When I use the term "liberal Judaism," I am here referring to a variety of Jewish communities in the United States that share a particular commitment to the ideology of "liberalism." These include the following denominational affiliations: the Reform, Conservative, Reconstructionist, and some Modern Orthodox communities. These specifically "religious" Jewish communities are committed to certain liberal principles, including the social contract, a faith in rationality, and liberalism's commitment to a kind of universal discourse. These ideological commitments were very much a part of the Jewish community I grew up in as well. The distinction I am now making is that the communities I became a part of were "religious." What I mean by this is that they shared a certain faith commitment that manifests itself in terms of a desire to engage in traditional and innovative Jewish learning as well as Jewish practice.[7]

In this liberal Jewish community I was trained as a Jewish scholar. Through my work at both the Conservative and Reform seminaries, as well as within the field of religion, I became an educated "religious" liberal Jew. I also became a feminist primarily in response to issues of exclusion in liberal Jewish texts and practices. Thus, my feminism and my Judaism are historically bound. For many years, I thought that all Jewish feminists came to feminism more or less as I had done, by first becoming committed to this kind of liberal Judaism and then wanting to be empowered as Jewish women.

I was wrong. Despite the close connections between liberal Judaism and much of mainstream second-wave U.S. feminism (see Eisenstein 1981), including a shared commitment to the promises of liberalism, I have learned, often painfully, that there are other options. Nevertheless, my Jewish feminism evolved out of this liberal Jewish community. As a liberal Jewish feminist I first wanted "equal rights": the ordination of women rabbis, the investiture of women cantors, women presidents of major Jewish organizations, as well as the inclusion of Jewish feminist readings of the tradition both critical and constructive in Jewish scholarship and Jewish worship. This kind of scholarship, in particular, nurtured me, but, because the Jewish feminists I identified with shared, by and large, my heterosexual, white-skin class and Jewish educational privilege, I was isolated from other Jewish women and other Jewish feminist possibilities. Looking back, I lacked a degree of both imagination and real agency in this regard. Liberalism, as a totalizing discourse, left little room for me to imagine Jewish feminisms outside of this particularly narrow liberal Jewish milieu. Moreover it did not allow me to explore the contradictions and differences within even my own liberal Jewish feminist identity—the tensions between my family's Jewish liberalism and the conflicting liberalisms of the Jewish institutions that trained me.

Thus, I share this particular telling of my history because it offers insights into my struggles with these various Jewish liberalisms and my turn to feminist literary theory. Although I am still very much tied to these traditions, often defining my own project as "postliberal" (Levitt 1992), I no longer work solely within Jewish Studies. I have reached outside of this discipline in order not only to account for the plurality of Jewish feminist positions, the differences among and between Jewish feminists, but in order to account for the differences and the contradictions within my own Jewish feminist identity.

What follows is my reading of Miller's attempt to speak "as a Jew." In it I will offer both a critique of what happens to "Jewish identity" within feminist literary theory[8] and show how this theory might be used to critique the legacy of the unified liberal Jewish self.

Part Two. What Difference Can Theory Make?

What difference can a theoretical text like Miller's make in addressing this complexity? In order to answer this question, I will now focus on that part of "Personal Histories" where Miller attempts to "speak as a Jew." This shift in positionality is a response to the failures of "Whose Dream?" As Miller writes,

> Since the disembodiment of that position seemed to work against my own desire for a dialogics within feminism, I decided that in my revisions of the work I would place myself—autobiographically—in relation to the material of identity already elaborated through the quotations. More specifically wanting to fracture the simplified profile of straight white woman, and in the spirit of a more locational feminist politics [she writes], I placed myself in the text "as a Jew." (1991, 95)

This "speaking as a Jew" takes two forms. She first presents a series of "anecdotal" accounts of what she calls "identity politics in the academy" and what they mean for her as a Jew, and concludes with a brief description of what happened when she included Jewish dreams and Jewish nightmares in a later version of "Whose Dream?" Having tried to speak "as a Jew" in these ways, Miller draws the following conclusions:

> I have not found a way to assume that rhetoric of identity (although I am both, I cannot lay claim to "Jewish feminist"): it is not a ground of action for me in the world, nor the guarantee of my politics—my writing. The fact, however, of being both Jewish and a feminist is a crucial, even constitutive piece of my self-consciousness as a writer; and in that sense of course it is also at work—on occasion—in the style and figures of my autobiographical project. (1991, 97)

I quote this passage in full because it is the most concise statement Miller makes about her identity "as a Jewish feminist" and it shows her ambivalence. She insists that she does not want to position herself or be positioned by others "as a Jew," yet Miller remains Jewish, claiming a Jewish and a feminist identity in the style and figure of her writing. Thus, as is her "style," she expresses this hesitancy and ambivalence formally. Here, as elsewhere in her text, she makes her most striking statements about these identities parenthetically. In the passage just cited, for example, she insists she cannot call herself "a Jewish feminist" in a parenthetical comment. Furthermore, although she writes directly that she does not want to be tied to her Jewishness as a kind of grounding, she elaborates on this in a note. It is in the note that she insists that she can not call herself "a Jewish feminist and a feminist Jew in every moment of my life" (1991, 100).

What is striking about the comment "I am not a 'Jewish feminist'" is that it comes from a feminist critic whose work generally resists such unproblematized notions of identity. Despite this, in "getting personal" and discussing her "Jewishness" as a response to her failure to communicate at Queen's College, Miller seems to lose her critical voice. Instead, ironically, she appeals to the same kind of liberal categories to talk about her Jewishness that I turned to feminist theory to critique, specifically, liberalism's notion of the "unified (in this case Jewish feminist) subject." In so doing, Miller rejects both the dreams of "identity politics" as well as "deconstruction," in terms of their shared critique of liberalism and their commitment to difference(s). Instead, she makes "Jewish feminist" into a single absolute term not unlike the liberal Jewish feminist position I have struggled to reject. In so doing she does not allow for instability. She also denies the possibility of other Jewish feminist positions as well as the contradictions within these identities. By referring to Judith Plaskow, the Jewish feminist theologian, as the paradigmatic example of "the Jewish feminist," Miller denies that she is a "Jewish feminist" since this is the only possible Jewish feminist position she recognizes. In so doing, she ignores not only her own complicated position but the evidence of at least one other possibility in her own text. She ignores her own reference to Evelyn Beck, a Jewish lesbian feminist literary critic who, as she noted at a conference on feminist theory in Milwaukee in 1985, "exhorted Jewish women to identify themselves (take back their names and their noses)" (Miller 1991, 96). In her initial statement, therefore, Miller's logic is simply to say that because she is not exactly like Judith Plaskow, she cannot be a "Jewish feminist." Since this position denies the complexity both among and between Jewish feminists, I find it extremely problematic.

Fortunately, however, Miller also makes a different point. She tells us that her Jewishness and her feminism are constitutive elements of how she understands herself as a writer. Thus, despite her ambivalence and her inability to control these aspects of her identity, they are at work in her writing. They are there "on occasion." I believe this point is crucial. This approach allows Miller to claim those places where her Jewishness is important in her work. And, contrary to her first statement, she can argue that being Jewish and a feminist are critical to the ways in which she positions herself specifically in her writing. Thus, she does not have to be a Jewish feminist *always* and *everywhere* to claim this identity.

I believe that this occasional approach is a more viable account of identity. It resists the romanticizing of the absolute nature of such statements as, "I am always and everywhere a Jewish feminist" and instead, allows for difference(s). Moreover, it appreciates the importance of context in making these kinds of claims. Being both Jewish and a feminist may affect "the style and figure" of Miller's autobiographical project, but this is not the only possible way of expressing one's Jewishness or one's feminism. For other Jewish feminists, the margins may not be the most apt description of our Jewish feminist identities.

Finally, in this context, I want to explain my own use of the term "identity/ies." I write about Jewish feminist identities in both the singular and plural in order to account for precisely those two things Miller argues for: first, the importance of context, and second, the multiplicity within and among Jewish feminists. On occasion it is important to lay claim to an identity both as a partial and temporary textual and/or political strategy. In claiming a subject position, one acknowledges that this is only one of many contradictory positions that could be taken.

Toward Some Tentative Conclusions: Identity/ies in Practice

In order to explain what this "identity/ies" might look like in practice, I will now turn to Miller's final rereading of "Whose Dream?" where she includes an attempt to speak "as a Jew." In this rendition, Miller claims an assimilated New York Jewish identity. She reveals in yet another parenthetical comment, "If not theorized [my Jewishness is] at least revisited by Woody Allen" (1991, 96).

She goes on to state that not only is she a New York Jew, but a Jew for whom Israel is "an almost mythic place" (96). In other words, "Israel" is not a part of her experience of being Jewish. Her Jewishness is marked by Israel's absence. The question is, if this is true, why does Israel appear at all in her autobiographical account? Miller answers this question indirectly by citing Jenny Bourne, a British Jewish socialist feminist critic. Miller uses Bourne's disturbing and often inaccurate critique of Jewish feminist identity politics, "Homelands of the Mind: Jewish Feminism and Identity Politics" (Bourne 1987),[9] to prove that she had no choice but to talk about Israel. "There is, in the end, *no stable* diaspora-based identity for us as Jewish feminists; *all* roads lead back to the question of Israel" (Miller 1991, 100; my emphases).

Allowing Bourne to define Jewish feminist identity, Miller leaves herself no other option but to present herself in relation to Israel.[10] In this way, Miller demonstrates quite poignantly how her first option, the absolute criteria for who is a Jewish feminist, denies her experience as well as her agency in these matters. As a result of this imposition of an absolute, Miller no longer writes in her own voice. Since Israel is not a part of her New York experience, she is resigned to be without words.

Before relating what Miller actually did, I want to ask what would have happened had she actually addressed the problem of being held accountable to someone else's criteria for who is a Jewish feminist? This would have solved Miller's problem. She would have had a lot to say. Arguing against Bourne and others who make such claims, she could have claimed an unstable, in her case, diaspora-based Jewish identity.

Had Miller done what I am suggesting, she might have responsibly talked about the painful experience of being held accountable as a Jew in 1988 for Israeli policies, especially the occupation. Miller could have made explicit her complicated feelings about speaking "as a Jew" to an audience that included Edward Said, the prominent Palestinian cultural critic and activist.[11]   In other words, Miller could have used this opportunity to problematize the whole issue of being defined by *others*. She also could have argued that context is constitutive for identity by positioning her own remarks within a particular historical moment—what it meant to write "as a Jew," with little prior engagement with Israel, during the Intifada. Here she could have made explicit her moral and political trepidation. After all, even Woody Allen (in one of his more responsible moments)[12] did address precisely these kinds of issues when he wrote in the *New York Times* that "Jews don't go around breaking other people's bones."

Left without words of her own, Miller reinvokes her initial failed textual strategy. She once again resorts to "a politics of quotation" (1991, 97). This time, she quotes an Israeli psychiatrist's account of the dreams of Arab and Israeli children.[13]   As in her earlier efforts, Miller allows "quotations" to "speak for her," and without an "I," even a contingent "I," once again she fails to communicate. As she tells us, this time her use of quotations

> Generated a reaction in the audience that brought me up abruptly
> against both my personal anxieties about speaking "as a Jew" and
> the dangerous ambiguity underlined by Edward Said, produced by
> the politics of quotation itself. (The agonies of Middle East politics
> aside, it is true that I should have thought twice about giving a
> psychiatrist the last word, especially in a paper about dreams!)
> (1991, 97)

She then goes on to claim neither a willingness to speak "as a Jew" nor a willingness to speak "for others." She writes:

To some extent the difficulty of these two occasions was an effect of context; it was also, and more importantly, a symptom of the project of identity writing itself: *impossible* to elude: the co-implications, which *always* seems to find its borders in violence, of the "speaking as a"s and "speaking for"s. . . . It is for this reason that I have not tried, even in this space of written revision, to master the crisis by a conclusion that would put things back together again. This could *only* be done by a discourse of containment that depends *finally* on making an abstraction of that violence. (1991, 97; my emphases)

In this way, Miller ends her essay in resignation. She is ultimately unwilling to claim a subject position, if only for a time. According to Miller such a strategy is ultimately "impossible." As she reminds us, "this could only be done by a discourse of containment." Given this, as Miller suggests elsewhere, "What [is] there, really, to say once the structure of competing oppressions has been put in place in those [absolute] terms" (1991, 96)?

In contrast to this resigned stance, I have demonstrated that it is possible to "speak as a Jewish feminist."[14] I have argued that in the context of both Jewish Studies and Feminist Studies it is important for Jewish feminists to claim both the specificity and complexity of our own "identity/ies" so that we not lose our voices, but, rather, honestly and responsibly claim subject positions not as absolute or secure but as occasioned.

What does all this mean in the context of this volume of essays? What does this Jewish feminist reading of a text in feminist literary theory have to offer the production of postmodern Jewish hermeneutics? By highlighting the contradictions within feminist literary theory around issues of identity and difference—the tensions between deconstruction and identity politics—I bring to postmodern Jewish hermeneutics a feminist critique. Feminist identity/ies are not, as Miller's opening quote suggests, ever simply "deconstructionist figurations of a female subject . . . permanently deferred in the gap between her existence and the figure of a woman" (Miller 1991, 75). Instead, she is always already confronted by a political urgency, a commitment to resist domination. These tensions are constitutive. With this in mind, feminist literary theory offers postmodern Jewish hermeneutics not simply a "deconstructionist stance" toward Jewish identities, but a politics. Because feminist literary theory remains deeply political even as it appreciates and works with the tensions between what Fuss has called essentialist and constructionist positions, it offers Jewish Studies a strategy for claiming a Jewish position, for "taking a stand." In other words, by thinking about "Jewish identity/ies" we might begin to confront not only the "gap between the existence and the figure of the Jew" but the political urgency that is also constitutive of what it has meant to claim a Jewish identity at the end of the twentieth century.

NOTES

1. I apologize for this somewhat decontextualized reading of Miller, but I have chosen not to allow Miller's text totally to define the terms of this discussion. For a much more detailed reading of her essay, see Levitt 1993, chap. 4.

2. These works include Barbara Smith (1984); Audre Lorde (1984); Gloria T. Hull, Patricia Bell Scott, and Barbara Smith (1982); Cherríe Moraga and Gloria Anzaldua (1983); and Gloria Anzaldua (1987). What is striking about Miller's reading of identity politics is the virtual absence of any Jewish presence when, in fact, Jewish feminists, especially lesbian Jewish feminists, were actively engaged in these struggles. See, for example, Elly Bulkin, Minnie Bruce Pratt, and Barbara Smith (1984); Evelyn Torton Beck (1982); Irena Klepfisz and Melanie Kaye/Kantrowitz (1986); and Aurora Levins Morales and Rosario Morales (1986).

3. "Bell hooks" is a pseudonym for Gloria Watkins. As she explains:

    > One of the many reasons I chose to write using the pseudonym bell hooks, a family name (mother to Sarah Oldham, grandmother to Rosa Bell Oldham, great-grandmother to me), was to construct a writer-identity that would challenge and subdue all impulses leading me away from speech into silence. I was a young girl buying bubble gum at the corner store when I first really heard the full name bell hooks. I had just "talked back" to a grown person. Even now I can recall the surprised look, the mocking tones that informed me I must be kin to bell hooks—a sharp-tongued woman, a woman who spoke her mind, a woman who was not afraid to talk back. I claimed this legacy of defiance, of will, of courage, affirming my link to female ancestors who were bold and daring in their speech. Unlike my bold and daring mother and grandmother, who were not supportive of talking back, even though they were assertive and powerful in their speech, bell hooks as I discovered, claimed, and invented her was my ally, my support. (bell hooks 1989, 9)

4. This statement is itself somewhat ironic given hook's own difficulties speaking, or rather "talking back" to her mother literally in her own voice (see my n. 3 above).

5. I want to thank Steven Kepnes for pointing out to me the double irony

in this statement. "Nancy K. Miller just wants to 'go home.' She responds to hook's desire for 'home' with her own desire for home" (Steven Kepnes, personal correspondence, July 1993).

6. In offering such a stance, I am resisting the binary between "essentialist/constructionist." As Fuss argues,

> It is my conviction that the deadlock created by the long-standing controversy over the issue of human essences (essential femininity, essential blackness, essential gayness . . . [essential Jewishness?]) has, on the one hand, encouraged more careful attention to cultural and historical specificities where perhaps we have hitherto been too quick to universalize but, on the other hand, foreclosed more ambitious investigations of specificity and difference by fostering a certain paranoia around the perceived threat of essentialism. (Fuss 1989, 1)

Fuss then goes on to argue, as the quotation with which I open this paper suggests, that it is precisely these kinds of tensions that constitute feminist theorizing. For more on this whole question, see Fuss 1989.

7. On liberal Judaism, see, for example, the work of Eugene Borowitz (1990, 1984, 1983).

8. I am especially indebted to Evelyn Torton Beck for pointing out the overwhelming invisibility of "Jewishness" in Feminist Studies. See Evelyn Torton Beck (1988).

9. In this essay Bourne offers an "Old Marxist" critique of "identity politics." As Bourne argues,

> The shift in Jewish feminist politics towards a preoccupation with cultural identity found justification in, and was reinforced by, the New Marxism which, in its 'flight from class', had chosen the new social forces (of Women, Blacks, Gays, Greens, etc.) as the builders of the new Jerusalem. 'Classism,' in the new scheme of things, was no more than another autonomous force like racism or anti-Semitism or homophobia. Oppression, therefore, and not exploitation became the focus of attention. And capitalism was not so much 'a mode of production which can be reduced to one central contradiction—between exploited workers and capitalists'—as 'a set of oppressions including those of race, sex, and nationality.' (Bourne 1987, 3)

Thus, using this criteria, Bourne longs for "one central contradiction" and resents the assertion of differences. In her specific critique of Jewish feminist identity politics, Bourne offers a similar approach. Here again she presents an absolute criteria for a Jewish feminist politics. She writes that Jewish feminists

> refused . . . to take a stand on the crucial and painful contradictions posed by the material realities of the Middle East, and opted instead to internalize those contradictions into a crisis of Jewish feminism, to be resolved on the basis of our complex identities. Politics required us to take a stand on the issue, metaphysics

allowed us to escape it—but feminism allowed us to conflate the political and the personal, the objective and the subjective, the material and the metaphysical, and escape into Identity Politics. (4)

In other words, for Bourne there is one right answer, a single correct political stance toward the Middle East and, for that matter, the legacy of the Holocaust. According to Bourne, Jewish feminists should renounce, in this case, our ties to the State of Israel "in the name of a larger feminist politics" (4). Ironically, of course, it is in a negation of Israel that Bourne argues that "all roads lead back to the question of Israel" (18).

10. Another disturbing implication of Bourne's statement is that it presumes that Israel does offer "in the end" a "stable" identity. In sharp contrast to this seamless depiction of Israeli identity, see Laurence Silberstein and Hannan Hever's contributions in this volume. Each of these essays makes clear the complexities and contradictions within and among Israeli identities as well.

11. Miller presented this final version of "Whose Dream?" at a colloquium at the School of Criticism and Theory at Dartmouth College during the summer of 1988.

12. These references to responsibility in relation to Woody Allen in a feminist context are especially disturbing to me. I have made these references to Allen because he is cited on more than one occasion by Miller as expressing a Jewish identity close to her own. My concern is around Allen's treatment of women as reflected in his films. Reference to him in a text about Jewish feminist identity does raise certain suspicions for me. Nevertheless, he is quite prominent in Miller's text, and, therefore, I have chosen to acknowledge this connection.

13. These accounts are from David Grossman (1988).

14. In this brief paper I have only touched upon the problem of "speaking for" in my reading of "Whose Dream?" Questions remain. For a powerful and nuanced account of these issues, see Alcoff 1991–92.

REFERENCES

Alcoff, Linda. "The Problem of Speaking for Others." *Critical Inquiry* (Winter 1991–92): 5–31.

Anzaldua, Gloria. *Borderlands, La Frontera, the New Mestiza.* San Francisco: Spinsters/Aunt Lute Press, 1987.

Beck, Evelyn Torton. "The Politics of Jewish Invisibility." *NWSA Journal* 1:1 (1988): 93–102.

———, ed. *Nice Jewish Girls: A Lesbian Anthology.* Trumansburg, N.Y.: Crossing Press, 1982.

Borowitz, Eugene. *Choices in Modern Jewish Thought: A Partisan Guide.* New York: Behrman House, 1983.

———. *Liberal Judaism*. New York: Union of American Hebrew Congregations, 1984.

———. *Exploring Jewish Ethics: Papers on Covenant Responsibility*. Detroit: Wayne State University Press, 1990.

Bourne, Jenny. "Homelands of the Mind: Jewish Feminism and Identity Politics." *Race and Class* 29:1 (Summer 1987): 1–24.

Bulkin, Elly, Minnie Bruce Pratt, and Barbara Smith, eds. *Yours in Struggle: Three Feminist Perspectives on Anti-Semitism and Racism*. New York: Long Hall Press, 1984.

de Lauretis, Teresa. "Feminist Studies/Critical Studies: Issues, Terms, and Contexts." In *Feminist Studies/Critical Studies*, ed. Teresa de Lauretis. Bloomington: Indiana University Press, 1986.

Derrida, Jacques. *Margins of Philosophy*. Trans. Alan Bass. Chicago: University of Chicago Press, 1982.

Eisenstein, Zillah. *The Radical Future of Liberal Feminism*. New York: Longman, 1981.

Fuss, Diana. *Essentially Speaking: Feminism, Nature, and Difference*. New York: Routledge, 1989.

Grossman, David. *The Yellow Wind*. Trans. Haim Watzman. New York: Farrar, Straus, and Giroux, 1988.

Hall, Stuart. "Cultural Identity and Diaspora." In *Identity, Community, Culture, Difference*, ed. Jackson Rutherford. London: Lawrence and Wishart, 1990.

hooks, bell. *Talking Back: Thinking Feminist, Thinking Black*. Boston: South End Press, 1989.

Hull, Gloria, Patricia Bell Scott, and Barbara Smith, eds. *All the Women Are White, All the Blacks Are Men, But ' ne of Us Are Brave: Black Women's Studies*. Old Westbury, N.Y.: Feminist Press, 1982.

Klepfisz, Irena, and Melanie Kaye/Kantrowitz. *The Tribe of Dina: A Jewish Women's Anthology*. Montpelier, Vt.: Sinister Wisdom Books, 1986.

Levitt, Laura. "Covenantal Relationships and the Problem of Marriage: Towards a Post-Liberal Jewish Feminist Theology." Conference paper given at the American Academy of Religion, San Francisco, 1992.

———. "Reconfiguring Home: Jewish Feminist Identity/ies." Ph.D. diss., Emory University, 1993.

Lorde, Audre. *Sister Outsider*. Trumansburg, N.Y.: Crossing Press, 1984.

Miller, Nancy K. *Getting Personal: Feminist Occasions and Other Autobiographical Acts*. New York: Routledge, 1991.

Moraga, Cherrie, and Gloria Anzaldua, eds. *This Bridge Called My Back: Writings by Radical Women of Color*. New York: Kitchen Table–Women of Color Press, 1983.

Morales, Aurora Levins, and Rosario Morales. *Getting Home Alive*. Ithaca, N.Y.: Firebrand Books, 1986.

Smith, Barbara, ed. *Home Girls: A Black Feminist Anthology*. New York: Kitchen Table Press, 1984.

About the Editor

Steven Kepnes is associate professor of philosophy and religion and director of Jewish Studies at Colgate University, Hamilton, New York. He earned his M.A. and Ph.D. degrees at the University of Chicago. He received a Mellon postdoctoral grant from 1986 to 1988 and was a visiting scholar at the Hebrew University and at the Shalom Hartman Institute for Advanced Jewish Studies from 1993 to 1995. He is author of *The Text as Thou: Martin Buber's Dialogical Hermeneutics and Narrative Theology* and editor, with David Tracy, of *The Challenge of Psychology to Faith*. His articles on Jewish thought have appeared in such journals as *The Journal of Jewish Studies, Soundings,* and *The Harvard Theological Review.* He is currently Judaism editor for *Religious Studies Review* and working on a book entitled *The Jew in the Postmodern World.*

About the Contributors

Daniel Boyarin is professor of Talmudic culture at the University of California at Berkeley, where he holds the Herman P. and Sophia Taubman Chair in the Department of Near Eastern Studies. Author of numerous volumes, journal articles, and scholarly papers, he has recently published *Carnal Israel: Reading Sex in Talmud Culture* and *A Radical Jew: Paul and the Politics of Identity*.

Yudit Kornberg Greenberg, associate professor of religious studies at Rollins College, has recently completed a book on the philosophy of Franz Rosenzweig, entitled *Better than Wine: Love, Poetry, and Prayer in the Thought of Franz Rosenzweig*. Her article, "Franz Rosenzweig and Martin Heidegger on Poetry," appears in volume 16 of *History of European Ideas*.

Edward L. Greenstein is professor of Bible at the Jewish Theological Seminary of America. Author of *Essays on Biblical Method and Translation* and *Reader Responsibility in Biblical Narrative* (forthcoming), he has edited the *Journal of the Ancient Near Eastern Society* and the series, *Society of Biblical Literature Semeia Studies*.

Susan Handelman, professor of English at the University of Maryland, College Park, is author of *Fragments of Redemption: Jewish Thought and Literary Theory in Scholem, Benjamin, and Levinas* and coeditor of *Psychoanalysis and Religion*.

Hannan Hever is senior lecturer in the Department of Poetics and Comparative Literature at Tel Aviv University. His recent publications include *Poets and Zealots: The Rise of Political Hebrew Poetry in Eretz-Israel* and *Studies in the Poetry of Avraham Ben-Yitzhak*.

Martin S. Jaffee, associate professor of comparative religion and Jewish studies at the University of Washington, is coeditor of *Innovation in Religious Traditions* and author of three studies of Talmudic texts. His recent essays include "Halakhah in Early Rabbinic Judaism" and "How Much Orality in Oral Torah?"

Laura S. Levitt is assistant professor of religion at Temple University. She is author of *Ambivalent Embraces: Jewish Feminist Identities as Home* and coeditor of *Feminist Critical Studies and Judaism*, both forthcoming from Routledge. Her essay, "Reconfiguring Home: Jewish Feminist Identity/ies," appears in *Gender and Judaism: The Transformation of Tradition.*

Peter Ochs is Wallenstein Associate Professor of Jewish Studies at Drew University. He edits the Postmodern Jewish Philosophy Network. Among his publications are *Reading Pragmatism: Charles Peirce's Pragmatic Writing* and the edited collections, *Understanding the Rabbinic Mind* and *The Return to Scripture in Judaism and Christianity.*

Adi Ophir, senior lecturer at the Cohn Institute for the History and Philosophy of Science and Ideas at Tel Aviv University, edits *Theory and Critique*, an interdisciplinary journal for the critical study of Israel's culture and society. He is author of *Plato's Invisible Cities: Discourse and Power in the Republic.*

Laurence J. Silberstein is Philip and Muriel Berman Professor of Jewish Studies in the Department of Religion Studies at Lehigh University and director of the Berman Center for Jewish Studies. He is author of *Martin Buber's Social and Religious Thought*, editor of *New Perspectives on Israeli History* and *Jewish Fundamentalism in Comparative Perspective*, and coeditor of *The Other in Jewish Thought and History.*

Elliot R. Wolfson is professor of Jewish Studies at New York University and adjunct professor of Jewish history at Columbia University. His recent publications include *Through a Speculum That Shines: Vision and Imagination in Medieval Jewish Mysticism*; *Along the Path: Studies in Kabbalistic Myth, Symbolism, and Hermeneutics*; and *Circle in the Square: Studies in the Use of Gender in Kabbalistic Symbolism.*

Edith Wyschogrod is J. Newton Rayzor Professor of Philosophy and Religious Thought at Rice University. She is author of *Saints and Postmodernism: Revisioning Moral Philosophy* and *Spirit in Ashes: Hegel, Heidegger, and Man-Made Mass Death.*

Index